MISSIONARIES, MENTAL HEALTH, AND ACCOUNTABILITY

The mental health issues of missionaries are a topic that rightfully deserves our attention for missions in the twenty-first century. This publication sheds light on the dark and morbid problems hidden behind the heroic accomplishments far beyond our expectations. Both the missionary and the church communities will find the candid discussions and the alternatives presented herein vitally indispensable. The comprehensive and professional resources contained in this book unravel an inconvenient truth of missions in our time. All churches that are committed to missions should consult this publication.

Kyu Sam Han
senior pastor, Choong Hyun Church, Korea

I commend the publication of these honest reflections. This book is an essential resource for leaders of denominations, churches, and mission agencies as they wrestle with the significant challenges of sharing the Good News of Jesus across cultures in the twenty-first century.

Malcolm McGregor
former SIM international director 2003–2013
currently, seconded to Langham Scholars as Associate Director for Scholar Care

This collection of essays offers a fresh—and much needed—appraisal of the challenges of intercultural Christian ministry, especially in terms of the psychological and interpersonal challenges that arise. Of special value are the papers dealing with the phenomenal rise and expansion of Korean cross-cultural ministry the past four decades. One hopes this model of ministry will grow as a fruit and witness of the global body of Christ.

Wilbert R. Shenk
Fuller Graduate School of Intercultural Studies

These essays call the church to a new level of "best practices" regarding how we screen candidates for missionary service, the support systems at home and abroad which surround the missionary, the intentional provision for space, self-reflection and renewal, as well as ongoing pastoral care for missionaries and their families. This book may challenge our conceptions of what it is like to actually serve as a missionary, but it will be a "balm of Gilead" for those whom we have entrusted with that sacred work to make Christ known among the nations.

Timothy C. Tennent, PhD
president, Asbury Theological Seminary

MISSIONARIES, MENTAL HEALTH, AND ACCOUNTABILITY
Support Systems in Churches and Agencies

Editors

Jonathan J. Bonk
J. Nelson Jennings
Jinbong Kim
Jae Hoon Lee

Missionaries, Mental Health, and Accountability: Support Systems in Churches and Agencies
©2019 by Global Mission Leadership Forum (GMLF)

All rights reserved.

No part of this book may be reproduced, stored in a retrieval system, or transmitted in any form or by any means—electronic, mechanical, photocopy, recording, or otherwise—without prior written permission of the publisher, except brief quotations used in connection with reviews in magazines or newspapers. For permission, email permissions@wclbooks.com.

Unless otherwise noted, Scripture quotations are from the New International Version (NIV)®, ©1973, 1978, 1984, 2011 by Biblica, Inc.™. Used by permission of Zondervan.

Scriptures marked ESV are taken from The Holy Bible, English Standard Version® (ESV)®, ©2001 by Crossway, a publishing ministry of Good News Publishers. All rights reserved.

Scriptures marked KJV are taken from the King James Version.

Scriptures marked NABRE are taken from the New American Bible, revised edition, ©2010, 1991, 1986, 1970 by Confraternity of Christian Doctrine, Inc., Washington, DC. All rights reserved.

Scriptures marked NASB are taken from the New American Standard Bible® (NASB), ©1960, 1962, 1963, 1968, 1971, 1972, 1973, 1975, 1977, 1995 by The Lockman Foundation. Used by permission. www.Lockman.org.

Scriptures marked NRSV are taken from the New Revised Standard Version Bible, ©1989 by National Council of the Churches of Christ in the United States of America. Used by permission. All rights reserved.

Scriptures marked NKJV are taken from the New King James Version (NKJV)®, ©1982 by Thomas Nelson, Inc. Used by permission. All rights reserved.

Published by William Carey Publishing
10 W. Dry Creek Cir.
Littleton, CO 80120 | www.missionbooks.org

William Carey Publishing is a ministry of Frontier Ventures
Pasadena, CA 91104 | www.frontierventures.org

Dorothy R. Carroll, copyeditor
Katie Koch, Mike Riester, interior design
Yena Hwang, cover design
Dr. Craig A. Noll, indexer

ISBNs: 978-1-64508-284-2 (paperback), 978-1-64508-286-6 (mobi), 978-1-64508-287-3 (epub)

Printed Worldwide

23 22 21 20 19   1 2 3 4 5

Library of Congress data on file with publisher.

DEDICATION

*"But we have this treasure in clay jars,
so that it may be made clear
that this extraordinary power belongs to God
and does not come from us."*

2 Corinthians 4:7 (NRSV)

OTHER TITLES IN THE GMLF SERIES

Accountability in Missions:
Korean and Western Case Studies

Family Accountability in Missions:
Korean and Western Case Studies

Megachurch Accountability in Missions:
Critical Assessment through Global Case Studies

People Disrupted:
Doing Mission Responsibly among Refugees and Migrants

CONTENTS

Foreword 1–PAUL & LILA BALISKY ... ix
Foreword 2–JEONG-HO CHAE ... x
Foreword 3–TIMOTHY KIHO PARK ... xii
Foreword 4–MALCOLM MCGREGOR ... xiii
Foreword 5–SCOTT MOREAU ... xiv
Foreword 6–TIMOTHY C. TENNENT ... xvi
Preface 1–JINBONG KIM ... xviii
Preface 2–JONATHAN J. BONK ... xx

BIBLE STUDIES: By Christopher J. H. Wright

01 Elijah and the Healing of Depression and Fear ... 2
02 Jeremiah and the Healing of Disillusionment, Bitterness, and Self-Pity ... 11
03 Peter and the Healing of Failure and Guilt ... 21

SECTION A: Missionary Disillusion, Discouragement, and Depression

04 Finding a Way through the Darkness of ... Despair, Discouragement, Disillusionment, Despondency, and Disappointment–RUTH L. MAXWELL ... 34
    RESPONSE–KYUNGWHA HONG ... 42

05 A Journey toward Korean Missionaries' Mental Health–DO BONG KIM ... 47
    RESPONSE–THOMAS KEMPER ... 56

06 Missionary Anger: A Korean Cultural Perspective–JONATHAN S. KANG ... 59
    RESPONSE–BARBARA HÜFNER-KEMPER ... 72

07 Navigating the Challenges in International Missions–SOOHYUN KIM ... 75
    RESPONSE–PATRICIA LUCILLE TOLAND ... 85

SECTION B: Missionary Relational Dynamics and Tensions

08 Marital Conflict among Korean Missionary Couples–HYUN-SOOK LEE ... 90
    RESPONSE–BEN TORREY ... 98

09 Neurodevelopmental Disorders and Missionary Children's Mental Health
    –NANCY A. CRAWFORD ... 102
    RESPONSE–JENNY H. PAK ... 110

10 Sexual Addiction–RICHARD WINTER ... 115
    RESPONSE–SUN MAN KIM ... 122

SECTION C: Contextual Contributory Factors in Missionary Mental "Illness"

11 *Psychological Stress and Limited Access Area Missionaries*–Jeong Han Kim 128
    RESPONSE–Karen F. Carr 141

12 *A Courageous Call, a Confounding Crisis, and the Contours of Appropriate Care*
    –Stanley W. Green 144
    RESPONSE–Jinsuk Byun and Hyekyung Hong 154

13 *God's Wounded Servants: Exploring the Lived Experience of Trauma*–Young Ok Kim 158
    RESPONSE–Pamela Davis 166

14 *Spiritual Resources in Dealing with Trauma*–Frauke C. Schaefer
    and Charles A. Schaefer 169
    RESPONSE–Meesaeng Choi and Hunn Choi 177

15 *Happiness among Korean Missionaries and Organizational Care in the Missions*
    Community–Eunjung Um 181
    RESPONSE–Lois A. Dodds 192

SECTION D: Resources for Missionary Mental Health Care

16 *Organization-Centered Member Health*–Brent Lindquist 196
    RESPONSE–Nam Yong Sung 204

17 *A Study on the Emotional Stress and Mental Health of Retired Korean Missionaries*
    –Jae-Hon Lee and Sung Il Moon 208
    RESPONSE–Liz Bendor-Samuel 217

18 *Retirement Plans for Korean Missionaries: A Case Study of NamSeoul Church*
    –Jinbong Kim and J. Nelson Jennings 222
    RESPONSE–Lawrence Fung and John Wang 232

SECTION E: Workshop Papers

19 *Depression in the Old Testament*–Michel G. Distefano 238

20 *Missionary Kids: Who Rocks the Cradle?*–Lois A. Dodds 256

21 *How to Build a Multicultural Mission—Opportunities and Challenges:*
    A Case Study of WEC Korea–Kyung Nam Park and Kyoung A Jo 265

SECTION F: Summaries

22 *Our Pain Is Not in Vain*–Jung-Sook Lee 276

23 *"But We Have This Treasure in Jars of Clay" ... Mental Health and God's Servants*
    –Jonathan J. Bonk 286

Participants 301

Contributors 307

Index 319

TABLES AND FIGURES

Table 5.1
A Journey Map for Missionary Mental Health Care — 53

Table 11.1
A Comparison of GMS Missionaries' Locations with Countries That Persecute Christians — 130

Table 11.2
The Number of Deported GMS Missionary Families, 1979–2018 — 132

Figure 13.1
Four Aspects of Background Knowledge Necessary for Missionary Mental Health Providers — 164

Table 15.1
Number of Participants according to Referral and Organization Types — 185

Table 15.2
Correlation Coefficient of K-SPARE Variables, Mean, SD (N=154) — 186

Table 15.3
K-SPARE Subjective Well-Being Variables' Mean, SD according to Referral Types — 187

Table 15.4
K-SPARE Subjective Well-Being T-test according to Referral Types — 188

Table 15.5
Ministry Satisfaction T-test according to Referral Types — 188

Table 15.6
Themes and Sub-themes of Happiness and Dissatisfaction in Ministry — 190

Figure 21.1
WEC Korea's Membership Trend — 267

Table 21.2
Reasons for Resignation between 2000 and 2018 — 271

FOREWORD 1

The Korean missions movement in our generation is a significant phenomenon in the history of the world church. As this movement continues to expand, it is inevitable that cross-cultural challenges will remain. At present, the Korean church is the leading sender, per capita, of cross-cultural evangelists and workers.

In light of the challenges that accompany such a robust missionary movement, a biennial series of forums commenced in 2011 at the Overseas Ministries Studies Center (OMSC) in Connecticut. The collection of these seminal papers was edited by Jonathan J. Bonk in *Accountability in Missions: Korean and Western Case Studies*. A statement about that groundbreaking forum reads thus: "The practicality, the honesty, the professional and intellectual vigor, and the spirituality of both the intent and the outcomes of the forum made it clear that something *significant*—not huge, not mighty, not numerically impressive, but *seminal*—had been launched." During the following years, three additional forums were conducted in both Korea and the United States, which issued in both Korean and English publications. This present volume is another outcome of that 2011 groundbreaking symposium and contains fifteen case studies, presented by both professional Koreans and non-Koreans at a symposium held at the Kensington Stars Hotel in Sokcho from June 10–14, 2019. The first three essays deal with missionary disillusionment, discouragement, and depression. A second section holds four essays about missionary relational dynamics both within marriage and cross-cultural experience. Four chapters in category three are case studies that unpack contributing factors affecting the loss of mental health among missionaries. The final category of four chapters provides helpful resources for field missionaries struggling with stress and mental health issues.

During the latter part of our privileged career as SIM missionaries in Ethiopia (1967–2005), our lives were very much intertwined with Korean missionaries in various capacities—in theological instructing, evangelism, church planting, development projects, and administrative responsibilities. The ability of our Korean colleagues displayed in their cross-cultural adaptation was amazing. This was especially true of Korean couples who served in peripheral church-planting ministries. They were adept in Amharic, the national language, and became skillful with the indigenous languages. They had the ability to live simply and wisely in outpost areas. At the SIM Ethiopia bi-annual spiritual life conferences, the Korean missionaries felt a family spirit within the larger SIM body. At these conferences, they openly shared their stories in the larger group and were free to discuss the highs and lows, stresses and misunderstandings that occur within an international missionary agency. And, as could be expected in a multi-national group, we Westerners sometimes also faced conundrums while serving together with Korean brothers and sisters. As an example: Several Korean missionaries were incorporated into the semi-annual Ethiopia SIM week-long Council deliberations. Rather than voicing their opinions during our feisty conversations, the Korean delegates remained almost silent. It was only later, in private conversations, that they would express their strong feelings on certain issues. When challenged as to why they did not offer their candid opinions during the Council deliberations, they remarked, "We did not want to appear difficult." Thus, we had opportunities to learn from each other and appreciate the differences in cultural understanding.

This book presents fifteen chapters, by an equal balance of both Korean and Western writers, that reach into the complexity of missionary mental health, plus into accountability in church and agency support systems. There is an equal balance of Korean and Western writers, and four important areas of missionary relational dynamics are considered: 1) disillusion, discouragement, and depression; 2) relational dynamics and tensions; 3) contextual contributory factors in missionary mental illness; and, 4) helpful insights to resources for missionary mental health care. We found these presentations very applicable to our own experiences in the Ethiopian context, in such areas as the need for meaningful prayer within the body of Christ, the trauma created by neglect of family responsibilities in the cause of ministry, the need for professionals to give help to "wounded servants," and the value of rich relationships that enhance mental health and provide happiness and joy for all as we work together in world mission and church.

As a missionary couple who have served in various ministries and leadership roles in Ethiopia, we highly recommend this book, especially for leaders within the growing number of majority world agencies, who are presently responsible for burgeoning new cross-cultural mission endeavors.

Drs. Paul & Lila Balisky
Former SIM missionaries in Ethiopia
Residing in Grande Prairie, Alberta, Canada
paulilab@telus.net

FOREWORD 2

As Genesis 12:3 proclaims,[1] a missionary is a deliverer of blessings. The missionary must reflect and reproduce the character of Jesus, reinforcing the structures Jesus built on earth, and redelivering the gospel until all the peoples of the earth hear the message.

---

1 " ... all peoples on earth will be blessed through you."

Being human in nature, however, missionaries inevitably come face to face with many difficulties. Yet, at times, all we have done to help them is encourage them to overcome their troubles by faith. Thankfully, we are beginning to see that taking care of the mental health of missionaries is not an option but a requirement for maintaining healthy missions. The church, with the help of mental health professionals, is therefore called to care for the mental health of her missionaries.

The choice of "Missionaries, Mental Health, and Accountability in Church and Agency Support Systems" as the topic for the Korean Global Mission Leaders Forum (KGMLF) 2019 was a timely one. Especially when the support structure for missions is poor, taking care of mental health on an individual level can be difficult. It is thus crucial to build adequate support structures. In that light, I find it encouraging that the forum provided an opportunity for the Korean Christian Psychiatric Association and KGMLF to connect and to work cooperatively.

The forum topics included not only emotional challenges, such as stress, depression, anxiety, and anger, which missionaries face routinely on the field, but also various topics including marital conflict, problems with children, sexual problems, trauma, and risk management issues. The discussions exchanged in the forum, I believe, provided an important step toward breaking the pattern in which so many missionaries have found themselves: suffering from unresolved mental issues that have reached the level of severe illness, when many of their problems could have been prevented with proper diagnoses and earlier detection. It is my hope to see more discussions on missionary mental health occur—discussions that have so far been neglected, due to a general lack of awareness or differences in perspectives among churches and mission agencies.

We as Christians aim to have the purpose of Christ fulfilled in the world. And we are Christians with the world in view. Each one of us is essentially called to live the life of a missionary, whether we are heading toward cross-cultural mission fields, whether we are welcoming the migrant people from other cultures, whether we are supporting and sending outgoing missionary workers, or whether we are mobilizing people to live according to God's purposes. I believe that the topics discussed in KGMLF's 2019 forum will be helpful as we work together toward the fulfillment of God's purposes in the world. I pray that the results of the forum will become widely known, to be used for the benefit of many. May God bestow his blessings on all those who were involved in this important forum, whether as staff, presenters, or participants.

Jeong-Ho Chae, MD, PhD
President, Korean Christian Psychiatrists Association
Professor, Department of Psychiatry, The Catholic University of Korea

FOREWORD 3

The number of Korean missionaries has increased greatly since 1980. Ministering to those missionaries by providing them with high quality member care is essential for the success of their missionary work but has been neglected by the Korean church for a long time. In earlier decades, we seldom heard about missionary member care, but in the past decade we have seen dozens of Korean missionary member care organizations emerge. Even so, there is more work to do: Korean missionary member care ministries must strive to provide more comprehensive and professional services to the missionaries they serve.

I am glad that the Korean Global Mission Leaders Forum (KGMLF) hosted a conference on "Missionaries, Mental Health, and Accountability in the Church and Agency Support Systems" in June 2019 at the Kensington Stars Hotel, Sokcho, Korea. Papers on diverse topics such as the spiritual, mental, emotional, psychological, sociological, cultural, and physical needs of missionaries were presented and discussed by experts in their respective areas of missionary member care. Together, the participants considered several complex problems relating to missionary member care, and solutions to these problems were suggested.

Sending out more missionaries is an important task for today's church, but caring properly for the missionaries who have already been sent out is no less important. Now is the time for the Korean church and missions, particularly missionary member care organizations, to work together in developing and implementing strategies that will improve missionary care. The number of missionary member care ministries must increase, and their ministries must become more comprehensive and professional. Each organization should be unique, having its own area of specialty within the broader community of member care providers.

This book, written by both Koreans and non-Koreans, gives us a comprehensive perspective on missionary member care. I recommend this book to Korean missionaries, missionary candidates, missions leaders, local church leaders, and all who are truly concerned with missionary member care. God cares for his servants, whom he calls and commissions to work for the coming of his kingdom. The Korean church and Korean missions organizations must therefore develop support systems that provide the care that their kingdom workers need.

Timothy Kiho Park, PhD
Senior Professor of Asian Mission
Fuller Theological Seminary School of Intercultural Studies

FOREWORD 4

Throughout the centuries, the baton of mission engagement has passed from one nation or region to another, as the Spirit of God touched people's lives, compelling them to step beyond their home contexts and "Go." Andrew Walls captures the dynamic qualities of God's mission as it moves between cultures:

> … [C]ross-cultural diffusion has always been the lifeblood of historic Christianity; that Christian expansion has characteristically come from the margins more than from the centre, that church history has been serial rather than progressive, a process of advance and recession, of decline in areas of strength and of emergence, often in new forms, in areas of previous weakness.[2]

An important part of mission history in the twentieth and twenty-first centuries has been the role of the Korean church. It was at the margins of the global church in the early twentieth-century, when the Holy Spirit awakened the nation through the Pyongyang Revival of 1907, resulting in the church enthusiastically embracing the cause of God's mission. Now, Korean missionaries are working all over the globe, taking the Gospel to many of the hardest places and least reached peoples, planting churches and ministering to people in great need.

Visit Seoul, and you will be struck by the dynamism and energy of Korea. This city was devastated during the 1950–53 Korean War, yet today it is one of the most modern and progressive cities in the world—a testament to the hard work, energy, and commitment that is characteristic of the Korean people. These same qualities, and more, have been invested in the cause of God's mission.

Yet, in very subtle ways, our strengths can so easily become our weaknesses: qualities overplayed can undermine our foremost abilities.

I honor the Korean church for taking a critical look at its mission engagement through the 2019 Korean Global Mission Leaders Forum (Sokcho) and for publishing this important book. It takes great courage for any culture to look at itself and to evaluate such areas as Mental Health and Accountability. Topics like anger, marital conflict, sexual addiction, and lack of care for fellow missionaries are not the usual stuff of missionary biographies, but by reflecting on these realities, important lessons can be learned for future gospel engagement.

As a mission leader looking back on more than forty years overseas, I recall some significant challenges, casualties, and sadness along the way: a friend killed in a plane hijacking, tropical infections that took the lives of colleagues, one person severely disabled following an accident, some scarred by wounds inflicted through interpersonal and team conflicts. But I am also reminded that such suffering is not new. How did the early church process the aftermath of the death

---
2 Andrew Walls, *The Missionary Movement in Christian History* (Maryknoll, NY: Orbis, 2007), 145.

of its first martyr, Stephen? What kind of counseling did Barnabas need, following the conflict with his strong-minded mission partner, Paul? What about Paul's last letter to his trusted colleague, Timothy (2 Timothy)? Was this a man struggling with depression and a loss of hope—"everyone in the province of Asia has deserted me,"[3] "no one came to my support"?[4] And what about his team member Demas, who "because he loved this world, has deserted me"[5]—what was the backstory to this statement?

Throughout Jesus' ministry, he sought to prepare his disciples for the magnitude of the challenge ahead. The upper room discourse of John 14–17 is perhaps the climax of this preparation. Jesus says, "I have told you these things, so that in me you may have peace. In this world you will have trouble. But take heart! I have overcome the world."[6] He was calling his disciples to a troubled existence, yet assuring them that he had overcome this broken world. He promised them the power of the Holy Spirit; with the coming of the Holy Spirit, they would have not the power of "Immanuel, God with us"[7] but of Immanuel, God within us.

I commend the publication of these honest reflections. My prayer is that it will lead to the enhanced preparation of Korean missionaries and to increased engagement in the mission of God by the people of this great nation.

This book is an essential resource for leaders of denominations, churches, and mission agencies, as they wrestle with the significant challenges of sharing the Good News of Jesus across cultures in the twenty-first century.

MALCOLM MCGREGOR
Former SIM International Director 2003–2013
Currently, seconded to Langham Scholars as Associate Director for Scholar Care

FOREWORD 5

The fifth publication stemming from a series of biennial conferences that bring together church, agency, and missionary leaders, this book provides rich, significant insights into both Korean and non-Korean missions and missionaries.

In this volume, the fifteen chapters offer case studies, surveys, and personal reflections, which together portray the state of the art in member care for Korean missionaries. Every chapter demonstrates courage, personal conviction, and judicious honesty.

---

3   2 Timothy 1:15.
4   2 Timothy 4:16.
5   2 Timothy 4:9.
6   John 16:33.
7   Matthew 1:23.

Foreword

One of the more challenging areas being confronted in global missions today is that of caring for missionaries and their families. From recruitment to retirement, missionaries lead challenging lives that require a type of attention not needed for the general population of Christians. Missionaries cross linguistic, cultural, and ministry boundaries. Doing so as a single person is challenging: learning a new language, adjusting to a new culture, engaging in ministry in a place where ministry needs to be done differently than in your home culture, dealing with loneliness—all of these present significant challenges. The process of culture shock, which includes emotional, psychological, and even physical trauma, is a normal part of the adjustment process. The fact that one of this book's chapters deals with the traumas of kidnapping and murder clearly shows that the intensity and effect of caring for missionaries can be off the charts.

When the missionary unit includes not only the missionary but also a spouse and one or more children, the complexities multiply. Each person in the family undergoes similar stressors (though from varying vantage points), and each must face the added dynamic of family engagement, whether that dynamic is healthy or unhealthy.

For Korean missionaries, as the essays in the volume show, performance pressure, hierarchical relationships, senses of obligation, ideals of the missionary "hero," the undercurrent of Confucian relational values, and the concepts of shame and face each place their own pressures on missionaries and their families. Further, needing psychological or psychiatric help remains a stigma for Korean missionaries today, making it not only a challenge to get help but a challenge to even admit that one needs help.

As you will see throughout this volume, Koreans experience member care challenges similar in many respects to the challenges faced by non-Korean missionaries—depression, addictions, marital strife, disillusionment, organizational tensions, challenges with colleagues, family trauma, medical issues, and the like. However, they experience and perceive these challenges through Korean cultural lenses and need mediation, facilitation, and empowerment that make sense in light of Korean culture. As if all of this were not enough, you will see that Korean churches and missions have yet to give significant attention to providing missionaries with the adequate means to retire after their active service in cross-cultural ministry has concluded.

As you read this book, I invite you to bear in mind that the case studies and stories presented within it are those of real people. They do not represent just numbers or hypothetical situations—these stories involve the lives of Christ's dear servants, who desire to make the name of Jesus known among the nations. In the vast majority of cases, they tell of ordinary people, who choose to follow an extraordinary call to serve God cross-culturally and often pay a great price. Their stories demand that we appropriately care for them and those who serve alongside them. May God richly bless—and perhaps even convict—you as you read these fascinating cases and learn firsthand the member care concerns and challenges facing contemporary Korean and North American missionaries.

Scott Moreau
Academic Dean
Professor of Intercultural Studies
Wheaton College Graduate School

FOREWORD 6

The title *Missionaries, Mental Health, and Accountability: Support Systems in Churches and Agencies* may appear at first glance to represent an esoteric discussion of theoretical issues surrounding the life of a missionary by people far removed from the field. However, the remarkable gift of this book is nothing less than a deep dive into the actual lives and ministries of those brave men and women in the church who are most committed to the extension of the gospel. These essays give us a treasure trove of actual case studies into the lives and reflections of the missionaries themselves, as they seek to navigate the unfamiliar terrain of cross-cultural life and work. The insights of this collection of essays and research is a clarion call to the church that we have done a far better job in inspiring and sending out workers into the harvest than we have in caring for and sustaining the ministries of those who respond to the missionary call. Healthy recruitment *and* sustainable retention should be an important concern for the whole church.

These essays examine the special challenges of missionaries who go forth with what many of the writers refer to as "hero status", and yet face the formidable challenges of initial entry, cultural adaptation, and the often neglected anxieties of home assignment. Furthermore, the challenges highlighted in this volume are not limited to the external challenges of cross-cultural engagement but also include the equally powerful internal forces that erode one's spiritual equilibrium and family systems in a job with no clear boundaries, no place of daily refuge, and little space for reflection and renewal. Yet, these essays do not merely point to pathological realities, which should awaken the care teams of every missionary organization, but also to the equally admirable growth in the lives of many missionaries who undertake the arduous and often misunderstood lives of cross-cultural workers committed to extending the gospel into new contexts. In other words, there are clear, positive pathways offered to the church in these essays, which can promote health and wholeness in the lives of the missionary community who often labor in isolated contexts, whether in restricted access countries or among peoples where the missionary can openly serve as a Christian worker. Both contexts present formidable and definable challenges, to which many of those who send missionaries have paid insufficient attention.

While many of these essays focus on the experience of Korean missionaries, the application is far broader and should be carefully read by churches and mission sending agencies around the world. These essays call the church to a new level of "best practices" regarding the screening of candidates for missionary service; the support systems at home and abroad that surround the missionary; the intentional provision for space, self-reflection, and renewal; as well as ongoing pastoral care for missionaries and their families. This book may challenge our conceptions of what it is like to actually serve as a missionary, but it will be a "balm of Gilead" for those with whom we have entrusted that sacred work to make Christ known among the nations.

Timothy C. Tennent, PhD
President
Professor of World Christianity
Asbury Theological Seminary

PREFACE 1

My God, my God, why have you forsaken me?
Why are you so far from saving me, so far from the words of my groaning?
—(Psalm 22: 1, NRSV)

While preparing for the fifth KGMLF on *Missionaries, Mental Health, and Accountability: Support Systems in Churches and Agencies* I was mildly rebuked by a Korean pastor, who asked me: "Why are you having a forum on a topic like this? Aren't missionaries by definition spiritually, mentally, and physically whole?" This book is a response to such idealizing and glamorizing of missionaries, placing them on a pedestal above and beyond ordinary humanity. Dr. Jonathan Bonk and Dr. Nelson Jennings, who have been working with me for years, provided great encouragement in the planning and undertaking of the forum. Rev. Jae-Chul Chung, chairman of Asian Mission, who has been helping missionaries around the world for decades, also encouraged and supported the development of the forum in many ways. It was he who initially suggested this year's topic.

This book is much more than simply a compilation of papers written by forty authors. The authors have shared years of professional knowledge and experience, accompanied by countless personal testimonies. On behalf of the Global Mission Leadership Forum, I extend my sincere thanks to all the authors who prepared their papers in the midst of already busy schedules, and then traveled all the way to Sokcho, South Korea to participate in the forum. It is also my honor to acknowledge with thanks the one hundred participants who came from all over the world to share in and contribute to the rich intellectual and spiritual feast of the event. This book would not have been possible without them.

In 2008, when I first shared my vision for KGMLF, Dr. Jonathan Bonk not only supported the idea, but he also became an integral part of growing the KGMLF and expanding the forum into what it is now. I am deeply grateful for the guidance and encouragement of the GMLF Board and Trustee members, especially for that received from Dr. Nelson Jennings. I hope God will continue to bless our work together.

Tears ran down my cheeks as I read the stories, recalled in this compilation, of God's great servants such as Elijah, Jeremiah, and Peter. They experienced brokenness, depression, despair, failure, and spiritual collapse. I received great comfort while reading the Bible study papers by Dr. Christopher Wright, who was my principal and professor at All Nations Christian College in England more than twenty years ago. Dr. Wright served as the Bible instructor at the first KGMLF, held in New Haven, Connecticut in 2011, and at the KGMLF 2017 and 2019 meetings, which were held in Sokcho, Korea. I am very grateful for his insightful and practical application of the Bible.

Preface

My little experience with mental illness suggests that prevention is very important; but if this is not possible, active care and recovery—with the help of specialists, if possible—are needed. Without the help of specialists, I would not be writing this preface. Dr. Jonathan Bonk's reflections, made during a personal conversation, bring me joy:

> Mental illness is not merely mental illness. It's also a path to empathy with the weaknesses of others. It's a way of exposing ourselves–not as superheroes but as weak men and women saved by grace and utterly reliant on God's strength made perfect in weakness. This is what it means to be *authentic* people. This is what it means to be *interdependent* members of the Body of Christ. Independent people are no more use than independent members of a human body. It is only through deep interdependence that we can be of any help to those around us.

This is also the teaching of the Apostle Paul in 2 Corinthians 1:4–11. I thank Dr. Lois Dodds for her encouraging assessment of KGMLF 2019:

> It was truly the most meaningful conference of my life! It was inspiring and informative … Learning in the four ways … was both effective and enjoyable. Reading the case studies, hearing the lectures and respondents, and then participating in the Q & A session for each presentation was genius. Furthermore, I was deeply impressed by the Onnuri Church staff who poured out their hearts and resources to make this forum successful.

I would like to emphasize that the KGMLF has been able to develop over the years due to the servant leadership of Rev. Jae Hoon Lee, senior pastor of Onnuri Church, together with the active support of the church elders. Rev. Lee's emphasis that "we only play a catalytic role" is the central message of the Bible. We are all catalysts and should be like John the Baptist: "only Jesus" should be shown through our lives. I must once again acknowledge Asian Mission, which continues to play a catalytic role in KGMLF. Rev. Jae-Chul Chung's belief that "the investment for KGMLF is an intangible investment for the invisible kingdom of God" is attested to by the extent of the support of his organization. It is he who recommended that KGMLF 2021 should be held in Pyeongchang Kensington Hotel, a hotel used in the 2018 Pyeongchang Winter Olympics, and we have accepted with appreciation his sound advice and generous offer of a venue. The sixth KGMLF, focusing on "Missions and Money," is set for November 9–12, 2021 in Pyeongchang, Korea. I am so grateful to Onnuri Church and Asian Mission. I pray that God will keep using them as catalysts in the history of world mission. I pray that God will bless Onnuri Church and Asian Mission abundantly.

Heartfelt thanks are due to the staff of KGMLF 2019 for their cheerful and efficient effort in support of KGMLF. In particular, I want to thank the more than forty Onnuri Church members who devoted their time to serving this forum under the gentle leadership of Rev. Hong Joo Kim (head mission pastor of Onnuri Church

Mission Headquarters) and mission pastor Kyunghee Lee. I would also like to acknowledge Rev. Sang Joon Lee of Asian Mission, who attended to KGMLF 2019's practical needs. All the staff were unstintingly cheerful and uncomplaining as they rendered service to the forum participants throughout the event. What a truly fantastic group of men and women!

I would also like to express my gratitude to DG Wynn of William Carey Publishing, who facilitated the English publication of this book, and to the Duranno Press staff, who handled the publication of the book in Korean. I also want to thank Mrs. Dorothy Carroll for her English editorial work, and Dr. Soonuk Jung for heading up the Korean translation of the book. Lastly, I wish to thank my family, who supported me in countless ways behind the scenes.

In the near future, the fifth KGMLF English book will be placed on the shelves of the Yale University Library in New Haven, Connecticut, where I have lived for about fourteen years. But my ultimate wish for the book is quite different. I pray that the book, *Missionaries, Mental Health, and Accountability: Support Systems in Churches and Agencies* (William Carey Publishing, 2019), will be an encouragement and comfort to missionaries who serve in places of darkness amidst mental pain. This book is dedicated to them and to pastors and congregations who care deeply for their missionaries—the earthen vessels through whose weakness and brokenness the power of God is revealed. This book is offered up as a sacrifice to God on behalf of such men and women and the supporting congregations who attend carefully to the care of God's servants. Lord, help us make sure that these things happen! Amen.

Jinbong Kim
Managing Director of GMLF
Coordinator of KGMLF

PREFACE 2

It seems scarcely possible that the seed from which this, and four other books, sprang germinated ten years ago at the prestigious Seoul Club in South Korea.

Fourteen key Korean mission executives and mission pastors took part in the first planning meeting for the Korean Global Mission Leaders Forum at the Seoul Club on March 1, 2010. The meeting was hosted and paid for by the late Mr. Young Hyun Jung and his wife, Mrs. Sook Hee Kim, faithful and generous supporters of the then fledgling enterprise, and the parents of Soon Young Jung, wife of my colleague, Rev. Dr. Jinbong Kim. Those taking part included Dr. Keung-Chul (Matthew) Jeong, Dr. Hyun Mo (Tim) Lee, Rev. Dr. Shin Chul Lee, Rev. Wonjae Lee, Dr. Sang-Cheol (Steve) Moon, Rev. Dr. Nam Yong Sung, Rev. Dr. Yong Joong Cho, Rev. Shinjong (Daniel) Baeq, Dr. Kwang Soon Lee, and Rev. Dr. Seung Sam Kang. It was there agreed that a modest international working forum would be convened at the Overseas Ministries Study Center in New Haven,

Connecticut to explore by means of case studies the theme, "Missionary, Mission, and Church Accountability: Implications for Strategy, Integrity, and Continuity."

With the assistance of my colleague Dr. Jinbong Kim, serious planning for the inaugural forum to be convened from February 10–14, 2011 got underway. This little event succeeded beyond our modest hopes! Forty-eight mission and church leaders gathered to present and discuss case studies and responses, bravely tackling complicated issues relating to financial, administrative, strategic and pastoral accountability practices and lapses related to mission organizations and their supporting congregations.

For those of us who took part, the forum was a great encouragement. Through the publication of Korean and English versions of the ensuing book—*Accountability in Missions: Korean and Western Case Studies* (Wipf & Stock, 2011)—its blessings spread wider still. The practicality, the honesty, the professional and intellectual vigor, and the spirituality of both the intent and the outcomes of the forum made it clear that something *significant*—not huge, not mighty, not numerically impressive, but *seminal*—had been launched. It was our *"cloud as small as a man's hand rising from the sea"* (1 Kings 18:44), signaling God's blessings to come. A model of vigorous cross-cultural interaction, constructive cross-cultural collaboration, and sharing both through multilingual publications had been born, one that could be employed to address other complex but overlooked issues bedeviling missions regardless of the sending or receiving country, mission society, or denomination involved.

Four more biennial forums followed: one more in New Haven in 2013, and the next three in Korea—thanks to the leadership of Rev. Jae Hoon Lee, senior pastor of Onnuri Church in Seoul, which joyfully hosted the KGMLF in 2015, 2017 and 2019. The KGMLF 2017 meeting, the first hosted under the new GMLF organization, took place at Kensington Stars Hotel in Sokcho. KGMLF's success was largely due to the generous financial and personnel support provided by Jae Hoon Lee, senior pastor of Onnuri Church, Jae-Chul Chung, chairman of Asian Mission, and other Korean churches.

With the benefit of experience, successive forums improved upon earlier ones. At each gathering—by means of challenging Bible studies and insightful open-ended case studies and responses by key mission leaders from Korea and from around the world—a range of complex, mission-related accountability challenges issued in several more Korean and English publications: *Family Accountability in Missions: Korean and Western Case Studies* (OMSC Publications, 2013); *Megachurch Accountability in Missions: Critical Assessment through Global Case Studies* (William Carey Library, 2016); *People Disrupted: Doing Mission Responsibly among Refugees and Migrants"* (William Carey Library, 2018); and now this volume, *Missionaries, Mental Health, and Accountability: Support Systems in Churches and Agencies* (William Carey Publishing, 2019).

This is how it came to be that from June 10–14, 2019—marking the culmination of nearly two years of careful planning for presenters, respondents, facilitators, travel, accommodations, hosting, and all of the other details crucial to a successful forum, and with the generous support of the sponsoring congregations and mission organizations—approximately one hundred mission and church leaders, missionaries, psychologists, psychiatrists, and professional caregivers from around the world were welcomed to Sokcho by two hosting agencies, Onnuri Church and Asian Mission.

Onnuri Church mission staff and volunteers—a team of more than forty individuals in all—handled all of the logistics entailed in hosting and serving forum participants. Words cannot convey our deep respect and appreciation for this team. Nor do words seem adequate to convey our deep appreciation for the indispensable generosity of Rev. Jae-Chul Chung, chairman of Asian Mission, in providing the accommodations and facilities for this fifth forum.

With Dr. Jinbong Kim, we prayed and prepared for this occasion for two years, and the presence of these scores of leaders was evidence that God had answered our prayers. Some gave generously, even sacrificially, of their financial resources; others joyfully devoted their time and intellectual energies; many shared their gifts of wisdom and knowledge in the presentations and responses that constituted the presentations of this forum and the chapters of this book; others—especially Mrs. Dorothy Carroll and Dr. Soonuk Jung—toiled diligently behind the scenes, editing and translating the manuscripts, correcting errors, clarifying meanings, and making sure that each offering was the best that it could be, and making sure that all the manuscripts were available in both Korean or English, so that the book would be available in both languages.

Special acknowledgments must be made of the indispensable role played by Dr. Jinbong Kim, whose inspiring vision, personal sacrifice, organizational gifts, and unstinting effort were the essential catalyst whereby all other contributions combined to create this well-formed and useful forum.

As we look back, it is with thanksgiving that all of us who have been in any way associated with the forum and with the book that you hold in your hands acknowledge a verity that has been attested throughout the history of our Lord's merciful dealing with those who seek to follow him faithfully. For as Paul reminds us and as our own experiences testify, "We have this treasure in jars of clay to show that this ... is from God, and not from us ..." (2 Corinthians 4:7). To God be the glory!

Jonathan J. Bonk
President
Global Mission Leadership Forum

BIBLE STUDIES
by Christopher J. H. Wright

# 01

1 Kings 19
ELIJAH AND THE HEALING OF DEPRESSION AND FEAR

by Christopher J. H. Wright

In our three Bible expositions at this year's KGMLF gathering, we shall look at three men who had significant encounters with God at points of critical need. All three were godly servants of the Lord, faithfully obedient and true to his call. But each of them went through experiences of brokenness, depression, despair, failure, and spiritual collapse—as do many loyal servants of God today. However, all three of them also experienced God's touch of personal healing in the deep springs of their persons and in relation to their mission for God. Perhaps considering each of them will reveal areas of our own inner lives and mission, where we may likewise stand in deep need of God's personal touch this week.

First of all, then, let us meet Elijah. The story of his collapse and restoration can be read in 1 Kings 19. It comes as quite a surprise to us as readers. For, in 1 Kings 18, we see Elijah at the pinnacle of his ministry. There he is on Mt. Carmel, taking on the whole army of the prophets of Baal single-handedly in the name of the living God of Israel, and achieving a stunning, fiery victory. We see a man in the prime of his strength and the peak of his success as a prophet of the true God. It is a high point of his mission, in leading a national turning back to Yahweh by the whole people, and it is a personal vindication by God of his calling and ministry. That is an easy chapter to preach from! But here in chapter 19, we find what seems like a different man altogether. Here he is in the depths of suicidal despair, defeat, and fear, literally running for his life and actually praying to die.

Let us consider first the ingredients of Elijah's despair and, then, the ingredients of God's therapy.

A. THE INGREDIENTS OF ELIJAH'S DEPRESSION

Emotional factors

Shock (vv. 1–2). After Mt. Carmel, Elijah probably had high expectations. Such a signal defeat of the god Baal must surely lead to a full-blown national revival. After all, the people had shouted out for hours, "The LORD, he is God!" Elijah himself had been vindicated. So, perhaps, he was planning a preaching tour, to take the word of God and the news of what had happened at Mt. Carmel all around the country. He had been mysteriously absent for three years, but now Elijah was back. Instead, the next day, he received news of this terrible threat to his life from Queen Jezebel. It must have been a severe and unexpected shock, going from being the hero of the moment to being a wanted man with a death-threat hanging over him. It was the ruin of all his hopes and plans. What if he did get killed? Who, then, would carry on the essential mission to bring the people back to the Lord?

Fear (v. 3a). This too is unexpected. We think of Elijah as an incredibly courageous man—a man who could walk into the palace of King Ahab and Queen Jezebel and announce God's judgment on them and their whole system of government (and walk out again alive!), a man who could survive in solitary hiding for months, fed by the miraculous generosity of ravens. Yet, here he drops into the very opposite: "Elijah was afraid and ran for his life!" Whatever plans he had been considering, whatever God had told him to do next, whatever the next phase of his mission was supposed to have been—he dropped it all and ran away in sheer panic.

Elijah was shocked and scared. Christians, including pastors and missionaries, are not immune to such emotions. We are not insulated against sudden bad news or real threats. And we are not (and should not be) emotional stoics who feel nothing (or pretend to). James tells us that Elijah was a man of like feelings as the rest of us. He felt what we can easily feel, and it drove him into massive despair and flight. It can happen to any of us. Maybe it already has.

2. Physical factors

Isolation (v. 3b). Perhaps it was out of kindness to his servant that Elijah left him behind at Beersheba. Perhaps it was just that his emotional state was such that he needed to get away from all human company. Perhaps it was to spare his servant's life, in case Elijah got caught. We do not really know, but the result was that Elijah was on his own. Now, he had been on his own before, of course. He had spent months by the brook Cherith with nobody but the ravens (and God) for company, which had led him into deep dependence on God and his provision. But this time, in his present frame of mind, his isolation became an insidious thing. Loneliness can be a real cancer. It can breed doubt and despair and unbelief. Remember Thomas, who was not with the other disciples when the Lord first appeared to them—somewhere out on his own where his doubts could fester. Isolation is a perfect incubator for anxiety and depression. And you do not have to be literally *alone* to be lonely, of course. A crowd can be a very lonely place. Even a jolly Christian fellowship, where everybody else seems to be doing just fine, can be terribly lonely for the fearful believer. Pastors and missionaries are vulnerable to a very particular kind of loneliness, even in the midst of their work that seems to be so filled with other people.

Exhaustion (vv. 4–5). Just think for a moment of that long, tense day on Mt. Carmel, followed by his marathon run to Jezreel (18:46). Then, immediately, he decides to head south to Beersheba, which is in the extreme south of Judah. He spends yet another whole day of lonely hiking farther into the wilderness in the scorching heat. We do not hear of him taking any food or drink in this whole time. The man was physically shattered. In such circumstances, with the added fear for his life at the hands of Jezebel's possibly pursuing thugs, it is not at all surprising that Elijah sinks into deep despair.

Spiritual depression is quite often linked to physical factors such as weariness, hunger, and lack of sleep. Such things in themselves do not cause depression, but they certainly can exacerbate it and make it even harder to resist or just 'shake it off' (which is not something we can do or should ever tell others to do).

3. Psychological factors

A "total-failure" complex (v. 4b). Read between the lines of what Elijah says to God. "I've had enough, Lord. I've done everything I can, and it's no use. Nothing has changed. I'm getting nowhere, in spite of what seemed like a great success. I'm a failure after all. And your mission is a failure too. Indeed, I'm no better than all the rest of the people for generations now. I'm no better than the people I condemn. So, I give up. You might as well let me die now, for all the good I'm doing. If you really love me, shoot me!" It is interesting that Moses had the same feelings of being overwhelmed to the point of preferring death to carrying on (Num. 11:14–15). This is a total collapse of nerve, a sense of utter failure, leading to suicidal depression. And it seems so irrational (as depression often does).

He had run away to save his life—but now he wants to die anyway, let God do what Jezebel had threatened to do! We need to use our imagination to grasp the mental turmoil in Elijah's head as he ran, walked, trudged, stumbled, maybe eventually crawled, on and on, far out into the wilderness—all the way from Jezreel to his juniper tree, finally all alone and in the depths of despair.

Distortion of the facts (vv. 10, 14). When someone is depressed it usually does no good to tell them that they are only imagining things, because probably they are not (and even if they are, imagined and perceived things become reality for them). Depression is not just fanciful. Sometimes it is related to facts but involves a distorted or partial reading of the facts. Look at what Elijah says, and compare it with the real situation. He is selective and partial on some facts. For example, he makes much of his own zeal for the Lord. But there were others too who had not been unfaithful to Yahweh, and he not only knew it, he had met some of them, such as Obadiah (18:1–15). He mentions how the Israelites had destroyed God's altars—but forgets that he had just repaired the one on Mt. Carmel. He says that they had killed the Lord's prophets, which was true, but Obadiah had kept 100 of them alive (18:13), and Elijah knew, and he exaggerates some other facts. For example, he complains, "I alone am left" (NRSV). But what about his own servant, and Obadiah, and the 100 prophets in a cave somewhere? "And now *they* are trying to kill me too," he adds, as if an army were searching for him, when all he had was a message from Jezebel (though she may have seemed as scary as a whole army!).

Here, then, is another frequent ingredient in spiritual depression among hard-pressed, exhausted servants of God. We see only part of the whole picture—and usually the worst part. We make a wrong selection of facts, or we twist and exaggerate some facts. We get things out of perspective or out of proportion. What we think and say and imagine may well have elements of truth—but not the whole truth. And when we sink into that bog of damaging and depressing thoughts, sometimes God has to take us aside and bring us back to his view of reality—which is what God eventually did with Elijah.

4. Spiritual factors

Failure to believe God's answer to his prayer. On Mt. Carmel, Elijah had prayed that God would give unmistakable proof that "these people will know that you, LORD, are God, and that you are turning their hearts back again" (18:37). In other words, he wanted unmistakable evidence of national repentance. And that proof had come with the shouts of the people when the fire of the Lord fell on the restored altar and the sacrifice: "The LORD [not Baal!]— He is God." Over and over again those words had rung in Elijah's ears. But now, in his depression and fear, he cannot even believe that it had really happened or that they had really meant it. His complaint in verse 10 completely bypasses the events of Mt. Carmel and goes back to the state of the Israelites beforehand.

His faith fails, even in the face of the evidence he had prayed for and had seen and heard for himself. This is astonishing. And yet it is not untypical. For in the throes of spiritual depression, even God's past answers to prayer, however wonderful and even spectacular, can seem like unreal, mocking memories.

Satanic attack. Now this is not mentioned explicitly, of course. The Old Testament does not give much attention to "the satan" (as he gets called; the word means, "accuser"). However, the worship of Baal and the whole system of Canaanite idolatry was unquestionably bound up with the work of the one whom the Bible calls the devil or Satan. Its worship of nature, its immorality and sexual depravity, its callous oppression and injustice (as typified in the behavior of Jezebel)—all these things bear the fingerprints of the dark kingdom of the evil one. *And Elijah had challenged it!* Elijah had made a laughing stock of Baal and his prophets. He had taunted the futility of Baal's claim to be some kind of god. He insisted that the law of Deuteronomy 13:1–5 should be carried out: that false prophets who led the people away from the worship of their living, redeemer God should be executed. And Satan fought back. Satan is a defeated enemy but never accepts defeat (until the time he will finally be destroyed). Look at the way he constantly plagued the ministry of Jesus. In the same way, we may discern his hand here in the circumstances that produced Elijah's suicidal thoughts, fear, and despair.

We hardly need to be reminded that Satan, though defeated by Christ at the cross, is still alive and active in today's world. He still fights back viciously against those who dare to challenge his dark world or who release captives from his bondage in the power of the name of Jesus. This is one reason why acute depression quite often follows after some signal spiritual victory or "successful" period of ministry for the Lord.

These, then, are some of the ingredients of Elijah's depression. These were some of the things that were breaking into his relationship with God, destroying his confidence in the mission God had given him or in his own ability to carry it out.

Let us turn, with relief, to the Master Therapist—God the healer at work. How did God deal with his exhausted, despairing, suicidal servant?

B. INGREDIENTS OF THE DIVINE THERAPY

I marvel at the beauty and simplicity of the way God gently and yet firmly nursed his ailing servant back to wholeness and active service. Of the four things that God does, we can start at the most basic level.

1. God gives him sleep, food, and drink (vv. 5–7)

God meets Elijah at the point of his most pressing and urgent need—his physical exhaustion, hunger, and thirst. God did not turn up demanding a serious spiritual counseling session. God did not rebuke him, call him out as a failure, or tell him to turn around and get back to work. On the contrary, not just once but twice, God refreshed Elijah with the gift of sleep and the provision of food and drink.

Now *sometimes* (but by no means always), that is all that is really needed to cure an episode of spiritual depression, if it is primarily linked to physical factors such as exhaustion. We ought to remind ourselves that sleep is not merely "natural" (any more than food and drink are). Sleep itself is a gift of God (also like food and drink). As Psalm 127:2 puts it, "He grants sleep to those he loves." So, God showed his love for Elijah in the simplest possible way. He let the poor man sleep!

And the food! The menu and table service are provided by an angel this time (which meant that God even gave Elijah some company for a time at least), not scraggy old ravens with bits of meat in their beaks, not the daily minimal rations of a poor foreign widow. Those were the ways in which God had provided for Elijah in the days of his obedience. But now, here he is running away from his mission in disobedience and despair—and at such a time as that, God sends him *an angel* with fresh baked bread and a jar of clean, cold water. What a tender touch! Here is God effectively mothering his servant. We may notice with regret that there is no mention of Elijah saying even a word of thanks. He just ate, drank, and went back to sleep! And God let him. For that was his greatest need at that moment. It may well be yours too. If so, receive God's permission, and let him care for you as his beloved in the simplest gifts of his grace—sleep, food, and drink.

2. God takes him back to the roots of his faith and his mission (vv. 8–9)

Refreshed by the sleep and food, Elijah sets off for Mt. Horeb, or Mt. Sinai (it was just an alternative name for the same place). That was another long journey farther south. But why did God take him to Sinai? Well, because it was a very appropriate place for God to put Elijah together again and restore him to his mission. Here are some aspects of the significance of the place, which we can read in-depth in the accounts in Exodus and Deuteronomy especially.

Sinai was the place where God had revealed himself to his people, with great power and many signs. It was the place where God had established his covenant with the descendants of Abraham, saying to them, "you will be my people, and I will be your God." It was the place where God had given to the people of Israel their identity and mission as his priestly kingdom and holy nation in the midst of all nations on the earth (Exod. 19:4–6). It was the place where God had given instructions for the tabernacle, in which God had come to dwell in the midst of his people, a mark of their distinctiveness from all other nations. It was the place where God had given Israel his law—that is, the "torah," meaning guidance or instructions for how to live as a redeemed and holy people.

Sinai was, in a sense, the birthplace of Israel as a redeemed people with a mission for God, in relation to God's ultimate purpose to bring blessing to all nations on earth. For that reason, then, it was also the starting point of the mission of Elijah himself, since God had sent him precisely in order to bring Israel back to their true identity and mission and to their calling to worship Yahweh alone as their God. Israel itself needed to return to the God of Sinai.

So, God brings Elijah back to Sinai, as if to say, "This is where you need to see things afresh. This is where you need to remember who I am, the LORD God of Israel, the I AM WHO I AM God. This is where you need to see your own people from my perspective and to understand my purpose for them, and through them, for all nations. This is where you need to see your own calling as my prophet, in the light of what happened at this place centuries ago through my servant, the prophet Moses. Stand here with me, as he did. Let's get back to the fundamental truths that were revealed here. Let's get back to basics, Elijah."

Sometimes this is also what depressed and broken Christians need to do, especially those called into frontline work in ministry and mission. Go back, with God. Perhaps go back to the Mount of Ascension, to hear again the authoritative words of Jesus, "All authority in heaven and earth is given to me, so go and make disciples …" Certainly, go back to those words of promise, spoken by God and then Jesus to so many of his servants, "Look, I am with you." Perhaps go back to that point in your own life where you heard that specific calling of God to the work he has given you to do, and hear again the words that he spoke to you then, the vision he laid on your heart, the Scriptures that confirmed it in your mind, and the encouragement that you received from other believers. Go back to the Bible itself, and to that great overarching story of the mission of God—the story within which God has called you to play your part. Go back, with God. Back to basics. Back to the foundations of the faith and the roots of your own faith, back to the rock that is more enduring than Mt. Sinai.

3. God questions his behavior in the light of his mission (vv. 9, 13)

Only when he has got Elijah back to Sinai does God begin the real probing work of healing Elijah's depression and restoring him to service. And God does so in a typically surprising way. We can be sure that Elijah was very familiar with the stories of what happened at Mt. Sinai and how God came down there with spectacular cosmic and creational effects (read Exodus 19). So, the God of Sinai lived up to his reputation and put on quite a show—wind, earthquake, and fire, such as Moses of old had witnessed. But "the LORD was not in" any of those phenomena. So, clearly God was not trying to *scare* Elijah back to work. God can certainly use and speak through such natural forces, but God has other ways of speaking also. The God of Sinai can be as quiet as "a gentle whisper" (though I do prefer the old translation, "a still small voice").

But a whisper can be as penetrating as a thundering shout, when it is God asking the questions (which God is accustomed to doing rather often—starting in the third chapter of the Bible). So it is here: into Elijah's brokenness, depression, fear, and negative self-pitying thoughts, God drops this persistent question. God forces Elijah to explain his behavior, in the light of the mission God had given him.

"What are you doing here, Elijah?" Every word counts.

"*You* … Elijah"—whose name expresses your mission, "Yahweh is my God," what are *you* doing? What is all this running away from the job Yahweh gave you? What kind of behavior is this for *you* to be doing, when someone like Obadiah (whose name means "servant of Yahweh"), has been faithfully serving me right in the jaws of Ahab's court, under the nose of the queen you are running away from?

"And what are you doing *here*," in the light of all that this place stands for? How do you square your behavior with the knowledge of God and his people that you know is resonant in this place?

It is a somewhat mysterious, probing, searching question. It may hold some implied rebuke, but mainly it seems to be inviting Elijah to explain himself, to articulate the thoughts in his mind. At least, that is how Elijah took it, for twice over he trots out his reasons in verses 10 and 14—without much apparent change of mood. But the question simply bounces back after the first time, and somehow Elijah's mere repetition of his complaint sounds less convincing the second time around. Did he realize that himself? Did he get tired of playing the tape over and over again?

Sometimes this is how God deals with us also. Sometimes he uses the gentle rebuke, coupled with a question that allows us the freedom to express our inner thoughts (like a skilled counselor). For sometimes it is only when God gets those thoughts out into the open, when we are willing to speak them aloud rather than burying them in the echo chamber of our internal conversation with ourselves, that God can break through that vicious cycle of repetitive complaint and negative thinking. But God does it so gently, in a gentle whisper. "What is all this about, my child? What are you doing in this place or in this mood? What happened to the task I gave you? Where is that clarity of vision and mission you once had?"

If such gentle divine questioning (whether in our own hearts or through the faithful ministry of a perceptive friend or pastor) leads to the stirring of repentance, then that is the first step up and out of the bog of self-pity and despair. That may be the gentle therapy of the Lord. "A bruised reed he will not break," and a bruised Christian he will not shatter further with a heavy hand. Rather, he will lead us back to wholeness through a process of gentle, persistent, inescapable questioning, in which we find that the answers we have to give are part of the restoration.

4. God sends him back on his mission with reassurance (vv. 15–18)

God did not drop Elijah from his service just because of this collapse and failure. God did not say, "If you can't face the threats, you'd better go back home to Tishbe." No, God puts Elijah back together again and then sends him back to work. In fact, he sends him back with an even greater mission than the first (that is also typical of God). God gives to Elijah three specific new tasks to accomplish—in relation to the international scene, the next phase of Israel's history, and Elijah's own successor. Each of the three anointings he was to perform would play a part in God's plans for the purification of his people. It would be a ministry of judgment, for sure, but that in itself meant that God's plans for Israel would continue. There would be purging but not total obliteration. God was preserving a faithful remnant.

So, not only was Elijah not alone as the sole servant of God (there were at least 7,000 others in the nation), he would also not be alone in his personal ministry. God would give him a companion and a successor—Elisha (whose name means, "God is Savior").

And so, refreshed, rebuked, recommissioned, and reassured—Elijah sets off on the long road back to his mission for the living God.

And Elijah's mission goes on, for Elijah's God is our God—the God who, centuries later, would send another "Elijah" before his face, John the Baptist, who would prepare the way for another "Elisha"—Jesus, whose name means the same, "The LORD is Salvation." It is this God who knows our every weakness, who meets us in our frailty and sometimes in our failure and defeat, and who gently refreshes, restores, and reassures us too, with fresh work to do for him.

02 Jeremiah 15:10, 15-21

JEREMIAH AND THE HEALING OF DISILLUSIONMENT, BITTERNESS, AND SELF-PITY

by CHRISTOPHER J. H. WRIGHT

This passage is one of several in the book of Jeremiah that are commonly called "The Confessions of Jeremiah," though they are more like protests and laments than confessions. They are intensely personal prayers in which Jeremiah pours out his heart to God, exposing the costliness of his experiences as a prophet. If you want to feel the raw emotional depths of Jeremiah's heart, you could read also 12:1–3, 17: 5–8, 14–18, 18:18–20, 20:7–18. It is tough reading.

No wonder Jeremiah became known as "the weeping prophet"! But in case we judge him too harshly, we need to see all these outpourings against the background of long years of being a prophet, from his early youth to middle age—with no apparent success. Instead, he was the target of unrelenting rejection, ridicule, and hatred, along with bouts of physical violence. Forbidden by God to marry, he suffered intense loneliness, with very few faithful friends. And the pressure of these circumstances, on top of the frighteningly unpopular messages he was given to deliver, ate into his soul at times and drowned him in moods of intense disillusionment, self-pity, and rejection of the task he had been given. The amazing and encouraging thing is that not only did Jeremiah have the honesty to express such feelings directly to God, but that God ensured that they were recorded in his book for us all to read and learn from.

Let us try to analyze and "label" at least three elements in Jeremiah's distress in this passage, then see what God says in response.

DISILLUSIONMENT WITH HIS MINISTRY (VV. 10 AND 16)
This could be labeled as failure to come to terms with his tough situation.

In verse 10, Jeremiah wishes that he had never been born. He repeats that wish even more forcefully and crudely in 20:14–18. But Jeremiah knew (because God had told him) that God had chosen and appointed him to be a prophet from before he was born (1:5). So, this longing not to have been born at all was in effect a rejection of his whole calling to be a prophet. He has become disillusioned with the very ministry he was born to do. Why? Because of what he describes in the rest of verse 10: all he gets is strife, contention, hatred, and cursing. That is never easy to bear—especially if it goes on and on and feels totally undeserved. He has done nobody any wrong, yet everyone hates him. Very tough!

Jeremiah's disillusionment is made even worse by what he tells us in verse 16. He remembers back to the early days of his ministry. Even if he had been rather overwhelmed when God called him as a young lad, it had brought him joy and delight to be the bearer of God's word. He devoured God's word like sweet food. He was proud (in the right sense) to speak in the name of the Lord God of Israel—in the long line of those who had done so before him. Perhaps back in those early days, he had had high hopes and expectations. What a challenge! What a mission: to be God's "prophet to the nations"! "I bear your name, LORD God Almighty," he says. That was his divine commission and authority. Once, it had seemed like a priceless privilege. Now, it had become an intolerable burden and a daily torture.

So, Jeremiah falls into disillusionment. He cannot cope with the pressure of his situation. He knows God has called him to this task. And he knows he has really no other choice and nowhere else to go. But still he hates it and wishes he had never been born to such a life. Any dreams he may have had, even perhaps his childhood hopes of becoming a priest like the rest of his family, are shattered. Life had become a misery of disappointment and frustration. He had sunken in disillusionment.

And such disillusionment easily strikes at many a servant of God. A freshly ordained pastor goes to what he thought was a spiritual and mission-minded church with a great reputation for life and growth. Then, he soon discovers that underneath the reputation lies all kinds of deadness, dysfunction, personality clashes, power struggles, even corruption and immorality. What happens then to his enthusiasm for pastoral ministry? A young student goes to an evangelical seminary with a high reputation, expecting a wonderful life of enhanced godliness and discovers that not only is she required to clean toilets, but all kinds of unfair practices and lack of integrity permeate the faculty and administration. She becomes disillusioned with her fellow students and even her teachers. What happens to her sense of calling and mission for the Lord? A missionary couple head off to some foreign country, with great hopes of their own and great expectations of their sending church. But within a few years, they have returned home, having faced all kinds of cultural barriers that they had not been adequately prepared for, probably feeling (quite unjustifiably) that they have failed and, certainly, feeling very disillusioned.

Many of us have become utterly disillusioned with the way some high-profile "evangelical" leaders of churches and missions behave, obsessed with greed and money, and with complete disregard for Christ's teaching about humility, integrity, and servanthood. Or we become disillusioned with the way some churches or mission agencies treat their staff and missionaries, and wonder if the same fate awaits us eventually.

Disillusionment has several manifesting and very negative symptoms. Disillusioned Christians see no good anywhere. Instead, they tend to be always critical and characteristically pessimistic about everything. They can be very sarcastic, enjoying a kind of dark and negative humor about their colleagues. They pour cold water on other people's enthusiasm and zeal ("I used to be as excited as you are, but you'll grow up soon"). They sneer at good ideas or suggestions ("We tried that years ago, and it didn't work then"). Worst of all, disillusionment tends to be infectious. It poisons the minds and quenches the hopes and visions of others. Negativity spreads.

What, then, is God's response to this particular dimension of Jeremiah's need? It comes in verse 19, after Jeremiah has a few more things to say that we shall consider in a moment. (It is quite difficult to see how verses 11–14 relate directly to what Jeremiah says in verse 10.) There are two aspects to God's reply.

First comes a call to repent: "If you repent, I will restore you that you may serve me ..." God is rather firm with his disillusioned servant. This is not just a vague command. The second half of the verse shows that it was directed specifically at what Jeremiah had been *saying*. All his talk had become negative, destructive, and "worthless," which is characteristic of disillusionment, as we just pointed out. God checks Jeremiah on this and gently but firmly rebukes him. It is interesting: God allows him to speak his mind, but then challenges his words. Incidentally, this affects our understanding of what is meant by "the inspiration of Scripture." Not everything that Jeremiah is recorded as having said is, in itself, "the word of God" in a direct sense. Rather, the word of God (to us) in this section of Scripture comes through the honest recording of Jeremiah's negative, disillusioned thoughts and words, and the way God then rebukes them. We can be honest before God, but we need also to hear what God says in response.

The second dimension of God's response is the positive counterbalance to the first. God pulls Jeremiah back to his proper job as a prophet: "If you utter worthy, not worthless, words, you will be my spokesman"—which was, of course, the very essence of his calling and mission as God's prophet. Jeremiah will carry on with his ministry (whether he wants to or not), but only if he pays attention to what he says and does not allow his disillusionment to govern all his thoughts and words. Mind you, from all the other passages in which Jeremiah pours out his pain, God's rebuke in 15:19 clearly did not inhibit him from more bursts of agonized protest and lament. The man was human, after all.

2. BITTERNESS AND RESENTMENT AGAINST OTHERS (V. 15)

This could be labeled as failure to come to terms with opposition.

Jeremiah had been warned. Right at the time of his call, God had told him that he would need to be like an iron pillar in order to stand up against the opposition and rejection he would encounter (1:8, 17–19). He started out as a young man, and his message was uncompromising and unpopular. He had to be tough just to carry on. But surely, Lord, thirty years of it is a bit much for anybody to endure! And remember—it was not just polite theological disagreement in some friendly academic debate. People did not put their arms round Jeremiah's shoulders and sympathetically say, "We see your point of view, young man, and we're very sorry, but we just can't really go along with you there." No, Jeremiah was laughed at, rejected, ostracized, physically threatened, beaten, imprisoned, falsely accused, and almost lynched ... On and on and on it went, year after year. And worst of all, some of it came from his own kinsfolk, who seem to have regarded him as a traitor to them and the whole country. In the end, Jeremiah could bear it in silence no longer. He became bitter and resentful and cried out to God for vengeance on those who were making his life a misery (at best) and seeking to actually kill him (at worst).

We need to use our imagination and think into the emotions that lie behind passages like 12:3; 17:18; 18:19–23 and 20:12. There is a frighteningly frank honesty in the way Jeremiah expresses his feelings and his longings in such texts, which are echoed also in some of the Psalms. But before we point a self-righteously accusing finger at him, we should look deep into our own hearts, where we may sometimes find similar thoughts about other people who treat us with opposition and hostility—even if we would never speak them aloud. How amazing it is that such sentiments are actually recorded in our Bible!

There are several things about bitterness and resentment that make them dangerous.

First of all, they come high on the list of the most poisonous and lethal of emotions. We talk about being "eaten up" by bitterness, or "burning" with resentment—and those are metaphors that express exactly what these emotions do. They take a heavy toll on our health: psychological, spiritual, and even physical. There was a short period in my own life when my wife and I with our very young family went through a time of acute financial struggle and stress. We became bitter at God for allowing it and resentful of other Christian friends who seemed to be so well off and comfortable. We suffered rather helplessly at the mercy of those destructive emotions, till we faced them very honestly before God in repentance.

Secondly, bitterness and resentment are among the longest lasting emotions. People can bear grudges throughout their whole lives. Anger is usually short-lived. It can flare up and die away quite quickly. But resentment smolders on. I have met people in late adult life who have been crippled spiritually and emotionally (and in one case even disfigured physically) by resentments that began in childhood experiences. No wonder the Bible speaks of "the root of bitterness" (Heb. 12:15–16). It goes down deep, grows overlong, and bears perennial fruit—unless it is dealt with.

Thirdly, bitterness and resentment together raise one of the hardest and most resistant barriers to personal wholeness and spiritual health. This is because they usually include, at their core, a refusal to forgive some other person for a wrong or hurt (whether real or imaginary). And that refusal to forgive in turn prevents one from being forgiven, which in turn blocks off the flow of cleansing and healing. Jesus was quite specific and insistent when he warned us about this. Those who will not forgive others will not experience God's forgiveness themselves (Matt. 6:14). And without forgiveness, there is no true healing or restoration. There is a terrible cost to pay for nursing resentment.

So, what is God's answer to this part of Jeremiah's problem—his bitterness and resentment and vengeful desires against others? Well, one part of God's answer can be seen here, but the full answer lies beyond the horizon of the Old Testament.

In the Old Testament, people who felt aggrieved by their enemies through being attacked in one way or another were warned not to take vengeance themselves. Rather, they should accept that ultimately all "vengeance" (in the sense of righting a wrong and punishing the wrong-doer), all justice, all "putting things right," belong to God. God is the judge of all the earth, who will do justice—even if not immediately. So then, if there is some *real* cause for bitterness because some real wrong has been done, if there is a genuine grievance that cries out for redress—then hand it over to God and appeal to him to sort it out and put it right. This does not, of course, remove the need for the proper exercise of justice within the limits of human ability—through judges and courts and so on.

Indeed, God demands that society should seek to do justice and see that wrong-doers are punished and the innocent vindicated. But when that does not happen? When judges are corrupt? When money and power win the day? Then, appeal to God. Do not take the law into your own hands and act in violent vengeance. That is the road to blood feuds, accumulating violence, and social collapse.

So, Jeremiah, suffering all kinds of unjust hurt and wrong, including threats on his life, appeals to God to deal with his enemies and to punish them as the wrong-doers they are. Now, notice carefully what God says to Jeremiah in response, in 15:20–21. God does not dismiss Jeremiah's appeal as mere paranoia, "Of course nobody is out to get you!" On the contrary, God *agrees* with Jeremiah. There are indeed "wicked" and "cruel" people out there, who are intent on harming or silencing Jeremiah. But, God says, I will deal with them. Trust me. God says the same in 11:21–23.

So, in the Old Testament, the righteous are the ones who refrain from taking personal revenge on their enemies, but rather commit their cause to God and appeal to God to do justice on their behalf. That is the stance of the Servant of the Lord (Isa. 49:4, 50:7–9). And that, in turn, becomes the model for Jesus himself—and for his followers, when we suffer unjustly (1 Pet. 2:21–23).

Now, even if we were to go no further, this principle in the Old Testament stands out in contrast to the chronic tendency for human beings to fight back and "get even." Sadly, Christians often behave in the same way. We jump to defend ourselves, or to denounce others. We are fiercely loyal to our own group or party and engage in despicable political maneuvers to bring down those we see as "enemies." But should we not learn from Jeremiah (and Jesus and Paul), that even if real wrong has been done to us, rather than defending ourselves and / or seeking vengeance, we should leave it to God to vindicate the innocent and deal with the wicked? We may not like the tone of Jeremiah's prayer, but that is what in fact he was doing.

Of course, the New Testament does go much further than this. It not only repeats the Old Testament command not to retaliate, but it calls us to replace the spirit of vengeance with love. "Love your enemies and pray for those who persecute you," said Jesus (Matt. 5:43–48). Love your enemies! Why on earth should we do that? Because God, your Heavenly Father, does. But how can we do it? Surely, it is impossible to love those who are hating and attacking you? Yes, of course it is—apart from the supreme example, command, and empowering Spirit of Jesus himself. For, it was Jesus who, suffering the worst miscarriage of justice in human history and the horrendous torture and death that followed, could pray, "Father forgive them." And it is in his name alone that Paul could appeal to us to "Forgive one another, as God in Christ has forgiven you" (Eph. 4:32). We are commanded to forgive. It is not just a nice option. For forgiveness is the only remedy for bitterness.

Bitterness and resentment are a kind of bondage. They enslave, cripple, and paralyze us. But to expose that bondage to the incredible forgiving love of the crucified Christ is to have it melted away and to be released instead to forgive as we are forgiven. It is a most blessed and life-changing release. It produces amazing spiritual and psychological transformation in a person when he or she is released from the bondage of bitterness. I have seen someone whose whole physical appearance—the person's whole countenance—was transformed through the experience of forgiving and being forgiven.

Is it perhaps time for you to experience this for yourself, if your own life is being stifled and crippled by bitterness and resentment and an unforgiving spirit toward someone else? If the problem lies very deep, perhaps even deep in the past, then be humble enough to seek wise spiritual counsel and help. Do not go on nursing these life-sucking emotions. It is not worth the cost.

3. SELF-PITY

This could be labeled as failure to come to terms with his own feelings.

Verses 17–18 are redolent with self-pity. Jeremiah is lonely and broken hearted and wants God to know how he feels. If we want to know why he was so lonely, we only have to read chapter 16, where we find that God not only prohibited him from getting married (which was almost unheard of for men in his time and culture; Hebrew has no word for "bachelor"), but also instructed him not to participate in normal village social events like wedding or funeral feasts. So, whenever the village was gathering for community rejoicing or weeping, Jeremiah was noticeably absent. It must have been both socially offensive and severely isolating.

Now, Jeremiah had done plenty of weeping and groaning before. But in the earlier chapters of his book, we find that his grief was being poured out for the suffering of others. That is the clear focus of his tears in 8:18—9:1. Jeremiah felt deep sorrow at the persistent sin of his people and the terrible judgment they were storing up for themselves. So, he wished his whole head were made of water so that he would have enough tears to shed for his people. But now, it seems that all his emotions are introverted, turned in upon himself. He is weeping for his own pain (which is understandable, we might easily agree), wallowing in self-pity. At least, that is how I read his words here, in contrast to earlier words of grief for others.

Self-pity is another crippling, unhealthy emotion. It usually involves some element of wounded pride or suppressed arrogance. It dwells on the perceived conflict between what I am experiencing and what I think I deserve. And if you are in some form of ministry for God, you may well think (as Jeremiah did) that it is simply not fair to be pouring yourself out for him and still suffering so. "Here am I, called to a great ministry, destined for greater things, and yet look what I'm going through! I deserve better than this. I'm doing my best for the good of others, and yet they all hate me! Who do they think they are treating like this! Woe is me!"

Self-pity also has a strong element of self-centeredness. When it is given outward expression, it usually invites everybody else to feel sorry for me and bemoan what I am going through. It seeks sympathy and compliments. In fact, self-pity can be a very subtle form of sin, precisely because it is not recognized as sin at all by the person in the midst of it. On the contrary, it usually has the effect of making somebody feel, "I am the one who is being sinned against! I am the victim of other people, or of some undeserved circumstances." So, it becomes a powerful barrier to repentance and wholeness.

Jeremiah gets so bound up with himself and his own pain at this point, drowning in such a pit of despair and self-pity, that he even accuses God of being a failure. Just look at his astonishing outburst in verse 18b: "And as for you, God," he explodes, "You're a disappointment too. Just when I need you most, you turn out to be like a dried-up river bed!" Contrast that for a moment with the beautiful picture God had given Jeremiah in 2:13, that he, God, was like a spring of living water, never failing, always there to refresh and irrigate. But now, says Jeremiah, God seems like a wadi that looks like it should have water, but when you get there, it is all dried up. "That's you, God," says Jeremiah—"full of promises, but delivering nothing. Where are you God? You cannot be trusted!"

Now doubtless, we might protest, Jeremiah should not have even thought such things, let alone said them out loud and in prayer. But he did. That is what he was feeling and thinking, and he let it all out, expressing his very raw emotions with remarkable transparency to God himself. And this makes me think of how well Jeremiah must have known his God, how confident he was in his relationship with God, to have the boldness to be so brutally honest with him.

After all, God himself says, "I the Lord search the heart and examine the mind" (Jer. 17:10). So, God knows our innermost thoughts anyway. What, then, is the point of holding them inside ourselves, trying to conceal them, or pretending that we do not actually feel and think what is going on inside us? I cannot help thinking that some Christian worship (especially in our songs) consists of pretending to feel what we really do not feel, while simultaneously pretending not to feel what we really do feel. We may fool other people, and even ourselves, but we do not fool God. And since God knows, the far healthier way is to be totally honest in his presence and tell him exactly what we feel and think, for then we have a better chance of hearing what he might have to say in response.

What we find in this passage is that Jeremiah's outburst of honesty (vv. 15–18) leads to God's response of rebuke, restoration, and renewed promise (vv. 19–21). The lesson surely is that honesty with ourselves and God is the first step on the road to healing. There is no healing without repentance, but equally there is no repentance without honesty—even if that honesty involves giving vent to anger with God, questioning, protesting, and appealing. There is plenty of that kind of honesty with God in the Psalms, which God himself has given us to use. God wants us to be real in his presence, so that he can make himself truly present in our reality.

I remember a lady in a church where I was pastoring, for whom the first step back from deep-seated nervous and emotional collapse was a half-hour she spent raging with hitherto unexpressed anger against God—shouting at God, beating a cushion and myself quite liberally in the process.

The trouble is, we are often afraid of our own emotions, or we are afraid to share or receive the emotions of others. We get embarrassed and perhaps offended by them. We try to suppress them or deny them, which is really rather silly when you think that God created our emotions just as much as every other dimension of our embodied human life. But if we bottle up our true feelings and demand that others do the same, then it is no wonder if our human relationships are shallow and brittle and our relationship with God impersonal and routine. Let us rather pray to be able to accept what we feel and express it honestly to God. If there is something wrong or sinful in what we are thinking, then God will show us that, just as he does here for Jeremiah. He will respond not to drive us away in condemnation, but to gently bring us back to wholeness and renewed service.

God's answer to Jeremiah's outburst of self-pity in verses 17–18 are his words of repentance, recommissioning, and renewed promise in verses 19–21. And, again, they begin with the call to repent, which, in the case of self-pity, is a very hard word to hear.

Years ago, my wife and I went to a Christian medical practice for a full medical check-up before we left for service in India. I was out of the doctor's room in a matter of minutes—nothing wrong with life or limb. It seemed like my wife, however, did not come out for ages, and when she did, her face was white and disturbed. What on earth had they discovered to be wrong with her? I feared. Well, nothing physical was wrong. But the discerning Christian doctor had asked questions that got underneath some of my wife's deeper feelings, in response to the difficult circumstances we had faced in the previous few years of preparation. In the car on the way home, she told me the doctor had told her (with gentle truth) that she was filled with self-pity (which she admitted she was). And then he said to her, "The only thing to do with self-pity is to repent of it," which was very hard to hear, and still is. But it is true. The trouble is, of course, that self-pity is an emotion that makes us feel it is all the other people who need to repent, not me! I am the victim here; I am not the one who is doing anything wrong. It is hard to repent of self-pity because it can be a rather cozy emotion, giving you a kind of false comfort. You can wallow in it and enjoy it for a while, making everybody around you miserable, too. That is the trap—it becomes yet another sinful self-centeredness that quickly becomes a kind of bondage, with unhealthy results. The tentacles of self-pity can wrap themselves around you. And only specific repentance can break them off.

Self-pity is a state of mind that I personally find very easy to give in to, often because of some circumstance that ruins my plans; or because of frustration, stress, exhaustion, or disillusionment. And at such times, that doctor's words to my wife pierce my self-pitying thoughts: "the only thing to do with self-pity is to repent of it." So, I turn to self-accusation instead, and talk to God very directly: "Lord, you know how I am feeling right now, how dejected and frustrated and angry I am. But I repent of failing to see your hand in my circumstances and of assuming that all my own plans must be the best and must be fulfilled. Thank you for all the good things that I have been overlooking at the moment. Fill me with a gratitude that will drive out the self-pity. Restore to me the joy of serving you, even when things are not the way I would like them to be for my own convenience."

It is so encouraging, then, to read that God's response to Jeremiah did not stop at calling him to repent of the things he was thinking and saying. God restored Jeremiah's mission: "that you may serve me… . You will be my spokesman." This is effectively a recommissioning of what God had given to Jeremiah at the time of his original call to be a prophet in chapter 1. Not only does God renew the commission, he also renews the promise that went with it, "I am with you to rescue and save you… . I will save you… . and deliver you." These are wonderful words for Jeremiah and for us. But notice that we read them in the context of the despairing words that Jeremiah himself had spoken to God. Jeremiah's honesty meets God's healing.

Disillusionment, bitterness / resentment, and self-pity are a terrible trio of destructive emotions, miserable symptoms of sick and struggling Christians, even in the midst of their working hard in service to God. Yet, when we honestly express these feelings to God, then he can do his healing work—through repentance, recommissioning, and renewal of his precious promises to us.

May God the Holy Spirit help us not only to diagnose such symptoms when they manifest themselves in our own lives or the lives of those we love, but also to turn to God, our healer, and hear his gentle words of rebuke, restoration, and hope.

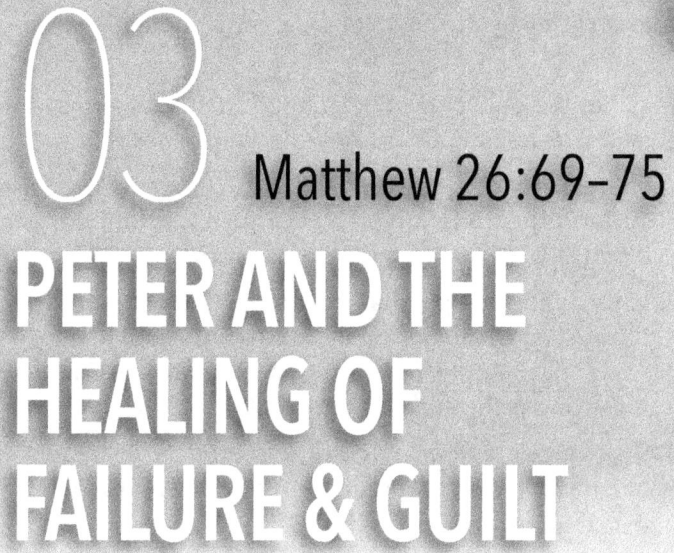

03
Matthew 26:69-75
PETER AND THE HEALING OF FAILURE & GUILT

by CHRISTOPHER J. H. WRIGHT

Note: This sermon was first preached at All Souls Church, Langham Place, London on March 30, 2003, and was first published in *Let the Gospels Preach the Gospel: Sermons Around the Cross* (Carlisle, PA: Langham, 2016), and *To the Cross: Proclaiming the Gospel from the Upper Room to Calvary* (Downers Grove, IL: InterVarsity, 2017). It is reprinted here with permission.

One of my favorite books is *The Book of Heroic Failures: The Official Handbook of the Not Terribly Good Club of Great Britain,* by Stephen Pile. Here is how he introduces the book:

> Success is overrated.
>
> Everyone craves it despite daily proof that man's real genius lies in quite the opposite direction. Incompetence is what we're good at: it is the quality that marks us off from animals, and we should learn to revere it …
>
> I am sure that I am not the only one who cannot do things and the slightest investigation reveals that no one else can do anything either.… .
>
> So, in 1976 the Not Terribly Good Club of Great Britain was formed, with myself, cocooned in administrative failure, as president.
>
> To qualify for membership, you just had to be not terribly good at something (fishing, small talk, batik, anything) and then attend meetings at which people talked about and gave public demonstrations of the things they could not do.
>
> In September 1976, twenty members hand-picked from all fields of incompetence gathered for the inaugural dinner at an exquisitely inferior London restaurant …[1]

The book then goes on to describe the most spectacular failures that historical research could uncover: the most unsuccessful bank-robbery, the worst bus service, the least successful firework, the worst performance of Macbeth, the fastest defeat in a war, and so on. It is a brilliantly funny book.

Of course, in real life, failure is usually very far from funny, except sometimes when we look back on minor moments of our own fallibility. Failure can be tragic and even desperately sad. We can think of marriages that have failed or of important exams that have been failed. We think of brave rescue attempts that have tragically failed or times when people failed to keep important promises. We are hardly even surprised when politicians fail to keep the promises of their election manifestos. Failure can be disappointing, cruel, tragic—and, sadly, sometimes simply predictable.

In Matthew 26:69–75, we read the story of Peter's great failure. It is so significant that it is one of the few events that are recorded in all four gospels. All four gospels note that Jesus predicted Peter would fail and that Peter did, indeed, fail.[2] Right in the middle of the story of Jesus' suffering and death, Peter's

---

[1] Stephen Pile, *The Book of Heroic Failures: The Official Handbook of the Not Terribly Good Club of Great Britain* (Abingdon-on-Thames: Routledge & Kegan Paul, 1979).

[2] Matt. 26:31-35, 69-75; Mark 14:27-31, 68-72; Luke 22:31-34, 54-62; John 13:37-38; 18:15-27.

denial, along with Judas's betrayal, makes that tragic story even more painful. The greatest story ever—the redemption of the world—is punctured by this moment of squalid human treachery.

Peter's failure is certainly tragic. Yet, of course, as I am sure we would all agree, it is very understandable. We can identify with Peter. Surely, only the most brazen of us would want to claim that we would have stood firm where Peter caved in.

Let us relive the story, shall we? Imagine the scene and put ourselves in it. Here is how Matthew tells it.

> Now Peter was sitting out in the courtyard, and a servant girl came to him. "You also were with Jesus of Galilee," she said.
>
> But he denied it before them all. "I don't know what you're talking about," he said.
>
> Then he went out to the gateway, where another servant girl saw him and said to the people there, "This fellow was with Jesus of Nazareth."
>
> He denied it again, with an oath: "I don't know the man!"
>
> After a little while, those standing there went up to Peter and said, "Surely you are one of them; your accent gives you away."
>
> Then he began to call down curses, and he swore to them, "I don't know the man!"
>
> Immediately a rooster crowed. Then Peter remembered the word Jesus had spoken: "Before the rooster crows, you will disown me three times." And he went outside and wept bitterly.
>
> Matthew 26:69-75

Matthew's story is full of irony and shock. Look at the contrasting images he puts before us when we put the Peter incident in the context of the rest of Matthew 26:

- There, on the one hand, is Jesus–in danger of his life, and yet he stands firm before the highest authorities in the land while they threaten him. On the other hand, there is Peter–in danger of probably not very much except embarrassment and possibly a bit of a beating, but he gives way before no one more threatening than a couple of servant girls.

- There, on the one hand, is Jesus–under oath to speak the truth about himself, and he does so. And there, on the other hand, is Peter–calling down oaths in order to deny the truth about himself and Jesus.

- There, on the one hand, is Jesus–falsely accused of blasphemy (an incredible thing in itself–the Son of God, accused of blasphemy!). And there, on the other hand, is Peter–actually guilty of blasphemy in the very presence of the Lord.

In fact, the text says that not only did he falsely swear an oath (taking the name of the Lord in vain in order to tell a lie), but it says he "called down curses." Some Bibles add, "on himself," but Matthew just says that he called down curses. So, it is perfectly possible that he called down curses on Jesus, saying something like, "I swear to God I don't know him. Curse the fellow!"

- When a slave girl looks at Peter with threatening recognition, he manages to curse and swear his way out of it. Yet, when Jesus looks at him (as Luke tells us), Peter can only rush out into the darkness as the cock is crowing, reminding him of the words of Jesus.

So, then, here is Peter, the anti-hero of our story:

- Wielding a sword in the darkness of the garden in front of a squad of soldiers, but only a few hours later, withering before a servant girl in the light of a fire;
- Hauling in a whole net full of fish single-handedly, but melting in fear when asked a few suspicious questions;
- Swearing that he would die for Jesus, but later swearing that he did not even know him;
- Bursting with courage and good intentions, and only a couple hours later, overflowing with shame, bitterness, despair, and tears;
- Hearing Jesus call him "the rock," but now finding himself a sobbing blob of jelly.

In short, Peter failed. Suddenly, surprisingly, shatteringly, Peter failed.

And as far as Matthew's gospel goes, that is the end of the story. Of course, we know more about Peter after this from the other gospels, but as far as this narrative in Matthew's gospel goes, Peter never reappears. Peter is last seen out in the darkness, weeping and gnashing his teeth. End of story (in Matthew).

What does this tell us? How do we respond, not only to what this story tells us about Peter, but also to what it tells us about ourselves? Why has Matthew reported it? Why have all the gospels reported this story? I think the story of Peter's great failure tells us three things at least, of which the first is very simply this:

1. FAILURE IS A FACT

Failure is a fact in the Bible. Think about it. Do a mental scan through the Bible. Adam and Eve failed, even though they were in a perfect environment. Abraham failed; he told lies about his wife and abused Hagar. Samuel failed to get his own sons to behave properly, even though he started out his own career condemning Eli for the same thing. Gideon failed, even after his great victory over the Midianites, when he said that he would not become a king and then behaved as if he were one and made an idolatrous object. Moses failed in the wilderness, to his own great regret. David failed, appallingly, not only in his acts of adultery and planned murder, but in failing to control his own family all the rest of his life. Every king of Israel failed in one way and another. The people of Israel as a whole failed, for generation after generation through the Old Testament—God's covenant people, God's redeemed people. Failure runs through the Old Testament like a ragged thread.

The New Testament, as well, shows us people failing all over the place. Even here in this story, why is it that we blame Peter for *his* denial of Jesus when, in fact, Matthew tells us that *all the disciples* forsook him and fled? Peter, poor man, was the only one (well, almost the only one, as we will see in a minute) who was actually in a position where he *could* deny Jesus. The only reason the other disciples did not deny Jesus is that they were not even there. They had fled. And yet, as Matthew tells us very carefully in verse 35, they had *all* said the same thing as Peter. "We won't disown you, we won't deny you." But when it came to the crunch, they all—except for Peter and, as we shall see, one other—deserted him. They were a collective failure.

You see, the whole Bible, from beginning to end, is a story of human failure (with the single exception of the Lord Jesus Christ himself). In fact, you could say that the title of Stephen Pile's book would be a very good title for the Bible— *The Book of Heroic Failures* (except that most of them were not particularly heroic). Certainly, its subtitle fits the Bible: "The Official Handbook of: the Not Terribly Good Club of Humanity"—except that the Bible does not tell us that we are just "not terribly good." It actually tells us that we are radically and terribly flawed. Sin has wormed its evil way into the depths of our human nature. Indeed, mere failure is only one of the least of our problems. Genesis 6 tells us that God saw that "every inclination of the thoughts of the human heart was only evil all the time." Jeremiah observed, probably from his own honest knowledge of himself, "The heart is deceitful above all things and desperately wicked. Who can understand it?" (Jer. 17:9). Paul tells us that whether you are a good Jew or a wicked pagan makes no difference. "There is no difference between Jew and Gentile, for all have sinned and fall short of the glory of God" (Rom. 3:23). John tells us, "If we claim to be without sin, we deceive ourselves and the truth is not in us" (1 John 1:8).

So, if you are ever tempted to imagine that you have never really failed, get real! You are only deceiving yourself. Failure is a fact. It is certainly a fact in the Bible.

Failure is a fact of experience. Most of us have some idea of the great story of the history of the Christian church. We know that the Gospel has spread from country to country and from continent to continent. We know something of the origins and growth of the great missionary movements. Maybe we have read some missionary biographies and admire the great things that courageous people have done for God down through the centuries. We can tell that great story of the past two thousand years as a testimony to the success of the Gospel by the power, grace, and sovereignty of God.

But looked at from another angle, church history is also a history of failures—some of them pretty ghastly. Rather like the stories of the Old Testament, we sometimes have to stand in amazement at what God accomplished *in spite* of the weakness and failure of the people he used, rather than *because* of their marvelous achievements. Sometimes (unlike the Bible) missionary biographies gloss over those less inspiring moments of failure.

I have another book of heroic failures.[3] This one is actually rather bigger—a lot fatter than Stephen Pile's little paperback. It is called *Too Valuable to Lose: Exploring the Causes and Cures of Missionary Attrition.* "Attrition" is the rather polite word used for missionaries who return home earlier than they expected or originally intended—for whatever reason. The book has researched those reasons and sought to analyze and address them. It is the product of an extensive research project, followed by a conference that was held at All Nations Christian College some years ago, to examine that reality—the problem of missionary failure (or apparent failure).

But missionaries? Here are people who, we might think, have the very highest motivation and calling and all good intentions to serve God in Christian mission. Some of them have had intensive training. Most of them are strongly supported and prayed for by others. And yet some of them also fail in one way or another. Some of them return home broken and disillusioned. Some fall into ungodly relationships. Some fall ill. Some just give up. The reasons are very varied, and not all of them are in any way blameworthy.

Failure is a fact.

The great tragedy is that so often we do not, or we will not, admit it. And, to be honest, we are usually rather embarrassed when other Christians start confessing their failures, afraid we may have to join the confession with a few of our own. We would rather cover up our shame and keep up some sort of pretense of "victorious Christian living," "Spirit-filled Christian living," or whatever phrase is popular at the time.

After all, we have read the books. We have been to the conferences. We have been up at the front or down at the back. We have been there, done that, bought the T-shirt—all in the effort to be a successful Christian.

We are not about to admit, after all that, that we still do not have it together. We are not going to admit that we still fall for the same old sins. We are not going to admit that we are uncomfortable being too visible as a Christian in a hostile world. We would not go so far as to say we have ever actually *denied* knowing Christ. We just do not say much about it at all. We are not going to admit the way we talk and think when nobody is listening or what we look at when we are alone or the way we treat those closest to us in our own families.

---

3 William Taylor, ed. (Pasadena, CA: William Carey Library, 1997).

We are not going to admit that, in short, we still fail.

Except that we do fail. And we know it.

It grieves me that in some Christian churches and communities there seems to be a whole culture of pretense, a constant celebration of glittering success stories ("testimonies") and a denial of the reality of failure. I think it can be pastorally disastrous, and it can even come close to denying the truth of the gospel. I have been in worship services where there was no confession of sin at all in the whole service—nothing but a diet of triumphant songs, testimonies, and the preaching of "success" and "faith" and "victory."

Have you ever reflected on this odd paradox in some Christian circles? It seems that *in order to become* a Christian, the *first* thing you have to do is admit that you have failed. But somehow, *once you have become* a Christian, the *last* thing you are ever expected to do is to admit that you fail. It seems that in order to enter the church, you must accept that you are a sinner, but the only way of staying credible within the church is by pretending to be a success. Certainly, there is something wrong there. Are we not missing something of the ongoing reality of grace in our lives—not just at the moment of coming to faith but in every step of the journey that follows?

Let us come back to our story of Peter. Surely, I think, one of the reasons that this story is in the Bible (recorded four times) is that it forces us to admit and accept the reality of failure. And this is a very liberating thing to do. Peter—one of the foremost of the first disciples of Jesus—failed. I fail. You fail. So does every other Christian on the planet. What a relief! Because, you see, the truly liberating thing that this story tells us, secondly, is that failure is not only a fact, but failure is also foreseen.

2. FAILURE IS FORESEEN

One of the shocking points of Matthew's account in chapter 26 is that Jesus knew beforehand about both Judas's betrayal and Peter's denial.

Look at verse 21. Jesus says, "Truly I tell you, one of you will betray me." At this, the disciples were all appalled and said, "It couldn't be me! What, me? No way! It's not me, for sure!" Jesus' prediction was a huge surprise, and apparently, even at this stage, none of the rest of the disciples suspected Judas.

Next, look at verse 31. Jesus says, "This very night you will all fall away on account of me." Another big shock! And they all said, "No, no, no. Of course we won't!" Peter especially protested, saying, "Me? Never! I won't disown you even if all these others do! You know me, Lord! I'll die for you if I have to!"—to which Jesus replied, "This very night, before the rooster crows, you will disown me three times."

The failures of Judas and Peter (and of all the others, too, of course) were foreseen by Jesus. Tragically, that fact seems to have made no difference for Judas, but as far as Peter is concerned, I think it is probably what saved him. Even as he went outside into the dark and wept bitterly, he must have been remembering,

"Jesus knew! Jesus said I would do that." That probably made his tears all the more bitter. And think of that look of Jesus (Luke 22:61). Peter knew that Jesus knew what he had just done—but Jesus had known all along. Indeed, Jesus had quoted Scripture (Matt. 26:31) to show that even Peter's denial and the desertion of all the disciples were in some mysterious way a fulfillment of what the Scripture had said. The whole scene was, therefore, in some sense, still under control. Jesus has it covered in more ways than one.

One of our old hymns includes the line, "Jesus knows our every weakness."[4] That is not a put-down. It is not a veiled threat. It is a word of comfort. Because if Jesus *knows,* then Jesus can cope with it. There is hope. There is light at the end of the tunnel. Failure is foreseen. Our failures certainly *grieve* the Lord, but they do not *surprise* him. He knows what is inside us. He knows what we are capable of.

I wonder if you have ever reflected on the way the story of the prediction of Peter's denial is told in John's gospel. I find it remarkable. Turn to John 13. It is a narrative filled with emotional tension. There is painful embarrassment as Jesus washes the disciples' feet. Then there is the shock of the prediction of the betrayal. Then there is the mysterious word about how Jesus is going to leave them. And, finally, there is the shock of Jesus predicting that Peter will deny him. Peter protests, but Jesus insists, "Will you really lay down your life for me? Very truly I tell you, before the rooster crows, you will disown me three times."

Now, remember, in John's original writing there were no chapter divisions. There was no heading, as in our Bibles, announcing, "Chapter fourteen, verse one, *Jesus Comforts his Disciples.*" Those breaks and titles were added much later to help us find our way around the Bible. Unfortunately, they sometimes make us read from the start of what we now call John 14 as if it has nothing to do with what we have just read in chapter 13. But in John's gospel, as he originally wrote it, Jesus went straight from having the discussion we see at the end of chapter 13 to saying, "But do not let your hearts be troubled."

What? How could he say that, after what had just happened?

"One of you is going to betray me, I'm going to die for you, and one of you is going to deny me, but—listen, don't let your hearts be troubled! Don't worry. Don't panic. Trust me. You trust in God; trust me. I know what I'm doing. I know where I'm going. And even your betrayals and your denials cannot destroy or derail what I am now about to do for you and for the world. I know all about what's going to happen, so don't let your hearts be troubled."

Failure is foreseen, and Jesus can be trusted even in the midst of it.

And that is what leads to the third and last truth that Peter discovered in this story (or, after this story, as Matthew tells it, for in Matthew's gospel, this is the last that we see of Peter; the other gospels, however, give us a happier ending). Peter discovered that not only is failure a fact, not only is failure foreseen, but failure is also forgiven.

---

4 It comes from the hymn, "What a friend we have in Jesus."

3. FAILURE IS FORGIVEN

Peter's tears were undoubtedly tears of remorse. But they must also have been tears of repentance that ultimately led to his restoration. How did that happen? Well, Luke and John give us the answers. Luke tells us that Jesus prayed for Peter's faith, and John shows us how Jesus probed for Peter's love. These factors were the keys to Peter's restoration.

Jesus prayed for Peter's faith (Luke 22:31–32). Luke records that Jesus said to Peter, just before warning him that he would deny Jesus three times, "Simon, Simon, Satan has asked to sift all of you as wheat. But I have prayed for you, Simon. I have prayed for you, that your faith may not fail. And when you have turned back, strengthen your brothers." And that prayer of Jesus was surely answered.

Yes, of course, Peter's nerve failed. Yes, Peter's courage failed. But somehow, Peter's faith did not fail. I do not know how, and I do not suppose that Peter knew how either, but somehow and somewhere inside himself, Peter went on trusting Jesus, even through this ghastly, shattering experience. Peter's faith did not fail, because Jesus prayed that it would not fail. I wonder, even as he went out into the darkness, if Peter heard in his agonized ears not just the taunts of the people he was running away from, but also the echo of those words of Jesus just a few hours before, "You trust in God. Trust also in me … Trust me, Peter. Go on having faith in me as you did on that first day you followed me. Trust me. Trust me."

Have you failed Jesus? Of course you have. The more appropriate question to ask would be, when did you last fail Jesus? Then, the key question is, do you still trust Jesus?

Have you let Jesus down again? Of course you have. Of course I have. The question is, do you still trust him?

Have you felt the deep shame of that failure? The embarrassment of it? Have you found yourself almost unable to face Jesus in prayer again because of it? The shame of failing—again? Of course you have. The question is, do you still trust Jesus?

After all, it was when you first decided to trust Jesus, when you first chose to put your faith in him, that you began your life as a Christian. Why stop trusting him now in the face of this latest failure, when you have trusted him to carry on the cross all the failures and sins of all your life?

The older I get and the longer I go on in the Christian life, and the more times I experience my own personal failure usually known only to myself but sometimes to others, the more I have learned how important it is not to trust myself, but to constantly come back and say, "Lord, it's *you* I trust." You see, Peter thought he could trust himself, did he not? He protested boldly that *he* would never let Jesus down. He would go to prison! He would die! But deny Jesus? Never! Peter trusted his own courage, his own strength. But he fell flat on his face, devastated and disgraced. The question is, where do you go from there? You go back to Jesus, who is praying for you, praying that your faith will survive. Peter knew that he could still trust Jesus—even if he could not have seen or imagined what that might mean. Peter's restoration depended on his continuing faith, and that depended on God's assured answer to Jesus' prayer.

Jesus probed for Peter's love. Jesus not only prayed for Peter's faith; he also probed for Peter's love. That comes out in the story at the end of John's gospel (John 21:15–19). It is a very familiar story; we know it well. Jesus makes breakfast for the disciples after their early morning fishing excursion and after yet another miracle involving a lot of fish. Then, when they have all eaten, and perhaps as they are starting to walk away from the lake, Jesus asks these three questions to Peter—really, he asks the same question once, then again, and again: "Peter, do you love me?"

I rather think that this occurred in a private conversation as they walked, for we read that "Peter turned and saw that the disciple whom Jesus loved was following them" (John 21:20), which suggests that Jesus and Peter were walking together, with John just behind them, possibly the only one able to hear the conversation between Jesus and Peter. Of course, I cannot be sure of that, and it is also possible that the conversation happened with all the disciples listening and before Jesus said (yet again), "Follow me."

No matter how the scene unfolded, have you ever wondered why it is only *John* who brings us the story of Peter's restoration? Why John? The answer, I feel sure, is that it was because John was the only one who witnessed Peter's failure (apart from Jesus, of course).

Turn to John 18. Jesus has just been arrested by the soldiers in the garden and is being taken off, bound, to the Jewish high court.

Simon Peter and another disciple were following Jesus. Because this disciple was known to the high priest, he went with Jesus into the high priest's courtyard, but Peter had to wait outside at the door. The other disciple, who was known to the high priest, came back, spoke to the servant girl on duty there and brought Peter in (John 18:15–16).

Now, that phrase, "the other disciple," is usually assumed to mean John himself. It is John's 'anonymous' signature for himself. He uses it a number of times in the gospel: "The other disciple whom Jesus loved." So, almost certainly, it was John who was known to the high priest, who came back, spoke to the girl on duty at the door, and let Peter into the courtyard where Jesus was on trial before Annas and then Caiaphas the high priest.

John was there.

John saw, and John heard, this horrifying moment of Peter's cursing denial of Jesus. John actually watched as Peter disowned Jesus—again and again. John heard Peter saying that he did not even know Jesus—this Jesus whom they both loved, this Jesus for whom they had both given up everything three years earlier. Peter, James and John—they were the innermost group of disciples, remember? Had they not walked and talked and eaten with Jesus? Had not Jesus even visited Peter's own house and healed his wife's mother? Had not Peter been the one to solemnly affirm that this Jesus was the Messiah, the Son of God? Had they not climbed the Mount of Transfiguration together? And had not Jesus crouched down and washed Peter's feet just a few hours before? And now, here is John, watching Peter with jaw-dropping astonishment, as the fellow denies—again and again—that he even knows Jesus at all and does so with oaths and blasphemy and cursing, with his coarse Galilean accent giving him away all the time.

John was there!

I sometimes wonder how Peter and John ever faced each other again after that terrible night. There must have been agonizing moments between them on the Saturday after the crucifixion. Did Peter beg John not to tell the other disciples? How could Peter ever again talk about loving Jesus if John were around and listening? And yet, that is exactly what happened, and John is the one who tells us. It did not happen because of Peter's initiative but under Jesus' probing, surgical question, "Peter, do you love me? Do you love me more than these? Peter, do you love me?"—asked three times, the same number of times that Peter denied Jesus. The connection is obvious. Jesus knew, Peter knew, and John was listening.

But look—who was this asking Peter the question? This is John chapter 21. It was the risen Jesus who questioned Peter—Jesus, who had already been on the cross and in the tomb. This was the Jesus who had taken upon himself all of Peter's guilt, failure, disgrace, humiliation, and sin. All of Peter's shame had been carried by Jesus on the cross.

> And all of your shame. And all of mine as well.
> Bearing shame and scoffing rude,
> in my place condemned he stood;
> sealed my pardon with his blood.
> Hallelujah, what a Saviour!

This Jesus asked the question, "Now then, Peter, do you love me?" And Peter says, "Lord, Lord, you know. You *know*. You know I love you. I have *always* loved you, and I still do. Even when I was denying you, I loved you. It broke my heart and yours. I hated myself, but I loved you. And I love you now, Lord. I love you, Lord."

And that was all Jesus wanted to hear this time around, not all that swearing that he would die for him (which he would do eventually), not all that great bluster, "Me? No, no, I'll never deny you!" All Jesus wanted to hear was, "Lord, you know that I love you."

It was all John needed to hear, as well. For, if Jesus had forgiven Peter, then he must forgive Peter, too. He could love Peter again, as they both loved Jesus. That is why John recorded it for the rest of us.

Peter the failure becomes Peter the forgiven. Have you been there? I have. I know what it is in my own experience, after an episode of particular and despicable failure of the Lord, to be literally flat on my face on the floor in tears before the Lord Jesus Christ, saying to him, again and again, "Lord, I love you. Lord, have mercy on me. Lord, forgive me. I want to go on serving you, if you will allow it. Lord, forgive me. Lord, restore me," and clinging on to Psalms 32 and 51. Then, too, I know what it is to get up from that experience, deeply repentant, deeply chastened, but knowing that the prayer is answered, knowing the warm relief of forgiveness and cleansing for the sins that have been washed away by the blood of Christ.

Well, that is the story of Peter's denial. It is a shocking story. But in the end, you see, it is a *safe* story. It is 'safe' because of where it is, embedded in the story of the cross. Yes, Peter's failure, like yours and mine, was a *fact* which he would never deny. Peter's failure, like yours and mine, was *foreseen* by Jesus. But most important of all, Peter's failure was *forgiven,* like yours and mine can be, because of the atoning, healing, and cleansing blood of the cross.

That is why the story of Peter's denial is in the gospel: because it is good news.

CLOSING PRAYER

I am sure that the Holy Spirit of God through his Word has touched our hearts—people and preacher alike. Now, the question is, what will we do with that moving of the Spirit in our hearts and conscience? Knowing, as we all do, that one way or another we have failed Jesus, in small things or in great things, we have disowned him and failed him again and again. Perhaps, even, for some of us, we have failed him in ways that are profound and significant, in things of which we are deeply, deeply ashamed at this moment. Perhaps there are tears to be shed even now about that. But that is all right. This is a safe place, and we are among friends. We are not in the courtyard of the high priest. We are not being mocked. We are not on trial. We are here, in the presence of God and the Holy Spirit. So, bring whatever is on your heart, and open it up to the Lord. He knows it anyway. He has known it all along. Do not hide it anymore. Instead, hear the question of Jesus: "Do you love me? Do you trust me?" Return to the cross and to the blood of the Lord Jesus Christ for his forgiveness. For, the same John, who told us that if we say we have not sinned, we are deceiving ourselves and the truth is not in us, that same John says that if we confess our sins, God is faithful and just and will forgive us our sins and cleanse us from all unrighteousness. That is the Gospel promise. Come back to that promise, receive it, and hear again that word of forgiveness from the Lord Jesus Christ himself. For his name's sake. Amen.

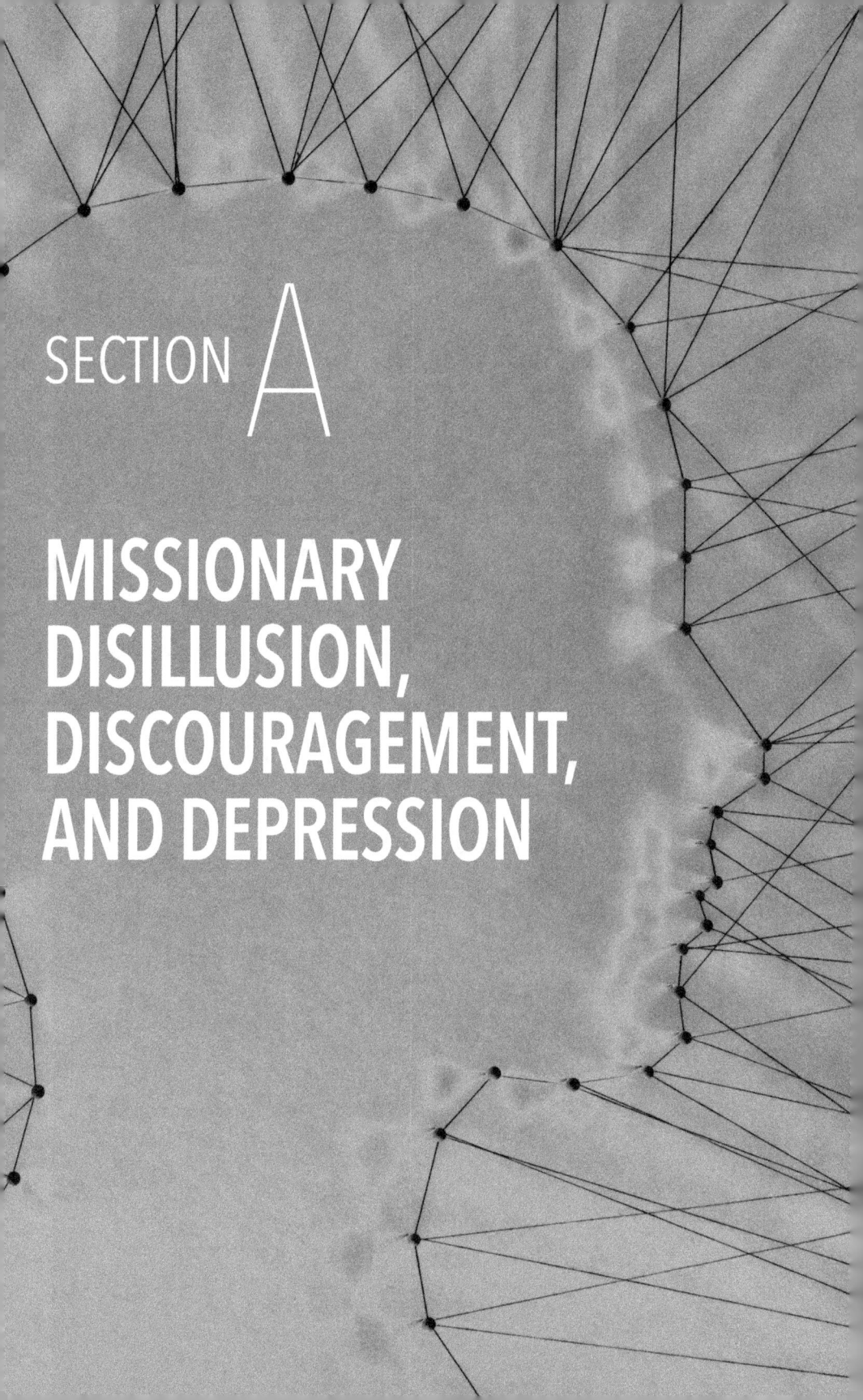

SECTION A

MISSIONARY DISILLUSION, DISCOURAGEMENT, AND DEPRESSION

04
FINDING A WAY THROUGH THE DARKNESS OF …
DESPAIR, DISCOURAGEMENT, DISILLUSIONMENT, DESPONDENCY, AND DISAPPOINTMENT

by Ruth L. Maxwell

I am not a mental health specialist and am not addressing a diagnosable mental health issue in this case study. However, I do have many years of member and leader care experience. What I have seen throughout those years is the premise for this case study, which is written from the perspective of seeing amazing workers struggle and, over time, reach a crisis in ministry. These workers were unable to find a way through the darkness of despair, discouragement, disillusionment, despondency, and disappointment. This case study is a compilation of such workers' stories, woven together, without exaggeration.

All names are fictitious.

Most workers will at some point encounter darkness. Many will become stuck and find themselves in depression. Others will go through these struggles and come out stronger, more resilient, and more aware of God's love and grace. Is there a way we can increase that number?

The statistics are unsettling. Sarita Hartz says, "80 percent of missionaries burn out and don't finish their term. 46 percent of missionaries have been diagnosed with a psychological issue, and of those 87 percent are diagnosed with depression."[1]

I contacted Dr. Debbie Hawker, who did initial research among foreign aid workers in 1997. In her reply to me, she quoted her earlier research, "About 50 percent of aid workers develop depression or another psychological difficulty while they are overseas or shortly after their return home (Lovell, 1997; Paton & Purvis, 1995; Paton, 1992). Around 30 percent may develop significant symptoms of post-traumatic stress (Erikson et al., 2001). Without debriefing, 18 months after returning home 25 percent still show significant symptoms of post-traumatic stress. With good debriefing, this can be reduced to 7 percent (Lovell, 1999b)." Hawker added, "I don't have very recent stats…. From experience, I think the figures remain fairly high."[2]

CASE STUDY

Pre-assignment. Frank and Amber individually and together knew God was calling them to cross-cultural ministry. Prayerfully, they chose a creative access country, an unreached people group, a well-established mission agency, and a ministry approach for involvement in this country.

Frank and Amber would not be serving alone. They would be part of a team, and relocating overseas would be a family adventure. Their pre-teen daughter, Joy, and teenage son, Justin, would be an important part of the ministry effort.

---

1 "What I Wish I'd Known About Missionary Burnout," on Sarita Hartz's official Web site, March 24, 2015, http://www.saritahartz.com/what-i-wish-id-known-about-missionary-burnout/.
2 Debbie Hawker, email exchange with the author, May 2018.

Their excitement grew, as Frank and Amber pictured leading people to Christ and discipling them into strong believers. The couple believed God had designed them for this, and their visa "platform" was an excellent means to this end.

Frank and Amber's church family were delighted to have one of their own going into cross-cultural ministry overseas. They anticipated sending short-term teams over, supporting them financially, and praying for them. Imagine the fruit that would come! The church believed in them.

The agency would provide the logistics and ministry support the family needed, and it was thorough in assessing their suitability for ministry. As a family, they passed with flying colors. The agency believed in them.

After the requisite language learning, Frank and Amber would establish a business. They wanted to relate to people on multiple levels. God would give them relationships: professional relationships in the local university, personal friendships with neighbors and fellow students, and hopefully spiritual relationships with seekers and maybe even a few believers. Their predecessors had done the same, and the team believed that Frank and Amber's family could do so as well. The team believed in them.

The more Frank and Amber shared, the more support and encouragement they received. Others believed in them. The more they received encouragement, the more they became excited. They started to believe in themselves.

As they began to save and raise funds, the couple found it taxing to make presentations on something about which they knew so little; simplifying their lifestyle was challenging too. As they envisioned living in a very different place, they began to form expectations about life in a different culture, on a multicultural team, attending classes and doing homework. What would family life look like in a hot place with expensive electricity, as they adjusted to homeschooling, new friends, limited menu options, and few amenities? They had to believe they could do this. Everyone else believed in them. As they saw all the evidence come together, it seemed that God believed in them as well. He was relying on them to join him in reaching these people.

When thoughts of uncertainty, anxiety, distress, or misgivings popped up, they dismissed them as not fitting with the planning, excitement, and anticipation that they were also feeling. They told themselves these were likely spiritual attacks, sent to discourage them. Who would understand if they mentioned them? Their pastor might doubt their call. The agency might wonder if they were suited for the work. What about those who might never hear the Gospel if they were delayed or did not go? And their team might think they could not cope, if just raising support stressed them out. Think of all the people they would disappoint! The right response was to trust God and keep going. The course was set. They would deal with these thoughts and feelings on their own. Or better yet, perhaps when they got settled, the thoughts would disappear. They just needed time.

Adjusting to life—newly arrived. The family's first weeks now felt like a distant blur of excitement, newness, curiosity, wonder, and adventure. Settling in went fairly smoothly. Getting set up had taken longer and cost more than they had planned, but it had been an adventure, and God had provided. They were surprised by the busyness of the other team members. It seemed that only the team leaders had time for them. Allen and Carmen were a wealth of information about life in this fascinating place and about integrating into this overwhelming setting. From banking to shopping, to ordering food, to getting around, to finding water and paying bills—Frank and Amber did not just feel like children learning everything all over; they were children, in that they were totally dependent on others to settle them in. Allen and Carmen really had it all together. Frank and Amber looked at them and wondered how long it would be before they too felt as at home. Doing "real ministry" felt far off.

Adjusting to life—early-to-midway in first term. Change happened constantly. No one had warned them about this. New government regulations meant leaving the country for visas. New friends were leaving for other assignments. Store shelves were emptying. Others assumed they were adjusting, because by all outward appearances, Frank and Amber looked normal, and everything seemed fine.

Joy quickly found a friend. Justin seemed lost. Homeschooling was less glamorous than anticipated and very difficult to make happen. Language classes and homework consumed their time. Family times were scarce. Teaching overtook parenting. The country's broken infrastructure was an added stress. Would there be water today? When would the electricity come on, and when would it go back out? Security concerns and government crackdowns in other places were reported daily. Attacks against churches and Christians were on the rise. The possibility of attacks by radical parts of society was becoming oddly normal. The more normalized it became, the more everyone's stress levels increased. Friendships with neighbors and fellow students became increasingly difficult. Trust seemed like a missing commodity in this culture. How was trust built in such a setting? Who could they trust?

Escaping from this context now became a daily desire. Maybe a family vacation would help ease the struggles. But vacations cost money—money they did not have. Instead, unhealthy alternate options surfaced—escapism into the Internet and into things dangerous to their souls, marriage, perspective, joy, and ability to hear God's voice.

Home assignment anxiety. Frank and Amber's preparation for their first home assignment began during a family crisis. Amber's progress in the language was remarkable, while Frank's progress left them wondering if he would ever be able to communicate at a heart level. Justin was failing his course work. Joy was doing well and enjoying her friends, but both children were bored, and they argued often. The adventure they had anticipated had not blossomed.

At the same time, there was a team crisis. Between a cancer scare, a car accident, and discouragement because of little-to-no results ("lack of fruit"), the whole team was struggling. What was wrong? Someone needed to take a short home assignment to allow for continuity. Frank and Amber offered to go. Joy was not excited, Justin could hardly wait, and none of them realized how much they had changed or how far others had moved on in their absence.

What would they tell their supporters and churches? Could they reveal the real story? If they did, they were certain that the church would be disappointed in them.

What expectations would be put upon them—multiple visits, seeing everyone, glowing reports, lots of "fruit," victorious stories of faith against all odds, church growth stories, lions killed, Goliaths defeated … ? The expectations had been palpable in the emails coming from home.

Could they hope for personal and family time—time to regroup; time to sleep and rest; time to reflect, process, and refuel—before speaking in churches? Or would people see them as lazy and spiritually weak if they asked for this? After all, people in ministry do not take vacations! Breaks are taken if something is "wrong." Besides, people had made financial sacrifices for them. Had those sacrifices been worth it? Had they even done ministry during this term? Frank and Amber felt totally useless.

What did God think of them? If how they felt about themselves was an accurate reflection of what God, churches, supporters, and the agency might think of them if they knew the real story, then Frank and Amber needed to rethink everything. Maybe now was the time to consider moving on. They felt like failures, and therefore they must be failures. Can "failures" serve God? Surely now was the time to transition and "follow God's leading"—to further education, new ministry opportunities, or better options for the kids' schooling. As they prepared to leave for home assignment, Frank and Amber told Allen that they were not sure whether they would come back, but they would pray about it.

Home assignment experience. Somehow, they made it through home assignment. They smiled. They reported. People were fascinated. They talked about the challenges of language learning and adjusting to a new culture. They kept smiling. The prayer meetings went a little deeper. They shared about the slow response to the Gospel and the need for faithful workers. They prayed silently for themselves and their future. When they shared about a colleague who had left the team because of depression, they were shocked when the response they got was simply, "Were they really a Christian?" They had not anticipated defending a coworker's salvation over a struggle with depression! Thankfully they had not told their full story. What would the church have thought of them? Frank and Amber found it difficult to keep smiling.

No one noticed what Frank and Amber did not say. No one wondered how their souls were doing or what robbed or encouraged their sense of joy. And if they had asked, Frank and Amber could not have answered without feeling guilty for not having endless joy in ministry. The truth was, they were still learning the reality that comes with trusting God's call and being inadequate: experiencing and resting in God's enabling power, finding God's presence amid their inadequacy, and standing in awe of him. They had not found words for their experience of darkness, their feelings of failure and inadequacy, or words to answer the question, "Where is God in this darkness?"

Interestingly, Frank and Amber felt most free to be vulnerable at a conference where other workers were also in attendance. They felt at home and in their own culture—understood at a deeper level and accepted, imperfections and all. This community lived in the gap between expectations and realities, in the challenge of being human while doing a divine task by faith. They walked in the shadow of the faith-challenging question, "How can failures serve God?" In this community, the measure of success was not "fruit," but drawing near to God. The measure of usefulness was availability, allowing God to determine the impact and the results.

Perhaps going back would be better than staying in their passport country. Frank, Amber, Justin, and Joy had indeed changed more than they had realized. For them, going "home" now meant going back to their adopted country.

Justin and Joy were ready to go back. They felt left behind by their own culture. At least in their adopted country, familiarity had begun to feel like home. They had changed, and change was okay. It was going to be good to return.

Next term. But life in the gap would still be filled with challenges. As is often the case, second termers are considered "experienced." Care of short termers and newcomers was added to Frank and Amber's list of responsibilities. Along with researching a business, they continued studying the local language. Their own family still needed attention. College was ahead for Justin. Joy's friend had moved, and there were no other young people her age within the foreign worker community. More friends and coworkers were leaving. Grief set in for Frank and Amber. Frank desperately studied language. Amber's isolation and loneliness grew and soon evolved into despair. Second term was turning out to be no better than first term. Exhaustion was their new companion. Chronic illness hounded them—infections, colds, headaches, rashes, asthma, and allergies. Where were these coming from?

As "experienced" workers, Frank and Amber had to turn in reports to their church and agency. The questions they were supposed to answer boggled their minds. The gap between expectations "at home" and realities "on the ground" were huge. How many converts? Tell a story about sharing your faith today. What are your five- and ten-year strategic plans? Have you planted a church yet? For Frank and Amber, language was still a struggle. (Why had they chosen such a difficult language?) Why had no one asked whom they were praying for? Did prayer count? Was it only about numbers? Strategic plans? Asking about their survival plan might have been a more useful question! Churches planted?

Was that not God's job? Where did these expectations come from? Suddenly Frank and Amber felt like servants, whose "success" on the field was to satisfy others' expectations. Had they become the means by which others vicariously received satisfaction for being "involved" in God's kingdom? Where was mutual sharing? Or was it only workers who must give account for how they are doing?

Word from Amber's family came that her father was ill and in hospital. They decided to wait and see how he responded to treatment. Justin and Joy wanted to go immediately, but were told no. The ocean had never felt so large.

One bright spot was a national coworker they especially enjoyed. Jonathan worked hard, wanted to be discipled, understood the cultural differences between them, taught them about his culture, and became the trusted friend they wanted. They even wrote home about him. A few workers warned them about trusting him too quickly. Then he changed. He became silent and withdrawn. He found fault with them often. Other things changed, as well. Their financial accounts did not quite balance. Things disappeared. Where once there had been fun and friendship, now there was distrust. When had all this started? What had they done to contribute to this breakdown? What was the culturally appropriate way to handle this? What was the biblical way of handling this? Some workers blamed them for not being careful, for being too trusting. Were they wrong to trust? Was this a spiritual attack?

In fact, was everything a spiritual attack? If not, then what was a correct view of what they were facing? Should they rejoice that they were suffering? Should they denounce this as an attack and expect to "rise above it?" They grieved that someone they loved, had stumbled. They too had stumbled. What had helped them at difficult times in the past? Who could they talk to? Maybe saying nothing was the best approach. They did not want to appear (or be) defensive. They wondered what it would be like to have someone walk alongside them—much like they were walking alongside the newcomers. Now that they thought about it, considering all their struggles, were they even qualified to walk alongside the newcomers?

For Frank, this term was more difficult than the last one had been—the exhaustion, deeper; the stress, greater; the expectations, higher; the sense of failure, more intense; the disappointments, sharper; and, anger about everything, just beneath the surface. What if that anger exploded? It could not! He would work harder at caring for others, at sharing Christ, and at fulfilling everyone's expectations. However, the struggle of his heart continued. The harder Frank worked, the more he asked, "Who cares for me?"

No one knew Frank was asking that question. If he had voiced it, others would have been surprised and shocked. From their perspective, he was doing an excellent job. They could not imagine the team without Frank and Amber. But Frank had no sense of that, and even if he had, it would not have resolved the ache that framed thoughts of "Nothing I'm doing is making any difference," or, "I could leave, and it wouldn't matter." Frank was dying inside, even while he was busy working hard on the outside. The aliveness that comes from simply being valued as a person worthy of being loved had died in the midst of meeting all the expectations around him—the expectations he placed on himself, the expectations others placed on him, and the churches' and agency's expectations regarding the outcome of his work.

Re-awakening. A breaking point was looming. Amber saw it first. The silence. The mechanical way Frank went about doing routine things. His lack of engagement with the children, and his impatience with her. Amber began to ask questions for which she had no immediate answers, but which she knew they as a family needed to answer. To whom could she go for help? Once again, she felt her isolation.

Then she did something intentionally different.

Amber turned to God and used the full extent of their experiences to inform her prayer. She began to lament—pouring out her heart to God. She named failure, as they perceived it. She named the growing darkness. She asked hard questions about dishonoring family, supporters, churches, the agency, and God himself. She voiced her fears and her hunger for her family to flourish as they journeyed with God through these difficult circumstances. She did not ask that God show them an easy path, but that they would be those who accessed his grace deeply. Prayerfully, she wondered where God was in all this. How did failure and darkness fit with his plans? What was his agenda for them personally—not just his agenda for their mission work? What were they responsible for? If they knew, they would surely act on it! What was the right way to think about all this? What if this darkness did not lift, and like others, they did not see fruit for their labor? Did God not also want fruit? Did anyone else feel this way, or were they the only ones? Were they destined to be one more attrition statistic? (The thought gave her chills!)

Something inside Amber had shifted and made her want to lean into this broken and shattered space, hoping for an encounter with God. She was not perfect, and never would be, no matter how hard she tried. No longer would she count on trying hard. Now was the time to lean hard.

Amber reached for her Bible and ran her thumb across the soft edges of the pages. She knew what she thought of their situation—not effective and not joyful. She was pretty sure she knew what God thought of them—another statistical failure. (Thankfully, God was a merciful God.) Had she asked him what he really thought, or had she assumed she knew? A flicker of conviction changed to a flame of desire. She wanted to know what he thought. She began to hope for something worth passing on to others, but what that was, she could not fathom. Not knowing, however, did not stop her hope or her awareness of God's love for her. How would she convey this new hope to Frank? Maybe together they could experience God amid these struggles, and be held by God's love. Maybe they would discover a life-message to invest in others. Would coworkers, church leaders, agency leaders, and supporters understand? Did it matter?

Amber remembered hearing one couple say that when they started singing one song together each evening, something shifted in their home. Maybe this could bring a fresh beginning to Frank and Amber's family, as well—even if they argued at first. Amber could sense a renewed excitement within herself, and her hope was growing into expectation that she and her family would see God working in and through the challenging circumstances that had come with his calling of them to cross-cultural ministry.

RESPONSE by Kyungwha Hong

Dr. Ruth Maxwell presents a vivid and realistic picture of a missionary family's journey. Her case study gives us a glimpse into what many missionary families in cross-cultural settings go through. Her detailed description is particularly helpful, since it depicts various challenges a missionary family may face during the different phases of mission work, starting from pre-assignment and moving on through a second term in one's host culture.

As Dr. Maxwell poignantly describes, most missionaries will encounter "darkness." Some may become stuck. Others, as Dr. Maxwell notes, will "come out stronger, more resilient, and more aware of God's love and grace." Dr. Maxwell asks a crucial question: "Is there a way to increase that number?" I consider this a question that overarches this entire forum.

In my response, I will describe general challenges that complicate the adjustment process for cross-cultural missionaries. I will then summarize the emotional issues that the case study family faced in each phase. Lastly, I will present two suggestions that could help missionaries "find a way through the darkness."

COMPOUNDING CHALLENGES FOR CROSS-CULTURAL MINISTRY

There are many compounding challenges that missionary families need to navigate in cross-cultural settings. Foremost is the issue of acculturation, as they adjust to their new mission field. On top of the differences in language and food is the loss of the familiar signs and symbols of social interaction.[3] Sometimes, one's version of common sense is no longer common sense. Thus, adjusting to a different culture, while at the same time balancing family and ministry responsibilities, can be overwhelming.

Related to acculturation is the issue of cultural identity for missionary kids. Figuring out who they are is a developmental task that all adolescents face. However, missionary kids face the extra difficult task of establishing their cultural identity while living amid two or more cultures.[4]

---

3 David Livermore, *Cultural Intelligence: Improving Your CQ to Engage Our Multicultural World* (Grand Rapids, MI: Baker Academic, 2009), 217.

4 Danica Hays and Bradley Erford, *Developing Multicultural Counseling Competence: A Systems Approach*, 3rd Ed. (Boston: Pearson, 2018).

Another challenge concerns the nature of the missionary job. Unlike most other jobs, ministry for missionaries often encompasses all aspects of life, including one's family and personal life.[5] Sometimes the boundaries between public and personal get blurred. When such ambiguity lasts 24/7, it becomes emotionally taxing. Furthermore, as Dr. Maxwell describes, there is a common misconception that when missionaries take vacations, something is "wrong," which discourages missionaries from taking breaks. Without ministry boundaries, limits, or breaks, burnout is to be expected.

When these compounding variables present themselves simultaneously, a person's stress-tolerance level may be lowered, resulting in mental health concerns.

THE DIFFERENT STAGES OF THE JOURNEY

Here, let me recapture the different challenges and emotions that the family in Dr. Maxwell's case study experienced.

Pre-assignment and Newly Arrived. The family starts their journey with excitement, curiosity, and a sense of adventure. This is what most people feel in the first stages of acculturation, called the honeymoon stage. People at this stage are motivated and feel they will not have any problems adjusting to the new culture.

They also dismiss negative thoughts that arise, such as anxiety and misgivings. Informing the family of what to anticipate in the acculturation process, as well as addressing any negative emotions they have dismissed is helpful for their adjustment.

Once the family arrives in their ministry field, they "feel like children learning everything all over," as Dr. Maxwell so accurately describes, and they are totally dependent on others. It would be beneficial to educate missionaries ahead of time that this feeling is normal and part of the process of acculturation. Their feeling of "real ministry" being far off is quite understandable in this stage. However, it would be helpful to rethink what "real ministry" means for them and to acknowledge that adjusting is, in fact, part of the "real ministry."

Early-to-midway in First Term. In this phase, we see that uncertainty and instability penetrate the adjustment period, with things like daily necessities, government regulations, security, and emotional support-systems being in a state of constant flux. On top of the uncertainty and instability is the added stress of language learning and home schooling.

The differences in adjustment levels among the family members is another potential problem, with Joy doing better than Justin in making friends, and Amber doing better than Frank in language acquisition. As the head of the household, Frank may feel the most pressure and have a heightened sense of failure, which then could quickly spread to other family members. All these issues could result in increased stress levels, which will take their toll both emotionally

---

5   Amy Cousineau, Elizabeth Lewis Hall, Christopher Rosik, and Todd Hall, "Predictors of Missionary Job Success: A Review of the Literature and Research Proposal," *Journal of Psychology and Christianity* vol. 29, no. 4 (2010): 354-363.

and physically. However, the most troubling aspect is, as Dr. Maxwell portrays, the "escapism into the Internet" and other "dangerous" practices, which could include many forms of addiction.

Home Assignment and Next Term. The family finds themselves living in the gap between two different worlds: expectation vs. reality; their own culture, in which they feel left behind, vs. their adopted host culture; being human vs. undertaking a divine task of faith. They feel like the gap between expectations and reality is huge, and thus, their senses of failure and anger are intensified. In addition, with constant goodbyes to friends and coworkers and the added responsibilities they now receive as "experienced" missionaries, the family members experience grief, isolation, and exhaustion.

Furthermore, a betrayal from a trusted friend devastates and confuses them. Instead of voicing their concerns, they lean toward not saying anything. Dr. Maxwell points out that no one knows Frank is feeling inadequate, uncared for, and like he is "dying inside." The emotional toll, instead of becoming an important topic for discussion, expresses itself in a more acceptable way: somatic symptoms.

Dr. Maxwell's descriptions make it clear that "experienced workers" also need systematic emotional support, a place to voice their confusion and their intense emotions. In addition, she highlights how easy it is for the church and mission agencies to forget that a missionary is a human being, who needs to "be valued as a person worthy of being loved."

Re-awakening. Frank exhibits symptoms of burnout. Thankfully, a turning point occurs when Amber starts to "name" and "voice" the failures and her fears to God. She seeks God and asks what God's agenda is for them personally and as missionaries. She displays hope and awareness of God's love for her. Dr. Maxwell illustrates how healing starts with identifying and acknowledging the darkness, honestly voicing not knowing, and seeking help. She also points out the importance of remembering God's unfailing love, not only for them as missionaries bearing "fruit," but also as valued persons. And, of course, the importance of having hope.

SOME SUGGESTIONS

Going back to Dr. Maxwell's question, what are some of the ways to increase the number of missionaries coming out of the darkness, stronger and closer to God? There is no easy, one-fits-all answer. The challenges are multilayered and multifaceted. I would like to suggest two things that could be part of the solution: changes in perception and systematic support for missionary families.

Changes in Perception. Mission organizations and churches need to change their perception and their standards of success. The fact that missionaries lived and endured in a cross-cultural setting should be acknowledged as ministry in and of itself. Missionaries need to be valued as people, not as tools or as robots that accomplish goals. Dr. Maxwell says it well: the measure of success needs to be drawing near to God, not how much fruit one bears. The measure of usefulness needs to be availability, "allowing God to determine the impact and the results." Based on this standard, we need to contemplate changing mission reports' contents and missionary communication systems so they reflect ontological reporting—not just reports of how many converts and church plants the missionaries have done.

Systemic support. Many mission organizations provide member care before and after mission work. However, this case study illustrates the need to systematize member care for missionaries active in the missionary field. The spiritual and emotional support needs to be consistent and continuous for these families. Moon and colleagues[6] and Lee[7] suggest operating a ministry team that visits the missionary families in their host culture. Lee suggests offering diverse spiritual and emotional support, including debriefing, counseling, and psychological tests.[8]

Another issue concerns who conducts the debriefing. Moon and colleagues found that more than half of the missionary participants wanted ministry debriefing to be conducted by mission organizations, while they wanted family debriefing to be done by counseling professionals.[9] There is a growing trend to have counseling teams within mission organizations. Although this is very positive and encouraging, there are some attending difficulties. For example, since counseling teams are part of the mission organizations, issues of confidentiality and dual relationships could arise. This can be solved by clarifying the role of the counseling teams within the mission organizations and referring missionaries to third parties, such as professional counseling teams, for personal concerns and family debriefing.

---

6 Steve Sang-Cheol Moon, Chan-Eui Park, Kyung-Seop Shin, Hee-Joo Yoo, and Nan-Sook Cho, *Hankuk Seonkyosa Member Care Gaesun Bangan (Improving Member Care for Korean Missionaries)* (Seoul: GMF Press, 2015) ,120-122.

7 Eunha Lee, "선교사 상담의 현황 및 상담추구의도모형" (Seonkyosa Sangdameui Hyeonhwang mit SangdamchoogooEuidoMohyung; "Status of Missionary Counseling and Model of Missionaries' Intention to Seek Counseling") (PhD dissertation, Torch Trinity Graduate University, 2013).

8 Ibid.

9 Steve Sang-Cheol Moon, et al., *Hankuk Seonkyosa Member Care Gaesun Bangan (Improving Member Care for Korean Missionaries)* (Seoul: GMF Press, 2015), 39.

As Dr. Maxwell gracefully presents, there is much hope for restoration and growth after the darkness. I would like to express my deep gratitude to the courageous missionary families who go forth out of their comfort zones and into the unknown for God and his kingdom. I would also like to thank Dr. Maxwell for her insightful and practical case study.

05
A JOURNEY TOWARD KOREAN MISSIONARIES' MENTAL HEALTH

by Do Bong Kim

The following is the story of a pastor, whom we shall call Mr. Sorak. He first served as a missionary in "P" country for twelve years, planting twenty-six churches and constructing several church buildings. He supported and participated in a theological education-by-extension program for local ministers. He also served as a faculty member in "U" seminary for two years to train ministers. He gained a good reputation from the local churches and their leaders by directing an effective ministry that utilized partnerships with fellow missionaries.

With no time to spare for rest or recharge, he lived as a "superman," developing the local ministries and continuing his own education at the same time. An ongoing lack of sleep and some discomfort in his digestive system caused him to feel drowsy during the days. In June 1998, he had a car accident while dozing off at the wheel, severely damaging both his car and the other vehicle. He was not able to drive after the traffic accident for about six months, possibly due to PTSD. According to his belief system, however, he had to overcome these difficulties with faith. His peers nicknamed him "the Phoenix," an immortal bird, and the nickname became his prescription for overcoming the crisis.

Mr. Sorak also suffered from hemorrhoids during his first missionary term in "P" country. For this, he received a special surgical operation in Korea in 1993, and had three days of hospital treatment and seven days of stabilization.

After his assignment as a missionary, Mr. Sorak ministered at a Korean immigrant church in Canada. He was diagnosed with multiple gallstones in January 2007 at age fifty. The plan was to have a simple laparoscopic surgery, get discharged in the afternoon, and rest at home for three or four days. Three days after the operation, however, Mr. Sorak's condition turned critical, and he had another operation. His life barely hanging by a thread, he was hospitalized for ten days. He was discharged, but it took many years for him to fully recover. The surgery had damaged blood vessels, which induced internal bleeding. The abrupt surgery also caused the gut contents to go bad, which led to irritable bowel syndrome. Mr. Sorak had to use the bathroom as often as fifteen times each morning. His body became fragile, and his quality of life collapsed. He had to step down from church ministry and stop attending the clinical pastoral education (CPE) program at the university hospital. His plans were all falling apart. He was filled with deep despair.

In October 2007, Mr. Sorak returned to Korea. He set his mind on serving in a hospital as his new mission field, where he would complete his unfinished ministry from his previous mission assignments. The CPE program he attended in Canada qualified him for this specialized ministry in the hospital. He believed that he could provide special care and support for missionaries' medical and mental health needs by ministering in the hospital. He wished to share his experience as a veteran missionary, as well as provide communication and relationship skills for self-care and cultural adaptation. This ministry has now been going on for eight years (as of the writing of this article).

Based on more than 1,000 interviews conducted during those eight years, Mr. Sorak learned that the belief systems of many missionary devotees, including himself, were tainted by the hero myth, and that this was a ticking time bomb, a likely cause of conflict that would ruin the lives of missionary families sooner or later.

MERITOCRACY IN KOREAN MISSIONARY CULTURE

Mr. Sorak grew up in Korean society that has experienced class conflict and condensed economic development in their recent history. The Korean church has also undergone explosive growth in a short period. There are two opposing views on this. Some people view the proliferation of churches in Korea as the result of a dynamic movement of the Holy Spirit, like that in the early church; others see it as a deformed growth, following the illusion of successism. The way the

Korean church understands people and society is disconnected from Christian spirituality. Things related to self and God are considered pure and spiritual, but human relationships and social engagement are classified as secular. Strangely, however, the desire for recognition and approval from others is so strong that Koreans are inclined to associate materialism and success with blessings from God. Much effort is given to "showing" and "doing," while "being" and "reflecting" are often neglected. This has led to patterns in the church, in which the Great Commission (Matthew 28:18–20) is emphasized, while the Great Commandment (John 13:34–35) is ignored.

As a missionary, Mr. Sorak had a misconstrued view of himself and tried to evaluate his abilities and faith by measuring visible achievements. Mr. Sorak held onto a Korean-made faith system that emphasized the rallying cry of "only by faith" and waved the banner of zeal, while bowing the knee to meritocracy. Zeal and passion are based on emotion, not rationality. Thus, when others discussed or criticized Mr. Sorak's opinion, he was likely to react defensively, considering it a rejection. When he felt that he was rejected, he either showed anger or avoided the situation by being silent. It was difficult for him to self-reflect or to maintain a dialogue to understand others' intentions. He would rather justify himself or turn to third parties, trying to get approval from them. Instead of seeking self-reflection or trying to improve communication and relationships with others, he would isolate himself in a cave of a prayer room, trying to find a solution from God.

THE MULTI-FACETED EFFECTS OF MERITOCRACY ON MISSIONARY HEALTH

With such a background, Mr. Sorak provides good examples of both pathological (undesirable, unhealthy) and developmental (desirable, healthy) phenomena that can occur when a missionary is separated from one's own culture and moves into a cross-cultural environment. For example, one pathological phenomenon is that a missionary propagates one's own cultural traits in the mission field, without being aware of the damaging effects thereof. A developmental phenomenon, on the other hand, would be to have a clear understanding of one's own culture and to establish healthy relationships in the new mission field. Impatience is one of the damaging effects caused by condensed growth and materialism, and, under its spell, missionaries can have difficulty waiting for the Cause-Process-Result cycle to complete. They may also struggle to distinguish between waiting and laziness. In such condition, missionaries can easily feel pressured to show their supporting churches a list of achievements, instead of taking time to develop a ministry fit for the local people. There looms a danger of pursuing secular goals, erecting a Tower of Babel, rather than building a tower based on the Bible, after the faith of Abel. Visible achievements, like constructing churches or school buildings, are often interpreted as a sign of a missionary's competence. Therein lies a temptation to misuse material resources and the power of one's authority to embark on short-term projects with conspicuous results. While emphasizing the importance of the attachment to one's primary caregiver during the growth process, John Bowlby made distinctions between healthy developmental pathways toward maturity upon experiencing separation and loss.[1] He mentioned that mourning is needed upon experiencing separation and loss. Similarly, a ministry must grow via healthy means for it to bear the eventual fruits of maturity. Further, the pathway to maturity at times involves not just growth, but mourning.

On the outside, Mr. Sorak was clad in the dysfunctions of Korean church and society. On the inside, he harbored hidden and unacknowledged worries, shame, and anger, which had formed within him as he grew up in a dysfunctional family. He had not undergone a proper mourning for the grief and loss he had experienced in his original family. Thinking that accepting Jesus as his Savior would settle all the problems of his past, he barely communicated with his original family and gave most of his attention to people related to his mission and ministry. Sadly, Mr. Sorak's pathological grief was manifested as a "demon lover complex" and developed into a "bad object addiction," i.e., respectively, a work addiction and a goal addiction. The minister was insensitive to the problem that a people can be "drawn magnetically towards the demon lover, resulting in their being repeatedly hurt, deeply wounded, and traumatized through tantalization and abandonment."[2] He lost the opportunity to integrate his internal and external selves by humbly and honestly laying down his problems, which would have been a far greater achievement than any other accomplishment in his ministry. Perhaps God would have wanted Mr. Sorak to throw off the self of his original culture (or the memories from his original family) through developmental mourning—enduring, surrendering, and releasing. Then he would have been free to establish new relationships within the new culture of the mission field, growing in the spirituality of wilderness by learning the lifestyle and environment of the local people. The example of Mr. Sorak has implications for other Korean missionaries who need professional support for their mental health. Mental health lies at the junction between the phenomenal, physical, and social elements and the invisible elements of religion and culture.

Returning to Korea, Mr. Sorak worked for the missionary care ministry at Member Care Network (MCN). Fortunately, Korean churches, denominations, and mission agencies were interested in mental health. Seminars and resources on missionary member care became widely available in the 2000s. Many books were translated to increase awareness of missionary member care. Experts, such as clinical psychologists, pastoral counselors, veteran missionaries, and medical doctors, joined in collaboration. One of the first domestic books on missionary

---

1 Jeremy Holmes, *John Bowlby and Attachment Theory*, trans. Gyungsook Lee (Seoul: Hakjisa, 2005).

2 Susan Kavaler Adler, *Mourning: Object Relation View of Psychoanalysis*, trans. Jaehoo Lee (Seoul: Korean Psychotherapy Institute, 2009).

care in Korea was, *Morning from the End of the Earth: Eleven Gifts of the Heart for the Missionary* (2007). Missionaries, psychiatrists, medical doctors, and counselors participated to write about physical care, pastoral care, psychological care, and mental health care. The significance of this book was that most of the content was based on the actual counseling of active missionaries, with many cases like Mr. Sorak's.

This book focuses on the seriousness of the problems of Korean missionaries, one of which is conflict between peers. It recommends the following: to prohibit competition at all times, to respect single female missionaries, to set the principle of partnership, to respect the boundary of each person's life, not to be obsessed about one's own principle, to give up special treatment, not to take any situation too seriously, to live by purpose, etc. (pp. 140–161). A missionary is not different from any other person except that God called him to the mission field. Acknowledging and accepting this is important for mental health (p. 71). Let us undertake the ministry that befits our talents and ability. Let us not compare ourselves with others. Accept the imperfection of man. Accept that a missionary is not different from others (pp. 72–74). In the life of a missionary and in ministry, there is a time of day when one moves actively with passion for God, and then there is also a time of night when one refrains from work due to physical, psychological, social, and spiritual reasons. Our task is to make the night time a time for growth instead of spending it as the period of inactivity filled with pain (p. 11).[3]

As a missionary, Mr. Sorak had maintained good relationships with his fellow ministers on the mission field in "P" country. But as a pastor at a Korean immigrant church in Canada, he faced conflicts. Principle-based administration and pastoral care were well managed until a certain point, when conflict between him and the church officers erupted. Mr. Sorak began to reinforce his own belief that resistance and confrontation were just. While his conflict with the church officers was deepening, he had to undergo a cholecystectomy. Several months later, he gave up both CPE and his pastorate position and left Canada.

Psychiatrists and mental health specialists emphasize that "missionary trainees are required to have [a] good understanding of one's own personal information, growth background, training process, life experience, and personal difficulties through personality tests, and foresee what influences these might have in the ministry. In the isolated environment of the mission field, missionaries face numerous relational challenges, including conflicts related with marriage, children, personality, habits, and the negative experiences from childhood. If there are any serious marital problems, deep bitterness due to broken relationships, or addiction-related issues, then it is better to postpone going to the mission field for some time."[4]

---

3 Missionary Care Net, *Morning from the End of the Earth: Eleven Gifts of the Heart for the Missionary*, (Seoul: Duranno, 2007).

4 Ibid. 33-35.

Gaining lessons from his unwise experience and from the analytical survey of Korean missionaries, Mr. Sorak produced a mental health care journey map for missionaries, in which diverse elements, such as holistic care, systematic life-cycle care, and proactive care were included. In this model, mental health care was viewed at a junction between the visible realm of physical and social elements and the invisible realm of religion and culture. Spiritual care was openly identified as a universal norm. The trend in missions has changed from having a simple member-care model to utilizing a multi-faceted member-care ministry.

THE ORGANIC RELATIONSHIP BETWEEN MENTAL HEALTH AND OTHER AREAS OF HEALTH

Mr. Sorak made a journey map for missionary mental health care, based on his experience and on what he observed while helping other missionaries, incorporating information he gleaned from various books and theses. (Many veteran missionaries wish to be useful as creative resources—"as upcycling material"—after their work on the mission field is done.) The columns in the map (**Table 5.1**) represent the personal, relational, professional, and spiritual domains. Spirituality is divided into religious and cultural parts: missionary work takes place in a multicultural environment, and it aims to strengthen the leadership capabilities of the local people so that they may spread the Gospel inclusively through their own cultural theology. The questions in this stage are, "Who am I?" (self-identity), "What is my worth?" (self-esteem), and "What can I do?" (self-efficacy). Across these domains, a missionary needs to experience communal growth through respecting and cooperating with others, for healthy experiences from one's original culture flow naturally into other cultures, along with healthy values, a healthy belief system, and a healthy worldview. The diversity of a multicultural environment, when one is separated and detached from one's original culture, becomes the seed of transcendence that fulfills God's kingdom. We are all God's people, with our roots planted in heaven.

MENTAL HEALTH CARE BY TIMELINE

The rows of the journey map represent the chronological stages of mission work (Stage). The lists in the intersection of rows and columns correspond to missionaries' positive, neutral, and negative behaviors. The lists indicate the signs of a missionary's mental health status—highlighting recurring behaviors and providing checklists for missionary mental health. When bad things happen in the mission field, we often focus only on putting out fires. But this list should be helpful in focusing us on the healing and rehabilitating of missionaries and their families, which in turn will minimize the loss of mission resources. Providing healing and rehabilitation for missionaries will also help to foster preventative measures for curbing missionary suffering in the future, as we begin to apply

Table 5.1. A Journey Map for Missionary Mental Health Care

Stage	Domain	Personal Care - Family Story	Personal Care - Self Awareness	Relational Care - Presence Family	Relational Care - Peer Group	Professional Care - Psycho-socio	Professional Care - Multi-disciplinary	Spiritual Care - Belief Centered	Spiritual Care - Cultural Based
Pre-Field	Recruit	Personal Identity (Attachment Type)	Calling	Consent (Expectation, Anxiety)	Recommendation	Research & Visit	Information	Personal Piety	Experimental
Pre-Field	Selection		Personality Type			Self-Assessment Tool	Talents for the Field		Multicultural Awareness
Pre-Field	Training		Communication	Participation	Peer Evaluation	Psychological Test	Language & Culture	Peer Support	Learning
Pre-Field	Deployment		Relationship	Encouragement/ Kids' Education	Support		Medical Check-up	Family Unit	Aquisition
On Field	Assimilation		Anger/Anxiety/Fear (Language/Culture) Family Issue (Kids' Education) Work-oriented/ Goal-oriented	Attachment/ Addiction Unfinished Issue Adult-Child Good Boy Syndrome Need of Approval Conflict with Kids *Empty Nest	Work-oriented Competition Power Abuse Malfunction of Leadership	Coaching Mentoring	Field Visit Care Crisis Care Debriefing	Value System/Belief System/ World View Confusion & Conflict *Synagogue type Culture & Faith	
On Field	Self-Operation	Relationship				Prevention of Burnout			
On Field	Vitalization					PTSD			
On Field	Collaboration								
Reentry	Furlough	Visiting/Staying Residency	Boundary Set-Up	Reentry Syndrome Relative Deprivation Negative Feeling Menopausal Disorder	Collaboration & Conflict Management	Resilience Community (Guesthouse) Filing	Lacking of Malfunction Family Care Lacking Welfare	Debriefing for Reentry/Sense of Guilt Reentry Maladjustment (Negative Critic, Isolation & Alienation) *Wildness Spirituality	
Reentry	Home Ministry	Family Conflict							
Reentry	Closing Work	Dysfunctional Family Issue	Stress Management						
Reentry	Documentation								
Retirement	Work End-Up	Residency Transportation	Refuse Powerlessness Worthlessness Self-Despised	Lacking of Communication No Alternation		Loss & Grief Isolation	Self-efficiency Retirement Village (Recycling/ Upcycling) Medical Care (Physio-Psychiatry)	Meaninglessness/Helplessness/Mistrust/ Maladjustment/Egotism/Loneliness/ Disease or Suffering Written Bucket List Written will including Medical Intent *Wildness Church	
Retirement	Contribution	Loss/Grief/ Mourning							
Retirement	Focusing								
Retirement	Preparation								

the lessons we learn while providing care. However, negative experiences cannot be completely avoided in the mission field. Some of the negative behaviors included in the list above are inevitable when responding to diverse variables in the field, even if missionaries are carefully selected in the recruiting, training, and placement processes.

As the stages progress, the information and the resources the missionaries have obtained should become a subject of interest to the locals (Power), and the accumulated experience of the missionaries and the cooperative relationships they have built among their peers and the local people should generate a reasonable agreement (Principle). Also, the ministry should endeavor to help both the missionaries and the local people become mature (Person). Further, our approach to missionary mental health needs to maintain balance, instead of falling over to the extremes of either faith or medical models. The medical model is (1) based on evidence-based rationality for multidisciplinary teams to work together (multidisciplinary), (2) divided into treatment, rehabilitation, and prevention, with attention to preventive medicine, (3) patient and family-oriented service, and, (4) directed toward holistic/integrative treatment with scientific and mystical elements. These are valuable lesson points for a missionary's mental health care model as well.

Mr. Sorak's wife had served with joy and satisfaction in "P" country as a missionary family member. But she had many difficulties in Canada, where she was treated several times for anemia and arrhythmia. She also had uterine myoma, which was the suspected cause of her anemia. A specialist then diagnosed her with hyperthyroidism, treating her with medication for over a year; but she ended up needing a hysterectomy. After that, her anemia improved slightly, but her lethargy and irritability persisted. After returning to Korea, her condition became worse, and she needed psychiatric support to recover peace of mind. The problem was that she had to take care of her aged mother, who had dementia, while she herself needed care. The demands of caring for herself and her mother accumulated as stress and internal conflict within her, which finally exploded. At that point, the doctors came to understand that the illnesses of Mrs. Sorak's immune system, nervous system, endocrine system, and psyche were all interconnected.

> Modern holistic nursing requires understanding of the patient[s] as human beings from a holistic point of view. That is, human beings have a mind, a body, a society, a culture, and a spiritual realm, and needs [sic] to satisfy the desires of each realm. When spiritual well-being is divided into religious well-being and existential well-being, religious well-being does not show significant correlation with any of [the] sub-areas of menopausal symptoms, but existential well-being has [a] negative correlation in all three domains of mental-physical symptoms, physical symptoms, and psychological symptoms. … In this study, it was at first expected that if the religious well-being

and existential well-being are high, then there would be less reports of menopausal symptoms. Existential well-being was in accord with the first expectation, but religious well-being was different from the initial expectation.[5]

Mr. Sorak's wife was also in need of healing with holistic care. Mr. Sorak's personal crisis spilled over to his wife and family members, exposing them to the dysfunctions of his family of origin along the way. Today, Mr. Sorak's family understands they must balance the soundness of their ministry with the soundness of their family. Mr. Sorak and his wife, his son and daughter-in-law, and his granddaughter are all striving together towards rehabilitation.

CONCLUSION

All servants of God need to invite God's presence and walk with him through "Vulnerable Mission" in the mission field. Mr. Sorak believes that God is making a mosaic with the broken pieces in the lives of missionaries. God does not overlook these broken pieces; he is making them into a masterpiece, in part through the help of health specialists who possess God's wisdom and have learned sophisticated treatment techniques. Missionaries are not end products just because they are sent to the mission field following their calls and their training. They are always **becoming beings** and **learning beings.** They are **living beings**, who live out missional lives, regardless of their locations.

QUESTIONS FOR REFLECTION

1. What can be done to dissolve the hero myth that wreaked havoc in Mr. Sorak's life and resulted from a particular cultural background of the Korean church?
2. How would you comment or give advice, from the viewpoint of mental health, regarding the tendency of Korean missionaries to be work-centric in their ministries?
3. How can missionaries create learning, healing communities in the mission field that will help to maintain their mental health?
4. What are some ways in which missionaries can live missional lives creatively, by "upcycling" their experiences upon returning home?

---

5 Mi Hyang Kim, "On the Relationship Between Menopausal Symptoms and Spiritual Well-being," *Korean Society of Women Health Nursing,* Book 4, vol. 1 (1998): 38-51.

RESPONSE by Thomas Kemper

"You're like lambs in a wolf pack"
(Luke 10:3b, *The Message*)

In "A Journey toward Korean Missionaries' Mental Health," Dr. Do Bong Kim gives us a great deal to think about regarding the psychological ramifications of Christian missionary service. His case study of "Mr. Sorak" has implications not only for the church in Korea but also for the worldwide missionary community, especially the Protestant missionary community that it most clearly reflects. Mr. Sorak's assumption, supported by his social and theological context, that he must be a mission "superman"—a missionary hero—is widespread in our Protestant history and mindset. It is at base a question of the source and use of power.

The historical prevalence of the "missionary hero" myth is attested by a considerable body of literature. In the tradition of which both my organization, the United Methodist Board of Global Ministries, and Korean Protestantism are part, the image of the missionary hero is rooted in the mid-eighteenth century evangelistic outreach of England and America. In the United States, we can date the origins to a particular book, *The Life of David Brainerd,* written by the revivalist Jonathan Edwards right at the middle of the eighteenth century. Brainerd was a physically frail young man who spent three years as a missionary among Native Americans, until struck down by disease. He lived the few remaining years of his life in the Edwards' household.

The book made a folk hero of Brainerd, and his story became the model for tales of missionary heroes, hundreds of epics about missionary giants of faith—men and women larger than life—around the world. Sunday school literature and missionary society publications would become significant conveyors of these stories, often aimed at children and youth, and frequently soliciting donations. Such collections of missionary hero stories were common in general publishing well into the twentieth-century. I found an 83-page volume from 1913, *Fifty Missionary Heroes Every Boy and Girl Should Know*, recently reissued on the Internet.[6] The public image of the missionary in general and, perhaps, the personal self-images of individual missionaries have been strongly influenced by this heroic literature.

Of course, reaction against the missionary hero myth is not new, and the imagery today is more common in some parts of the mission movement than others. The presentation of missionaries as heroes and heroines has largely dropped out of the mainline churches of the West. My wife and I were not confronted or judged by it when we were United Methodist missionaries from Germany in Brazil twenty-five years ago. The myth lingers primarily in more evangelical circles but is being questioned there too.

---

[6] Julia H. Johnston, *Fifty Missionary Heroes Every Boy and Girl Should Know* (New York: Fleming H. Revell Company, 1913).
http://www.temkit.com/13-Missionary/Fifty%20Missionary%20Heroes.pdf.

A September 2015 article in *Christianity Today* magazine argues for an evangelical "Farewell to the Missionary Hero." Author Amy Peterson maintains that overly romanticized portraits of missionaries fail to take account of the real struggles of faith that real missionaries face and paint a false picture of what it means to respond to the call to be God's servant in mission.[7]

How do we best guard against the debilitating aspects of the old hero imagery and still honor the missionary vocation of being sent as participants in the *missio Dei*—God's mission? (And I would submit that such participation in God's mission is heroic, if we understand "heroic" as describing bold commitment to the Great Commandments of loving God and neighbor.)

I think that the answer is to be found in large part in an insight Dr. Kim, and through him Mr. Sorak, makes on the last page of his paper, where he writes: "All servants of God need to invite God's presence and walk with him through 'vulnerable mission' in the mission field." He goes on to say that missionaries are not "end products"—heroes—but are "always becoming beings and learning beings. They are living beings... ." And to be a living being, even one sent by God for a task, is to be vulnerable—to be exposed to potential threats. It means to find power in the experience and example of Jesus, the God who died on a cross.

Jesus himself recognized the vulnerability, the humanness, of the first class of missionaries he commissioned, the seventy described in Luke 10. The passage is well known. Jesus sends the seventy in teams of two "like lambs in a wolf pack" with no luggage or money. How much more vulnerability is possible—dependent on strangers for food and lodging; stuck in a host's house, like it or not, eating what is put before them; and expected to heal the sick and bring good news of God's abiding presence? Dr. Kim's sentence rings of truth as we consider Luke 10:1–11: "All servants of God need to invite God's presence and walk with him through 'vulnerable mission' in the mission field." The seventy are, as Dr. Kim wrote, "becoming beings and learning beings. They are living beings." They are not heroes, and Jesus knows that. The last verse anticipates the possibility of failure, of not being welcomed, of being rejected, and of wiping off the dust of a place from their feet.

German theologian Phillip Hauenstein argues that this strangeness, this foreignness, this vulnerability in Luke 10 is for missionaries a charisma, a gift or blessing, helping them and those to whom they witness and with whom they serve to see their situations through the eyes of the other. It mitigates the need to become missionary action heroes with power over people, instead preparing the way for the power of the Gospel of love in real human lives and communities.[8]

Luke 10 is hardly the only New Testament passage that supports vulnerability—genuine humanity—as a quality of authentic missionary life and power. The vulnerable,

---

7 Amy Peterson, "Farewell to the Missionary Hero," *Christianity Today* 59, no. 7 (Sept. 2015): 76, https://www.christianitytoday.com/ct/2015/september/farewell-to-missionary-hero.html.
8 Phillip Hauenstein, *Fremdheit als Charism* (Neuendettelsau: Erlanger Verlag für Mission und Ökumene, 1999).

honest, down to earth reality of the missionary vocation is a frequent theme in the letters of the Apostle Paul, the greatest of the New Testament missionaries. Paul was constantly becoming, learning, and living as a vulnerable person. The letters give clear indication that Paul was tempted at times to think that the revelations he received and the travails he endured gave him heroic, powerful status. Second Corinthians contains some notable examples, which are highlighted by the plain language of *The Message,* the Bible paraphrase by Eugene Peterson.

Speaking in 2 Corinthians 4:7–12 of the glory of God's love in Christ, Paul writes, "If you only look at us, you might well miss the brightness. We carry this precious message around in the unadorned clay pots of our ordinary lives. That's to prevent anyone from confusing God's incomparable power with us. As it is, there's not much chance of that. You know for yourselves that we're not much to look at. We've been surrounded and battered by troubles, but we're not demoralized; we're not sure what to do, but we know that God knows what to do; we've been spiritually terrorized, but God hasn't left our side; we've been thrown down, but we haven't broken … Our lives are at constant risk for Jesus' sake, which makes Jesus' life all the more evident in us."

Second Corinthians 12:7–10 focuses on Paul's self-image in terms of his sense of being singled out for messages from God. He wrote, in Peterson's paraphrase: "Because of the extravagance of those revelations, and so I wouldn't get a big head, I was given the gift of a handicap to keep me in constant touch with my limitations … at first I begged God to remove it. Three times I did that, and then he told me, 'My grace is enough; it's all you need. My strength comes into its own in your weakness.'"

Paul, with his limitations and vulnerabilities, lived in the hope that God would fulfill his purposes in his good way, as he wrote in Romans 8:24, "For in hope we were saved."[9] As we, as missionaries, place our hope in God, we are saved from hero myths to become earthen vessels of God's grace and power.

The power of the Gospel—and the strength of faith that enlivens missionaries, as Paul so well knew—is linked to the image of a broken, dying God reigning from a cross, which was a total scandal and absurdity in the first century Roman world. It still is today. It seems too vulnerable, too real. However, to be vulnerable is not to be powerless, but it means to appeal to a power greater than that of the iconic hero. Christlike vulnerability invites the power of God to work.

Colin Morris, British Methodist theologian, journalist, and long-time missionary in what is today Zambia, puts it this way:

> If your purpose is to dominate, to coerce–power over people–then the Roman machine was power, and the cross spelt impotence. But if your aim is to change human hearts without smashing the human will–power through people–then the cross has proved to be the power of God to salvation.[10]

---

9 NRSV.

10 Colin Morris, *Bible Reflections Round the Christian Year* (London: SPCK Publishing, 2005), 48.

06
MISSIONARY ANGER: A KOREAN CULTURAL PERSPECTIVE

BY JONATHAN S. KANG

Got anger? Anger is an instinctive reaction and natural human emotion, primarily designed to safeguard an individual from danger or threats. For most people, experiencing anger several times a day is nothing out of the ordinary.

Should we suppress anger as much as possible? Anger ranges from mild annoyance or dissatisfaction to extreme rage or fury. People often think anger is dangerous because it can lead to violence or to impulsive, out-of-control behavior. In fact, excessive rage negatively affects physical health, psychological well-being, and interpersonal relationships. Unmanaged anger can cause anything from throbbing headaches to more serious concerns, such as insomnia, severe depression/anxiety, heart conditions, and even substance abuse. If not controlled, anger can cause fear and anxiety in the people who witness it, especially loved ones. With its adverse physical and psycho-social effects, it is no wonder people insist that anger should be controlled or suppressed at all costs.

However, anger is a powerful emotion that can positively affect human life too—protecting and preserving us from danger. It also signals the individual that something is not right with the present situation or circumstance. Anger plays an important role in the human survival mechanism (a.k.a. the fight or flight response), which pushes us to deal with immediate problems as they arise, including internal and external demands and threats, whether perceived or real. In brief, anger can act as a catalyst for moving us toward positive ends, though all the while potentially wreaking havoc if it ceases to be an agent of protection and preservation.

Anger dynamics become even more complex when one considers the relevant cultural elements, the ethos of the particular environment, and the personalities of the people involved. How the unique cultural characteristics of Korean missionaries play a role in their experiences and expressions of anger is the main topic of this study.

JONAH AS AN ANGRY MISSIONARY

The Bhagavad Gita[1] is not psychological literature but surely gets to the point when it says that having desires is the root of anger. Frustrated desire causes anger, and anger blinds people to irrational thinking, even leads to destruction. Anger is the disappointment and frustration that comes when expectations fall short, like they did in the case of Jonah.

It is difficult to pinpoint the factors at play in Jonah's cultural context, work environment, and personality, but anger had evidently gotten the best of him. This missionary found himself angry at three things (Jonah 4:1–5)—God who had commissioned him, the people to whom he was called to minister (i.e., the mission field), and the discomfort he experienced when his sheltering plant withered—because, whether for right or wrong reasons (we know that it was unwarranted), things were not panning out the way he wanted or expected. Jonah, for sure, did not like the Assyrians and had good reasons for it. Why did Jonah run away to begin with when he was commissioned to go to the mission field? Perhaps the history detailed in the book of Nahum offers a window into the deep undercurrent of hatred and trauma the ancient Hebrews had to endure, which seems to justify Jonah's willful disobedience and fleeing from the scene. Jonah was angry with God for sending him into the heart of the enemy's territory, whose evil deeds were well chronicled as being the bloodiest and most vicious kinds of cruelty in ancient times, and who victimized the Israelites time and time again.[2]

Jonah did not want anything to do with the Assyrians, let alone to see them spared from God's judgment and wrath. What further angered him was the fact that

---

1 The Bhagavad Gita is an ancient Indian literary work that became an important foundation for the literature and philosophy of the Hindu tradition.

2 Gordon Franz, "Nahum, Nineveh and Those Nasty Assyrians," The Shiloh Excavations, Associates for Biblical Research, biblearchaeology.org, May 28, 2009, accessed September 3, 2018, http://www.biblearchaeology.org/post/2009/05/28/Nahum2c-Nineveh-and-Those-Nasty-Assyrians.aspx.

he knew God was a God of mercy, who would save the enemy if they repented from their evil ways. Jonah was blinded by the emotions arising from his nationalistic ethnocentricity. Engulfed by hatred and burning rage, he had no place in his heart for fulfilling God's command to reach out to Israel's violent enemies.

UNIQUE KOREAN PSYCHO-CULTURAL CHARACTERISTICS

Korea bears the undesirable distinction of having the highest suicide rate among all OECD countries for nearly the past decade and a half. The prevalence of depression and anxiety runs at a high rate as well, against a backdrop of dramatic economic growth. Korea has become one of the world's leading technology users and one of the leading manufacturers of telecommunications, home appliances, semi-conductors, digital IT, automobiles, and ships. For the past decade or so, Korea's economy has ranked thirteenth in the world, and the Korean Olympic team has been in the world's top ten. Korean pop culture has also become a global phenomenon. K-dramas, with subtitles, are watched all over the world, bringing joy and tears to many viewers. K-Pop and other idolized celebrities are stealing the hearts of young people, and many not so young, from global stages. K-food and K-cosmetics are also making a splash in the world market, as never before.

Where else can you find a nation like Korea? From the ashes and ruins of WWII and the Korean War, "the miracle of the Han river," along with the country's democratization, transformed a war-torn, impoverished country into one of the world's richest countries, within the span of a single generation. The economic and political successes of South Korea have been nothing short of miraculous. Korea is regarded as an exemplary model for developing countries, in terms of rapid advancement in economic growth and democratization.

Despite the accolades and achievements, and the exponential improvement in quality of life, why then is the happiness index of Korean people at rock bottom among all OECD countries? Why are suicide, divorce, alcohol consumption, traffic accidents, and plastic/cosmetic surgery rates at the top? Why are store shelves overflowing with self-help books and dietary supplements of all varieties? Underneath the remarkable economic success, Korean people are mourning, groaning, and hurting, and seeking relief from real and perceived physical and mental health maladies. Sadly, stress, fatigue/tiredness, depression, anxiety, and anger have become psychological key words in the everyday life of Koreans. Certain unique and enigmatic Korean psycho-socio-cultural characteristics underlie the Korean psyche and may shed light on the extant anger of Korean missionaries.

Jeong

Jeong (정) is a combination of many individual emotions that bind individuals together; it is a type of deep attachment, a deep-seated bond. It is a feeling of affection, interest, understanding, loyalty, warmth, and emotional connection. You can feel *jeong* for family, friends, lovers, relatives, colleagues, classmates, strangers, or even places or objects—like the home in which you used to live, your hometown, your cars, your furniture, or your pets. *Jeong* is difficult to describe—it is more easily felt than explained. It is a "you know it when you experience it" kind of feeling, an indelible sense of affinity and "we-ness." *Jeong* is often communicated through unspoken but powerful actions that enable Korean people to experience a sense of "being" in a shared, collectivistic culture or kinship.

Jeong also has its dark side. There is a saying in Korea, "You live and die with *jeong*." It is that important to be included in the *jeong*-structure, bound by loyalty; otherwise, you face being marginalized or alienated from the collectivistic society. *Jeong*'s primary predicament lies here: "boundarylessness" between individuals connected by *jeong*. At times, the *jeong* dynamic can put an individual into a binding situation, where he or she may be forced to deal with blatant manipulations and coercion, being taken for granted, or being taken advantage of, paying a heavy price for *jeong*. Often the continuation of favors being asked that are too taxing or risky or the absence of reciprocity between the parties in this *jeong*-transaction can leave the individual(s) on the other side feeling hurt, betrayed, disrespected, hateful, and yes, angry.

Anger is a universal emotion, and it exists for a reason. Though anger may at times seem unwarranted, subjectively, one has a reason for feeling angry. Usually anger arises when an individual's boundaries have been violated in some way—a line has been crossed, or a "rule" has been broken, regarding what is acceptable or unacceptable, fair or unfair, or right or wrong. When another person does not have or hold to such rules, the one who does, becomes insecure and vulnerable, and anger is a natural reaction. Overbearing *jeong* can encroach on one's protective boundaries with unreasonable demands, making one feel guilty, burdened, and culturally unable to deny the unwanted requests for favors.

When these boundary-related stressors are present, even if one is not cognizant of how much the tension is mounting within, anger is likely to take root within the person over time. But, all too often, especially in Christian faith communities led predominantly by first generation leaders accustomed to the "old fashioned" way of conducting business, Korean culture has not caught up with the paradigm change allowing individuals to maintain healthy personal boundaries. Furthermore, according to the cultural norm, people should not feel free to express negativity or anger resulting from the violation of their personal boundaries, for doing so violates *jeong*-based practices, especially when a situation involves senior members, superiors, or someone in a position of power. Hence, suppressing anger has become a normal way for junior missionaries to handle emotions. Showing anger or displeasure is considered an unacceptable way to behave toward God and his anointed leaders and agencies. But unexpressed, pent-up anger can be tolerated or suppressed only for so long. Many missionaries I run into are desperately seeking ways to resolve it or at least put out the "fire" they feel no longer capable of managing, as they describe their feelings as analogous to a candle burning from both ends.

Han

Han (한) has been described as the "feeling of unresolved resentment against injustices suffered, a sense of helplessness because of the overwhelming odds against one, a feeling of acute pain in one's guts and bowels, making the whole body writhe and squirm, and an obstinate urge to take revenge and to right the wrong—all these combined."[3]

It has been theorized and speculated that *han* evolved with the flow of the Korean historical timeline. Its genesis may go as far back as the time of the Yi or Chosun dynasty (early 1390s to early 1910s), which had a hierarchical class system of four major classes—the Yangban, or nobility; the Joongin, or middle class; the Sangmin, or commoners; and the Cheonmin, or social outcasts with the lowest social standing. Society was ruled by the privileged Yangban class, while the peasants (of humble birth, slaves, even most commoners) had to earn a living in hard ways—restricted, oppressed, deprived, maltreated, and abused—all because of their inherited low social status.

Some historians have counted, during Korea's 5,000 years of history, more than 1,000 foreign invasions and intrusions into the territory, by nations such as China, Mongolia, and Japan.[4] In particular, thirty-six years under the Japanese occupation (1910–1945) had a major impact on shaping *han* in the soul and spirit of Koreans. Strong emotions of *han*, which harbored deep hostility and vengeance toward the Japanese for their subjugation and maltreatment of the Korean people during the Japanese colonial period, can find a parallel in how Jonah felt toward the Assyrians. In the ensuing tragedy of the Korean War, collective bitterness and sadness were further reinforced.

With the passing of time, much has been forgotten and forgiven, and quite frankly, people in their early sixties and younger are not as attuned to *han*. They might not know what people of the older generations mean when they say, "We are a people full of *han*." One should be reminded, however, that *han* is not something tangible or apparent, but like still waters, it runs deep in the lives of the Korean people, even in mundane, everyday life.

How *han* plays out can and does differ from one individual to the next. Many Koreans still harbor *han* deep within for their humble birth, e.g., being born out of wedlock or coming from certain geographical regions such as Jeollado, the southwestern part of the Korean peninsula, which is easily distinguished by the accent of its local people. Some people who lack academic credentials or were born into poverty may continue to live as victims, begrudging and holding on to

---

3 Boo-wong Yoo, *Korean Pentecostalism: Its History and Theology* (New York: Verlag Peter Lang, 1988), 221.
4 "우리나라가 역사에서 외세에 침략이 몇번 있었나?" ["How many times in history has Korea ever been invaded?"], tip.daum.net/, accessed August 24, 2018, www.tip.daum.net/question/99361511. Translation by author.

unresolved *han* all their lives. On the other hand, some are compelled by their *han* to break the vicious cycle of being poor and uneducated, by sacrificing their lives to arduous labor and toil so that their children do not have to experience what they went through.

When one considers *han* as a backdrop in the development of Korean history, it is easy to understand why Koreans are feisty, fiery, emotional, passionate, and easily angered, and why they relentlessly pursue becoming better and greater. *Han* can be said to be a collective emotion that evolved and became ingrained in the souls and minds of the lowly Cheonmins, the ignoble classes, and the poor and uneducated, as well as the victims of foreign invasions and regional conflicts throughout history. Even in modern history, frequent wars and political and social unrest have been the norm for most Koreans; today's older generations have experienced destruction, suffering, personal loss, and unbearable pain over extended periods of time throughout their lives. When *han* is suppressed and allowed to brew under the surface over time, a person who may appear mild, subdued, and passive can detonate like a bomb—the unresolved emotions mounting, then depressurizing, like in a volcanic eruption. Koreans have a way of saying, "I feel a strong surge of anger rise up" (울화가 치밀어 오른다). Unfortunately, the longer a "*han*-related wound" is left unattended and the repressed (unconscious) ill lies dormant, the worse it gets. It festers and gradually morphs into a more destructive force, becoming more conducive to the development of *hwa-byung*, a psychosomatic syndrome common among Koreans. *Hwa-byung* feeds on unresolved *han*, like a sponge soaks up water. Accumulated, unresolved *han*-associated emotions always become toxic, which consequently requires our conscious and unconscious minds to spend more energy denying, forgetting, or forcefully repressing our desires and thoughts. This process adds even more layers of *han* and sets the stage for an eventual surge of irrepressible rage or becomes internalized as *hwa-byung*.

Hwa-byung

Hwa-byung (화병) literally translated is "fire illness (*hwa*-fire and *byung*-illness)." Sometimes it is better known as *ul-hwa-byung*, with "*ul*" added as a prefix to *hwa-byung*, together rendering the meaning, an illness with pent-up, depressed and heavy feelings ("*ul*") and fire ("*hwa*") inside the chest or body. It is a Korean-specific emotional disorder (though there remains room for debate as to whether this syndrome should be classified as culture-bound[5]), resulting from suppressed anger and depression or stress, which includes many somatic elements.

Hwa-byung cannot be clearly understood apart from the psychology of *han*. The two concepts are inseparable. Where *han* is a culture-specific, collective emotional state of suppressed anger or frustration, *(ul)hwa-byung* is a culture-related or culture-bound psychosomatic illness, stemming from suppressed anger

---

5   The Diagnostic and Statistical Manual of Mental Disorders (DSM) currently lists *hwa-byung* as one of the culture-bound illnesses.

or frustration. Simply put, pent-up, unexpressed, and accumulated *han* is one of the major culprits of *ul-hwa-byung*. In Korean culture, relieving or expressing emotions, whether positive or negative (but especially anger), has been frowned upon as immature, ignorant, or indicative of a lack of education. Such behavior is perceived as antagonistic to the Confucian ideal of harmony in familial and social relationships.

The Korean people have long suffered from an inferiority complex, which I believe is a major contributor to the "fiery disease" of *hwa-byung*. As a small country (even smaller now that the country has been divided in half for over seventy years) lacking military might, Korea has been a frequent target of the avarice of powerful neighboring countries throughout its long history. Nonetheless, Korea has remained resilient and intact, persevering and prevailing as a racially homogeneous nation, a source of national pride and validation for Koreans, even as they begrudge the frailty of their historical identity. But the repercussions of their survival are many, one of which is the formation of psychological defense mechanisms. While Koreans are known for being resilient, resourceful, and persistent, the psychological defenses at play underneath the façade of their cultural disposition make their presence felt as passionate emotions that can be excessive, intrusive, confrontational, and competitive—all to protect and preserve a threatened ego.[6]

This spirit of inferiority and insecurity is pervasive in Korean culture and history. It is the common denominator of issues pertaining to *han* and *hwa-byung*. As an old adage goes, "When a cousin buys land, you get a stomach ache,"[7] many Koreans would admit to feeling bitterness over someone else's success. Suffering from a stomach ailment is a psychosomatic manifestation of that envy. For people with an inferiority complex, seeing others succeed or turn fortune to their favor can cause anger and physical pain—*hwa-byung* symptoms that are visible and common among Koreans.

Che-myun

Che-myun (체면) literally means "body-face," a term used in conjunction with the "face saving" behavior integral to public and social relationships in the collectivistic Korean culture. One's sense of dignity and honor, respectability and reputation is protected and maintained through *che-myun*, as are harmony and reciprocity in social group dynamics. However, when *che-myun* behavior goes beyond societal norms, and often it does, it can become pretentious, or an opportunity to "show off." *Che-myun* may even force an individual to behave contrary to one's true self and reality. An idea that corresponds to *che-myun* might be *che-tong*, literally meaning "body managing." It is a term used in the context of

---

6 Y.K. Harvey and S. Chung, "The Koreans," in *Peoples and Cultures of Hawai'i: A Psychocultural Profile*, eds. J.F. McDermott, W. Tseng, and T.W. Maretzki (Honolulu: University of Hawai'i Press, 1980), 135-154.

7 The Korean adage, "사촌이 땅을 사면 배가 아프다," is somewhat similar to the old proverb, "The envious man grows lean at the success of his neighbor."

keeping one accountable to the standard of conduct suitable for one's social status or reputation. A person can go overboard with *che-myun* behavior and cross into the hypocritical. For example, a couple may want to assure others of their social status (or, save face) by showing off and living beyond their means (e.g., going into debt to drive a fancy car, live in an extravagant home, or throw an extravagant wedding for their child; or fighting to pick up the tab for meals).

Noonchi Culture

The literal translation of *noonchi* is "eye-measure."[8] *Noonchi* is the ability to read, gauge, or pick up on things quickly by sensing nuances surrounding the given moment or situation, i.e., "eye-measuring." Specifically, *noonchi* encompasses multiple traits and abilities, such as being tactful, sensing others' moods, gaining understanding quickly, being intuitive, and reading non-verbal cues and body language well. By the same token, lacking *noonchi* means being clueless, slow-witted, or tactless. Considered a skill necessary to communicate effectively in the high-context culture[9] of Korea, *noonchi* is also a survival tactic of the weak or inferior in this hierarchical society. Some have speculated that, as social classes were formed during the Yi dynasty era, the weak or "lesser classes" had to develop and rely heavily on *noonchi* to read the minds of the upper classes, so that they could survive under their leadership and make ends meet. Even today, *noonchi* plays a critical role in Korean organizations, including churches and mission organizations. For the junior staff member, being able to read the mind of a boss or senior staff person is critical for survival, in this culture where social and professional relationships are hierarchically structured.

WHY DO MISSIONARIES GET MAD?

Work ethos. Korean missionaries are work-focused and task-oriented. Their sense of identity hinges on "what they do" and on their tangible accomplishments, rather than on "who they are" as individual beings. They often find themselves caught in the middle of the never-ending, proverbial tug-of-war between "to be" and "to do" and the question of "orthodoxy" or "orthopraxy." Finding a balance between work and rest has also been a difficult challenge. Some say that this has to do with people valuing the Confucian virtues of hard work and loyalty to the collective cause much more than they value "working smart," per se.

---

8   Sonja Vegdahl and Ben Hur, *CultureShock! Korea: A Survival Guide to Customs and Etiquette* (Singapore: Marshall Cavendish International Asia Pte Ltd., 2008), 36.

9   A high-context culture relies on implicit communication and non-verbal cues. In high-context communication, a message cannot be understood without a great deal of background information. See Brian Neese, "Intercultural Communication: High- and Low-Context Cultures," Southeastern University Online Learning, August 17, 2016, accessed August 25, 2018, https://online.seu.edu/high-and-low-context-cultures/.

Korean mission organizations, like business and social institutions, are highly hierarchical in nature. To fare well, one must develop a sense of *noonchi* and be able to read the terrain of situations quickly, including the superiors' feelings, and act accordingly. In times past, most indigenous missionary organizations lacked organizational guidelines (such as goals, objectives, policies, and procedures), and many rookie missionaries were asked to commit their lives to kingdom causes without the benefit of the "missionary tool box." In the eyes of some ardent senior missionaries, using such guidelines seems "secular" and "not of faith," a practice only necessary for someone not relying on faith and the work of the Holy Spirit. Therefore, this intuitive, difficult to teach, and culturally inherited ability of being able to "pick up nuances," "figure out without asking questions," and "get it done using your own discretion"—*noonchi*—is an indispensable and irreplaceable skill for a junior staff person. Nonetheless, however valuable it may be, *noonchi* cannot be equated with genuine wisdom or Spirit-led acts of faith.

Constantly engaging in *noonchi* behavior has its costs. One can easily become known as a person who only gets by because he is a "*noonchi* master," one who is shrewd and crafty but not hardworking. The psycho-social cost of relying on *noonchi* is even higher. A high level of mental energy is required to operate *noonchi* effectively, since it is never straightforward. Furthermore, the person using *noonchi* as a primary tool for problem solving is not operating out of self-confidence, but out of passive insecurity and heightened anxiety or hypervigilance. This person is likely to engage indirect or implicit sources and strategies and may thus be labeled as manipulative and approval-seeking, especially with regard to people in positions of power. And when someone puts forth that much effort, only to see his or her plans fail, anger is the likely result.

How they work. Bbali-bbali (빨리 빨리) literally means "hurry-hurry." Getting things done quickly has been a trademark of the Korean work culture. More recently, *bbali-bbali* has morphed into *bbali-maani* (빨리 많이), or, "hurry-much." Getting things done fast is not enough; now we need to "get a lot done, faster." *Bbali-bbali* has become a way of life and survival in the cutthroat, pressure-cooker culture of Korea. This mindset permeates not just the workplace, but most aspects of Korean society.

Some attribute the etiology of Koreans' hurriedness to the old days when, to make a living, farmers had to work hard and quickly through the change of seasons. Poor in natural resources, Koreans traditionally engaged in agriculture, prior to the country's miraculous industrialization. The "hurry" syndrome is also believed to be closely related to the country's rapid urbanization and economic development, as many major changes took place during a short period of time. During that transformation, the obsession with "hurriedness" spread like wildfire throughout the workplaces of Korea, with a pervading sense that the quality of one's work would be valued only when the work was completed quickly. "Speed" became second nature for Koreans in all matters, even within the faith community—"O Lord, please teach me how to be patient RIGHT NOW!" One's ability is often judged based on "expeditiousness," productivity, and results, not the quality of the work process. What matters the most is not how you get there, but getting there FAST, faster than everyone else. This is true among missionaries, too. The processes involved in mission work are overlooked and undervalued, as missionaries burn out from the task-oriented, results-driven, often superficially focused culture of mission work. Churches and mission organizations, as well as missionaries themselves, evaluate their work using tangible, outwardly visible measures of success, contrary to Hebrews 11:1, which says, "Now faith is confidence in what we hope for and assurance about what we do not see." Placing confidence in outcomes and achievements, no matter the cost, has become the driving force for Koreans, Korean missionaries in particular.

Unfortunately, far too many Korean missionaries are paying the high price for this way of life. The high-energy anxiety attending the "hurriedness" disorder causes maladaptive social behaviors such as rudeness, apathy, and even violence, along with various physical and psychological ailments, not to mention anger.

How they relate: Jeong-Chemyun-Noonchi at work! Dr. Jekyll, please meet Mr. Hyde. The Dr. Jekyll-Mr. Hyde dynamic epitomizes how Koreans can be both highly task-oriented and highly relationship-oriented, which are contrasting traits. How is it so? As alluded to earlier, Koreans emphasize results and performance yet rely heavily on relational connections to get things done. They are highly social but in a hierarchical manner, as shaped by the Confucian emphasis on social order. This is especially noticeable in the Korean honorific language structure, with its multi-levels of formal and informal speech, each used with different people in different situations. The requisites of Confucian hierarchy are evident and practiced on a daily basis in myriad ways, governing acceptable behavior and social etiquette. Age, wealth, education, social position, and gender are among the many variables factored into establishing one's standing within the complex, hierarchical social structure.

However, all cultures evolve with the change of time, and Korea, too, has started to loosen its adherence to the dearly held and socially reinforced traditional ideals and norms, particularly among its postmodern, westernized generation.[10] Even so, the strongly hierarchical work culture persists to this day. Accustomed to the respect, loyalty, and humility prescribed by hierarchical social norms, those in positions of authority expect deference and obedience from their subordinates. On the flip side, *che-myun* and *jeong* oblige the seniors in an organization to take care of the junior members, for example, by supporting them in the workplace, treating them to nice meals and drinks after work, or providing the social and

---

10 The younger generation of the Korean workforce is in a state of flux; they feel ambivalent about and struggle with dealing with bosses/senior members of an organization who adhere to the traditional collective culture, even as they hold themselves out to be more modern, Westernized, and individualistic and less ideologically inclined towards Confucianism.

personal connections (인맥) critical for survival and advancement in their *jeong*-based, collectivistic culture.

In this *jeong*- and connection-based work culture, conducting work performance evaluations takes on an arbitrary aspect, with social connections, relationships, and *che-myun* at play. Such cultural and interpersonal elements can and often do take precedence over the objective quality of one's work. Furthermore, with the culture valuing *noonchi*—as opposed to formal protocols and guidelines—as the way to get things done right, objective evaluation becomes problematic.

Myung-bun (명분), which means justifying or upholding one's cause, is an important attempt at "face saving," as is *che-myun*. Since failure to justify oneself will bring shame and guilt, and neither party (superior or subordinate) knows how or wants to deal with such negative and awkward emotional situations, people often choose not to confront others or speak openly about problems. Instead, they hold back their true feelings, which fester inside, becoming a root of bitterness and an eventual source for inappropriate expressions of anger.

A junior missionary faces a dilemma when forced to work with underperforming or incompetent leaders. The same is true if a junior missionary becomes aware of a senior missionary's moral or ethical failures. The junior missionary's stress level rises, and the missionary feels stuck in a rut, unsure of what to do or how to handle the situation at hand. Not only is preserving the *che-myun* of senior missionaries important but, perhaps, what is more critical is not to violate the norms of relational hierarchy. Whether it is appropriate or not, whether it is godly or not, many missionaries are forced to practice their *noonchi* skills here, rather than utilizing their godly discretion to discern ways to resolve the problem. More often than not, they cover up and ignore the issue until it resolves on its own, or they dismiss it entirely, which can have serious repercussions later.

CONCLUSION

Coming to terms with their cultural legacy and how it has affected mission work, the Korean missionary community has begun a return to the biblical basis and foundations for their work. They have begun to call for redress, as the old, results-oriented paradigm for missions placed undue pressure on them, engendering many physical, psycho-social, and spiritual ills. But to effect meaningful change, a church culture that treats its missionaries as a commodity must first be changed. The leaders of Korean churches and mission organizations must halt their "*gap-jil*"[11] and their relentless pursuit of lofty goals in the face of declining missionary productivity and cease viewing their junior missionaries as mere cogs in the organizational machine, with no right to personal happiness and well-being.

---

11 *Gap-jil* refers to the arrogant and authoritarian attitudes or actions of people who are in positions of power.

Anger is not only an essential human emotion designed to protect an individual from threat or harm; it is more so a secondary emotion, fueled by primary feelings that threaten our egos, such as fear, shame, and anxiety. In such cases, we use anger as a cover to conceal, control, and manage the feelings that make us vulnerable. In the case of missionaries, their emotional state can be weighed down by the trepidation they feel not only about the mission work itself, but even more so about the sponsoring faith communities they count on for support and sustenance. Their senses of identity and well-being depend on these relationships. However, traditional Korean culture and the "faith community" culture demand that they suppress their fear and anger. Hardly anyone dares to speak up, even in the face of mounting *han*, an amalgamation of strong emotions preceding fiery anger and even rage. This psychological "defense" system, perhaps conditioned by the culture, hinders desirable and constructive attempts to deal with underlying anxiety and its accompanying emotions and desires.

The *han* that develops as a result of emotional wounds is blanketed with anger. The underlying emotions can range from feeling inferior, mistreated, ashamed, guilty, invalidated, rejected, and insignificant, to a deep sense of loss, failure, and helplessness. It is not uncommon to see missionaries habitually and inappropriately expressing anger, for anger can easily become addictive when it provides regular relief from intolerable feelings. However, providing an outlet for these primal feelings and desires can be dangerous!

Perhaps every transient generation has its own cultural idiosyncrasies to endure. All cultures change through time. Missionary culture, too, has changed, however slowly. But expecting a dramatic paradigm shift to occur quickly will only bring disappointments. People's attempts to shape missionary culture by altering just a few existing elements of mission communities have met with much resistance, however prudent the suggested changes may have been. Changes in a "glocal"[12] culture do not take place in a vacuum. Cultures consist of multiple interdependent components, and changes in global culture may necessitate changes in the local culture as well. As the economies (not just in terms of finance) of mission communities change, the rest of the missionary culture changes in response, again, with great reluctance and resistance, for people not only fear change, but many genuinely believe that when things have been done the same way for a long time, that must be the right way of doing things. "Why fix something that is not broken?" is a mentality that the current generation of missionaries is up against. Culture change is complex, with far ranging causes, effects, and consequences. One hopes that missionaries do not abandon, in their frustration, their godly attempts to create at least a subculture that reflects their call to be the "salt and light" of the world.

---

12 "Glocal" is a portmanteau of global and local, rendering a definition of "Reflecting or characterized by both local and global considerations." See "Glocal," Oxford Living Dictionary, accessed July 29, 2018, https://en.oxforddictionaries.com/definition/glocal.

Then, what about anger? Anger is a universal emotion, yet it is greatly shaped by culture. Not anger itself, but the expression of anger (or lack thereof), is the culprit behind both personal and relational struggles in the lives of Korean missionaries. Cultural demands, as well as pressure from mission agencies, sponsoring churches, and supporting individuals, can be overwhelming at times, and missionaries sometimes have little or no control over those things.

However, missionaries can be equipped with psycho-spiritual resources with which to validate themselves and be strengthened to confront and deal with any personal or relational lapses or inadequacies. Replenished with a fresh supply of psychological ammunition, they will be able to withstand and deal well with both internal and external cultural threats.

Missionaries face the challenge of practicing self-efficacy and self-care, with a healthy dose of self-control, which is a fruit of the Spirit. Scripture admonishes us, "Be angry and do not sin; do not let the sun go down on your anger,"[13] encouraging missionaries to control what they can—that is, expressing anger appropriate to their situations and to their level of Christian maturity. It might also be fitting to quote Jim Elliot to bring the matter to an end, for he knew what he could control and what he could not: "He is no fool who gives what he cannot keep to gain what he cannot lose."[14]

---

13 Eph. 4:26, ESV.
14 Jim Elliot, *Journal, October 28, 1949*. Journal entry. p. 174, Billy Graham Center Archives, Collection 277.

RESPONSE by Barbara Hüfner-Kemper

Thank you, Dr. Jonathan Kang, for your brilliant reflection on anger among Korean missionaries. It has given us a lot of valuable insights in the complexity of the uniquely Korean psycho-cultural context.

It appears that in Korean culture, anger is perceived as predominantly negative, "an unacceptable behavior toward God and his anointed leaders and agencies."

I would like to start our reflection with a short self-assessment exercise:

- Please write on a sheet of paper the first ten words that come to your mind when you hear the word "Anger."
- Are your associations more positive or negative?

Dr. Kang distinguishes in his paper between negative and positive assumptions regarding anger. "Out of control" behavior and violence are obviously negative; however, life preserving actions are seen in a positive way.

Whenever I do the self-assessment exercise with my clients (who come from a wide range of cultural backgrounds), most of them see anger as a negative emotion. It is obvious that such an understanding has a significant impact on how we handle our own anger and how we accompany or coach adults, adolescents, and especially two- to three-year-old children when they show anger.

Dr. Kang describes in his remarkable study how people can get stuck between suppression and explosion when it comes to anger. I am especially impressed by the very body-oriented Korean language that describes feelings in such a precise and vivid manner, as the following:

The phrase, "we are people full of *Han*" describes "feelings of unresolved resentments … a sense of helplessness and… . acute pain in one's guts and bowels, making the whole body writhe and squirm …"

Suppressed anger results in an emotional disturbance inside the chest named *Hwa-byung*—fire illness.

"And a slowly brewing and suppressed *Han* can make a person who may appear mild, subdued, and passive on the surface detonate … like a volcano."

For most of my clients, the feeling of anger starts in their guts like fire and is constantly rising. "Pressure cooker" and "volcano" are their favorite expressions for describing their inner, uncomfortable state of mind. There is very often a felt sense of helplessness, as well, like being stretched between the two poles of suppression and explosion. Suppression leads to depression; explosion, to losing one's face in the community.

TWO EXAMPLES OF LIFE-TRANSFORMING RESPONSES TO ANGER

Jesus. In Mark 3:1–6, Jesus heals a man with a shriveled hand on the Sabbath. Jesus asks the man to stand up in front of everyone and then heals his hand, an action that reconnects the man to the community and restores his capacity to handle his life again. Yes, but this is work on the Sabbath.

And Jesus asks, "Which is lawful on the Sabbath: to do good or to do evil, to save life or to kill?"[15] He challenges his listeners to distinguish between good and evil, between anger as a life-saving energy or a destructive one.

People answer first with silence and suppressed anger and, later, with explosive anger, preparing to kill him.

Jesus, however, gives us a great example of not suppressing anger. He becomes angry and shows this moving emotion[16] in a controlled manner, while looking openly at the people with stubborn hearts.

Jesus uses his anger in a constructive way: not acting out, but acting for; moving from suffering "handlessly" to suffering proactively; using his angry energy in favor of life and healing.

Non-violent Communication. Dr. Marshall B. Rosenberg, the developer of Non-violent Communication (NVC), offers insights on the positive implications of anger.[17] He sees anger and conflict as a tragic expression of a need not met. "NVC is to totally divorce the other person from any responsibility for our anger," he says.

In Dr. Rosenberg's five-step program, anger is transformed into need-serving feelings. I will concentrate here on the first three steps, since they describe an internal process: we can work on anger successfully on our own, not saying anything out loud. This approach is useful in high-context cultures like Korea and takes *noonchi*—the ability to read between the lines and not express yourself verbally and directly—into consideration.

Rosenberg's first step is to identify the cause of our anger, without confusing it with interpretation or evaluation. For example: a person is complaining about someone, saying, "I am angry because he/she is not answering my emails; he/she is not taking me seriously." The person has made an immediate jump from the observation of unanswered email to the judgmental conclusion of not being taken seriously. The person's unchecked evaluation of the other's motive is the cause of the person's anger here.

The second step is to identify thoughts and assumptions that trigger anger: "I am angry because I think / judge / evaluate / assume that [fill in the blank]." It is important to ask myself: "What am I telling myself that is making me so

---

15 From Mark 3:4, ESV.

16 Emotion comes from the Latin word "movere" and means to move and to mobilize us.

17 Marshall B. Rosenberg, *The Surprising Purpose of Anger* (Encinitas, CA: PuddleDancer Press, 2005).

angry?" And while asking that question, we quickly get in touch with the need behind that judgment.

Therefore, the third step toward transforming our anger is to search for our unmet need.[18] As we begin to recognize our needs, our angry feelings very often shift toward more controllable feelings, such as sadness, frustration, or grief. This course can lead us to a greater sense of peace and can prepare us for the next steps toward life-transforming action.

Let us follow Jesus' example, expressing anger wisely and honestly, transforming it into a non-violent and non-judgmental attitude, doing good for ourselves, for others, and for the kingdom of God.

QUESTIONS FOR REFLECTION

1. Is there healing for our anger issues?
2. How can we follow Jesus' example of handling anger–transforming it into a life-saving energy, instead of reacting with suppression or explosion?
3. How can we create a healthy distance between us and our angry feelings, so that we avoid being dominated or controlled by them?

---

18 See the NVC website with a helpful list for considering feelings and needs. https://www.cnvc.org.

07
NAVIGATING THE CHALLENGES IN INTERNATIONAL MISSIONS

by SOOHYUN KIM

AN EPISODE

In 2007, I met a Korean missionary who was about to serve on the field as a long-termer, after having completed a few short-term trips with an international organization. She said to me that she would not serve with an international organization again and discouraged me from joining an international missions group. I was immediately curious about the basis for her opinion, but I could not directly ask her. I sensed that there was something she did not feel comfortable sharing. As time passed, a chance came to discuss the issue with her again. After hearing my inquiry, she kept silent for a minute. She was hesitant to answer because she knew that her answer could plant a seed of prejudgment in my mind.

"Because of racial issues," she answered with a deep sigh. "If you are a Korean, you cannot move on to leadership positions. Even for a married couple, if one of them is a Korean, they cannot be promoted further, even if they have spent a long period of time on the field. Newcomers from the Western hemisphere will take over all the important positions."

Her frustration was evident.

The above episode happened more than ten years ago; the current situations in various international missions should be far different from what this woman experienced. However, I still meet some Korean missionaries who have stopped working with international missions, although they continue working on the field. Whenever I come across them, I can sense their disappointment with international missions. Moreover, there are still a few Korean missionaries in international missions who are wrestling with a feeling of "racial discrimination," because the racial code is an easy way of explaining the marginalization they experience within their missions organizations.

MINUTES TO PONDER

If the above is a reality on the field, Korean missionaries will need to ponder the following questions carefully:

- What causes the dropout or marginalization of Korean missionaries in international missions? Is the racial issue really at the center?
- Why do Korean missionaries need to continue working in international missions? Is it worth investing our times and efforts? What are the benefits of working in multicultural teams for Koreans?
- If Korean missionaries are called to work in multicultural teams, what can we do to thrive in international missions?

After reviewing a case study, I will address these three respective concerns.

A CASE STUDY[1]

J joined an international mission ten years ago. In the beginning, she enjoyed various social meetings within her mission, although there were few other Koreans there. She was able to maintain positive social relationships, as she had acquired advanced English proficiency before serving on the field. She loved her Western coworkers' smiley faces and gentle manners. Compared to Korean missionaries, they looked happier and seemed more content. J was impressed at their joyfulness and warmth.

As time passed, J and her colleagues started to run small classes, teaching various practical skills to an unreached people group. In the workplace, J

---

1 Please note that important personal information has been changed to maintain confidentiality.

was often taken aback by the unfriendly attitudes of her colleagues. First of all, she felt shocked at their direct "No" statements. She was embarrassed whenever she heard, "I am sorry; I cannot do that," or, "I don't think so." She was disappointed at others' "unwillingness" to step out of their comfort zones, so she took more responsibilities for which no one else would volunteer. Secondly, she felt disconcerted when others asserted themselves straightforwardly. They appeared to be good at self-promotion, so she began to wonder where their sense of humility was. She longed for a colleague who would behave more like her.

A few years later, J came to get easily frustrated at small things. She was pressured to carry on with the responsibilities for which she had volunteered. She shared her challenges with her colleagues at regular team meetings. However, she did not feel like they were hearing her out, as every meeting started on time and finished on time, regardless of how much she shared about her hardships. She assumed if she shared more, the others would support her more, so she talked more about her difficulties, even in various social gatherings. She was desperate for someone to resonate with her. But she realized that everyone was laughing and enjoying fun activities at these gatherings, except for her. One person even said directly that she attended these gatherings to relax, but felt unable to because of J. After hearing that, J felt deeply alienated and betrayed. She stopped participating in such gatherings, except for mandatory team meetings.

In the end, J could not trust any of her colleagues in the mission. She could not trust herself anymore either. She thought she had failed to gain the others' hearts, although she had done her best in everything. She was confused about what she was doing wrong. She became isolated and marginalized. She missed the company of people with whom she could be "one of *us*." She regretted that she had not developed close relationships with other Koreans nearby. She felt that she was being punished because she had pretended to be a Westernized Korean.

REVIEW OF THE CASE

Perspectives from Social Studies

In general, it is a challenging task to thrive well in a team that embraces diversity. Theories from social science show how difficult this task really is. *Evolutionary Approaches* by Sng, Williams, and Neuberg suggests stereotyping and having prejudices against others is one of the innate human tendencies that help human beings survive and thrive efficiently over history.[2] It says, "We stereotype because we need to quickly and easily predict, with some degree of accuracy, the opportunities and threats afforded by others."[3] According to this theory, a community that consists of diverse subgroups will segregate quickly if

---

2 O. Sng, K. E. G. Williams, and S. L. Neuberg, "Evolutionary Approaches to Stereotyping and Prejudice," in *The Cambridge Handbook of the Psychology of Prejudice*, eds. Chris G. Sibley and Fiona Kate Barlow (Cambridge: Cambridge University Press, 2017), 21,46.

3 Ibid., 38.

no intentional efforts are made to maintain the unity that overcomes prejudices against each other. *The Social Identity Perspective* by Reynolds, Subasic, Batalha, and Jones, proposes that this social change eventually comes by resolving these prejudices so that we should not be afraid of these interactions.[4] It clearly indicates that these interactions are the only way to bring about the social change that promises a better atmosphere for its all members.

Perspectives from Intercultural Studies

Intercultural studies provide us with an effective tool to understand J's disconnection, as we can see significant collisions in values that provoked J's confusion:

Categorical Thinking vs. Holistic Thinking: J was not aware that social time and relationships are different from working time and relationships for Westerners. "Westerners tend to categorize time between work time and personal time."[5]

Guilt vs. Shame: J was not accustomed to assertive and detailed verbal communication, as she had grown up in high-context cultures, where the communicators express more of the information without speaking it. " ... [M]any of the Two-Thirds World people think holistically—they do not differentiate between criticism of an idea and criticism of a person. To criticize my thought is to criticize me and that causes me shame or loss of face."[6]

Time vs. Event: J did not feel heard, since every meeting started and finished on time, regardless of how much she shared about her hardship.

Individualism vs. Collectivism: J's identity as an individual was weaker than her identity as a member of a certain group. She constantly longed for the presence of others who were similar to her in many ways. "In much of the world, one does not think in individualist terms but more as a member of a group, as part of the collective whole ... Collectivistic people do not make important decisions on their own."[7]

I believe intercultural studies should be the starting point to understand J's case. However, I also believe that we need other tools to grasp the whole picture of J's disconnection. Regrettably, most papers in Intercultural Studies reflect a person's experience adapting from a Western culture to some other culture, since most of this research has been done by Westerners. Also, most articles reflect a person's acculturation process rather than a group's acculturation process, as most of the research designs were individualistic in approach. Thus, I would like to address two major weaknesses of current intercultural

---

4   K.J. Reynolds, E. Subasic, L. Batalha, and B. Jones, "From Prejudice to Social Change: A Social Identity Perspective," in *The Cambridge Handbook of the Psychology of Prejudice*, eds. Chris G. Sibley and Fiona Kate Barlow (Cambridge: Cambridge University Press, 2017), 47, 64.

5   D. Elmer, *Cross-Cultural Connections: Stepping Out and Fitting in Around the World* (Downers Grove, IL: IVP Academic, 2002), 97.

6   Ibid., 114.

7   Ibid., 91.

studies: 1) The discipline does not pay significant attention to *the power differences between Western culture and other cultures,* and 2) Its starting point is *how I can get connected with others, rather than how we can get connected with others.* I assume the following perspectives from sociology and psychology will help us to resonate with J further.

Minority Identity Development Model

The Minority Identity Development Model was developed by Atkinson, Morten, and Sue when they were working with American minorities in the United States.[8] They suggest that five stages should occur before a minority population feels comfortable with its own group and with the dominant group as well. Let's say a woman moves to a foreign country, where people from her cultural background are a minority population. In the *Conformity Stage,* she prefers the dominant culture over her own. In the *Dissonance Stage,* she begins questioning her beliefs formed in the Conformity Stage, as she encounters some experiences that challenge her formal beliefs. In the *Resistance and Immersion Stage,* she sinks into her group's values and rejects anyone from the dominant group. In the *Introspection Stage,* she begins recognizing the limitations of the Resistance and Immersion Stage. In the *Integrative Awareness Stage,* she becomes connected with her own group and with the dominant group, by admitting that there are some acceptable aspects and some unacceptable aspects in all cultures.

This model gives us us meaningful insights into why Korean missionaries choose to leave international missions. In other words, Koreans are supposed to accomplish this minority identity developmental task on their own and in addition to their other work, if they wish to remain in international missions. Western missionaries appear not to face these significant challenges. Some could argue that Westerners also proceed through this developmental task when they enter new cultures. However, I would not agree with this argument, since I believe Westerners' experiences of being a minority group cannot be easily compared with the identity crisis that Koreans face in international missions. For example, if a Korean were surrounded by ten Americans, the Korean would do his/her best to learn English. In contrast, if an American were surrounded by ten Koreans, the American would probably start teaching them English. The American may be the "literal" minority, but he/she is the majority in terms of cultural influence, as there is a significant power difference between Western culture and other cultures.

According to the Minority Identity Development Model, J seems to reach the Resistance and Immersion Stage. She started out admiring the atmosphere surrounding the Westerners, but she ended at depreciating the dominant culture. Many Koreans are likely to leave international missions at this stage, rather than move forward to accomplish the full task of minority identity development.

---

8 D. R. Atkinson, G. Morten, and D. W. Sue, *Counseling American Minorities: A Cross-Cultural Perspective,* 4th Ed. (Dubuque: WBC Brown & Benchmark Publishers, 1993), 19-39.

Some of them choose to remain in missions, but fatigued by the minority identity development process, they prefer to be segregated like an island and serve only with other Koreans.

Transformation from "We" to "I"

Can a Korean survive alone without being accompanied by other Koreans in international missions? The answer is, "Yes," but I would like to add another sentence, such as, "but, it will take time for the person to learn how to stay alone with comfort." Gaining the competence of staying alone does not happen without intentional efforts, although these efforts are regrettably overlooked by Westerners. This is the second extra task that Koreans must accomplish, if they wish to remain in international missions.

Staying alone does not mean that a person stays precisely alone, but it means *a person can stay there without having a shared identity with others.* Staying alone with comfort means *a person has established an individual identity* (who I am) *instead of maintaining the previous communal identity* (who we are). Furthermore, having learned how to stay alone means *a person has built up a new form of attachment after being painfully detached from previous close relationships.* Sue Johnson, the developer of Emotionally Focused Therapy, points out how depressed and aggressive a person becomes when the person's deeper connectional needs are not met within intimate relationships.[9] I believe Korean missionaries' experiences of detachment are far more traumatic than this type of relational discord, as Koreans are shaped as persons within community. If I may explain this process with a bit of exaggeration, it is similar to the process of diminishing a boundary and rearranging persons: diminishing a distinctive boundary between a family and others and arbitrarily rearranging the placement of the family members and others, in order to prevent a person from having a strong sense of belonging to his or her family.

It is interesting that mainstream developmental psychology does not pay significant attention to communal identity development. It seems that Western researchers do not even think about the presence of certain groups that develop together and simultaneously form communal identities. However, Western scholars are providentially paying more attention to interpersonal relationships than biological factors in human development studies. For example, Gergen questions common psychological ground and states, "We typically employ such terms as thought, emotion, motivation, and self-esteem as if they referred to existing states or entities within the individual."[10] He argues, "It would not be selves who came together to form relationships, but relational process[es] out of which the very idea

---

9 S. Johnson, "Emotionally Focused Couple Therapy," in *Clinical Handbook of Couple Therapy*, 5th Ed., eds. A.S. Gurman, J. L. Lebow, and D. K. Snyder (New York: Guilford Press, 2015), 97-128.

10 K. J. Gergen, "The Social Construction of Self," in *The Oxford Handbook of The Self*, ed. Shaun Gallagher (Oxford: Oxford University Press, 2011), 639.

of the psychological self could emerge."[11] Barresi and Martin write, "It seems to us that an integrated theory of the self, was one feasible, would have to consider three major dimensions of selves, which we will call the experiential dimension, the ontological dimension, and the social dimension."[12] Daniel Siegel, a psychiatrist who is creating the expression of Interpersonal Brain Development, states, "A relational self is a fundamental aspect of who we are," and, "Science reveals our deeply social and neutrally embodied minds."[13] Thus, I am positively expecting that advanced development research based on collectivism will be coming soon, as the current research paradigm seems to be moving in that direction.

The reason that I have written the lengthy paragraphs above is to emphasize that there are no well-established psychological theories that explain the process of transforming one's identity from "us" to "me." If there are no theories on communal identity development, how can there be theories on its transformation? There are some sociological studies regarding different relationships between within-group relationships and intergroup relationships, but these studies do not touch on interpersonal attachment or the related identity development deeply.[14,15] I regret that Korean missionaries' agony over this process is largely overlooked by our Western colleagues, because there is no theoretical lens available through which they can view and understand our challenging task.

THE ADVANTAGES OF WORKING IN INTERNATIONAL MISSIONS

Until now, I have explained why Korean missionaries become more vulnerable in international missions. Now, it is time to ponder if it is still worth investing our time and effort in international missions, regardless of these various challenges. I would like to propose that there are two great benefits to be gained by working in multicultural teams.

Multicultural teams will help Korean missionaries to fulfill the responsibility of evangelism. Lianne Roembke writes about the advantages of multicultural teams clearly from this perspective.[16] First, multicultural teams reflect the

---

11 Ibid., 645.

12 J. Barresi and Raymond Martin, "History as Prologues: Western Theories of the Self," in *The Oxford Handbook of The Self*, ed. Shaun Gallagher (Oxford: Oxford University Press, 2011), 53.

13 D. J. Siegel, *The Developing Mind: How Relationships and the Brain Interact to Shape Who We Are, 2nd Edition* (New York: Guilford Press, 2012), 349, 387.

14 M.B. Brewer, "Intergroup Discrimination: Ingroup Love or Outgroup Hate?" in *The Cambridge Handbook of the Psychology of Prejudice*, eds. Chris G. Sibley & Fiona Kate Barlow (Cambridge: Cambridge University Press, 2017), 90, 110.

15 A.T. Maitner, E.R. Smith, and D.M. MacKie, "Intergroup Emotions Theory: Prejudice and Differentiated Emotional Reactions toward Outgroups," in *The Cambridge Handbook of the Psychology of Prejudice*, eds. Chris G. Sibley & Fiona Kate Barlow (Cambridge: Cambridge University Press, 2017), 111, 130.

16 Lianne Roembke, *Building Credible Multicultural Teams*, edition afem: academics BD.4 (Bonn: Verlag für Kultur und Wissenschaft Culture and Science Publ., 1998), 56, 59.

body of Christ comprehensively to non-Christians or new Christians.[17] Non-Christians or new Christians can easily witness a diversity of Christians, without misunderstanding that one type of spirituality is better than the others. Secondly, multicultural teams have a variety of resources with which to communicate the Gospel to non-Christians or new Christians efficiently.[18] They can explore which way of communicating works best in new cultural contexts, as each team member has already brought various ways from their countries that may or may not work well in new contexts. Thirdly, these teams communicate the "purer" Gospel to non-Christians or new Christians—a message of the Gospel that does not carry the proclaimers' cultural baggage.[19] It is evident that non-Christians or new Christians respond to the Gospel better when the Gospel with which they are presented is purer. When multicultural mission team members work together, they too become increasingly able to see the Gospel in its purity; for, although people carry their cultural baggage naturally, when people of different cultures interact, each culture can help each other culture to recognize where its own blind spots have distorted the Gospel.

Additionally, multicultural teams help Korean missionaries to fulfill the responsibility of social action. John Stott points out the importance of social action alongside evangelism by showing parallels in the parables of the Good Samaritan and the Prodigal Son.[20] In the parable of the Prodigal Son, the lost son is a victim of his own sin (personal sin), and he is rescued by his father who displays love and reaches the lost son (evangelism). In the parable of the Good Samaritan, the mugged person is a victim of others who sinned against him (social sin), and he is rescued by a Samaritan who displays compassion after overcoming a certain prejudice (social action). The call to social action is obvious throughout the Bible, but not all Korean missionaries are enthusiastically following it. Perhaps this is because we cannot fully resonate with oppressed minority populations if we have not shared similar experiences. Thus, I believe that taking the position of an ethnic minority in intercultural mission teams will help us to be more compassionate to social minorities, which will lead us to carry out more social action.

PRACTICAL GUIDELINES FOR KOREANS IN INTERNATIONAL MISSIONS

As a final step, I would like to submit the following six practical guidelines that would help Korean missionaries to thrive better in multicultural teams. Lianne Roembke describes three factors that prevent cross-cultural workers from being adjusted to each other in multicultural teams: *ignorance, personal inability to*

---

17 Ibid., 56, 58.
18 Ibid., 59.
19 Ibid., 59.
20 John Stott, *The Contemporary Christian* (Leicester: InterVarsity, 1992), 346.

change, and *unwillingness to change*.[21] There might be a few Korean missionaries who cannot adapt themselves well to international missions because they have a psychological inability to do so, which is rooted in their insecure upbringing. There could be some Koreans who are not keen to work in multicultural teams. However, I think that there are more Korean missionaries who are competent and willing to work in international missions than there are those who are unable or reluctant to. Given the above, I believe *ignorance* is the most important factor that hinders Koreans from being adjusted in international missions. Thus, the first guideline for Korean missionaries is *to remember the importance of working in multicultural teams*. Working in international missions is one of the critical calls for carrying out evangelism and social action efficiently.

The next guideline is *not to compare Koreans' slow adjustment speed with others*. Social science researches and intercultural studies show that working in cross-cultural contexts in multicultural teams is considerably challenging for every missionary. On top of these findings, the perspectives from sociology and psychology prove Korean missionaries become more vulnerable in these steps for various reasons. Thus, as Korean missionaries, we should not feel guilty for our slow progress or doubtful about our adaptation competency.

The following guideline is *not to leave international missions until having developed a reasonable sense of belonging*. A time of loneliness comes after the honeymoon period in the beginning, regardless of how long the honeymoon period lasts. However, the lonely time is the best time to learn different styles of interpersonal relationships with people from diverse backgrounds. A child will eat something unfamiliar if he/she becomes hungry. But if the child instead visits the neighbor's house to find some familiar fare, how will the child learn to enjoy new dishes?

The fourth recommendation is *to volunteer for leadership roles*. Without being involved in various leadership roles, Korean missionaries will not be able to see other parts of international missions, since international missions are mainly governed by their policies. It is common that information on how an organization works is passed on to certain persons who are involved in specific roles only. The more responsibilities for which a person volunteers, the better the person will understand how the organization works.

The fifth is *to keep improving English over the years,* instead of dropping that focus after a few years of investment at the beginning. The power of English is greater than we normally expect, as the scope of our thoughts is significantly influenced by our languages. The more fluent the English we speak, the more precisely we understand thoughts that are generated by English. I understand that there is some controversy over the extent to which this is true (how much does our language influence our thoughts?). For example, linguistic scholars who support *Linguistic Determinism* believe that "language structure controls thought and cultural norms. Each of us lives not in the midst of the whole world but only in that part of the world that

---

21 Lianne Roembke, *Building Credible Multicultural Teams*, 82.

our language permits us to know."[22] Scholars who support *Linguistic Relativism* say, "Culture is controlled by and controls language ... Language provides the conceptual categories that influence how its speakers' perceptions are encoded and stored ... The basis of linguistic relativity is that the difference between languages is not what can be said but what is relatively easy to say."[23] However, regardless of this controversy, all linguists agree that if we would like to understand different thoughts, we need to learn the languages that generate those thoughts.

The last is *to remind ourselves frequently of the personal blessings of becoming multicultural persons.* God calls Korean missionaries to build multicultural teams on the field to fulfill his missions to non-Christians or new Christians. But I also trust that he commands us to accomplish this task for our interests. For example, some scholars say, we will gain beneficial psychological outcomes while we are managing two group loyalties, bilingual communications, and cultural identities at the same time.[24] One scholar writes that we will come to grasp the Gospel in greater depth when we stop seeing the Gospel exclusively through the lens of Korean culture.[25] We will become closer to God as our relationships with others are intimately interwoven with our relationship with God. The more we connect with others, the closer we get to our Lord. Are there any additional personal blessings that come from being a multicultural person? It is your turn to discover the blessings that may be in store for you.

---

22 F. E. Jandt, *An Introduction to Intercultural Communication: Identities in a Global Community*, 4th Ed. (Thousand Oaks, CA: SAGE Publications, 2004), 150.

23 Ibid.

24 S. X. Chen, V. Benet-Martinex, and M. H. Bond, "Bicultural Identity, Bilingualism, and Psychological Adjustment in Multicultural Societies: Immigration-based and Globalization-based Acculturation," *Journal of Personality* 76, no. 4 (August 2008): 803-838.

25 P. G. Hiebert, *Anthropological Reflections on Missiological Issues* (Grand Rapids: Baker Books, 1994). Also, P. G. Hiebert, *Transforming Worldviews: An Anthropological Understanding of How People Change* (Grand Rapids: Baker Academic, 2008).

RESPONSE by Patricia Lucille Toland

CURRENT REALITIES

I commend Dr. Kim for her excellent and encompassing analysis of the different facets involved in J's case study. As she stated, missions have changed in the last ten years and have become more diversified. Now, most international organizations fully embrace non-Westerners. The first minorities to integrate into culturally dominated organizations are pioneers who face many challenges. As more nationalities join, the integration of ideas and values slowly change the organization's sub-culture, creating shared basic assumptions among members.

Today, international mission agencies with Western roots that emphasize multiethnic integration and mutual understanding have Koreans and other minorities as leaders. This is a phenomenal testimony to the power of Christ in mission agencies.

Fortunately, with many Koreans in missions, soon there will be complementary research from Koreans to add to intercultural studies, specifically in the area of identity loss and transition. Westerners cannot write on transitioning from a communal to an individual identity, since Westerners have never done so. However, Westerners have transitioned from an individual identity to a communal one; some missionary autobiographies specifically mention this struggle. My own experiences involved adjusting from an individual to a communal mindset, which took years and was extremely frustrating and exhausting.

Groups. Westerners do not grasp group-based identity easily because "self" in the Western mind is not defined by social relationships and expectations.[26] Therefore, Westerners do not understand the feelings of honor and shame when expectations are upheld or violated. The following characteristics can help Westerners understand collectivity: conformity, protection, belonging, solidarity, support, acceptance, status, meaning, value, dignity, unity, shared values, consistent norms and structure, reciprocity, shared honor and shame, shared identity, and unspoken expectations, among others. Fostering these characteristics within mission teams will help Koreans feel more included as team members.

In addition, when Koreans and Westerners understand the unspoken expectations of the team, mutual appreciation results, forming a cohesive bond. A tightly knit team, where each nationality feels valued and understood, generates a desire to please others out of respect and honor, no matter one's nationality.[27]

If expectations are violated, the member who did not meet the others' expectations may feel shame through discomfort, alienation, isolation, or

---

26 Christopher L. Flanders, *About Face: Rethinking Face for 21st Century Mission* (Eugene, OR: Pickwick, 2011), 45-46; 55-56.

27 David A. DeSilva, *Honor, Patronage, Kinship and Purity: Unlocking New Testament Culture* (Downers Grove, IL: IVP Academic, 2000), 35.

minimization in relation to the group.[28] In contrast to J's experience with a mostly Western team, some international agencies with teams made up of mostly Koreans see the opposite happen. The complaint is similar to J's, but the non-Korean feels marginalized and leaves the team. Thus, we face the reality of human nature and the challenge of bonding with those who are different from us. God wisely calls us to unity amidst diversity.

Adaptation. The Minority Identity Model, which Dr. Kim details, parallels the stages of culture shock. Leaving the field while in the rejection phase is parallel to the "Resistance and Immersion" stage with which J struggled. All nationalities respond the same way, i.e., when trying to acculturate to a host culture, preferring to isolate themselves and spend time with those who are homogenous to them in worldview and patterns of relating. Like-mindedness provides an escape from the stress of grappling with new values and beliefs.

Working in multicultural teams requires a long-term mindset. There is no step-by-step process for how to become less group-oriented and more individualistic or vice versa. Acculturation is learned through trial and error and is a process of frustration and victories. One of the best ways to approach this transition is by finding a "cultural friend of peace," someone to consult and to ask for interpretations of conversations or voice intonations, who can also advise how to respond appropriately.

A Korean missionary told me that the Asian culture in which she worked was so group-oriented that it made her, even as a Korean, feel individual-oriented. This shows that the depth of change is different for each context. Another of my Korean colleagues, who had worked overseas on multicultural teams for over ten years, commented that adaptation came more quickly when there were no other Koreans on the team, because it forced them to assimilate so they could enjoy ministry. Many Koreans have shown that adjustment can be done, but it takes time and purposeful effort.

Identity. Koreans suffer a deep loss of identity whenever moving into a cross-cultural context causes them to lose their Korean community. Westerners suffer an identity loss as well, because they were "somebody" in their home context and now are "nobody." However, Koreans do not have the advantage of coming from a diversified culture; hence, multicultural teams are new and sometimes overwhelming. Expecting to be fully adopted by the team, they may find conditions that can magnify their identity loss. Yet, all missionaries let go of known ways of doing, thinking, and perceiving when integrating into a new culture. It is an unavoidable part of becoming bicultural or, in this case, multicultural.

Identity re-formation can take years for a Korean adapting to an individualistic community or for a Westerner adapting to a group-oriented community. Either

---

28 Stephen Pattison, "Shame and the Unwanted Self," in *The Shame Factor: How Shame Shapes Society*, eds. Robert Jewett, Wayne L. Alloway Jr., and John G. Lacey (Eugene, OR: Cascade, 2011), 9, 18.

way, re-forming one's identity requires identifying as an "I" rather than a "we," or a "we" rather than an "I." This is where mutual understanding can be birthed. Paralleling the Westerner's adaptation process and losses with those of Koreans, I believe that phases can be identified to help Koreans recognize what is happening and what to expect while developing a new identity. Praise God for our identity as sons and daughters in Christ, which can carry us through when we are feeling alone.

Attachment. How can Koreans fill the identity "vacuum" while waiting to bond with a new group? It is important to note that people with broken attachments in their background may have a more difficult time adjusting later in life.[29] However, a person can make new attachments.[30] Missionaries on the field, for example, can have extra difficulty adapting to their team, if they suffered from broken attachments earlier in life. Different from primary attachments, transitionary attachments may thus be important for helping Korean missionaries through the adjustment phase, since attachments can be formed with "extended family, teachers, friends, coworkers, lovers, and pets."[31] The more multicultural teams become, the more opportunities there are to form attachments with other language students and team members who also share community identity.

Member care. Member care that supports Koreans during their cultural transition periods is crucial. Successful transitions depend, in part, on the person's response to the transition.[32] There are six interrelated dimensions of care, each addressing preventable problematic areas that cause missionaries to leave the field prematurely.[33] In addition, there are five levels of care—master, self, sender, specialist, and network—which provide care from different sources to keep a person healthy and thriving.[34] Proper care provides missionaries with resources, counsel, encouragement, companionship, spiritual strengthening, and re-confirmation of call, along with an understanding of the cross-cultural adaptation process. Adapting to a new culture is a journey from struggling to thriving, both personally and ministerially, on the field, and it is a process that all nationalities face. Proper member care would help Korean missionaries during the period of identity loss to eventually thrive and become resilient. However, a word of caution: care administered by Koreans who live nearby can turn exclusive and instead of fostering cross-cultural

---

29 Karen Carr, "Normal Reactions After Trauma," in *Trauma and Resilience,* eds. Charles and Frauke Schaefer (Fresno, CA: Condeo Press, 2012), 45-46.

30 Graham Barker, "The Effects of Trauma on Attachment" (Christian Counsellors Association of Australia, 2012), 4, https://www.ccaa.net.au/documents/TheEffectsOfTraumaOnAttachment.pdf.

31 Ibid., 2.

32 Laura Mae Gardner, "A Practical Approach to Missionary Transitions," in *Enhancing Missionary Vitality,* eds. John R. Powell and Joyce M. Bowers (Palmer Lake, CO: Mission Training International, 1999), 94-95.

33 Lawrence and Lois Dodds, *Caring for People in Missions: Just Surviving–or Thriving?* (Liverpool, PA: Heartstream, 1997).

34 Kelly O'Donnell, "Going Global: A Member Care Model for Best Practice," in *Doing Member Care Well,* ed. Kelly O'Donnell (Pasadena, CA: William Carey, 2002), 15-19.

adaptation, can merely forge deeper Korean bonds, hindering the transition process. Therefore, virtual member care may be more effective.

SUGGESTIONS

Working in a multicultural team necessitates that each member understands the characteristics, worldview, power base, and basic assumptions of the other members. Below are suggestions to facilitate mutual understanding:

1. Give the team specific training on cultural similarities and differences, including leadership styles, decision making, confrontation styles and reactions, power distance, hierarchy expectations, demonstrations of care, work relationship vs. friendship expectations, individual vs. collective expectations, and long- and short-term outlooks, balancing team values between ministry and compassionate relationships.

2. Engage in team building activities to help team members understand how the other members perceive things and why they react as they do.

3. Create sensitivity by learning and practicing various indirect and direct communication strategies as a team.

4. Have team events in which members practice utilizing collectivistic traits, then alternate and practice utilizing individualistic ones.

5. Purposefully create an environment of compassion.

6. Join agencies that have non-Westerners in leadership.

7. Identify a "person of peace" from whom interpretations of conversations and examples of how to respond can be explained and provided.

8. Use Internet video calling and cellular texting to provide transitionary attachment opportunities.

9. Receive member care from experienced Koreans.

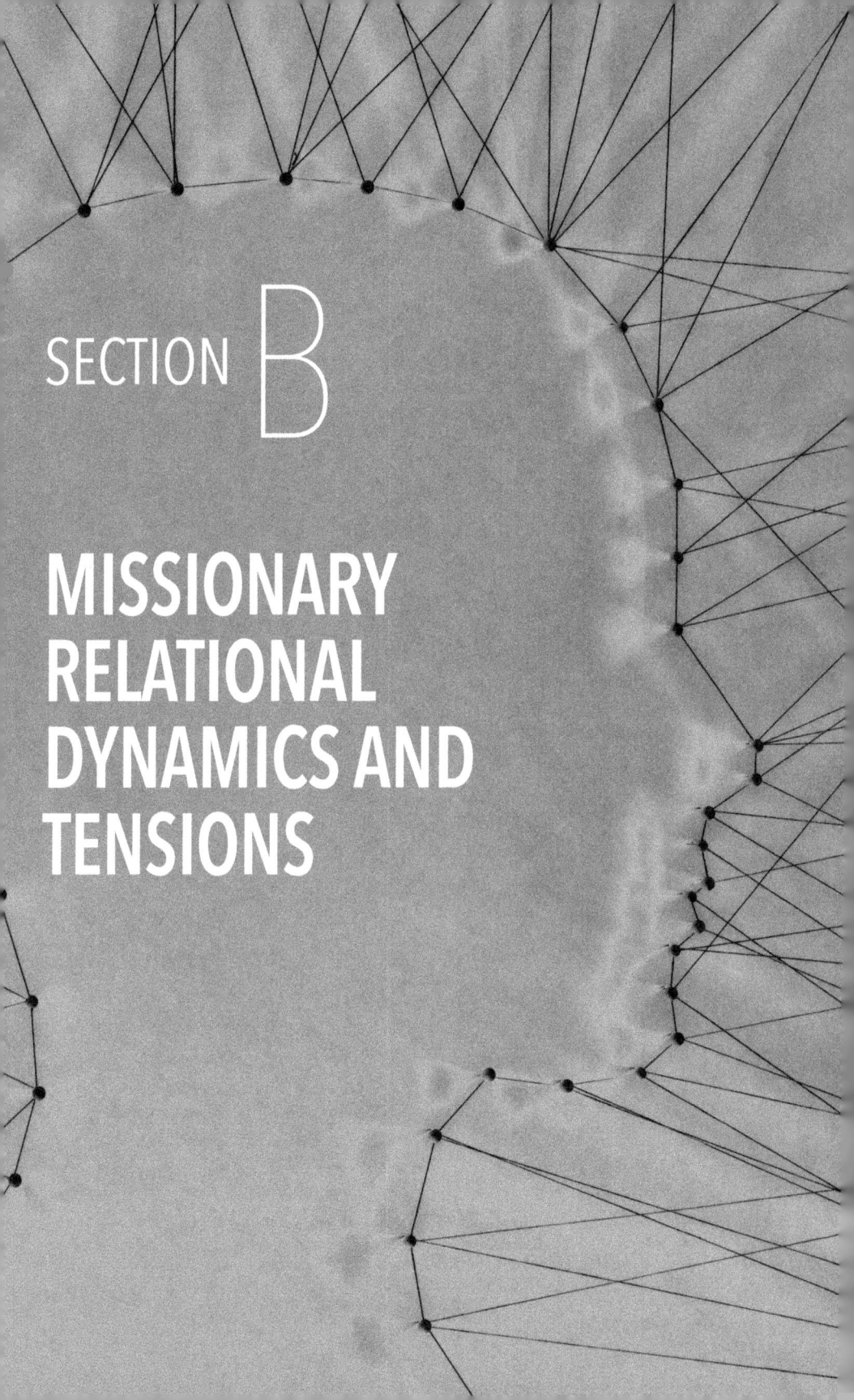

SECTION B

MISSIONARY RELATIONAL DYNAMICS AND TENSIONS

MARITAL CONFLICT AMONG KOREAN MISSIONARY COUPLES

by Hyun-Sook Lee

INTRODUCTION

As the divorce rate in Korea is the highest in Asia,[1] marital conflict is becoming an important social issue there. Marital problems are not limited to unbelievers; Christian families face severe conflicts as well, and missionary families are no exception. Therefore, conflict within married missionary couples is a critical area

---

1 "Divorce Statistics, 2017," Korea National Statistical Office, March 21, 2018, kostat.go.kr/portal/korea/kor_nw/3/index.board?bmode). The number of divorces in Korea peaked in 2009 and then declined to 107,300 in 2016, down 1.7 percent (1,800) from the previous year. On the other hand, the crude divorce rate gradually decreased from 2.5 in 2009 to 2.1 in 2016, but then spiked to 4.4 in 2017 (*Judicial Almanac of Korea*).

of focus for member care (MC) workers. Further, marital strife not only causes difficulties for the couples themselves; it also has a significant impact on their children. The following are some specific cases[2] of Korean missionary couples—revealing what their relationships are like and what the causes of their conflicts are. After the case studies, we will discuss some proposals for improving Korean missionary couples' (and therefore also families') relationships.

MARRIAGE CONFLICTS AND THEIR CAUSES

According to research, almost half (49.4 percent) of Korean missionary family members feel that their families are emotionally "in harmony, even though, from time to time, there are some conflicts which are manageable within the families." The next largest group, 37.1 percent, describe their families as "in harmonious relationships and happy;" while 5.3 percent say that there is discord in their family relationships, but it can be resolved because the problem is temporary (such as a child's going through puberty). Finally, 1.2 percent say that they are experiencing serious conflict and discord and need help. A quick glance at these numbers seems to indicate that Korean missionary families are generally happy and are able to deal well with conflict when it arises. However, in in-depth interviews conducted for the study, seven women missionaries out of the twenty participants described having marital conflicts that had been hurting them very much.[3]

After meeting many missionaries in support groups and in counseling sessions of married couples, Lee Hyun-Sook summarizes the factors that contribute to a missionary couple's conflict as follows:

- Culture shock and cross-cultural adaptation
- Prioritization of the ministry over the family
- The need for couples to depend heavily on each other in the mission field
- The patriarchal Confucian culture of Korea
- Problems stemming from the family of origin
- A lack of ability to communicate and empathize well

Case 1. Mr. and Mrs. Kim, a missionary couple, had worked for seven years in a school ministry, located in a remote, outlying Muslim country, where few other Koreans lived. While they were suffering from mental and emotional isolation,

---

[2] The names used in the following cases are aliases, and the cases do not present the stories of any specific missionary couples, but rather examples of scenarios that are common among Korean missionary couples.

[3] Steve Sang-Cheol Moon, et al., *Hanguk seongyosa member care bangan* [*A Plan for Improvement of Member Care for Korean Missionaries*] (Seoul: KRIM, 2015), 47-48.

a robber broke into their home and took money that they had reserved for the construction of the school. While the robbery was occurring, Mrs. Kim went in to see what was happening, risking being raped. She was not harmed, but after this event, Mr. and Mrs. Kim became fearful, suffering from panic disorders and burnout, and they ended up returning to their home country. Everything, from their daily routines to their work in the school, had become difficult for them because of the differences between their home culture and the surrounding cultures and because of the ever-present dangers of robbery and terrorism.

Before going to the mission field, Mr. Kim had been a pastor of a church, assisting the senior pastor, and his wife had been a homemaker. His grandmother had raised him, and he had lived alone from junior high school on. He had never had the opportunity to experience an affectionate relationship with his mother. He tried hard to be a good child, in hopes of receiving recognition from the people around him. As an adult, due to his hard work, he did earn the recognition of his colleagues. However, he and his wife had many conflicts. He became easily irritated with her, even though he knew she was having a hard time too.

Case 2. The Lees, a missionary couple in their forties, were ministering in a restricted area. Mr. Lee had grown up as the youngest child in his family; Mrs. Lee had been the oldest in hers. Soon after they entered the country of their assignment, the couple learned that Mrs. Lee had thyroid cancer, and she had to have surgery. Later, the Lees experienced another traumatic event, when their whole family was suddenly deported, forcing them to return to Korea from the mission field. However, Mrs. Lee showed strength and resilience over the next several years, starting a business as a ministry for women in the area. It was evident that she was a gifted businesswoman.

On the other hand, Mr. Lee was a passionate evangelist, who used to preach the gospel on the streets of Korea but felt helpless when he was unable to do similar ministry on the mission field. He also felt that his wife did not respect him, and there was no intimacy between them. Gradually, Mr. Lee fell into hopelessness and became addicted to pornography and Internet games. Furthermore, he was oppressive in rearing his children, so the couple often fought about parenting concerns. They frequently broke into quarrels because of their first daughter, who was struggling emotionally because of the discord between her parents.

Case 3. Mr. and Mrs. Park were a middle-aged missionary couple, who had been working for 18 years in a relatively free country. A few years ago, Mr. Park had returned home, as he was exhausted from relief work. However, after having a three months' vacation, not a full sabbatical year, Mr. Park returned to the mission field. He had grown up as a model student, very courteous and exercising good manners. Later, as a hard-working missionary, highly respected by his colleagues and the locals, he looked to his home to be a place of rest. Mrs. Park was three years younger than him, so Mr. Park expected her to show him respect and be polite, not asserting her opinions strongly. Thus, her assertiveness and disregard hurt him badly. Mr. Park's family of origin had been very traditional and, not being a girl, he had not been expected to do most of the household chores. Years later, his wife became frustrated because he was unwilling to help her around the house and did not pay much attention to her or their children.

Among the six factors leading to conflict within Korean missionaries' marriages (listed above), let us now consider the three factors that are most closely tied to Korean culture and society.

THREE CULTURE-RELATED CAUSES OF CONFLICT

1. A *work-centered life*. Korean missionaries often prioritize ministry over their families. This value can cause or deepen conflict between a husband and wife. Most husbands who are also missionaries leave family matters mainly to their wives and dedicate all their own time and energy to ministry.[4] As they search for the full reward of their missionary efforts in the fruits of their ministries, they frequently become immersed in work and cannot rest. They become exhausted because they are unable to enjoy even institutionally guaranteed rests, such as furloughs and vacations.[5] Many regard caring for the family as a private concern that has nothing to do with public ministry, and this is reflected in the mission field, as well.

My wife and I went back to the mission field before she had recovered sufficiently from cancer surgery. I thought that I had to learn to speak the local language quickly. I wanted to start my ministry as soon as possible. I was unaware of my wife's difficulties, so I did not help her. Later, I realized that my wife was having trouble taking care of two young children on her own. But while we were learning the language, there was a deep conflict between the two of us, and both of us became exhausted. (Mr. Lee)

I was exhausted while doing relief work, and I did not even know that I was exhausted. I remember sitting in a library to write a paper and being unable to read or write a single line. However, I wanted to write my paper quickly, because I wanted to help others… . When I went home, I was too tired to help my wife do the housework, so she was having a hard time, too. (Mr. Park)

Korean missionaries do generally value caring for their families and taking time for rest and privacy.[6] When the amount of conflict between a missionary mother and her children is low, the level of anxiety in their home is also rather low.

---

4 Hyun-Sook Lee, "Seongyosaei daeingwange stress hoebokgwajung yongu" ["A Study on the Restoration Process Regarding the Interpersonal Stress of Missionaries"] (PhD diss., Baekseok Univ., 2014), 58–59.

5 Steve Sang-Cheol Moon, et al., *Hanguk seongyosa member care bangan*, 134.

6 Hyung-Joon Kim, "Tamoonhwagwon seongyosaei taljingwa bubujeokeung" ["A Study on Burnout of Missionaries"] (PhD diss., Korea Presbyterian Seminary, 2009), 2–3.

Moreover, the longer a missionary works abroad, the lower the level of anxiety in the family becomes.[7] Thus, a caring and stable home environment decreases the missionary family's level of stress.

However, those who come from a work-centered perspective, which places a higher priority on ministry than family, tend to focus on their roles and responsibilities as missionaries and do not take the time to develop relationships with their spouses outside the contexts and burdens of work.[8] This approach can cause severe marital conflicts, especially in a cross-cultural context.[9] Lee Eun-Joo pointed out that missionary wives are more depressed than their husbands, and their frustration levels within marriage are high. Moreover, when missionary couples have many children, their anxiety levels are even higher. Thus, when missionary fathers are so preoccupied with their ministry work that they cannot help at home or take time to develop relationships with their spouses and children, their homes become increasingly full of discord.

The above findings suggest that work-centered values have had a major negative influence on the emotions of missionaries and their families. Missionaries would do well to recognize that what kind of participants we are in God's mission (being) is more important than how much we do for his mission (doing).

2. *Confucianism and its values.* Generally, Confucianism has had a more significant influence on Korean culture than anything else. It also influences Korean missionaries, as they grow up with patriarchal values, such as filial duty(孝), seniority and hierarchy, and fear of losing face. These values influence family relations and behavioral norms and, as a result, are a major player in marital conflicts.

In Case 3 (above), Mr. Park's patriarchal values became a source of conflict for him and his wife. According to Confucianism, a wife should serve and honor her husband, but this patriarchal perspective makes it difficult for a couple to have an intimate relationship. As a result, the wife often becomes depressed, which has an additional adverse emotional effect on the couple.[10] Such a scenario is common.

3. *Continuation of problems rooted in the family of origin.* According to Lee Yoo-Kyung, conflict within some Korean missionary couples stems from problems that existed within their families of origin.[11] Further, family-of-origin problems can spawn

---

7 Eun-Joo Lee, "Buinseongyosadulei simlijeok galdeunggwa bulani wooule michinun younghyang yongu" ["A Study on the Impact of Psychological Conflict and Anxiety on Depression of Women Missionaries"] (PhD diss., Chongshin Univ., 2017), 130.

8 Hyun-Sook Lee, "Seongyosaei daeingwange stress hoebokgwajung yongu," 110-116. (The study shows that the way for missionaries to find restoration in the face of their interpersonal stress was "to escape from the bridle of the role of a missionary and then to live as myself, a child of God, created uniquely as I am.")

9 Ibid., 58, 110.

10 Sarah Kim, "Bubu galdeunggwa wooul, bulan gwangeeseoei yongseoei jungjaehoygwa" ["Relationships Among Couple-Conflict, Forgiveness, Depression, and Anxiety: Moderating Effects of Forgiveness"], *Hanguk Kajunggwanri Hakhoeji* [*Korea Journal of Family Management*] 28, No. 4 (2010): 55-56.

11 Yoo-Kyung Lee, "Hangukseongyosaei bubu galdunggwa gukbokgyunghume gwanhan younku" ["A Study on the Experience of Marital Conflicts & Recovery among Korean Missionary Couples], *Korean Journal of Christian Counselling*, vol. 27, no.1.

new problems for married missionaries, causing them even greater interpersonal stress and conflict.[12] In Case 2 (above), the Lees' marital conflicts were also rooted in their families of origin.

> I was the eldest daughter of my parents. My dad died early, and my mom depended on me. So I had to take care of everything in my home and protect my mom. I became very independent and self-assertive. I had to conceal my status as a missionary in the mission field. Therefore, I started a soap-crafts shop for the women in the area as my ministry, and it turned out to be a good ministry. My husband was a passionate evangelist, who used to preach the gospel on the streets of Korea but felt helpless when he was unable to do similar ministry in the mission field. He seemed to become daunted and passive. I usually did not ask my husband's opinion, and I think I ignored him a little. (Mrs. Lee)

In her family of origin, Mrs. Lee was a family hero. Not only was she the oldest daughter, she also functioned as the head of her household. In contrast, as the youngest in his family of origin, Mr. Lee was like a lost child. These family roles continued to play out in the Lees' marital relationship, which further amplified their conflicts. While Mrs. Lee was active in ministry and expressed her opinions freely, her husband was not good at expressing what he wanted. In his family of origin, his position had not given him the platform to do so. Even in his marriage, Mr. Lee did not express his opinion, so his wife usually did things without consulting him. Her disregard for his opinion frustrated him, though: she did not seem to respect him as the head of the family. So, their marital conflicts intensified.

Unresolved problems from one's family of origin can have serious detrimental effects on a marriage and can easily aggravate marital conflict. This is especially the case when people do not receive enough attention from their families or when their parents do not treat them with warmth and care; such circumstances often lead to a variety of addictions and abuses, including domestic abuse and Internet addiction. Husband-wife relationships that are troubled by such things elicit problems in their children's lives as well, such as Internet and gaming addictions, rebellion, religious skepticism, poor peer relationships, and in extreme cases, suicide. Such outcomes are severe, so prevention is essential.

SUGGESTIONS FOR IMPROVING THE MARITAL RELATIONSHIPS OF KOREAN MISSIONARY COUPLES

Even today, Korean churches are inclined to expect missionaries to achieve "successful" ministries, rather than personal maturity and growth. This is partly because they think that missionaries should be "spiritual giants," even though they have seen that that is not true at all. Among other things, through member care, we need to help missionaries grow, heal, and become more resilient in the face of the post-traumatic stress[13] that can develop from severe marital conflict.

---

12 Hyun-Sook Lee, "Seongyosaei daeingwange stress hoebokgwajung yongu," 57-58.
13 Frauke C. Schaefer and Charles A. Schaefer, eds., *Gotonggwa eunhye* [*Trauma and Resilience*], trans. Moon-Gap Doh (Seoul: Timothy Press, 2016), 34-43.

Unfortunately, Korean missionaries are inclined to consider emotional pain or severe stress a part of daily life, rather than seeking help to alleviate it.¹⁴ Also, many of them are ashamed to reveal their inner difficulties and weaknesses to others, because their Confucian values will not allow them to do so. Therefore, in many cases, one's personal problems cannot be dealt with appropriately before they become severe. Considering this situation, we need to propose the following to improve member care for Korean missionaries.

1. *Careful screening.* The missionary selection process requires careful screening of those who have been abused or addicted. As we saw above, even those who have been doing well in their home countries can experience difficulties and severe stress in the mission field. According to Gardner, the missionary selection process requires an assessment of spiritual, relational, and physical health, as well as emotional vitality and resilience; methods for screening applicants include assessment tools, life interviews, and community life observation.¹⁵ Through careful selection, finding those who are especially vulnerable to stress and having an appropriate course of treatment available for them ahead of time (assuming they are accepted as members) will be the best way to promote health and thriving for the missionaries, their sending agencies, and the supporting churches.

2. *Sufficient self-reflection and self-understanding.* Self-understanding is crucial to missionary health. During training, and before candidates go overseas, member care providers must help the prospective missionaries to reflect on themselves and their stories. The candidates' training should include participation in programs, such as missionary support groups or group counseling sessions, that would help them recognize—through lectures, readings, and the experiences of other missionaries—any potentially problematic values they hold, for instance, a patriarchal, Confucian approach to marriage.¹⁶ Further, missionary candidates are less likely to experience unnecessary marital conflict if they go to the mission field with insights gained from individual or husband-wife counseling. Many senior missionaries are reluctant to get help with their marital conflicts because they are afraid of losing face, but in these cases, the missionaries must pursue help despite their fears, for the sake of their marriages, ministries, and mental health.

3. *Training in communication and reconciliation skills.* Missionaries should also learn communication and reconciliation skills. Communication and reconciliation courses/seminars for couples and families can help missionaries develop healthier marital relationships. Through such training, couples who have been resentful of each other can find forgiveness and reconciliation, begin communicating more

---

14 Jonathan Shung Kang, "Mental and Emotional Health of a Missionary Family," in *Family Accountability in Missions*, ed. J. Bonk (New Haven: OMSC Publications, 2013): 154-167.

15 Laura Gardner, *Seongyosa member care handbook* [*Healthy, Resilient, and Effective in Cross-cultural Ministry*], trans., Ruth Baek and Hunbok Song (Seoul: Abba Press, 2016), 44-59.

16 Hyun-Sook Lee, "Seongyohyunjang sayokihooei seongyosaei jungsingonganggwa member care" ["Mental Health and Reentry Member Care"], in *Compendium of Bangkok Forum 2014-2015* (Seoul: Mission Partners, 2015): 183-193.

effectively, and learn to show each other greater empathy. Many missionaries feel empathy for their spouses but do not know how to express themselves. They ask for reconciliation and forgiveness in unhelpful or ineffective ways. And when this happens repeatedly, in many cases, couples become frustrated, unable to forgive and reconcile properly, resulting in the accumulation of negative emotions. Thus, many couples end up living side by side, but in a state of emotional divorce. They need external help to break their habituated patterns of relating.

4. *Establishing and utilizing a counseling system.* When faced with difficulties in ministry, missionaries are often unaware of how to get help. Even if member care services are available, they may not know about them. To minimize such cases, we need to establish a system that can provide immediate mediation and counseling for couples with marital conflict, either face to face or online. Member care organizations such as Turning Point are already available to serve in this way. It may not always be possible to visit troubled missionaries in person, but we should at least be able to offer timely professional help through Skype or email.

5. *Acceptance of a community.* For missionary couples to recover from exhaustion or emotional difficulties, acceptance from their community is critical. Many missionaries are struggling to live as model missionaries, rather than living as children of God; rather than living out their identity as children of God, they are trying to live a life that matches what they perceive to be the role of a missionary.[17] In one study, as missionaries participated in group recovery sessions, they all started to live more as themselves, as children of God, rather than focusing on what they should accomplish as missionaries. The participants' relationships with their spouses, children, and peers improved, too.[18] This growth was due, at least in part, to the way in which the sense of community within the group provided the missionaries with a safe environment for honest reflection and sharing. The participants felt safe to share vulnerably about themselves, as they all accepted each other unconditionally. Korean churches and mission agencies should have a deep interest in supporting such communities, both at home and in the mission field, so that ministry workers can experience unconditional acceptance in a spiritually, emotionally, and physically safe environment.

6. *Other suggestions.* Missionary couples who are hurt and damaged in their marital relationships are very likely to feel depressed and frustrated, and they cannot expect to bear the fruits of continuing and effective ministry. Therefore, it is essential for Korean churches, sending agencies, and MC organizations to support and encourage missionary couples in the endeavor to develop and maintain healthy marital relationships. They must also provide better systems and programs, through which to prevent marital problems within missionary couples. To do this, first, participation and cooperation between churches, sending agencies, and MC organizations is

---

17 Hyun-Sook Lee, "Seongyohyunjang sayokihooei seongyosaei jungsingonganggwa member care," 190.

18 Hyun-Sook Lee, "Seongyosaei daeingwange stress hoebokgwajung yongu" ["A Study on the Restoration Process Regarding the Interpersonal Stress of Missionaries"]. *Korean Journal of Christian Counselling 27*, no. 1(2016): 215-216.

crucial. Second, churches and sending agencies must provide missionary couples with support and systems that ensure their times of rest, including furloughs and vacations. Third, the training and securing of counseling specialists, as well as other professional MC workers, is an urgent need.[19]

RESPONSE *by Ben Torrey*

"If the foundations are destroyed, what can the righteous do?"

–Psalm 11:3

Dr. Hyun-Sook Lee has clearly identified several problems that Korean missionary couples face. She has also included a number of valuable suggestions. I would like to highlight her fifth suggestion: "acceptance of a community." This is, in my mind, one of the most important ones. God did not mean for us to be alone. He put us in families, and he placed families together in communities. Our fundamental community, beyond our biological families, is the church, the body of Christ, the people of God. Passages such as Romans 12, 1 Corinthians 12 and 13, Ephesians 4, and others emphasize how important are our community and our relationships with each other. Isolation is, to put it bluntly, deadly. We need each other. The preacher put it succinctly, "Furthermore, if two lie down together they keep warm, but how can one be warm alone? And if one can overpower him who is alone, two can resist him. A cord of three strands is not quickly torn apart" (Eccles. 4:11-12, NASB).

Moreover, when Jesus sent his disciples out on their missions, he sent them two by two. This pairing into twos was not a pairing of husbands with their wives; since the husband and wife become one flesh (Gen. 2:24), they go as one. No, the "two by two" sending was a sending of two separate partners, working as a team. Paul always worked with a team. The modern pattern of individual missionary couples serving in isolation has no foundation in Scripture.

I believe that community is critically important for missions and the health of missionaries, so I strongly endorse the author's fifth recommendation. All her suggestions are clearly important, but community is where our help comes from.

I would like now to move beyond the author's suggestions and consider foundational issues, such as God's intent for the family and for husband-wife relationships. If the foundations are destroyed, there is little that God's people (the righteous) can do. Anything built on a shaky or destroyed foundation will not stand, no matter how well designed it is.

Where do we learn what the foundations for missionary care should be? I believe that most, if not all, evangelical missionaries would agree that the Holy Scripture provides the answer. Therefore, let us look at what the Bible says about these issues and take it seriously.

---

19 Hyun-Sook Lee, "Hyunjangeseoei member care" ["Member Care in the Mission Field"], *Hanguk Seonkyo* [*Korea Mission Quarterly*] 17, no. 4(2018): 65-78.

I would like to start at the beginning with the story of creation in Genesis 1. First of all, we see in verses 1–3 the triune God. We know this from John 1:1–3, where we learn that the creative word of God, "and God said …," was the second person of the Trinity, God the Son, the Word made flesh. Skipping down to the creation of man and woman in verses 26–28, we see that mankind is created in the image of that triune God. "Let us make man in our image …" He then gives them their first command, "Be fruitful and multiply." This is a command to fill the earth with the image of God. Unlike all other living beings created by God to reproduce after their own kind, the man and the woman are to reproduce after the kind of God. We see in this that it is truly the family that can be considered the full expression of the image of God. Going over to the end of chapter 2, we read another key verse: "For this reason a man shall leave his father and his mother, and be joined to his wife; and they shall become one flesh" (Gen. 2:24). Jesus quotes this verse (Matt. 5:9–6; Mark 10:8); Paul quotes it in two separate epistles, 1 Corinthians 6:16 and Ephesians 5:31. Repetition indicates importance. Clearly, Jesus and Paul thought this principle of a man leaving his father and mother and being joined to his wife so as to become one was extremely important.

Dr. Lee identifies Confucian culture and expectations as being the source of a number of issues between Korean missionary husbands and wives. The principle stated in Genesis 2:24 cuts to the very foundation of Confucian assumptions and worldview. In Confucian ethics, a woman's primary role is to serve her husband's family. This assumption is built into the very fabric of the language. The ordinary term for a woman getting married is *shi-chip kanda*, going to the mother-in-law's house, where she is to become a helper, often a servant, to her mother-in-law. In that context, she is to care for her husband, who stays under the authority of his parents. We see this principle at work in the expectations of women, particularly, but in the expectations of men as well, as Dr. Lee's paper illustrates.

The biblical principle, on the other hand, is for the man to leave his parents and take his wife as his equal. This is the meaning of Eve being taken from Adam's rib, his side. It enables her to stand side-by-side with him as an equal before God. They are then able to propagate the image of God through building their own new family and bearing children. The husband and the wife are to work together in harmony, not one dominating the other. However, we know that sin changed this. Only after the fall (Gen. 3:16–19) do the woman and the man struggle with each other and with all other aspects of their natural lives. With our redemption from the fall through the cross of Christ and his resurrection, should not these patterns of struggle and domination be transformed back into that which was God's original intent?

God's plan for creation clearly shows the importance, the sacredness of the family. It also helps us to realize the vital importance of caring for, guarding, and building up the family—ours and all those that make up the body of Christ, the household of faith. Because of its sacred importance and the fact that the family is most fully the image of God, we may understand how thoroughly Satan hates it. The first object of Satan's hatred is God himself, the triune God. I believe that after his hatred of the Trinity, Satan's hatred is aimed toward the image of the Trinity, the human family. For this reason, he seeks to destroy it in every way he can. He began this attack in the Garden of Eden by tempting the woman and, through her, the man—causing them to disobey their God, in whose image they had been created. The attack continues in every attack on the family, from all sorts of sexual sin, to abortion (which destroys the image of God directly), all the way to neglecting or abusing spouses and children in the name of missions and ministry, sacrificing one's family for some religious ideal that is not required by God. While it may sound harsh, even extreme, I see a parallel here to the false worship that required the sacrifice of sons and daughters to the flames—something God never required and which, he declared, "did not come into my mind" (Jer. 7:31). God never conceived of this wholesale sacrifice of children—and wives—for apparently godly purposes. It did not even occur to him.

Other passages that show the biblical perspective on family include Deuteronomy 24:5: "When a man takes a new wife, he shall not go out with the army nor be charged with any duty; he shall be free at home one year and shall give happiness to his wife whom he has taken." (NASB) This indicates the vital importance of establishing the new marriage on a strong foundation of loving care that gives joy to the woman. Also illustrating the biblical perspective on family, Psalm 127:3–5 says, "Behold, children are a gift of the LORD, the fruit of the womb is a reward. Like arrows in the hand of a warrior, so are the children of one's youth. How blessed is the man whose quiver is full of them; they will not be ashamed when they speak with their enemies in the gate." Children are not to be viewed as a burden but a blessing and gift from God.

Unfortunately, missionary couples are often trapped in an abusive church system that forces young assistant clergy to neglect their wives and their children at the most critical time of family building, as they struggle under enormous workloads and expectations to sacrifice. It is also that system that causes a senior pastor's wife to tell an assistant pastor's wife that she is being selfish for having a third child, as happened to a friend of mine. This is not an isolated case. The system, with its Confucian worldview, sees the wife as the servant of her husband and his church or mission, the "Christian" "mother-in-law's house." God's intent is that they, like the Holy Trinity, work together in unity to discern God's will for family and mission.

In terms of the husband's responsibility toward his wife, it is also good to keep in mind the words of Ephesians 5:25–33 about a man loving his wife as Christ loves the church.

We see that the biblical worldview diametrically opposes the commonly held Confucian view, in terms of family structure. The Confucian perspective also elevates work and success to a level that jeopardizes the family. Knowing this, we can see the real need for a true shift of paradigms in relation to family and ministry within the Korean church—which leaves us with the question of how to bring about such a shift. All the careful selection, training in interpersonal communications, counseling, and other mechanisms of missionary preparation that a sending church or agency provides will not overcome this most foundational issue of basic assumptions, mindset, worldview. A change is needed.

The change begins with facing the problem squarely, talking about it, and examining all aspects of it. It would also be good for mission organizations to establish these principles as foundational and train missionaries in them. However, the change really needs to begin earlier, in the structure of the church system that recruits and sends the missionaries. The church needs to embrace and propagate a biblical family culture. This is truly a great challenge. A movement is needed, perhaps something like the well known Father School that has done so much already to bring about reconciliation and healing between generations in Korean families. Perhaps a "Family School" movement can be launched. I pray that God will raise up leaders who can and will address this challenge with wisdom and effectiveness.

09

NEURODEVELOPMENTAL DISORDERS AND MISSIONARY CHILDREN'S MENTAL HEALTH

by NANCY A. CRAWFORD

"*I regret to inform you that, according to my knowledge, adequate resources are not available here in East Africa to meet your child's needs, given this diagnosis of _____*" (fill in the blank with a diagnosis from one of the six classifications of Neurodevelopmental Disorders: Intellectual Disabilities, Communication Disorders, Autism Spectrum Disorder, Attention-Deficit/Hyperactivity Disorder, Specific Learning Disorder, Motor Disorders). I dreaded the times I had to say those words after completing psychoeducational assessments for missionary kids (MKs) in Africa.

During my years serving as a clinical psychologist at Tumaini Counselling Centre in Kenya, I assessed over 100 MKs who were struggling academically. My hope was that, with an accurate diagnosis, the families could then choose interventions to help their children reach their full academic and psycho-social potential. Even though the primary reason parents or MK schools usually requested a psychoeducational evaluation was due to the child's academic struggles, an equal concern was the child's mental health, because children with neurodevelopmental disorders are at risk for high levels of psychological distress and poorer overall mental health, especially depression.

By far, the two most common neurodevelopmental disorders I diagnosed in MKs were Attention-Deficit/Hyperactivity Disorder (ADHD) and Specific Learning Disorder (SLD). The following case studies are composites of times that I have been a witness to a) missionary families and their organizations responding in a supportive manner to their children, b) missionary families and their organizations not responding in a supportive manner, and c) missionary families who had circumstances that made it difficult to arrive at an accurate diagnosis, which then delayed treatment for their children. Delayed treatment for ADHD and SLD is especially regrettable, because early intervention can make a big positive difference.

ATTENTION-DEFICIT/HYPERACTIVITY DISORDER (ADHD): DESCRIPTION, TREATMENT, AND MISSIONARY REALITIES

Description. Robert,[1] age 15, spends up to six hours playing video games at a time and is very skilled at his favorite games; however, he consistently puts off doing his homework until the very last minute. It seems like he cannot get started on his homework unless he sees it as an acute emergency (e.g., "I'll fail the class if I don't get this paper done"). Even though he can focus on his video games, he has trouble focusing when he reads things he's not interested in, having to read the same passages over and over again to fully understand what he's just read. Robert especially dislikes having to write 3000-word papers. For his entire school history, Robert has been told that he is intelligent but does not apply himself. While Robert has never been disruptive in class, it seems as if he is always daydreaming and not paying attention. His grades are suffering, and once social, he is now withdrawing into himself and his video games. When Robert does speak, he often makes disparaging comments about himself and others.

I chose Robert as an example to describe ADHD, as he represents a type of it—ADHD, predominantly inattentive presentation—that is often overlooked and not diagnosed until adolescence or adulthood. Children with high intelligence can often mask symptoms for years and do not grab the attention of their parents or teachers as do the children with ADHD, predominately hyperactive/impulsive type (children who fidget, leave their seats in class, talk excessively, run about or climb in situations where it is inappropriate, etc.). Children, such as Robert, may have Attention Deficit symptoms (difficulties in organizing tasks and materials,

---

1 Robert is a composite of MKs I assessed for ADHD.

sustaining focus and effort, managing frustration, utilizing working memory, regulating self-action, etc.) that were noticeable during early childhood but were not apparent until they encountered the challenges of adolescence or adulthood.

Treatment. Based on the landmark National Institute of Mental Health Multimodal Treatment Study of ADHD in the mid-1990s, the primary treatment of ADHD is still medication, carefully monitored, in combination with psychoeducation for students and parents, behavioral treatment, and psychotherapy. Below is a selection of parents' responses that I heard after they learned that their MKs had been diagnosed with ADHD. Each response is followed by psychoeducation, based on recent research. Psychoeducation about ADHD is vital in helping parents, organizations, and the children themselves not to blame the children for things beyond their control.

"I don't think Robert has ADHD. He is just lazy. No treatment is necessary; he just needs to exert some willpower." **Psychoeducation:** A 2012 meta-analysis of 55 fMRI studies provided evidence of differences in several neuronal systems between children who were diagnosed with ADHD and those who were not. These neuronal systems affect Robert's brain's ability to organize, prioritize, and get started on his work, in addition to other aspects of attention.[2]

"I don't want my child to take medicine, especially stimulants. He will grow out of this naturally." **Psychoeducation:** Imaging studies have shown that stimulants improve the ability of individuals with ADHD to get activated for assigned tasks and to minimize distractibility while doing tasks.[3] For more than half of children, ADHD symptoms remain at least into their twenties. A 10-year follow-up study of boys who had received a diagnosis of ADHD in childhood found that 35 percent of those in their early twenties fully met DSM diagnostic criteria for ADHD, and 22 percent still met at least half of the diagnostic criteria and had significant impairment.[4]

"We can't leave our ministry here, and Robert is well liked by the Africans, who won't understand if we leave. I'm sure Robert will be fine when he returns home." **Psychoeducation:** Although anxiety disorders, major depressive disorders, and substance abuse disorders occur in a minority of individuals with ADHD, they occur more often in children like Robert than in the general population. Additionally, individuals with untreated ADHD are likely to experience unemployment, elevated interpersonal conflict, physical injury, traffic accidents, and obesity.[5]

---

2   Samuele Cortese, et al., "Toward Systems Neuroscience of ADHD: A Meta-analysis of 55 fMRI Studies," *American Journal of Psychiatry* 169, no. 10 (Oct. 2012): 1038-1055.

3   Thomas E. Brown, *A New Understanding of ADHD in Children and Adults: Executive Function Impairments* (New York: Routledge, 2013).

4   Joseph Biederman, et al., "How Persistent Is ADHD? A Controlled 10-Year Follow-up Study of Boys with ADHD," Psychiatry Research 77, no. 3 (May 2010): 299-304.

5   American Psychiatric Association, *Diagnostic and Statistical Manual of Mental Disorders*, 5th Ed. (Arlington, CA: American Psychiatric Association, 2013).

"We want to do everything we can to help Robert. What can we do?" The three-legged stool of ADHD treatment is psychoeducation, medication, and behavioral/environmental management. There are many quality Web sites, such as www.chadd.org, and books that provide greater understanding of ADHD, and with greater understanding can come greater empathy, along with practical management techniques. Medication must be carefully monitored in the initial weeks of treatment, to guide dosage and timing to fit the individual's body chemistry. Helping Robert may mean moving nearer, at least for a while, to a medical doctor who can provide him adequate medical support. Additionally, sometimes helping to meet Robert's unique educational needs may mean moving him from home school to day school or from day school to home school (or in or out of boarding school, as the case may be). Psychotherapy may also be needed to address relational health, self-esteem, parenting concerns, and stress and anxiety management.

With identification, proper treatment, and management, MKs with ADHD, like Robert, can lead successful lives and thrive. By ignoring ADHD symptoms and neglecting treatment, Robert may have substantial mental health concerns now and in the future. Often, missionary families will need the support of their mission organizations in securing the treatment of ADHD, especially if it involves medication management, a change in schooling, or psychotherapy.

Missionary Realities. Factors that occur in missionaries' lives can make it difficult to diagnosis ADHD confidently. Sometimes, home schooling families or teachers with small class sizes may not recognize the need for an ADHD assessment, because without other children to act as a comparison group, their students may seem to be functioning well. In these types of situations, what may appear to be normal in a small group may be very different from normal in a large group. In a small group, it can be easy to disregard ADHD symptoms because "Robert is just being Robert." Additionally, there is a strong genetic component to ADHD, and worrisome symptoms may be overlooked or exacerbated by a parent with similar symptoms. At times, missionary families may need the support of their mission organizations in even seeing the need for an ADHD assessment.

Other factors that may make it difficult to accurately diagnosis ADHD are trauma and transitions. Trauma may produce similar symptoms to ADHD, such as troubles with attention, as children's minds are occupied with the extraordinary events they have witnessed; or misbehavior, as children may express the sadness, fear, and anger they feel by hurting themselves or others with words or actions. Children who have experienced multiple transitions may also exhibit symptoms similar to ADHD's, for their minds may be preoccupied with the changes they are experiencing and with the sadness of saying goodbye to the people, places, and pets that define home for them.

Because of these missionary realities, and for the sake of their current and future mental health, MKs who exhibit ongoing difficulty in the following executive functions of the brain (with or without disruptive behavior) must receive a comprehensive psychoeducation assessment:

- Activation: Has difficulty organizing tasks and materials, difficulty estimating time, trouble getting started on work.
- Focus: Loses focus when trying to listen or plan, is easily distracted by internal and/or external stimuli, forgets what was read, and needs to re-read. Focus is situationally variable: tends to have some specific activities or situations in which it is not difficult to focus.
- Effort: Has difficulty regulating sleep and alertness, difficulty in completing tasks on time, especially in writing.
- Emotion: Has difficulty managing frustration and modulating emotions.
- Memory: Has difficulty remembering things when needed. Seems to have an inadequate "search engine" for activating stored memories and integrating these with current information to guide current thoughts and actions.
- Action: Has difficulty monitoring and regulating self-action, as well as difficulty slowing self and/or speeding up as needed for tasks.[6]

SPECIFIC LEARNING DISORDER (SLD): DESCRIPTION, TREATMENT, AND MISSIONARY REALITIES

Description. Rebecca,[7] age 10, frequently says that she hates school. She reads slowly and with a lot of effort and often cannot answer questions based on what she just read. When she is asked to read out loud, she leaves the room, complaining of a stomach ache. When she does read out loud, she has difficulty sounding out the words and will guess at many sight words (e.g., call, come, could, day, down—from Fry's List of 100 Words that make up 50 percent of all written English).[8] As a small child, she loved to be read to, but never showed an interest in learning to read. Rebecca appears to learn best when she can hear the material and appears happiest when she is drawing pictures or identifying birds. In fact, Rebecca can identify most birds from their calls and can recall the names of the birds after hearing them only once. Her grades are suffering, and she is beginning to call herself stupid. For the past six months, she has become very worried about her poor school grades to the point of not being able to fall asleep at night.

---

6 Thomas E. Brown, *Outside the Box: Rethinking ADD/ADHD in Children and Adults: A Practical Guide* (Arlington, VA: American Psychiatric Association Publishing, 2017).

7 Rebecca is a composite of MKs I assessed for SLDs.

8 Edward Fry and Jacqueline Kress, *The Reading Teacher's Book of Lists*. 5th Ed. (San Francisco, CA: Jossey Bass, 2006).

I chose Rebecca as an example to describe a Specific Learning Disability with impairment in reading (alternately known as dyslexia),[9] as she represents a type of SLD that has profound implications for children who are in an educational system that relies primarily on reading for instruction and on written language for demonstrating what the students have learned. Almost every school subject (e.g. math, science, history, etc.) uses written words to communicate basic concepts, and almost every school subject assesses students' mastery by a written examination that demands reading. Students, such as Rebecca, who struggle to read at grade level are likely to have poor grades in most subjects, with the accompanying discouragement and anxiety that often come when they cannot keep up with their peers.

Treatment. There is no known way to correct the underlying brain structures and processes that cause dyslexia. It is a lifelong problem. However, early detection and early intervention using specific educational approaches and techniques can close the gap between Rebecca and her peers. Often these interventions can be suspended once the student reaches mastery. Below is a selection of parents' responses that I heard after the parents learned that their MKs had been diagnosed with an Autism Spectrum Disorder (ASD). Each response is followed by psychoeducation, based on recent research. As with ADHD, psychoeducation about SLDs is vital in helping parents, organizations, and Rebecca, herself, not blame her for things beyond her control.

"I don't think Rebecca has an SLD or dyslexia. She just needs to work harder at reading." **Psychoeducation:** According to www.mayoclinic.org, dyslexia tends to run in families. It appears to be linked to certain genes that affect how the brain processes reading and language, as well as risk factors in the environment. Risk factors include a family history of dyslexia, premature birth or low birth weight, and exposure during pregnancy to poor nutrition, drugs, alcohol, or infection. Prenatal risk factors are important to consider for national children adopted into expatriate missionary families.

"We are in an isolated environment and cannot afford the time and money to provide the various interventions needed. Also, we can't leave Africa because we would be unemployable back home. Rebecca's an intelligent girl and will probably grow out of it and be fine." **Psychoeducation:** The treatment of dyslexia is more time intensive than it is materially intensive, and there are many high-quality resources online and elsewhere to draw upon. Students like Rebecca do need intentional, targeted interventions to learn how to read well. Untreated dyslexia may result in Rebecca's experiencing lower academic attainment and subsequent unemployment or underemployment. Dropping out of school and concurrent depressive symptoms would increase her risk for poor mental health outcomes, whereas high levels of social or emotional support predict better mental health outcomes for her.

"We want to do everything we can to help Rebecca. What can we do?" **Psychoeducation:** The primary treatment for dyslexia is targeted interventions that focus on the student's

---

9   The terms "SLD in Impairment in Reading" and "dyslexia" are largely interchangeable. SLD in Reading also includes poor reading comprehension; dyslexia also includes poor spelling.

specific struggles, such as decoding, reading fluency, word reading accuracy, and/or reading comprehension. A comprehensive examination by a reading specialist can result in specific strategies to help Rebecca. Some mission organizations and MK schools have relationships with Special Education teachers who can help with these assessments. For American MKs, US schools have a legal obligation to take steps to help children diagnosed with SLDs with their learning problems. Sometimes families need to return to their local school districts to get these assessments and specific treatment plans. Other times, Rebecca's home schooling family may need to consider boarding or day school, for her educational needs to be met; or perhaps, if she is already in a school, she may need the extra and targeted help a home schooling environment can provide.

With identification, proper treatment, and support, MKs like Rebecca with an SLD in Reading, Math, and/or Written Language can lead successful lives and thrive. By ignoring SLD symptoms and neglecting treatment, Rebecca may have substantial mental health concerns in the future. Mission families may need the support of their mission organizations in securing the treatment for these SLDs, especially if it involves a change in schooling.

Missionary Realities. For missionary (and all) families, one convoluting factor in diagnosing SLDs is that they commonly co-occur with other neurodevelopmental disorders (e.g., ADHD) and other mental disorders (e.g., anxiety and depression). Sometimes, once a student's trauma, anxiety, or depression is addressed, then the student's capacity to achieve academically is increased to the point where she no longer struggles to learn. A comprehensive psychoeducational assessment is necessary to discern if the SLD is the root of a student's educational difficulties or if it is a symptom of other mental disorders.

Similarly, sometimes what appears to be an SLD may actually be deficits or gaps in a student's academic instruction. Students who switch schools due to the multiple transitions inherent in missionary life are vulnerable to gaps in their academic instruction. And students who switch between US, International Baccalaureate (IB), and Cambridge International General Certificate of Secondary Education (Cambridge IGCSE) are especially vulnerable to experiencing gaps in their academic instruction. These instructional gaps are most likely to be seen in reading and math-related subjects, as various curriculums approach these topics differently in scope and sequence. For example, when assessing for a Math SLD, it is important to know if and when fractions were introduced, for students who have schooled in both the US and Cambridge IGCSE curriculums.

Finally, it can be challenging to know if a student has a true SLD or if the student has had inadequate academic instruction. In some cases, missionary home school families have forgotten that "school" is not just a noun, but is also a verb. Without external accountability, home schooling missionary families can become overwhelmed by ministry, as well as interpersonal and personal issues, and not attend to the schooling of their children. It is vital that the academic progress of the home schooling MKs be monitored.

FOUR OTHER NEURODEVELOPMENTAL DISORDERS

In this case study, I have focused on ADHD and SLD because they were the most frequently diagnosed neurodevelopmental disorders of the MKs I assessed. In East Africa, I also assessed MKs with Communication Disorders, Autism Spectrum Disorder, Motor Disorders, and Intellectual Disabilities. As my experience was limited in these neurodevelopmental disorders, what follows are some brief, general reflections:

Communication Disorder. Children with a Communication Disorder (e.g., Language Disorder, Stuttering, Speech Sound Disorder, and Social Communication Disorder) need frequent and early interventions with a Speech and Language Therapist. With such interventions, children have a good chance of improving and being able to function well, both educationally and occupationally. Such services were rarely available in East Africa.

Autism Spectrum Disorder (ASD). Children with ASD (persistent deficits in social communication/interaction and restricted, repetitive patterns of behavior) need intensive and early interventions from a team of mental health providers who specialize in providing behavioral, psychological, educational, or skill-building interventions. Without interventions, many individuals with ASD have poor adult psycho-social functioning, as measured by independent living and gainful employment. Such services were rarely, if ever, available in East Africa.

Motor Disorders. The range of types of motor disorders (from developmental coordination to stereotypic movement to tics) makes it difficult to generalize treatment and prognosis. What they have in common is that the disorders interfere with social and academic functioning, and the necessary treatments were rarely available in East Africa.

Intellectual Disability. Unlike the other neurodevelopmental disorders, the possibility of independent living in adulthood is highly unlikely for a child with intellectual disability. Depending on the level of severity of the intellectual disability, interventions may increase adaptive functioning to a limited degree. Once an intellectual disability is definitively diagnosed, then interventions to increase adaptive functioning can often be carried out by lay people. With adequate community support (both from mission organizations and nationals), MKs with intellectual disabilities may thrive as much in their cross-cultural setting as they would in their passport countries.

CONCLUSION

This case study opened with the words I most dreaded saying to missionary families. I will close with the words I most hoped I would hear from missionary families upon learning that their children had a diagnosis of ADHD or SLD. Given the mental health and functional difficulties in adulthood for those whose disorders went untreated as children, the words I most hoped to hear were *"We want to do everything we can to help our child, and we will trust God for the reactions of our African church, our mission organization, and our supporters. What can we do?"*

RESPONSE by Jenny H. Pak

I am pleased to respond to Crawford's thoughtful article, "The Neurodevelopmental Disorders and Missionary Children's Mental Health." Attention-Deficit/Hyperactivity Disorder and Specific Learning Disorder are the two most common neurodevelopmental disorders she came across during her work with missionary children (MKs). Through two respective case composites, she provides a brief description of the concerns, treatment issues, and factors relevant to the missionary context. As I have worked with families and children in clinical, missionary member care and ministry settings for many years, I am sympathetic to Crawford's opening line that she regrets needing to inform parents of their child's diagnosis. The situation, of course, is made worse when there is a lack of adequate resources available for treatment in mission fields. Unfortunately, the condition is not better for Korean MKs because of limited public awareness of neurodevelopmental disorders in Korea (in pages that follow, "Korea" refers to South Korea). There is a lack of developed research around children and ADHD/LD and even less research on how the neurodevelopmental disorder affects often neglected subgroups, such as missionary children. As research on Korean MKs with neurodevelopmental disorders is not available, I will briefly describe general publications on ADHD and LD in Korea to contextualize the challenges faced by Korean MKs.

ATTENTION-DEFICIT/HYPERACTIVITY DISORDER (ADHD) IN KOREA

Do cultural influences impact ADHD diagnosis and treatment? ADHD is among the most prevalent disorders of childhood and adolescence, and experts indicate that every culture has children with ADHD.[10] According to a comprehensive, systematic review of the literature conducted by Polanczyk and colleagues, the worldwide prevalence of ADHD centers around 5.2 percent,[11] but the rates across countries vary widely, ranging from 1–20 percent, which has led some to question whether the ADHD diagnosis is a Western cultural product.[12,13] Evidence of commonalities in etiology, symptom expression, and treatment outcomes, however, has supported cross-cultural validity of the diagnosis, and much of the variability across countries can rather be attributed to differences in diagnostic practices, medical systems, school policies, cultural attitudes, and access to services for ADHD.[14]

---

10 Russell A. Barkley et al., "International Consensus Statement on ADHD," *Clinical Child and Family Psychology Review* 5, no. 2 (June 2002): 89-111.

11 Guilherme Polanczyk et al., "The Worldwide Prevalence of ADHD: A Systematic Review and Metaregression Analysis," *American Psychiatric Association* 165, no. 6 (June 2007): 942-948.

12 Stephen V. Faraone et al., "The Worldwide Prevalence of ADHD: Is It an American Condition?" *World Psychiatry* 2, no. 2 (June 2003): 103-113.

13 Jessie C. Anderson, "Is Childhood Hyperactivity the Product of Western Culture?" *Lancet* 348, no. 9020 (July 1996): 73-74.

14 Stephen P. Hinshaw et al., "International Variation in Treatment Procedures for ADHD: Social Context and Recent Trends," *Psychiatric Services* 62, no. 5 (May 2011): 459-464.

In 1979, the Child Psychiatry Clinic at Seoul National University Hospital opened and marked the beginning of child psychiatry in Korea. Subsequently, the Korean Academy of Child and Adolescent Psychiatry (KACAP) formed in 1986 and made significant contributions to develop children's mental health services in Korea over the following twenty years. A recent, large-scale epidemiological study of the prevalence of ADHD among Korean children within a community of a medium sized city was reported to be 8.5 percent,[15] while previous studies of children in Seoul indicated a prevalence between 5.9 percent[16] to 9.0 percent.[17] In contrast to the high prevalence of ADHD, the incidence of ADHD diagnosis and medication use in Korea for ages six to eighteen years, based on the analysis of the nationwide (universal care) health insurance database, was only 0.357 percent and, during 2008–2011, 0.248 percent.[18] This suggests that less than one-fifth of children with ADHD were identified and treated in Korea and that more effort is required in this area.

Despite national education campaigns to raise awareness since 2004, public understanding of ADHD is still quite poor, and the stigma against psychological or neurodevelopmental diagnosis in childhood is high. The Korean Ministry of Health and Welfare did not recognize developmental disorders, learning disorders, or ADHD as disabilities until 2008.[19] For this reason, schools in Korea are still under-resourced to deal with children with ADHD and other neurodevelopmental disorders, as teachers tend not to know very much about the diagnoses or methods of treatment. One study found that Korean teachers have difficulties distinguishing ADHD from other disorders, including emotional disturbances.[20]

Similarly, most Korean parents have little or no understanding of neurodevelopmental disorders and commonly associated emotional and behavioral problems, such as depression, anxiety, low self-esteem, peer victimization and bullying, oppositional defiance, and conduct disorders. From educators to parents, a more effective network of community mental health, active consultation services, and preventive educational services are needed to ensure more successful treatment linkages and to overcome the stigma that is deeply rooted in Korean culture

---

15 Moon Jung Kim et al., "Prevalence of Attention-Deficit/Hyperactivity Disorder and Its Comorbidity among Korean Children in a Community Population," *Journal of Korean Medical Sciences* 32, no. 3 (2017): 401-406.

16 Subin Park et al., "Prevalence, Correlates, and Comorbidities of DSM-IV Psychiatric Disorders in Children in Seoul, Korea," *Asia Pacific Journal of Public Health* 27 no. 2 (August, 2014): 1942-1951.

17 Soo-Churl Cho et al., "Full Syndrome and Subthreshold Attention-Deficit/Hyperactivity Disorder in a Korean Community Sample: Comorbidity and Temperament Findings," *European Child & Adolescent Psychiatry* 18, no. 7 (July 2009): 447-457.

18 Minha Hong et al., "Nationwide Rate of Attention Deficit Hyperactivity Disorder Diagnosis and Pharmacotherapy in Korean in 2008-2011," *Asia-Pacific Psychiatry* 6 (October, 2014): 379-385.

19 Kyunghwa Lee, "Attention Deficit/Hyperactivity Disorder across Cultures: Development and Disability in Contexts," *Early Child Development and Care* 178, no. 4 (May 2008): 339-346.

20 Younghee Hong, "Teachers' Perceptions of Young Children with ADHD in Korea," *Early Child Development and Care* 178, no. 4 (January 2007): 399-414.

(e.g., individual's mental illness or disability perceived as the family shame). According to the recent Korean Ministry of Health and Welfare report, the lifetime prevalence rate for mental disorders in Korea is 27.6 percent (i.e., three out of ten adults experience mental disorders more than once throughout their lifetime). A more comprehensive and conscious effort must be made at a national level to promote and improve mental health services.[21]

LEARNING DISORDERS (LD) IN KOREA

The early development of special education in Korea can be largely attributed to Christian missionaries from the United States and European countries, who worked in the late nineteenth century, mainly with children with visual or hearing impairments. Since the enactment of the Special Education Promotion Act (SEPA) in 1977, which mandated free special education and related services (e.g., physical therapy, speech therapy, and medical services for children with disabilities), special education in Korea has made great progress, especially over the last twenty-five years.[22] In 1994, SEPA was completely revised to incorporate inclusive education for students with disabilities in general education. In 2008, SEPA was replaced with the Special Education Act for Individuals with Disabilities and Others (SEAIDO), which updated the LD definition (significant difficulties with learning abilities, such as listening, speaking, attention, perception, memory, and problem solving, or in academic achievement areas such as reading, writing, and mathematics) and moved the task of assessment and evaluation of at-risk students from individual schools to local school districts.[23]

Despite the rapid developments made by the Korean Institute for Special Education, a lack of consensus on the definition of LD and on the best assessment criteria for identifying students with LD persists. Additionally, the complexity of referral procedures, general low knowledge of students with LD among teachers and parents, and unclear processes for obtaining LD supportive services in school have contributed to the recent decline in students reporting LD (e.g., 6.8 percent in 2011; 4.7 percent in 2013; 2.7 percent in 2016).[24]

Poor academic achievement is a very complex construct, and attitudes toward disabilities differ from culture to culture.[25] The public perception of people with

---

21 Sungwon Roh et al., "Mental Health Services and R&D in South Korea," *International Journal of Mental Health Systems* (June 2016): 1-10.

22 Nari Choi et al., "Policies and Issues Surrounding the Identification of Students with Learning Disabilities in South Korea," *International Journal of Special Education* 32, no. 2 (April 2017): 439-457.

23 Special Education Act for Individuals with Disabilities and Others (2008). Act No. 8852. Retrieved from https://elaw.klri.re.kr/kor_service/lawView.do?hseq=16226&lang=ENG.

24 Dae Young Jung, "South Korean Perspective on Learning Disabilities," *Learning Disabilities Research and Practice* 22, no. 3 (July 2007): 183-188.

25 Matthias Grunke et al., "Learning Disabilities around the Globe: Making Sense of the Heterogeneity of the Different Viewpoints," *Learning Disabilities: A Contemporary Journal* 14, no. 1 (Jan 2016): 1-8.

disabilities in Korea is generally negative and stigmatized. For centuries, education was the way to improve social status under Confucianism. Consequently, academic success has been overvalued and emphasized.[26] Parents of students without disabilities have even opposed inclusion in regular classrooms, for fear of lowered academic standards and student achievement.[27] Even general education teachers who support the basic idea of inclusion feel unprepared and do not want students with disabilities in their classrooms. Schools and the government need to provide more administrative support and training to both general and special education teachers to improve LD screening, referral procedures, and intervention programs in Korea. More collaborative efforts could also be developed through local churches and mission organizations to educate and raise awareness.

KOREAN MISSIONARY CONTEXT

The number of Korean missionaries abroad has grown rapidly since the late 1970s (e.g., 93 in 1979; 1,645 in 1990; 10,422 in 2002; over 20,000 since 2013).[28] Reflecting this remarkable increase in the last two decades, Korean MKs around the world have also jumped to more than 17,675 as of 2014, where approximately 35 percent are in local schools on mission fields, 38 percent are in MK/International schools, 9 percent are homeschooled, and 18 percent attend schools in Korea or categorized their places of education as "other."[29] While Korean MKs now constitute a large percentage of students in MK/international schools, the cultural differences and non-English speaking background of Korean MKs pose a challenge for MK/International schools, which are based on a Western education system, use Western-style curricula, and employ English-speaking teachers/staff.

Many Korean missionary parents feel unprepared to tackle not only how they will educate their children, but also how they will help their children deal with cross-cultural adjustments and transitions, language barriers, multiple losses, rootlessness, and cultural identity issues. Acclimating to the mission site and academic difficulties are the two most commonly cited problems, with approximately 10 percent of Korean MKs indicating serious adjustment problems in school and 6 percent indicating professional counseling needs and mental health problems.[30] Repeated moves and separations are challenging for most MKs; however, children with ADHD, for example, who have difficulties building and maintaining interpersonal relationships, are particularly more vulnerable to feeling loneliness, a lack of belonging, and even

---

26 Juhu Kim et al., "Understanding of Education Fever in Korea," *KEDI Journal of Educational Policy* 2, no. 1 (June 2005): 7-15.
27 Jiyeon Park, "Special Education in South Korea," *Teaching Exceptional Children* 34, no. 5 (May 2002): 28-33.
28 Korean Research Institute for Mission (krim.org) recurring surveys.
29 Steve Sang-Cheol Moon, "Mission from Korea 2014: Missionary Children," *International Bulletin of Missionary Research* 38, no. 2 (April 2014): 84-85.
30 Ibid.

depression in the mission context. Studies have found a significant association between ADHD symptoms and depression, which may reflect various adjustment difficulties attributable to the cumulative effects of ADHD-related impairments and negative environmental circumstances.[31]

CONCLUSION

Overall, Korea has much work to do to become more inclusive and aware of neurodevelopmental disorders. With already limited resources devoted to studying its impact on children, this article on missionary children in particular hopes to serve as a starting point for greater dialogue around the subject. Further policy and research should look toward the educational system. With admission to good colleges and careers extremely competitive in Korea, most missionary parents have high expectations for their children's education. While parents may believe that educating their children is their most important duty, children experience enormous pressure to achieve academically. Students with ADHD and LD who are struggling with their academic performance and achievement tend to suffer from low self-esteem and underestimate themselves. Often, they also experience high levels of anxiety, especially surrounding the future (e.g., college, career, relationships). In addition to proper assessments, diagnoses, and education about neurodevelopmental disorders, students would benefit from individual or group therapy, promoting academic strategies (such as time management skills), as well as advocating for accommodations and resources in schools. Mission organizations can partner with schools and mental health services to educate, screen, and provide resources on ADHD and LD for Korean missionary parents and MKs through opportunities such as pre-orientation and reentry programs, mission conferences, and MK retreats. Every MK, with or without disabilities, should be able to succeed and thrive according to his or her fullest potential. Korean churches and mission organizations must actively work toward overcoming the shame and stigma surrounding neurodevelopmental disorders to better support MKs with ADHD and LD.

---

31 Rick Ostrander et al., "Attention Deficit-Hyperactivity Disorder, Depression, and Self- and Other-Assessments of Social Competence: A Developmental Study," *Journal of Abnormal Child Psychology* 34, no. 6 (December 2006): 772-786.

10
SEXUAL ADDICTION

by Richard Winter

THE BEAUTY AND BROKENNESS OF SEX

Our sexuality is one of the most beautiful and precious gifts that God has given us in creation. We are made with the ability to delight in and desire intimacy with another person. Our bodies and brains were designed for this. Adam knew that Eve was different from the animals, as he said (or sang), "At last, bone of my bones, flesh of my flesh," someone designed to meet me at the deepest places of body and soul. God made us with the ability to look at another and wonder at the person's physical beauty, become captivated by one's personal attractiveness. The Song of Songs is a poetic description and affirmation of erotic attraction and sensual imagination and delight. God made us with sexual organs that have incredibly sensitive nerve endings, hormones released with human touch that bind us together, and hearts with deep longings for closeness and companionship. And, as if this were not enough, sex produces the extraordinary miracle of new life and personhood, and marriage is thus the building block of family and society. Finally, sexual intimacy is a living picture of our relationship with God. From the beginning to the end of Scripture, it is the expression of the intimacy between God and his people (Israel and the church), with the ultimate vision and hope of the most profound mystery, the union of Christ and the church (Eph. 5:31–32).

So, it is hardly surprising that sex should be a prime target for the enemy. Where else can he do such devastating damage as in the arena of intimacy and relationship between men and women and between us and our loving God? This is a war zone. Christopher West puts it so well: "If we want to know what's most sacred in this world, all we need do is look for what is most violently profaned."[1] All over the world, the beauty and glory of good and God-given sex are shattered and turned into a tsunami of brokenness and grief in sexual slavery; prostitution; sexual abuse; intimidation and rape; sexually transmitted diseases; abortion; infidelity; premarital sex; pornography; sex with animals, machines, and robots; and sexual addiction. Far from the maker's instructions, now "anything goes."

And, sadly, the church through the centuries has not helped much. Early Church teachings, influenced by Gnosticism, tended to see the body and its pleasures as unspiritual and carnal in contrast to the soul, which was seen as godly and spiritual. Augustine's struggle with sexual addiction led him to be suspicious of anything good in sex. Later in life, he modified his views. Jerome, in AD 350, wrote, "Anyone who is too passionate a lover with his own wife is himself an adulterer."[2] In other words, you can have sex in order to have children, but do not enjoy it too much! Until recently, many churches have avoided speaking much about sex and have spiritualized the Song of Songs into a metaphor of Christ's love for us, not a real erotic relationship between two lovers. Many of our parents focused on the dangers of temptation and instructions of "don't …." Or, from ignorance, embarrassment, and silence, they handed down a lot of hang-ups, leaving us feeling that sex is shameful, dirty, and confusing. Everyone else in the culture is talking about sex, but until recently, the church has been very quiet.

Inevitably, once human beings turn away from the design of the creator and start to live independently of him, the enjoyment of his good gifts of food, sensuality, relationship, and sex become the ultimate source of pleasure. The gifts replace the giver and become idols in our hearts. Our relativistic sexual ethic arises from a view of human beings as complex animals + time + chance, and we try to ignore the serious consequences of neglecting the creator and his design for human flourishing.[3]

THE NATURE OF ADDICTION

This is where addiction begins. If sex is one of the most pleasurable experiences we know, why not try to get that pleasure as often and as intensely as we can? Intense experiences of pleasure are great for distracting us from other problems in life—boredom, loneliness, anxiety, depression, anger, fear, frustration, pain. We use drugs to do this, and sex can become like a drug, producing its own chemical high, as a result of

---

1   Christopher West, *Theology of the Body for Beginners* (West Chester, PA: Ascension Press, 2004), 12.

2   St. Jerome, *Against Jovinianus*, book 1, §49, trans. W. H. Fremantle, G. Lewis, and W. G. Martley. In *Nicene and Post-Nicene Fathers, Second Series*, Vol. 6, ed. Philip Schaff and Henry Wace (Buffalo, NY: Christian Literature Publishing Co., 1893). Revised and edited for New Advent by Kevin Knight. http://www.newadvent.org/fathers/30091.htm.

3   See Glynn Harrison, *A Better Story: God, Sex and Human Flourishing* (London: IVP, 2016).

the actions of the body. With orgasm comes a rush of dopamine and other pleasure hormones. But the pleasure does not last long. Our brains are so designed that we easily become habituated to repeated experiences of pleasure, and soon we do all we can to find ways to reproduce them. Like drugs, we need them more often and in higher and more exciting doses. And the more we use them, the deeper the pathway we create in our brains, so that it becomes more and more difficult to stop using them. They take over our brains and bodies. The healthy intimacy and pleasure mechanisms of the body are highjacked by the fast-food alternative of pornography or promiscuous sex that will eventually destroy body and soul. Millions are caught in the grip of such unwanted behavior. William Struthers describes these brain changes in his book, *Wired for Intimacy*.[4]

But it is not just the addictive power of sex or drugs that drives addiction. When soldiers returned from Vietnam, many of them addicted to heroin, 95 percent of them stopped using the drug. Away from the horrors of war, they did not need it. Dr. Gabor Maté, a psychiatrist, wrote, "Emotional isolation, powerlessness, and stress are exactly the conditions that promote the neurobiology of addiction."[5] Acknowledging that we self-medicate for the pain, Jay Stringer, a therapist and expert on sex addiction, says that there is also an addiction to the inevitable feelings of self-contempt, shame, and judgment, and we repeatedly re-enact the "formative stories of trauma, abuse, and shame that convinced us we were unwanted to begin with."[6]

The sex industry is huge, especially the pornography business. It is estimated that 3–5 percent of Americans are addicted to sex (9–16 million people).[7] And this depends on how addiction is defined, because 64 percent of thirteen to twenty-four-year-olds intentionally watch pornography at least once a week. Perhaps such usage does not indicate addiction, but it certainly represents a strong habit that could easily escalate. It is so often a slippery slope. Jay Stringer summarizes some statistics in this way:

- Approximately 35 percent of all Internet downloads are porn related.
- Porn sites receive more monthly traffic than Netflix, Amazon, and Twitter combined.
- Porn is a $97 billion industry, with as much as $12 billion of that coming from the US.
- About 57 percent of our pastors and 64 percent of our youth pastors struggle or have struggled with pornography.[8]

---

4 William Struthers, *Wired for Intimacy: How Pornography Hijacks the Male Brain* (Downers Grove, IL: IVP, 2009).

5 Gabor Maté, *In the Realm of Hungry Ghosts: Close Encounters with Addiction* (Berkeley, CA: North Atlantic Books, 2010), 142-145.

6 Jay Stringer, *Unwanted: How Sexual Brokenness Reveals Our Way to Healing* (Colorado Springs: Navpress, 2018), 11.

7 Approximately 8 percent of men and 3 percent of women.

8 Stringer, *Unwanted*, xvii.

- It is estimated that visitors to porn sites are 70 percent men and 30 percent women. A hefty 63 percent of 18–30-year-old men and 21 percent of 18–30-year-old women admit to viewing pornography several times a week. Sexual addiction among women is increasing. On average, children are first exposed to porn at ages 9–11, although with the use of cell phones, this is happening earlier. Young people increasingly believe that pornography is not harmful.[9]

We all struggle to be good stewards of the minds, hearts, and bodies that God has given us. We all live on the edge of addiction, tempted to allow some pleasure to master us—whether it is food, alcohol, nicotine, work, pain-killers, relationships, or some variety of sexual behavior. There is a continuum, moving from unhealthy habits through compulsive behaviors into outright addiction, where we lose all control.

UNDERSTANDING THE ROOTS

So why not call it what it is? Lust, rebellion, and sin! Just repent and stop. Put to death the sins of the flesh. Have your mind renewed. Pray. Study the Scriptures, and be obedient. Be accountable to someone on a daily basis. For some, this approach may work, but for the majority, it is a temporary solution and a repeated battle with only short-term victories. We are complex creatures, and it is important to understand why we do things in order to be able to truly find change and freedom. Sexual behavior is often driven by deep unmet longings, wounds in the soul, and shame, that emerge in aberrant desires and behavior. The sins of others in our lives, often when we were very young, have had a profound and damaging impact on our ability to have mature and healthy relationships and sexual expression. Jay Stringer, in his research involving 3,800 men and women, found that there were "five key childhood drivers of unwanted sexual behavior: rigid and/or disengaged family systems, abandonment, parents who were emotionally enmeshed with their children, a history of trauma, and sexual abuse (both overt and subtle forms of it)."[10]

Pastors and counselors need to be able to talk about the goodness and glory of sexuality, as well as the brokenness—the ecstasy and the agony. What is most sacred has been most profaned, and we are at war. To bring healing and hope, we need to be comfortable both talking about sex and the body and listening with curiosity, compassion, and grace to stories that will make us profoundly sad, angry, and often confused. Further, we need to start exploring the stories of our own bodies and hearts, finding clues to what has shaped our erotic fantasies, our addictive behaviors, our distorted relationships, and our shame, which will hopefully lead us to the foot of the cross and into the arms of our welcoming, gracious, and healing Father, God.

---

9 Covenant Eyes Porn Stats, 2018, accessed August 6, 2018, https://www.covenanteyescom/e-books/.

10 Stringer, *Unwanted*, 15.

CASE STUDY

Sam's sad story. The pathway into sexual addiction is different for each person, and it is different for men and women, but there are common patterns to these stories. Sam first discovered porn while playing a game on his grandfather's computer when he was ten. He found himself strangely excited and intrigued by it and began to find his own way to it on other unguarded computers in his home. In high school, it became a nightly obsession. His discovery of pornography opened up a whole new world and became, as it is for so many young men and women today, the primary source of his knowledge about sex and relationships. He spent more and more time on his computer, searching for increasingly erotic images to arouse him. Many of the scenes involved humiliation and degradation of women, and ultimately, he was looking at group sex and sex with animals. Initially he was disgusted and ashamed, but his conscience became insensitive. He began to chat with women online, and that led to occasionally meeting prostitutes. He was living a compartmentalized, double life. His attempts to control his sexual fantasies, urges, and behaviors did not last long. He knew this was not good for him, but he could not stop. When he felt shame, guilt, and despair, he would ease the pain with another "fix."

Sam got married, hoping that this would be the solution to his problem. He did not tell his wife of his struggle. Marriage helped for a while, but after some stress at his office, he relapsed back into some of his old patterns and became more and more deceitful. His secret addiction was gradually destroying his relationship with his wife, as he became bored with their sex life. Real, healthy relationships are complicated and more focused on giving than getting pleasure. Masturbation with pornography in a fantasy, virtual "relationship" is much simpler.

In his teen years, Sam had become cynical about God because his prayers for freedom from this addiction were not answered, even after repeated rounds of repentance, confession, and determination to change. Sam's struggle is an echo of Augustine's struggle with a similar addiction, many centuries earlier:

> [B]ut I was ... bound by the iron chain of my own will. The enemy held fast my will, and had made of it a chain, and had bound me tight with it. For out of the perverse will came lust, and the service of lust ended in habit, and habit, not resisted, became necessity. By these links, as it were, forged together—which is why I called it "a chain"—a hard bondage held me in slavery. But that new will that had begun to spring up in me freely to worship thee and to enjoy thee, O my God, the only certain Joy, was not able as yet to overcome my former willfulness, made strong by long indulgence. Thus my two wills—the old and the new, the carnal and the spiritual—were in conflict within me; and by their discord they tore my soul apart.[11]

---

11 Augustine, *Confessions*, trans. Albert Outler, in *The Library of Christian Classics*, vol. VIII (Philadelphia: The Westminster Press. 1955), 164.

Finding help. Now Sam, caught by the chains of such slavery, in his own flesh/spirit war, was feeling trapped, his soul was torn apart, and his panic grew. He was terrified of telling anyone, especially his wife. Fearfully, he approached the young pastor at their church and was greatly relieved to hear that the pastor had struggled with pornography all through his college and early seminary years. The pastor listened well to his story and suggested a local counselor and a support group of men who were in the same struggle.[12] Together, they planned how he would tell his wife, recognizing that this would be very disturbing and traumatic for her. She then found help in a support group of the wives of sexual addicts and was able to talk about her childhood abuse, and her sadness, shame, anger, and diminished love for her husband.

In talking about his childhood, Sam remembered the loneliness of being a latch-key kid with both parents working full time, late into the evenings. When she was around, his mother would often tell him of her own loneliness and of his father's failures. He also recalled his older brother introducing him to porn and making him watch him while he made out with his girlfriend in his bedroom. He remembered being bullied at school for his small size. Through talking with others about his past, he was finally able to name these incidents as sexual abuse. He saw how he had used the fix of pleasure that came with porn-inspired masturbation to ease the pain of loneliness and shame. He also saw how the fantasy of being powerful over submissive women in pornography was particularly attractive after his experiences of powerlessness. But all this took two years of individual counseling and the help of the group, exploring his fantasies and desires, recognizing the triggers that sparked a relapse, retraining his brain, and experiencing significant degrees of freedom from deeply engrained habits of the heart. Both he and his wife had to grieve the effects of other people's sins, as well as their own. They recognized their legitimate anger and were able to discern healthy and unhealthy shame and guilt.

Sam's early loneliness and deep God-given longings for affirmation and love left him vulnerable. Jay Stringer writes: "Lust blooms in the soil of disengagement."[13] Sam's parents' neglect may have come out of a real need to provide for the family, and they may have been naïvely ignorant of their lack of love and protection for their son. Sam's brother damaged him in awakening his sexuality too early and doing so in an unhelpful context. And the bullies cruelly added to Sam's confusion, subconscious anger, and shame—anger and shame being powerful drivers of pornography use.

Moving towards healing and health. For a while, Sam's wife thought of divorcing him, but as she was able to talk about her confusion with her group and with a counselor, the pain subsided, and they worked slowly to restore good communication and trust. Sam was repentant and deeply sorry for the damage he had done and eventually forgave his parents for their neglect and his brother for his harmful behavior. He was able to accept forgiveness from God and from his wife for his own sin. Both he and his wife

---

12 For an example of an organization that promotes such groups for men and women see http://www.firstlightstlouis.org/.

13 Stringer, *Unwanted*, 33.

needed education in developing a normal sexual relationship. His wife had come from an emotionally and physically inhibited family and had only bad experiences of sex in her past, including two incidents of being abused by an uncle. Sam's sexual education had come through pornography. With ups and downs, and over several years, Sam continued to heal and grow, and eventually he became able to help other men in the church who were struggling in the same way he had struggled.

INGREDIENTS FOR HEALING

Many people who are caught in addictions have never learned to rightly care for themselves or have relationships where legitimate needs are met. Jay Stringer writes:

> My research showed that only 27 percent of pornography users had a solid pattern of self-care (exercise, eating well, and time with friends). The majority of those who struggle with unwanted sexual behavior choose passivity over against asking for what they need or being honest about what they are experiencing. They roam through life feeling overworked or underappreciated, which sets up entitlement for experiences they believe they deserve.[14]

What will replace the vacuum in the soul that the unwanted sexual thoughts and behaviors filled? Certainly prayer; good biblical teaching about the body, sex, and relationships; having one's mind renewed; obedience; and accountability are helpful and necessary. But so also are the self-care remedies of music, art, healthy food, avoidance of too much alcohol and caffeine, regular exercise, time in nature, and time away from work (with family, with friends, and alone). Jay Stringer encourages us to move toward "beauty, wholeness and creativity" and away from "loneliness, frustration, futility, and boredom."[15] Other essential ingredients for healing are, if possible, a good counselor, a small group where you can share your story and struggle, and a grace-filled church community that recognizes that we are all broken, imperfect people in need of redemption.

Other Recommended Resources

> Blankenship, Richard, ed. *Spouses of Sex Addicts: Hope for the Journey*. Maitland, FL: Xulon Press, 2011.
>
> Carnes, Patrick. *Out of the Shadows: Understanding Sexual Addiction*. Center City, MN: Hazelden, 2001.
>
> Ethridge, Shannon. *Every Woman's Battle*. Colorado Springs: Waterbrook Press, 2011.
>
> Laaser, Mark. *Healing the Wounds of Sexual Addiction*. Grand Rapids: Zondervan, 2004.

---

14 Ibid., 89.
15 Ibid., 150-151.

Magness, Milton. *Stop Sex Addiction*. Las Vegas: Central Recovery Press, 2013.

Rosenau, Doug. *A Celebration of Sex*. Nashville: Thomas Nelson, 2002.

Steffens, Barbara, and Marsha Means. *Your Sexually Addicted Spouse*. Far Hills, NJ: New Horizon Press, 2009.

Thompson, Curt. *The Soul of Shame*. Downers Grove, IL: IVP, 2015.

RESPONSE by Sun Man Kim

INTRODUCTION

Sexuality is not unique to any particular people group, because God created all people "after His own image, that is, the image of God." The intimate unity between God and his people is implicit in the relationship between male and female.[16] Thus, the sexuality of male and female is at the very center of authentic humanity, and it has the dignity of being a divine gift. God created Adam out of the dust of the ground and Eve out of the man's body (Gen. 2:21, 22), so he let male and female sexually depend on and desire each other. Moreover, the man and woman have received a cultural mandate from the Creator to be fruitful and multiply (Gen. 1:28). Thus, sexuality itself is not immoral. However, the sexual behavior of humans often strays outside the bounds of God's creational order, bringing serious consequences.[17] Arthur F. Holmes states that a sexual relationship is not confined to the man and woman but involves their Creator, who created humans for his good purposes.[18] Therefore, love is not the only moral principle linked to sexuality; the principle of justice is included as well. Any sexual behavior violating the moral principles of love and justice is bound to cause numerous problems.[19]

In this regard, sexual issues among Korean immigrant church leaders in America and among overseas Korean ministers are not separate from those of other countries or people groups. In addition, the current world is facing more complicated issues of sexuality and more dangers through the emergence of the cyber world.[20] The significance of the sexual issues seen among Korean

---

16 Richard Foster, *Money, Sex and Power*, trans. Young Ho Kim (Seoul: Tyrannus Press, 1996), 106.

17 C. S. Lewis, *The Joyful Christian* (New York: Macmillan, 1977), 198. "Sex in itself cannot be moral or immoral any more than gravitation or nutrition. The sexual behavior of human beings can."

18 Arthur F. Holmes, *Ethics: Approaching Moral Decisions* (Downers Grove: InterVarsity, 1984), 108.

19 Ibid., 112-14. Holmes applies this moral principle of justice to several areas, including sexual abuse, taking advantage of others sexually, and sexual discrimination in relation to marriage partners.

20 David L. Delmonico and Elizabeth J. Griffin, "Online Sex Offending: Assessment and Treatment," *Sexual Deviance: Theory, Assessment, and Treatment*, eds. D. Richard Laws and William T. O'Donohue (New York: Guilford Press, 2008), 459-460. A rapid increase in the sexual use of the Internet is threatening. An estimated 322 million individuals use the Internet

immigrant church leaders and overseas Korean ministers cannot be overlooked and needs to be carefully approached.

FROM THE BIBLICAL HISTORICAL PERSPECTIVE

The fall of Adam and Eve caused them sexual shame, made them distant from God, and led them to be frightened of God (Gen. 3:7, 10). Their fear of God led them to cover themselves with fig leaves and hide in the trees of the garden (Gen. 3:7, 10). In the light of God's creation, sexuality is a beautiful and intimate way of communication. However, sexual unions that go astray from the creation order have caused people misfortune and judgment (Rom. 1:18).

The region of Sodom and Gomorrah was depraved to the point of its destruction (Gen. 13:13; 19:13, 25). Crowds would force strangers into homosexual relations without hesitation (Gen. 19:5). Lot, who dwelled among them, also experienced shameful sexual depravity (Gen. 19:33). In the age of the judges, a Levite took a concubine and gave her over to the men of the city as he was faced with homosexual threats, leading to her death the next morning as she was raped mercilessly. A tragic war ensued that resulted in staggering casualties in the entire land of Israel (Judges 19 and 20). Sexual depravity and contamination spread within the temple. Two sons of Eli the priest committed sins of adultery with female temple volunteers (1 Sam. 2:22). Divine judgment came upon the two sons and Israel for this kind of sin (1 Sam. 2:34; 4:21, 22).

The New Testament era was not exempt from this kind of scandalous phenomenon either (Rom. 1:26, 27; 1 Cor. 5:1b; Jude 8).

Richard Foster, quoting another theologian, claimed that the fall of sex brought about the demonic wandering between satanic eroticism and the complete absence of eroticism.[21] However, the Bible does not only show tragedies caused by distorted sexuality, but also validates and blesses sexuality. One theologian understood the Song of Songs as an extended commentary of Genesis 2:25. While Jesus pronounced the one flesh made within marriage as a oneness of both sexuality and of life, that is, "what God has joined together" (Matt. 19:6), he warned of impersonal sex, saying, "Everyone who looks at a woman with lust has already committed adultery with her in his heart" (Matt. 5:28). Foster interpreted this to mean that Jesus could not treat sex lightly for it was "too good, noble, and holy."[22] The Bible does not clearly teach asceticism or celibacy. Sexuality is evidently the creation and gift of God. But distorted sexuality or sexuality astray from the creation order causes misfortune and disaster.

(2006), of which 40 million adults admit to regularly visiting pornographic websites (2006). An estimated 4.2 million websites make a profit of roughly $2.5 billion annually (2006).
21 Foster, *Money, Sex, and Power,* 108.
22 Ibid., 113.

FROM THE SOCIOLOGICAL PERSPECTIVE

Korean society in America is still very much a "saving face culture," where people are limited and restricted in self-expression. To save face, people avoid mentioning sexuality or are overcautious about doing so and regard it as a virtue to avoid the topic. The Benjamites in the Book of Judges did not punish sex crimes but covered them up, which had terrible consequences. This kind of concealment can also be found in saving face cultures. Moreover, the tendency to turn a blind eye toward sexually immoral behavior is growing, as modern societies witness globalization, rapid population fluctuations beyond race and border,[23] and the emergence of cyber societies through the Internet.[24] The limitless expansion of people's abilities to conceal or ignore sexually immoral behavior is related to the character of cultures that are grounded on anonymity. Even so, unethical sexual behavior does not only occur in cultures that are less transparent. However, a society of concealment is reluctant to acknowledge and address such behavior, and its consequences and negative influences are tremendous.

KOREAN IMMIGRANT CHURCH LEADERS HAVE FALLEN

Pastor L., with eloquence and strong leadership, had just planted a rapidly growing church in Los Angeles. He then developed a private relationship with a church member and crossed the forbidden line. Her disclosure to the presbytery shocked the Korean immigrant society. Pastor L. was censured with deposition and excommunication, but he did not accept it. Instead, he and his fellows challenged the presbytery, which split in two, and eventually, the KAPC (Korean American Presbyterian Church) denomination itself split in 2013.[25]

Pastor K. in New York was a dynamic preacher and respected role model with a sharp ability to exegete the biblical text. But he became spiritually exhausted and ultimately crossed the forbidden line with a woman from church. Pastor K. confessed his sins of adultery before the entire congregation in 2007 and resigned. Leaders and members of the church were deeply hurt and saddened by his fall.

---

23 Robert K. Schaeffer, *Understanding Globalization* (Lanham, MD: Rowman & Littlefield, 2009), 103. Schaeffer claims the modern age as the third age of global migration since Europeans began migrating overseas. He states that this is not just one kind of migration but is the varied migrations that occur due to economy, environment, politics, cultural development, etc. The United Nations estimates that about 2 billion people are living overseas, having crossed over national borders as of the year 2009.

24 James E. Hart and Mark Owen Lombardi, *Taking Sides: Clashing Views on Global Issues* (New York: McGraw-Hill, 2012), 52–76. The authors present both negative and affirmative aspects to the question, "Does the global urbanization lead primarily to unwanted consequences?" A negative side is that the world's megacities are suffering from environmental disorders such as pollution, poverty, disease, and lack of water; a positive side is that global urbanization contributes to the creation of a global economic and industrial engine. However, it commonly also causes moral and ethical crises, such as inevitable social changes and human trafficking.

25 Rev. Seon Joong Kim, phone interview, February 8, 2019. Rev. Seon Joong Kim is the former stated clerk of the permanent judicial court of the General Assembly of the Korean American Presbyterian Church. The court is established with eight ministers and seven elders who are elected, of which no more than two members represent the same presbytery.

Pastor P. in New York, a Korean American leader, was censured with deposition and deletion by the AMI (Acts Ministries International) denomination for his affair with a woman from his church in 2015.

These reports are only a few of the extant cases; other leaders of Korean immigrant churches have fallen from sexual scandals across the US and within both first- and second-generation immigrants. A closer study of the damage done to pastors' marriages and families may be a separate big task, but as for the Korean immigrant churches and society, the spiritual contamination and damages caused by this "catastrophic sin" may not be possible to measure.

A CLUE TO THE SOLUTION

Pastor K., who had been serving in New York, was censured with a three-year suspension by his presbytery and is currently serving at another local church, made up of former church members who accepted his repentance and recommitment. When he was asked about his feelings in an interview, Pastor K. shared what he has been through: emotional pain, deep self-reflection, and discipline. Noteworthy is that he placed priority on restoring his relationship with God and with his family, so that he could be forgiven and put in the right direction for healing and recovery. He said, " … right after the case was brought about, I confessed all the facts to my wife and received her forgiveness, and we went to the prayer mountain [and] prayed for two weeks, asking God for grace of repentance and, as a result, I received the grace of forgiveness from God."[26]

Pastor K. also confessed his sins to his four daughters one by one, asking for their forgiveness, and they embraced him with comfort. A sincere repentance and apology are a great step toward recovery, even though many scars may not be fully erasable from the hearts of the offenders or the public. While punishment with different levels of censure is required for offenders, offenders (and all other ministers) should also be offered counseling and preventive seminars designed by professionals to help them.

Experiencing the Kingdom of God

The power of the Gospel is the power of the kingdom of God. Even distorted sexuality can be healed, and people can find complete recovery. Quoting Carl Jung, "I am not what happened to me, I am what I choose to become," Najavits claims that new experiences for healing can rewire the human brain for healthy directions.[27] God's loving-kindness and truth in the authentic Gospel is the divine power to make it happen. Rahab, a Gentile prostitute, experienced God's loving-kindness and truth and had a son, Boaz (Matt. 1:5). She brought him up

---

26 The Christian Research Association Against Heresy in America, "Pastor Lee Young Hee Resigned from the Presbytery in New York," December 27, 2008, http://craaha.com/board_1040/1571.

27 Lisa M. Najavits, *Recovery from Trauma, Addiction, or Both* (New York: Guilford Press, 2017), 1. "New experiences can rewire the brain in healthy directions" (120).

with loving-kindness and truth, so that her son could also practice those values throughout his life (Ruth 2:8–14). The lineage of Abraham and David also depicts a beautiful picture of the kingdom of God that is filled with loving-kindness and truth (Matt. 1:3, 5). Considerate discretion regarding the misuse and abuse of sex, along with the Bible's teachings on healthy sexuality, will prevent a collapse of social norms and will support the persistence of morality in society.[28]

Seven Proposals for Coram Deo Faith

The comfort and happiness of one's family is the royal road to sexual ethics. The strength with which Joseph overcame sexual temptation was rooted in his Coram Deo faith (Gen. 39:9).

1. One should discern and guard oneself from any vulnerable situation of sexual temptation. For example, one Korean pastor in LA installed surveillance cameras throughout the entire church premises, including his pastoral office, so that at any time, anyone could see whatever was happening in the church.

2. One should know that spiritual burnout or too much stress sets the stage for a sexual fall. Sunday nights and the hours after early morning prayer are vulnerable times.

3. One should plan time for one's family and spouse (Proverbs 5:18).

4. One should engage in sports or exercise as an outlet for stress.

5. One should try to remove stress by taking up a hobby like woodcraft, painting, or photography to develop creativity.

6. One should try to recharge oneself through fishing, mountain climbing, or traveling.

7. Earnest prayer is a power that surpasses all of these efforts. But real prayer does not always involve kneeling. One poet puts it this way; "after prayer is finished, that a door of more fervent prayer opens, grant that I may have such a soul."[29]

Should we say that we have made enough effort to overcome sexual immorality if we implement all of the above practices? I believe that climbing the mountain of holistic maturation will never end until we enter the eternal kingdom of heaven.

---

28 Choong Koo Park, "Christianity and Sexual Ethics," *GueMalSeum*. April, 1996 (Seoul: Tyrannus Press, 1996), 136-146. The author searches to understand human sexuality from the ethical perspective that sees issues of sex as related to issues of justice.

29 Nam Jo Kim, *Kim Nam Jo's Collection of Poems* (Seoul: Sang A Publication, 1967), 22.

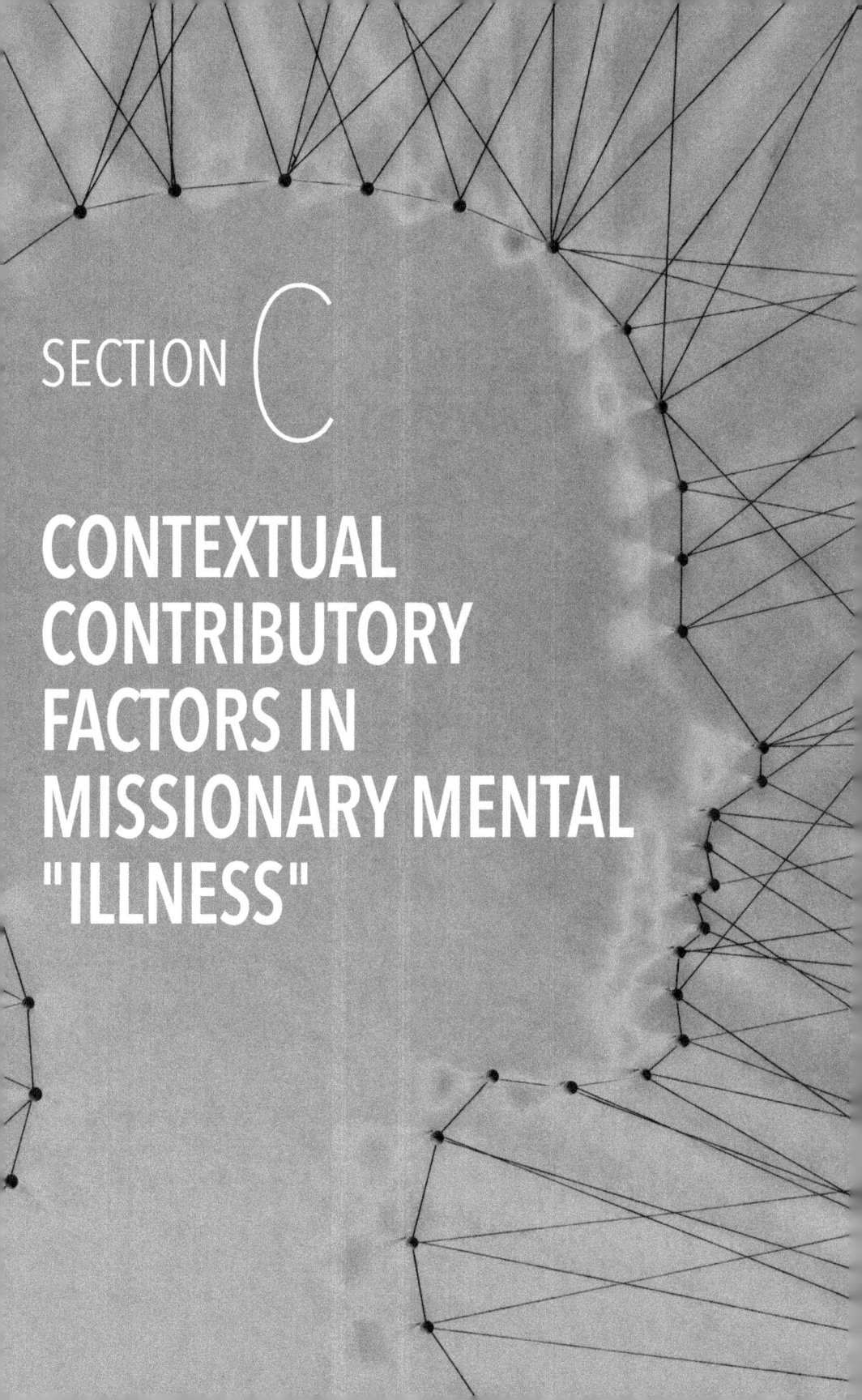

SECTION C

CONTEXTUAL CONTRIBUTORY FACTORS IN MISSIONARY MENTAL "ILLNESS"

11
PSYCHOLOGICAL STRESS AND LIMITED ACCESS AREA MISSIONARIES

by Jeong Han Kim

INTRODUCTION

What psychological differences exist between missionaries working in restricted access areas and missionaries working in open areas? Often, missionaries say that the longer they are in the mission field, the more they become like the locals there. Indeed, missionaries are affected by the local environments in which they serve.

Missionaries in restricted access areas feel more tension than missionaries in open areas. They can be forced to leave the mission field at another's discretion.

Before leaving the mission field, they may experience surveillance, summons, detention, interrogation, confrontation, or intimidation by the local security authorities. Global Mission Society (GMS) has more than 2,544 missionaries in 101 countries.[1] The psychological status of the missionaries serving in restricted access areas is clearly distinguishable from the psychological status of missionaries serving in open areas. This presentation explores the psychological stress of missionaries in restricted access areas through the cases of GMS, which has one tenth of all Korean missionaries as its members (about 27,205 missionaries in 172 countries, December 2016[2]). In particular, I will focus on the psychological state of deported missionaries and consider several appropriate measures for improving the care they receive.

RESTRICTED ACCESS AREAS AND MISSIONARY STRESS

Several factors contribute to the intense psychological pressure that missionaries in restricted access areas face. One of the biggest factors is the need to adjust expectations regarding the missionary's status in society. In Korea, people respect the job of a minister or missionary: it is a "proud job." If you, as a missionary, are accustomed to such an environment and suddenly move to a place where you would be unwise to reveal your line of work, you will feel psychological tension or pressure. If you have family members, the pressure your wife and children will feel is even greater. When missionaries have school-aged children, not only the parents but also the children tend to be extremely careful that their words and actions do not expose their family's missionary status. This cautiousness can cause maladaptation to the local life.

In general, the most worrisome thing for a Korean missionary is to be deported upon the execution of local law. There have already been cases of deportation in most of the restricted access areas in which Korean missionaries serve. Therefore, a missionary working in a restricted access community is haunted by the constant fear of deportation. These indirect experiences cause increasing anxiety. If a missionary is actually deported, the negative psychological impact on the missionary will only deepen. How, specifically, do missionaries react to being exiled? Here are some examples.

---

1 "Sending Status," Global Mission Society, accessed November 14, 2018, https://gms. kr/?d1=2&d2=1&d3=1.

2 "Theory / Strategy," The Korea World Missions Association, accessed December 2016, KWMA 2016년 연례 보고서, https://kwma.org/index.php?mid=tg_0102&category=1597&document_srl=11229.

I. The Status of Missionaries in Restricted Access Areas

According to Open Door's statistics, about 151 countries around the world are hostile to Christianity.[3] In particular, foreigners are not legally allowed to evangelize in some countries. In a large number of the 170 countries in which Korean missionaries are located, evangelizing is prohibited by law.

GMS sends missionaries to ninety-eight countries. About 30 percent of all countries prohibit foreigners from preaching or doing mission work. A comparison of GMS missionaries' locations with countries that persecute Christians is shown in Table 11.1.

Table 11.1. A Comparison of GMS Missionaries' Locations with Countries That Persecute Christians

Countries That Persecute Christians	Number of Countries Where GMS Missionaries Are Located	GMS Missionary Deportation Cases
Top 10 persecuting countries	7 countries	5 countries
Top 50 persecuting countries	28 countries	18 countries

Certain experiences, along with certain ways of thinking, feeling, and behaving, are peculiar to missionaries working in restricted access areas.

A Psychological Representation of Restricted Access Area Missionaries. GMS missionaries who work in restricted access areas express their feelings in various ways:

"Being a missionary in a restricted access area is like being 'locked in a boiling sauna.'"

"It's like carrying a big rock on your head."

"It's like living with heavy armor on."

A Behavioral Representation of Restricted Access Area Missionaries. The following behaviors are common to missionaries ministering in restricted access areas.

Watching the door: They tend to watch the door, no matter where they are. This has become a habit because they are constantly anxious that people might come to take them into custody or interrogate them.

---

3 "2018 Christian Persecution Trend," Open Doors, accessed November 2018, https://www.opendoors.or.kr/board/view.do?iboardgroupseq=1&iboardmanagerseq=1. Persecution of Christians is a global phenomenon which occurs in seventy-five countries. There are 151 countries that express hostility towards Christianity.

Talking too loudly: They often speak loudly in order to push their arguments.

Expressing themselves with exaggeration: Because they are usually oppressed, they tend to express their thoughts with exaggeration when they can express themselves freely in a public environment.

II. The Situation of Missionaries in Restricted Access Areas

It can be said that the suffering of a missionary in a restricted access area is greater than that of a missionary in a free mission country.

First, in Korea you can proudly declare that you are a pastor, a missionary, and a Christian, but in the mission field you must change your status, including your name.

Second, as a missionary in a restricted access area, you face legal sanctions. You continue your missionary work, but always with legal sanctions in mind, which keeps you under pressure whether the ministry is going smoothly or not.

Third, your ministry plan is always subject to change. The contents of your ministry, your method of ministry, your scope of ministry, the depth of your ministry, the deadlines in your ministry, and many other aspects of your ministry are uncertain.

Fourth, because of the nature of a restricted access area, as members of a missionary family, you cannot freely express your faith or talk about your ministry, so you need to warn each other about the possible dangers of sharing. You must always be careful not to inflict any inadvertent harm on your family. For example, if your children are young, their peers should not find out that they are part of a missionary family. This limits your children's ability to participate in school life and to pursue friendships. You are careful about your own relationships with colleagues, as well. For security reasons, you should not become too intimate with your colleagues, but, at the same time, you cannot not keep your distance from them, for they are members of the same organization. Your relationships with the locals must be conducted even more cautiously. The locals are the subject of the Gospel, yet, at the same time, they are the ones of whom missionaries should be most wary.

As described above, missionaries in restricted access areas undergo quadruple the pain of those serving in open countries. When there have been recent (twenty-first century) cases of deportation in the restricted access area in which a missionary is serving, or if a large-scale investigation of foreigners (missionaries) has recently been conducted, the mental stress of the missionary is even greater.

III. GMS Missionary Deportation in Restricted Access Areas

Since 1979, about 135 families (about 200 people) of GMS have been deported. (See Table 11.2.)[4]

---
4 Global Mission Society, "Crisis Management Team Report," GMS internal document, September 6, 2018.

Table 11.2. The Number of Deported GMS Missionary Families, 1979–2018

1979-2001	'02	'03	'07	'08	'09	'10	'11	'12	'13	'14	'15	'16	'17	'18	Total
17	6	3	2	1	5	5	3	7	11	2	16	5	21	31	135

Especially since 2002, the number of missionaries expelled from China has been increasing. Therefore, "deportation" is the main topic of conversation whenever missionaries have the chance to get together, whether for meetings, seminars, forums, or missionary conferences. They talk about why certain missionaries were deported, what the details of each scenario were, what the psychological state of the expelled missionaries is, how the sending church responded, where the missionaries relocated, and so on. And they are eaten up with anxiety (which has nothing to do with faith) that they, too, may soon become objects of deportation. As time goes by, the mounting pressure affects both their mental and physical health.

IV. The Psychological Expressions of an Exiled Missionary

The psychological expressions of deported missionaries vary widely among individuals. They differ greatly, depending on the mission field, the period of mission work, the health status of the missionary (physical, mental, spiritual), the missionary's financial situation, and the missionary's family relationships.

It took three years to recover. From the time I was deported, I wanted to go back to the mission field by any means possible. I even petitioned to the Korean Ministry of Foreign Affairs and visited some people who had political influence. I tried like crazy to find a way back. However, I realized that the deportation process could not be reversed. I suddenly panicked. I did not know where to go or what to do. When I met people, I had to listen to them saying, "How hard could it be, now that you've been deported?" I hated that too. So I exercised a lot. Three years have passed. I gradually grasped the reality of my situation and began to understand God's will in it. (Missionary A, deported from China)

I delude myself that I am on the way to China when I am on an airplane, and I am in tears when I am in the car. I am in tears when I'm alone. When I am with people, I don't feel it. But when I am alone, I start to think of China and cry. I am both angry and sad. When will I stop crying? (Missionary B, three months after deportation)

I had to leave the mission field after being refused entry at the airport. Then I moved to Thailand. My wife had gone to the mission field at age twenty-seven and spent about twenty years there. She did not accept that she could not enter China. However, I was forced to leave, so I began to minister in a third country. Six years have passed. I still dream of going to China at night. Cannot forget. I think it might be possible to reenter in five years, but I don't think I will be able to go back, considering the recent situation in China. (Missionary C, deported from China six years ago)

I cannot even watch a TV set with a black-colored frame. I hate anything of black color. Because those who interrogated me were wearing black uniforms. (Missionary D, interrogated alongside fellow missionaries and deported from the 00 area[5])

My sending church stopped supporting me. That was a great shock. Then I was denied entrance to the mission field. I wanted to die. I felt a "suicidal impulse" because of the economic hardship and the denial of entrance to the mission field that I was devoted to. (Missionary E, eight months after deportation from the West Asia region)

I understand it, but I cannot accept it. (Missionary F, expelled from India, six months later)

When I was deported and arrived at the airport to leave the mission field, I fell on my knees in front of the locals, who came out to say goodbye. At that very moment, I burst into tears. (Missionary G, in his fifties and expelled from the 00 region in 2018)

V. The Importance of Member Care for Deported Missionaries

A missionary was expelled from India. After the deportation, nine months had passed without his receiving proper care. The missionary expressed his mind like this: "The heart was torn into pieces, and our existence seemed to be worthless."

However, the missionary was invited to tea and to meals on several occasions, and he was given theoretical explanations on "the meaning of expulsion, the case of deportation, [and] the mission of a missionary." Since then, the missionary's state of mind has changed: "I am grateful and thankful that I can be used in a more precious form."

VI. A Deported Missionary's Desire for Member Care

A senior missionary in his sixties, who was deported from C and relocated to a third country, expressed his desire for member care to address the needs of deported missionaries.

A thorough debriefing is needed. Taking enough rest is also required. Specifically, taking a rest for about three months in an environment without acquaintance is recommended. Especially, my wife had a lot of trouble with her old wounds in the process of receiving counseling. I realized that the impact of the crisis of deportation would reveal even the hurt of the past. Therefore, it is necessary to have enough counseling.

In 2005, when a missionary was deported, one of his colleagues in a neighboring country invited him to come and rest there, which gave the deported missionary much comfort. He went, rested for several months, and recovered greatly.

GMS carries out the following care for deported missionaries.

---

5   The region is unspecified for security purposes.

First, airport reception: When a missionary is expelled, member care managers (more than two persons) from headquarters go to the airport and greet the missionary. At this time, a bouquet is presented to the missionary. If the missionaries are a couple, the bouquet is presented to the wife.

Second, housing accommodation: The member care managers escort the missionary to a prepared housing accommodation, such as the missionary accommodation in GMS headquarters (twenty-six rooms) or the missionary accommodation in Anyang city (ten rooms). GMS provides housing for at least one week and up to a month at its facilities. After that, the missionary can move to another place, depending on the individual situation. GMS provides basic amenities, including housing and money for food.

Third, communication: Care members communicate with the missionary and the member care staff. They seek to understand the psychological state of the missionary and try not to express too much encouragement or concern. They might suggest that the missionary participate in some cultural events, such as travel.

Fourth, psychological testing: Member care staff members communicate with the missionary from the time of the missionary's arrival at the airport. They also communicate with the member care managers, and if it is deemed necessary, they provide debriefing or psychological testing for the missionary at an appropriate time. (A resident psychology expert is available at the headquarters.)

Fifth, the sending church (sponsor): Member care staff communicate with the person in charge (pastor) of the sending church, explaining the psychology of the deported missionary and the subsequent procedure in detail, and providing necessary documents (on relocation and on understanding the deported missionary from the biblical, psychological, and mission historical viewpoints, etc.).

Sixth, the children's school: If there are children, the member care providers introduce them to the appropriate school(s).

Seventh, relocation: GMS has missionaries in ninety-eight countries. They investigate the mission resources needed in each mission field and relocate the missionary where necessary.

VII. Relocation

Relocation Area. Missionaries who are deported from restricted access areas should be relocated to open areas.

A missionary, once expelled from China, was then relocated to a restricted access area in Southeast Asia, where foreigners cannot legally engage in missions. "I am shaken when there is a stranger at the door. I'm afraid to be alone," said the wife of the missionary.

In this case, the missionary lives with the fear of a second expulsion, after having already experienced one. Psychologically, there is no choice but to feel greater pressure. Therefore, deported missionaries should be placed in areas where they can receive "missionary visas" or in areas that do not have legal restrictions on foreigners' missionary activities.

Relocation Time. Deported missionaries are all affected by major shock, but for varying periods of time. There is a big difference in the effect of deportation on each individual. Some people live in the shock of deportation for six years, while others have no problem getting back to their daily routines right after they are returned to their home country.

Regarding deported missionaries, it is common to think, "Go to the new mission field as soon as possible, so the shock of deportation can wear off sooner." But this perspective is clearly mistaken.

One missionary moved to another location in the tropical region a month after he was deported. However, due to the difficulty of adapting to the new culture and new ministry there, he appealed to the mission headquarters to make arrangements for him to leave. The missionary was in the midst of "serious spiritual, mental, [and] physical" suffering.

Missionary Lee Ki-pung[6] was a minister in Korea when he received a calling as a missionary to China. He left his Korean ministry and went to China, and several families who had been attending his Korean church went with him. Together, they started a church.

The church thrived, and the number of attendees reached over 1,000. Lee Ki-pung and his friends assisted Chinese locals both directly and indirectly. They also assisted other Korean missionaries to China in many ways.

One day in 2007, the government expelled foreign missionaries, along with others who were associated with them, and the church where Lee Ki-pung had been serving almost folded. The missionary, who returned to Korea, sought to reenter China through various routes, including the Korean Ministry of Foreign Affairs.

Returning to daily life was impossible for Mr. Ki-pung. He could not sleep or eat. It was hard for him to meet new people. He had a tough time facing the endless questions about "deportation" and the words of "comfort," which were, for him at that time, uncomfortable.

Mr. Ki-pung participated in debriefing and counseling. But they did not work. He exercised like a crazy. (He had to immerse himself in something.) He could not pray. He tried praying at a designated time and place, but still, he could not pray. He was engulfed in resentment, regret, and despair, and this went on for nearly three years. He could hardly believe that he was breaking down like this. The deportation had made his life dreadfully difficult.

One day, after three years, the missionary had gradually found his way to God's grace and said, "Who am I? I am a child of God. From now on, I will be grateful if I can be used in any way for God."

---

6 A pseudonym. The missionary's true identity is withheld for security reasons.

In Korea, he opened a new church. This church thrived, and more than 1,000 attendees gathered for worship there. Among the missionaries who had been deported from China, Lee Ki-pung chose those who had lost sponsorship from their sending churches, and his new church began to support them, re-sending more than ten missionaries to the mission field.

Because of his own experiences, missionary Lee Ki-pung now knows how deported missionaries feel and what their needs are. Knowing this will allow him actively to help other missionaries who face deportation in the future.

CONCLUSION

Missionaries in restricted access areas often describe their experiences in ways similar to this:

> "Ministering in a restricted access area is like having a big stone on your head."

> "I feel like I am wearing heavy iron armor. In the meantime, my mind, body, and spirit are also exhausted."

Getting deported is an indescribable shock. People know in their minds that they may be deported someday, but when they are actually deported, they may not be able to make a sound judgment or think properly because of the shock. Therefore, early care for a deported missionary is crucial.

As I described above, GMS has begun implementing customized care for missionaries who have been deported. I hope that through more thorough care in the future, missionaries will soon be able to escape the negative impacts of expulsion and move on to complete a new stage in ministry.

APPENDIX 1
Recommendations for the Deported/Visa- or Entry-Refused Missionary

GMS CRISIS MANAGEMENT TEAM

Missionaries can experience confusion in many areas of life because of "the azalea issue." Therefore, we recommend using the following basic guidelines to help direct them toward healthy behaviors and mindsets.

1. **Psychological (emotional) condition.**

    Do not feel guilty. / Do not be ashamed. / Do not try to reflect.

    Meet friendly people. / Encourage your family. / Communicate with your colleagues.

    Be proactive in getting help from an expert.

2. **Health**

    Do not fast. / Do not binge. / Do not retreat from daily life or become sedentary.

    Do some light exercise. / If you have any health problems, get a medical checkup immediately.

3. **Press contact**

    Avoid contact with the press. When asked for information, tell them to ask the Crisis Management Team (CMT).

    Do not try to explain to the people around you what happened.

4. **Children's school**

    Seek scholastic records from China and find a school suitable in Korea.

5. **Accommodation**

    Be proactive in working with the church, headquarters, and other facilities to secure accommodation.

6. **Spiritual Life**

    Pray, read, and meditate in a quiet space nearby, such as a church or living quarters, instead of going to prayer houses.

7. **Leisure**

    Try to enjoy good food, good places, good experiences (movies, concerts, theater, etc.) with your family whenever possible.

8. **Family**

    One's family is the best custodian, and mutual encouragement is needed. Actively encourage and comfort each other.

APPENDIX 2
Checklist for Missionaries with Expulsion/Entry Denial/Visa Rejection Issues

The purpose of this list is to help member care providers understand the situation of the missionary accurately and pursue solutions to the missionary's requests.

To be completed by the missionary:

A. Family Situation: Describe in careful detail your family situation, especially regarding the elderly and the children in your family.

number of families who were serving with you and where they are now:

your family members and their current situations:

age of your youngest child:

status of your parents:

B. Health Status: Circle all that apply.

healthy

chronic illness (any disease, treatment situation)

need immediate medical examination

C. Accommodation: Where are you staying?

home in Korea

parents' house

relatives' house(s)

with members of your sending church

guest house

unresolved

*If your accommodations are unresolved, your desired location:

D. Finances

flight ticket cost:

financial arrangement for staying in Korea:

current monthly sponsorship amount (average):

E. Ministry

types of ministry involved in your previous mission (church planting/seminary/North Korea/missions training/etc.):

how to reorganize ministry: delegate to local people/delegate to colleagues/complete dissolution/unresolved

F. Member Care

wish to receive consultation immediately (within one week)

no need for counseling

in need of counseling after taking a rest for a while (1 month)

other:

G. Relationship with the Sending Church

sending period:

sending church name:

sending church location:

communication with the sending church after the incident (circle all that apply):

contact from China to Korea

contact from within Korea

indirect or direct contact

request to the sending church (specify)

H. What are the most serious difficulties you are facing? (specify)

I. What help do you need most urgently? (specify)

J. Other: Please note any comments or requests that should be passed to the headquarters, sending church, or sponsors (write freely).

RESPONSE by Karen F. Carr

Jeong Han Kim has drawn our attention to the psychological stress of missionaries serving in closed access countries and the emotional reactions of those deported from these countries. Rev. Kim brings a unique perspective as a member of GMS, the largest mission organization in South Korea, with over 2500 missionaries, many of whom serve in restricted access countries. The dramatic increase in deportations in the last five years is striking. This raises a number of concerns for missionaries worldwide. We owe a debt of gratitude to Rev. Kim and GMS for taking the time to study and respond to the emotional and spiritual impact of deportation on missionaries.

Trauma and loss are no strangers to missionaries. What makes the crisis of deportation so difficult? Some of the pre-deportation chronic stresses that Kim highlights include:

- The constant threat of deportation and the corresponding anxiety
- The need to hide the real reason for being in the country
- Surveillance resulting in hypervigilance
- The loss of status as an "esteemed" missionary
- Isolation and suspicion; not knowing whom to trust

When missionaries are deported, both external and internal losses result in grief. In addition to the loss of ministry, home, and friends, there are also the less tangible but significant losses of dreams, hopes, roles, momentum, focus, and direction.

Kim helps us recognize that reactions to deportation will vary depending on location and length of service, health status (physical, mental, and spiritual), financial situation, and family relations. If the missionary feels that the deportation could have been prevented or was someone's fault, subsequent feelings of failure and guilt may complicate the recovery process. Unresolved past rejections may also emerge in the recovery process.

In his article, Kim provides quotations from GMS missionaries who have been deported, through which we gain insight into the inner pain and wrestling involved in processing this trauma. We see a process of shock, denial, fear, anger, and sadness, with gradual acceptance.

Kim discusses a number of effective member care strategies for deportees that address practical, emotional, and spiritual needs. I will highlight some of GMS's strategies and offer brief comments:

Airport reception—An airport reception honors the returning missionary with a gift and a supportive presence.

Accommodation and food—These practical supports facilitate rest and reduce stress.

Communication and rest—Encouraging restful and restorative activities is a wonderful way of giving missionaries the space and time to heal. The GMS protocol, which values rest, reminds me of God's response to Elijah, found in I Kings 19:3–18. It was only after sleep, practical care, and patient listening that God gave Elijah a new perspective and a new ministry assignment.

Psychological response—Since each missionary responds differently, it is important to assess the impact on each individual and family and design a response to match unique needs. How this is presented is important, however. If people think they are being offered counseling because the organization believes they are weak, they are likely to refuse help. Psychological services that are offered as a "standard way the organization cares for their own" are more likely to be accepted.

Communication with the sending church—Well-coordinated care will involve the missionary's entire support system and a point person who communicates with the missionary clearly and frequently.

Children's school—Minimizing disruption to the children's routines is a high priority. In addition to addressing their educational needs, the emotional impact of deportation on the children should be addressed. This may occur through counseling and/or parent education.

Relocation—As Kim notes, this decision should not be rushed, and missionaries must be given ample time to attain healthy closure. At the right time, finding a new focus will be an important part of the missionary's healing process. As much as possible, it seems wise for the missionary to have input and choice concerning relocation. GMS seems to have a policy that those deported from a closed country will be reassigned only to open countries. The rationale may be that returning to a closed country is likely to trigger post-traumatic responses. However, I wonder if there might be some exceptions, depending on the psychological health of the missionary.

The case study of missionary Lee Ki-pung is a clear illustration of how well-meaning words and conversations can be unhelpful and even hurtful to deported missionaries. "Endless questions about deportation and words of comfort which make the person feel uncomfortable" are common experiences and demonstrate the need to coach potential supporters in effective care for traumatized missionaries. It is interesting that ultimately for Lee Ki-pung, his healing needed to happen on a spiritual level. A deeper realization of God's grace and the reconstruction of his identity and worth in Christ resulted in a profound sense of gratitude and fruitfulness that had nothing to do with his own efforts and everything to do with God's amazing grace. We also see this in the beautiful words of a missionary expelled from India who initially felt his existence was worthless. After nine months, he was able to say, "I am grateful and thankful that I can be used in a more precious form."

I commend the GMS CMT for writing *Guidelines of Recommendations for Deported Missionaries*. I would highly recommend that all mission organizations consider developing comprehensive guidelines for traumatized missionaries.

There is one aspect of these guidelines which I feel could be improved, although it may be a cultural or language issue. Included in the guidelines are these directions: *Forbidden: Do not feel guilty. Do not be ashamed. Do not try to reflect.*

Feelings of guilt and shame are a natural response to deportation. Reflection or introspection, with many "what if" questions, is also common. In my experience, most people do not respond well when told what they should or should not feel. There is a subtle nuance here. We do not want to encourage the person to remain in these feelings, yet we need to come alongside them, expressing understanding and acceptance, before gently showing them that there is another path that will lead to healing. Laying down guilt and shame at the foot of the cross and allowing God's grace to wash away the pain and regret is a process.

I join Rev. Kim in hoping that as a community of believers, we can provide better care to deported missionaries, accompanying them on a path of healing that affirms God's love for them. With this kind of care, more missionaries will be able to affirm as Ki-pung said, "Who am I? I am a child of God. From now on, I would be grateful if I can be used in anything for God."

QUESTIONS FOR REFLECTION

1. Given that missionaries in closed countries feel constant pressure (like they are carrying a stone on their heads), what might be some proactive ways to care for them while they are still serving in the closed country?

2. Which of Rev. Kim's ideas for care of deported missionaries do you feel are most important, and what might you add to his list?

3. What would be examples of words of comfort that do not comfort? How can we coach and train those who are caring for deported missionaries?

12

A COURAGEOUS CALL, A CONFOUNDING CRISIS, AND THE CONTOURS OF APPROPRIATE CARE

by STANLEY W. GREEN

Note: Sensitive details that might jeopardize the security of those still working in Afghanistan have been curtailed. Some names and locations are intentionally obscured or changed, due to ongoing security concerns in the region.
*Indicates name has been changed.

AN UNEXPECTED TURN OF EVENTS

> *Surely God is watching over them, and as people all over the world pray for their release, we also pray that God's power and light would shine through this darkness.*[1]

In July 2007, Al and Gladys Geiser wrote these words, as they reflected on the kidnapping of twenty-three Korean aid workers who had traveled to Afghanistan. Their sentiments hinted at the kind of faith, hope, and trust in God that would carry them, if they should ever experience a similar crisis.

They could hardly have expected that one year and one month after their reflections, they would be the ones that Christians from all around the world would be praying for.

On Saturday, August 23, 2008, we members of the Mennonite Mission Network (MMN) sent an email prayer request to our network of supporters. We did so, driven by urgency, yet respecting the sensitivity of the circumstances we were facing and not yet sure what we should say. Taking care not to say too much, we mentioned the deteriorating conditions in Afghanistan and invited people to pray for the safety of Al and Gladys Geiser. In the following days, we informed our staff and our board of the hostage-taking of Al and his business partner, Al Shukur, asking that they hold the information with discretion.

CALLED TO SERVE

In lieu of military service, Al chose to serve with Mennonite Central Committee (MCC) after college, working for two years each in Korea and Pakistan. Later, again with MCC, he served for three years in Bangladesh, where he met Gladys Dyck, his future wife. In 1977, they married and together had two children, Andrea and Franklin. Later, Franklin and his wife Mary made Al and Gladys proud grandparents of their granddaughter, Kaitlyn Geiser.

In 1984, Al started his own company, Geiser & Geiser, Inc., in Ohio. He developed it into a business that included manufacturing, electrical and mechanical work, and heating and cooling. This business continued for 16 years, before Al and Gladys closed it to begin a new chapter in their lives. Sensing a call to again serve Christ in an overseas location, they joined MMN in February 2000 and left for Kabul, Afghanistan, where they worked for the next nine years, till 2009. Al built small water turbines and set up micro-hydroelectric plants to bring electricity to remote, rural villages. Gladys taught elementary students at an international school in Kabul. After a few years in the country, Al partnered with an Afghan coworker, who had begun his own workshop, and they established a company called Engineering Associates. This private company

---

1 Al and Gladys Geiser, letter to Mennonite Mission Network (MMN) Regional Director for Asia, John F. Lapp, July 2010.

made turbines, pipes, and all the parts needed for hydroelectric projects in remote villages of Afghanistan.[2]

THE KIDNAPPING AND SUBSEQUENT HOSTAGE CRISIS

At approximately 3:00 p.m. on Thursday, August 20, 2010, we received an unexpected phone call from the Executive Director (ED) of the agency through which we partnered for work in Afghanistan. He informed us that Al and two coworkers had been kidnapped in Wardak province, Afghanistan. Al, his partner, Al Shukur, and another worker had traveled by motorcycle to a certain region to service several micro-hydro projects. While there, they received an invitation to attend a funeral wake in a nearby location. They went by car, accompanied by a local man. On their way back to where they had left the motorcycle, they were stopped by two men, one armed with an AK-47. The men searched Al Shukur and Al, discovering from his documents that Al was an American, which then led to the hostage-taking. Initially, we assumed that the unknown group that had taken Al and his partner were the Taliban, but later we learned that the captors were affiliated with Hisb-e-Islami, a faction headed by the notorious Gulbuddin Hekmatyar. The kidnappers demanded a ransom for the release of Al and his partner.

Al Geiser's co-captive, Al Shukur, had relatives in the region, one of whom contacted Shukur's immediate family. The family then notified Gladys of the kidnapping. They also shared that between 50 and 200 people, who knew Al Shukur and Al, had immediately gone to secure the release of the captives. Both Gladys and the agency with which she was serving in Afghanistan believed very strongly that news of this incident should not be publicized in any way. They were convinced that media and any government attention would undermine negotiations already underway by locals. Al Shukur's family paid a ransom, and within two days he was released. Al Geiser ended up being held hostage for fifty-six days.[3]

ISSUES AND CHALLENGES IN DETERMINING OUR RESPONSE

News of the hostage-taking forced a host of troubling questions upon us. In a reflective piece that wrestles with what a faithful Christian response in the face of such an ordeal might look like, John Roth pinpoints some issues with which we knew we, as Anabaptists, would need to struggle.[4] Among them:

Paying Ransom—We were concerned for the well-being of Al. However, one of the most immediate challenges we faced was how to respond to the kidnappers'

---

2   Al Geiser's Obituary, *The Daily Record*, August 2, 2012, accessed July 10, 2018, http://www.the-daily-record.com/obituaries/20120802/alfred-al-geiser.

3   During the fifty-six days of Al's captivity, Al and Gladys' home church, Kidron Mennonite Church, assembled every day to pray for him and for his release. These prayers continued until Al's release and his return home to Ohio.

4   John Roth, "How should we respond to kidnapping?" *The Mennonite*, September 2014, https://www.goshen.edu/wp-content/uploads/sites/59/2014/04/September.pdf.

demands. Most non-governmental organizations have a clear policy against paying ransom money. So did we. If we complied with the demands of the kidnappers, some would argue, we would thus reward hostage-taking and encourage further kidnappings. When, however, human life is at stake and families are desperate, we feel pressure to explore whether we should be open to considering life-saving measures, even ransom payments.

Sanctioning Violent Intervention—Refusal to pay a ransom would force us to contend with other alternatives, violence among them. Should Christians, committed to the gospel of peace, encourage violent police or military actions to secure the release of the hostages?

Location of burial in event of death—In the face of the real possibility that the captors could kill their hostage, we needed to help the family anticipate their response, and, on a related note, determine where Al would be buried.

How should a mission agency react to these questions and others, surfaced by such a crisis? More importantly, how should we counsel the family, as they wrestle with how to respond in the face of the potential murder of their husband and father?

At 3:40 p.m. on August 20, soon after we were first apprised of the kidnapping, John F. Lapp, Rachel Stoltzfus (our Senior Executive for Human Resources), and I called the Executive Director of our partner agency to get a fuller briefing. At 4:00 p.m., I informed Terry Shue, who was the Geisers' pastor at Kidron Mennonite Church, Ohio, of the situation.

Later that day, at 9:30 p.m. (Eastern Time in the USA—6:00 a.m. August 21, Afghan time) key Mennonite Mission Network leaders gathered at my home to call Gladys Geiser to reassure her that we knew of the kidnapping and that we were going to do all we could to secure Al's release. We also asked her if she had any immediate needs that we could respond to. At 10:00 p.m. that same evening, we again called our partner agency's Executive Director, requesting any updates and briefing him on our call with Gladys.

For several years prior to these events, Mennonite Mission Network had put in place a Crisis Management Team. The Crisis Management Team was comprised of our Human Resources Senior Executive; our Global Ministries Senior Executive; our Director for Asia and the Middle East; our Worker Care Coordinator; our Director for Communications; and me, as Executive Director. On August 21, I convened the first of almost daily meetings by the Crisis Management Team during the hostage situation. In these early meetings, we made several critical decisions, among them:

As a result of conversations with Gladys Geiser (who initially resisted evacuation) and out of concern for her security (as she could have become a potential target also), we made the decision to repatriate her to the US.

Almost immediately, we contacted Crisis Consulting International. By then, Crisis Consulting International had experience working with mission/non-governmental agencies in sixty-five kidnapping incidents. Bob Klamser, our primary connection with Crisis Consulting International, advised that we should have a Crisis Management Team in place in Kabul (the Kabul Crisis Management Team).

On Wednesday, August 27, we flew John Lapp, our Director for West Asia and Middle East, who had been in daily contact with Gladys, to Afghanistan to be Mennonite Mission Network's point person on the ground. En route, John met Gladys in the Dubai airport and was able to get a briefing from her. He tried to encourage her in her time of uncertainty and in what we hoped would be the temporary loss of her husband.

On the day John left, the Crisis Management Team met in person in Newton, Kansas (our second office location), where Erwin Rempel (who had worked for Mennonite Mission Network previously in the Senior Executive role) and his spouse, Angela Rempel, were located. Sensing the need for proper documentation and the value of having a couple with both pastoral and administrative gifts in place, we invited Erwin (who had been a pastor in an earlier life) and Angela to join John Lapp in Kabul to help guide our response. Stunned, they nevertheless accepted the call and prepared to go to Kabul.

Other Kabul Crisis Management Team "members" arrived over the course of the next ten days: Erwin and Angela Rempel arrived on September 5. On September 2, Geoff*, a Crisis Consulting International staff person, arrived to serve as an advisor (he departed September 8). Anthony* arrived on September 9, as the Third Party Intermediary (the person who would handle the phone exchanges and negotiations with the captors).

In 2006, Tom Fox, a Quaker volunteer with Christian Peacemaker Teams in Iraq, had been kidnapped by a group linked to Al-Qaeda and was eventually murdered.[5] So, one of the first phone calls we made was to Carol Rose, the Executive Director of Christian Peacemaker Teams, to see what we could learn from their experience of dealing with the kidnappers.

COMMUNICATIONS WITH THE FAMILY AND THE CAPTORS

The first contact with the captors came on Monday, September 1. That evening, in a meeting at the Kidron Mennonite Church—with Gladys and her children (Andrea, Franklin, and Franklin's wife, Mary), their pastor, our Human Resources Senior Executive and Worker Care Coordinator, and me—we addressed several of the questions listed above. The family was clear that, should Al be killed, he must be buried in Kabul. In an emotional dialogue, we struggled for several hours through the tough questions, including whether a ransom should be paid and what level of government intervention was acceptable. By the end of the day, we (the family, the agency, and the church) agreed that:

The payment of ransom is not authorized, and the negotiations are to be developed and conducted accordingly.

---

[5] Joel Roberts, "Captors Kill American Hostage," CBS News, March 10, 2006, accessed July 10, 2018, https://www.cbsnews.com/news/captors-kill-american-hostage/.

The Crisis Management Team and negotiators are not authorized to conduct negotiations primarily crafted or intended to support an armed hostage rescue attempt by government forces.

Following that consultation, a letter was written to the US Government, addressed to Condoleezza Rice, US Secretary of State; and William B. Wood, US Ambassador, Embassy of the United States in Kabul, Afghanistan. In the letter, co-signed by their pastor, Terri Shue; another family member; Roland Geiser (Al's brother); and me, the family stated their hopes and convictions. The letter noted:

Al and Gladys have been working in Afghanistan since 2000, deliberately having chosen to work with the local people in peace building through reconstruction and close relationships with the Afghans. Al has partnered with an Afghan colleague and built up a business for him in the field of hydroelectricity. Together they have worked on many projects already, with more sites to work on in the future.

We have asked the American Embassy in Kabul for help in securing Al's release. In Gladys' conversation with Brendan O'Brien, Consular Chief, she said that although we need help, we do not want violent intervention on Al's behalf. Coming from an historic peace church, we believe this to be the right way to go. We have worked here for eight years and have come to spread peace, help, and hope to the people of Afghanistan through the work we are doing here in the fields of making hydroelectricity (Al) and teaching school (Gladys).[6]

During the first weekend in Kabul, John Lapp met with our partner agency, with staff at the US Embassy, with the Federal Bureau of Investigation, and with Al Shukur to brief them on our position.

From the first call until September 14, the team had fourteen calls with the captors in all. During these calls, they were able to establish that Al was still alive. They also received ransom amount demands, tried to offer reasons why the response to the ransom demand was delayed, and attempted to humanize the captive.

On September 19, John took an incoming call to Gladys' phone. It was Al, asking where Gladys was. John conferred with Bob, and Bob sent some scripting ideas for Gladys to use if she received another call. The next day, the captors called and said that Al would soon call back. John called Bob for advice, as a result of which Anthony did talk to Al extensively, with the captors close by, who also talked quite a bit. Al was able to give some visual clues about his surroundings. He talked about gathering a large ransom, but he mainly seemed to be trying to buy time, so that a rescue operation could be undertaken. He sounded very shaky. He asked for Gladys' number, continuing to give location description. Anthony stalled, saying that we did not have Gladys' number but would get it.

What followed was the most stressful and emotional time for the Kabul Crisis Management Team till then. The captors left a distinct impression that they had completely lost their faith in Anthony (our Third Party Intermediary) and were ready to kill Al that day. Bob Klamser's sense was that it was not credible to

---

6   Geiser family, letter to the US Government, September 1, 2008.

claim that the Kabul Crisis Management Team did not have Gladys' number, since there was supposedly daily contact with her during the negotiations. Bob further suggested that Gladys be contacted and advised to set up a cell phone voicemail so that Al could leave her a message. This was done with clear instructions that Gladys not answer the phone.

Bob contacted the Federal Bureau of Investigations at the same time and requested that they go to the Geisers' home to sit with Gladys during this time. As it turned out, the agent was on his way, talking to Roland by phone, when Al's call came. The agent recommended that Gladys answer the phone, so she did. Al and Gladys talked about twelve minutes, with Al giving bank account instructions for gathering and wiring money.

In an extraordinary phone conference on Sunday, September 21, we recognized that the captors' primary communication had shifted from talking to our TPI, to making calls, which were being monitored by the Federal Bureau of Investigations, directly to Gladys in Ohio. As a result, the Kabul Crisis Management Team began to disband.

On the morning of October 15, Kabul Crisis Management Team members received an unexpected, yet eagerly longed-for phone call. Al was free and resting at the US Embassy. A military special operations team had rescued Al during the night of October 14. Al had awoken to the sound of English voices calling his name before he was rescued and airlifted to freedom by a military helicopter. He was checked over at the Bagram air base and then taken to the Embassy in Kabul. Erwin and Anthony, members of the Kabul Crisis Management Team who were still in Kabul, were invited to meet Al that evening at the Embassy. They did so, but their conversation with Al was limited.[7] An Associated Press article from October 22, 2008 reported that US Special Forces soldiers had freed him during a nighttime mission, in which several insurgents were killed.[8]

Key Learnings and Considerations?[9]

For all those involved in crisis management and care-giving, especially the in-country Kabul Crisis Management Team, the level of stress was exceedingly high. Given the life-or-death stakes involved, it could not have been otherwise. The prospect that something we might say or fail to say in response to the kidnappers' demands could cost the life of our worker was daunting and felt dreadfully overwhelming at times.

Stress came not only from the fact that life and death determinations were involved, but also from a myriad of decisions, relationships, and unexpected changes in direction that arose.

---

7   Angela Rempel, Erwin Rempel, *Unexpected Invitations: Surprises, Adventures, and Opportunities in Mennonite Ministry* (Newton, KS: Mennonite Press, 2016).

8   Global Ministries, "Geiser, Partner Killed in Afghanistan," August 7, 2012, accessed July 10, 2018, https://www.globalministries.org/geiser_partner_killed_10_10_2014_1340.

9   A number of these learnings are gleaned from an unpublished document by John F. Lapp, dated November 5, 2008.

The demands of such an assignment absolutely require appropriate care for the crisis managers and care givers. We worked hard to provide appropriate levels of care.

Between the family and the Crisis Management Team, we never really arrived at what we considered appropriate compensation. We agreed that there would be no ransom, talking instead about an appropriate amount for "compensation." We had trouble, however, agreeing on the precise amount. In a September 6 meeting, we agreed to an acceptable "range" for compensation of up to $100,000, with a targeted offer amount of $40,000. On September 9, however, our partner agency indicated that it would consider any number above $5,000 to be a "ransom." They would have to disavow the Kabul Crisis Management Team if it made a higher offer, they warned. The Kabul Crisis Management Team agreed that the partner agency's voice be taken seriously and decided to reduce our "offer" to $5,000. Crisis Consulting International immediately began working on a script to incorporate this new offer.

The shift away from the Crisis Management Team (or Kabul Crisis Management Team) playing a primary role occurred following a series of uncontrollable events and developments, not because of any single decision or mistake. We are grateful to God, who guided us in our discernments.

MMN's crisis response policies were helpful only to a small degree. Most preparatory advice (such as how workers should prepare for evacuation) was not apropos. We needed the expert counsel and guidance that a group like Crisis Consulting International (CCI) provided.

From the outset, we were very hesitant to involve the Embassy/Federal Bureau of Investigations because of advice we received from those familiar with similar situations in other countries. While we did not approve the armed rescue operation, we also struggled with the dilemma of withholding information from the governmental authorities, who do have criminal justice responsibilities. That we were treated respectfully by the Federal Bureau of Investigations and given a fair degree of space to negotiate as we saw fit, only added to the complexity of discerning what an appropriate relationship with civil authorities should be.

The kind of crisis intervention we dealt with came with a significant financial and personal cost. During the seven-week period in which we used the services of Crisis Consulting International, booked expensive last-minute flights, and paid staff and other consultants for the many hours they invested, our costs escalated to high five-figure amounts. We are grateful that we did not need to use a for-profit crisis consultant group, which would have cost considerably more.

AL RETURNS TO OHIO

After his rescue and debriefing, Al traveled with a person from the US Embassy in Kabul back to Cleveland, Ohio, on October 20, 2010, two months after his capture. After 56 days in captivity, Al had lost about twenty pounds but was otherwise in remarkably good health. Mennonite Mission Network offered Al and Gladys counseling, recognizing their need to deal with the trauma they had experienced.

Return to Afghanistan

In the wake of the kidnapping and release, Mennonite Mission Network work in Afghanistan was discontinued. We did not have any other personnel on the ground in that country. Al, however, felt such a strong call to his work and witness among the people of Afghanistan that he made plans to return there.

> ... it wasn't long until he decided that God didn't save him just to be back in a safe place in Ohio. His partner, who also had been kidnapped and later released, didn't have a choice about just leaving the country and going somewhere safer to live. And Al didn't feel that it was right for him to do that. He very strongly felt that God was calling him to go back.[10]

Mennonite Mission Network, however, felt that the risk to Al's (and Gladys') life was inordinately heightened as a result of the deaths of some of his kidnappers. The likelihood of their being targeted for vengeance-killing seemed too real, especially since Al's work often took him into the less secure rural districts outside Kabul.

Al was, however, restless and could not still his sense of call to Afghanistan, despite all that had happened. As Gladys reports it:

> After six months, he left to go back to work in Afghanistan. I didn't go with him at the time, because I just didn't feel comfortable doing that yet. So he went and worked there for several months, and then he would come back to Ohio. And then he would go back again. We did that for two years.

The work seemed to be going well. There was lots of work and many big projects. They needed his help and expertise. Then in 2010, I went back with him.[11]

AL'S DEATH

On July 22, 2012, Al, his partner, and an employee of theirs traveled to a nearby village in the Parwan province to do some repairs. They decided to stay overnight and to return to Kabul the next morning. On their way back to Kabul the next day, their car was stopped and all three of the people in the car were shot and killed. Taliban spokesman Zabiullah Mujahid claimed responsibility for the killings.

According to a July 25 news release from the Daily Record of Wooster, Ohio, their pastor, Carl Wiebe noted,

> They were simply living out their lives following the model of Jesus, serving the needs of all people.... (T)he Geisers were aware of and accepted the risks in their work for peace in Afghanistan and have

---

10 "Gladys and Al Geiser–United States," Bearing Witness Stories Project, July 5, 2016, https://martyrstories.org/gladys-and-al-geiser/.

11 Ibid.

exemplified a lifestyle of Christian service having served internationally, nationally and locally for many years.[12]

According to the decision of his family, guided by Al's own wish, Al was buried in Kabul.

Al Geiser's life has ended, but his legacy lives on. We learned many things and resolved many others, while trying to make the best decisions regarding the crisis. One issue that persists, however, is the question about the level of risk we should take in exposing those whom we send to likely injury or death. The question is made more complex, considering our stated convictions, which pre-date this incident. In a special edition of Mennonite Mission Network's *Missio Dei*[13] series, we attempt to describe what we believe (a list of nine convictions), how we approach our work, and what role our work may have in pursuing God's vision of shalom in Christ. In the sixth statement we share our conviction thus:

> *The church expects opposition and is willing to suffer.* In a fallen world, the church expects opposition and hostility. Members of the church risk their lives to represent the love and presence of Jesus, regardless of the consequences. The church stands in solidarity with poor and oppressed people, trusts in God for its defense, and places its hope in God's faithful promises.

The early church father, Tertullian, who is reputed to have said "The blood of Christians is the seed of the church," offered the following observation:

> Yet no cruelty of yours, though each were to exceed the last in its exquisite refinement, profits you in the least; but forms rather an attraction to our sect. We spring up in greater numbers as often as we are mown down by you: the blood of the Christians is a source of new life.[14]

Tertullian's ancient declaration invites careful consideration of how we should respond. In our times, also, mission agencies will not be able to avoid the reality of suffering and even martyrdom. One of Al Geiser's lingering legacies is to force us as mission administrators to grapple with this question of the extent to which we tolerate risk to those under our care. How should we respond?

---

12 Bob Klamser, "Former Hostage Killed in New Afghanistan Attack," Crisis Consulting International, July 25, 2012, http://www.cricon.org/2012/former-hostage-killed-in-new-afghanistan-attack.

13 James R. Krabill, ed., *Together in Mission: Core Beliefs, Values and Commitments of Mennonite Mission Network. Missio Dei* No. 10 (October 2005).

14 Tertullian, *Apologeticus pro Christianis (Apology)*, trans. T.H. Bindley, accessed September 8, 2018, https://earlychurchtexts.com/public/tertullian_blood_christians_seed.htm, chaps. 48-50.

RESPONSE

by Jinsuk (Felipe) Byun and Hyekyung (Grace) Hong

Throughout our reading of Stanley Green's reflection, our hearts empathized with his suffering. In a world that seems like an ever-degrading mission environment, Rev. Green's writing speaks of our shared concerns. Our first mission field was to Ecuador in 1994. Even a cursory comparison of our time there shows that, since then, mission fields have changed unfavorably.

Currently, we serve at the Global Missionary Training Center (GMTC), where missionary candidates and career missionaries are trained. Every day at noon, all trainees and staff members pray for an hour for GMTC graduates and mission fields. Recently, there has been an increasing number of heartbreaking prayer requests for those who have been forced out of their mission fields. In response to Green's reflection, which dealt with missionary kidnapping / hostage-taking and death threats, we would like to discuss the essence of the crisis that missionaries face, as well as an appropriate response(s) and member care strategy.

COMMITMENT, CRISIS, AND THE DUTY OF THE MISSIONARY

No one, and of course, no missionaries voluntarily seek crisis. During almost all Crisis Management seminars at GMTC, we inevitably sense faces hardening and the atmosphere becoming serious. Why does God allow crisis? How should we deal with the problem of suffering?

Al and Gladys Geiser wrote about the July 2007 kidnapping of twenty-three Korean aid workers that occurred in Afghanistan. Who would have thought a similar kidnapping would happen to them? There are sacrifices and costs associated with our calling as missionaries, which make us humble. Doubtlessly a courageous man of faith, Al Geiser, having gone through the crisis of being kidnapped and held hostage, nevertheless returned to Afghanistan, being fully aware of the risk, and subsequently faced death. With conviction, he chose what he believed in and put it into practice. He left an important lesson for us—but also some uneasy questions we must now face.

Of the twenty-three short-term Korean workers taken hostage, twenty-one were returned, but only after two of them were murdered. The incident left a huge scar and many issues to deal with, not only for the Korean churches and mission community but also for the society at large. On the one hand, Korean churches and the mission community were blamed for their recklessness. On the other hand, the story caused controversy over how the government should carry out its responsibility to protect its citizens.

As Stanley Green mentioned, "In a fallen world, the church expects opposition and hostility." But we also believe, along with Rev. Green, that God's salvific work is accomplished when "the church stands in solidarity with poor and oppressed people."

Many of the kidnapped Korean aid workers stand in solidarity and have not lost their interest in serving the Afghan people. Since the incident, two of them were trained at our center, and from them, we heard many more stories unknown to the public.[15] In particular, one of those two became a missionary to Greece. Together with his wife, he planted a church and served the Afghan refugees faithfully. Unfortunately, he was killed in a traffic accident in 2017, while visiting Korea during the Christmas season. His life and his death testify that while the Afghan incident may have been passed over in the public eye, it has become a seed from which God's work for Afghanistan and its people has sprouted and is still growing. We would like to believe that it is yet another realization of Tertullian's prophetic words, "The blood of martyrs is the seed of the church."

We understand that the commitment of missionaries and the crises they face are directly connected to their duty. A missionary is not simply a private person but also a public representative of the church and mission community. The missionary's choices and decisions have implications for the society and a significant impact in kingdom work.

CRISIS MANAGEMENT POLICY OF MISSION AGENCIES

We are in complete agreement with Green regarding the problems with which he wrestled and the questions he posed as a leader of a mission community. As a responsible leader of a group, to what level of risk should he let their missionaries be exposed? What should guide the appropriate responses during crisis? All these questions are basically connected to the crisis management policies that the group has established. The basic issue is how to apply Jesus' word, "be wise as serpents and innocent as doves" (Matt. 10:16, ESV) into a practical context. It seems that Mennonite Mission Network (MMN) did the best they could in responding to the crisis that Al and his family faced. They showed prudence in a deeply challenging situation. They responded with full awareness of the risks and potential threats. Several years prior to Al's incident, MMN established the crisis management team and manual. The crisis management team did not act in isolation but solicited help from an international crisis consulting group, Crisis Consulting International (CCI). MMN maintained constant communication with Gladys Geiser, Al's wife, and other family members, which was very effective, in our view. While Green stated that "MMN's crisis response policies were helpful only to a small degree," undoubtedly those policies enabled MMN's swift response to the crisis situation.

In Korea, the Afghanistan hostage incident awoke the mission agencies to their need to create crisis management policies. As a result, Korea Crisis Management Service (KCMS) was established in 2010. In 2015, KCMS published *Missionary Crisis Management: Standard Policies and Manual*. The availability of crisis management policies is important. However, we need to remember that

---

15 The two individuals came to our center with their family and trained with their spouses as according to GMTC policy.

enforcement of policies should account for the character of the individuals involved. The policies anticipate various situations and affect a broad range of people, which makes it difficult for the policies to be comprehensive and cover minute details. Hence, the character, values, and standards of those who carry out the policies are as important as the policies themselves.

MISSIONARY MEMBER CARE

As evidenced in Al's crisis, MMN foresaw the possible stress and trauma caused by a crisis and took proper action, providing the needed care. Green's reflection, however, did not give details on how the psychological care was provided. Missionary care should be holistic, which includes but is not limited to physical, mental, social, and spiritual care.

On a practical level, missionaries should be able to care for themselves, while their family members, local churches, mission agencies, and member care organizations work to support the healing process. Ideally, a well-structured support system would be available to embrace and care for missionaries and respond to their practical needs. In the case of Al and Gladys, the home church seemed to play an important role. While member care should be deployed immediately upon the occurrence of a crisis, it should be done in the context of constant, regular member care, not only provided in times of crisis. Obviously, member care should also be provided continually after a crisis situation has ended, since trauma leaves a long-lasting psychological wound. In light of the above observations, effective missionary member care requires participation and cooperation among missionaries, their family members and relatives, local churches, mission agencies, and coworkers, as well as member care specialists and the relevant member care networks, all under God's sovereign care.

In the case of Korea, missionary member care still has a long way to go, even though the Afghanistan incident greatly increased awareness of its need. All the while, missionaries are still serving faithfully in the lands of their calling, even facing crises for the sake of expanding God's Kingdom. It is our hope that as we wrestle and struggle through the many issues that arise as we participate in God's mission, our efforts to provide excellent and effective member care will continue to progress, one step at a time.

QUESTIONS FOR REFLECTION

1. How should we embrace crisis and suffering when they accompany God's calling, and, in relation to this, what kind of responsibility does a missionary hold as a public representative of the church's mission?

2. In a crisis situation, what is the standard(s) that can guide a missionary who must make a decision, while seeking God's will (commitment) and considering practical concerns (e.g., safety)?

3. What is the limit of responsibility for missionaries, mission agencies, and sending churches as they establish and implement missionary crisis policies?

4. When should the appropriate missionary care start and stop, and to what extent should it be provided?

GOD'S WOUNDED SERVANTS: EXPLORING THE LIVED EXPERIENCE OF TRAUMA

by YOUNG OK KIM

All of us face some degree of suffering during the course of our lives. No one is exempt from it, including Christians who devote themselves to missions. Robert Grant stressed that a great number of missionaries may be frequently exposed to potentially traumatic events: "Being a missionary can be very dangerous … Overseas ministry can be peppered with years of direct experience with an exposure to crime, psychological intimidation, military and terrorist threats, kidnapping, armed coercion, torture, rape, and murder."[1] Currently, more than half of Korean missionaries serve in South East Asia, North Africa, and the Middle East, all of which are marked by unstable socioeconomic environments (e.g., poverty, high crime rates, and religious persecution).[2] Traumatic incidents often occur in these kinds of environments.[3] While working as a missionary from 1996 to 2005, I also witnessed many Korean missionaries suffering the losses of family members through accident; imprisonment; or physical, mental, emotional, and/or relational issues. Despite the frequency of Korean missionaries' experiences of trauma and the potential negative impact of those experiences, little research has been conducted on the nature of such suffering, particularly related to trauma among Korean missionaries. However, I never thought that I would be the one whom God calls to the member care of Korean missionaries, because I always desired to return to the mission field and work with the local people after finishing my studies in the USA.

GOD'S CALLING FOR MEMBER CARE

It was November 8, 2013 when I strongly sensed God's calling for me as a member caregiver for Korean missionaries. On that day, my missionary friend shared her own experience of trauma while serving on the mission field in the Middle East. She was imprisoned because of her missionary roommate's careless evangelism in the Muslim country and was unexpectedly deported from her mission field. After my friend returned to Korea, she suffered not only from that traumatic incident but also from a feeling of loneliness, not being understood or heard by others. It seemed to her that churches wanted to hear missionaries' success stories, not the stories of missionaries who were discouraged, hurt, and did not bear much fruit in their ministry. My friend asked me, "Who will listen to the wounded missionaries' stories and help them heal and become strengthened again to carry on the task God has given them?" At that time, I knew that through this friend, God was calling me to serve his wounded servants, and he had been training me in theology, missiology, psychology, and my own experience as a missionary, so that I could provide proper member care for Korean missionaries. I began praying and hoping that I could be God's instrument for the holistic healing of his wounded people until the day when he takes my last breath.

In this chapter, I will explore three Korean missionaries' experiences of trauma, including their suggestions for better member care for Korean missionaries. I will also discuss some implications for the effective training of member caregivers.

---

1 Robert Grant, "Trauma in Missionary Life," *Missiology: An International Review*, 23, no. 1 (1995): 71-83.

2 The Korea World Missions Association, "Statistics of Korea Missionaries as of December, 2017," *Korea Missions Quarterly* 17, no. 3 (Spring 2018): 138-145.

3 Robert W. Bagley, "Trauma and Traumatic Stress Among Missionaries," *Journal of Psychology and Theology* 31, no. 2 (2003): 97-112; Frauke Schaefer et al., "Traumatic Events and Posttraumatic Stress in Cross-cultural Mission Assignments," *Journal of Traumatic Stress* 20, no. 4 (2007): 529-539. doi:101002/jts.20240.

STORIES OF GOD'S WOUNDED SERVANTS

Here are Abraham's, Esther's, and Daniel's stories (their names were replaced with these pseudonyms). All of them are native-born Korean missionaries, and each of them experienced different types of trauma in different regions—the Middle East, Africa, and Asia. While these traumatic events were unexpected, the missionaries reported that in the face of them, they were unprepared, felt powerless, and remained unable to prevent the trauma.

Abraham's Story

Abraham has been serving in the Middle East with his family for eleven years, commissioned by a Korean denominational missions agency.

An unforgettable incident that I still remember happened around the sixth year of my work in the mission field. It was around 11 p.m. when I was kidnapped by four men in the vacant lot near my house. After being blindfolded and bound, I was driven to an undisclosed place, dragged from room to room, and eventually locked up in a rusted cell with iron bars, still not knowing why. Great fear arose inside me. Trains of fearful thoughts drove my mind, "Are they going to poison me? Are they going to make me lose consciousness through anesthetics and kill me?" With all of this in my mind, the only conclusion I could make was that whatever it may be, something terrible was going to happen to me. But I could not deny Jesus. The next morning, they interrogated me and led me to another room, while covering my eyes to take my picture and fingerprints. At that time, I overheard them saying that I had been arrested in suspicion of preaching the Gospel. On that day, I was released around noon, and my eyes were uncovered near the area of the intelligence head office. That was when I realized I had been kidnapped by the intelligence bureau. After that traumatic incident, I had to put a baseball bat by my bed for some kind of protection, I could not sing hymns or pray out loud at home as I had before, and I suffered from the fear of being kidnapped again. However, I stayed in that mission field for the next eight months and then returned to Korea for a sabbatical. When I visited my missions agency headquarters, I told them about my kidnapping, but they did not seem to consider it a serious concern because I had been released after fourteen hours unharmed. But from my perspective, I had been in peril of losing my life. The terror I had experienced was not something anyone else could fully understand because I had experienced it alone.

Esther's Story

Esther is a single missionary who has served for twenty-one years overseas and in Korea. She has been working with an international mission agency.

Two years after I began serving in the country Q in Africa, I had a car accident while traveling in a remote area with an outreach team from Korea. A male team member was driving the vehicle and did not see the truck parked on the street because it was night time and his sight was blinded by an oncoming vehicle's headlight. My left arm was smashed into pieces when our car and the truck collided. I tried hard to stay conscious with all my strength after the accident because I was the only person who could speak Swahili. After arriving in a hospital run by a German missionary, I lost consciousness. The next morning when I woke up, I found that my left arm was gone. After the car accident, I began to ask, "Why did such things happened to a missionary like me? Did I commit some great sin? What did I do wrong?" I felt like God had abandoned me. Then, I returned to Korea for treatment. A pastor came for a visit while I was hospitalized and said, "It must not be terribly inconvenient, since it's your left arm rather than your right arm." How can a pastor say something like that? I was very upset. I thought that the pastor was trying to encourage me that I was fortunate not to have lost my right arm, but I felt that it would have been better if he had not come. One of the most challenging things after the accident was that I felt like there was no one who was willing to listen to me. People came and shared their struggles with me because of my role as a pastor in the church, when I really wanted to tell them that I was having an extremely difficult time as well. I could not lay down the burden in my heart for two years. I felt so lonely and uncared for.

Daniel's Story

Daniel is affiliated with a Korean missions organization and has been serving in Asia with his family for twenty years.

While serving on the mission field, our family experienced an earthquake that resulted in around 500,000 deaths and 3,000 aftershocks. We would hear the walls rattling and would push our bodies against them in the direction from which the quake was coming. My daughter's MK school was in the region of the earthquake as well. The school itself was ok, but dead bodies were carried to the lot in front of the school by helicopters, and the students saw this. I think my daughter saw it, too, and that might have been when her eating disorder began. She was twelve years old at the time. Then, two years after the earthquake, my wife was diagnosed with cancer. So, our family returned to Korea for two years for my wife's surgery and treatment. About eight months after we returned to the mission field, the school doctor and the administrators at my daughter's MK school informed my wife and me that my daughter's bulimia and purging were so severe that her life was at risk. We were strongly encouraged to leave the mission field immediately to save my daughter's life and get treatment for her. However, our missions board in Korea told us that we could not change our mission under any circumstances. It felt like I had no choice. We could not leave or stay. Eventually the principle of the MK school wrote a letter to our missions board, and our family was able to move a country where my daughter could receive good treatment for two years, after which we were moved to a new mission field. I felt like I had failed as a missionary and as a husband and father. With this, I fell into depression, but because I had to care for my daughter and wife, I tried my best not to show any signs of it.

COPING WITH TRAUMA

Although all three missionaries coped with their trauma differently, common themes that emanated from the interviews indicated both negative and positive coping strategies, including religious coping strategies. They used the more negative coping strategies (e.g., self-blame, minimization/avoidance, isolating oneself) in the early stage of their trauma, and they eventually switched to more positive coping strategies (acceptance, positive thinking, sharing with others, getting social support, and seeking mental health). Abraham stated that after his release from his abductors, he avoided any anxiety provoking situations and minimized the negative impact of the incident, although he suffered from the symptoms of Posttraumatic Stress Disorder (PTSD). Esther reported isolating herself from others for years because she felt she was not being understood or heard by others. Daniel blamed himself for his family's suffering from the cancer and the eating disorder.

However, all three missionaries reported that they gradually began to use more positive coping methods and to share their stories with others, with the support of their Christian communities and mental health professionals. Abraham and Daniel shared that the love they received from Christian coworkers really helped them overcome times of suffering. Esther reported that sharing her experience with others was very helpful. She commented, "I had a chance to open up to an old British missionary couple that knew all about my situation, and I felt safe. It took almost two years for me to be able to reveal my wounds and openly process them with others." Abraham and Daniel reported that receiving help from mental health providers was the biggest help to them in processing their feelings and thoughts related to their traumas and moving on with their ministries. Unfortunately, they had to seek out professional help themselves because their mission agency did not provide any counseling for trauma.

All three missionaries also reported having used religious coping methods, both negative and positive, after experiencing their trauma. The negative religious coping pattern involved questioning God and faith and thinking that they deserved the trauma as punishment from God, while the positive methods included fostering a sense of spiritual connectedness with God and others through prayer and God's word. Their religious coping strategies changed over time from negative coping methods to positive ones. Abraham shared that Matthew 28:20 was a great comfort to him while experiencing unbearable fear and anxiety: "This passage really touched my heart. Even though nobody knew about my situation and what exactly was going to happen to me, I was at peace because of his promise; I knew God was with me." Esther also shared that her initial thoughts about the car accident were, "'Did I commit any great sin? What did I do wrong?' However, while I was meditating on Romans 5:8 about God's love—[that he loved us] while we were still sinners—I came to understand that in this situation, asking the question, 'Oh, does God really love me?' is quite foolish."

SUGGESTIONS FOR MEMBER CARE

At the end of each interview, missionaries were asked if they had any suggestions to improve member care for Korean missionaries. Most of them shared suggestions based on their own experiences. The common themes that emerged from the interviews can be categorized into three main areas of need: (1) better member care systems, (2) active prevention and crisis intervention, and (3) more mental health professionals.

Desire for Better Member Care Systems. All three missionaries described an urgent need for having a better-established member care system as a starting point of member care and development. Abraham and Daniel shared that international sending agencies probably do a better job with member care (e.g., offering psychotherapy when it is needed) than Korean denominational and missions agencies. Daniel commented, "Our mission organization has a very short history, unlike OM, WEC, or SIM that have more experience. These international organizations have more methods of helping out the missionaries in difficulties, while our organization has no experience in solving problems." Esther also shared that her international mission agency lacks in member care compared to other international mission agencies. However, she believes that the international missions agencies are usually more aware of the need for member care and have better strategies than the Korean denominational or missions agencies. Daniel reported struggling to find and connect with an appropriate counselor for his daughter when she was desperate for help: "When the missionary him- or herself has to figure out how to find help, it can take a very long time, resulting in many missionaries leaving without receiving counseling … I wish information on mission care was more readily available."

Desire for Active Prevention and Crisis Intervention. Abraham discussed what could be done to prevent missionaries from experiencing mental and emotional issues. He suggested proactive education on the importance of mental health for Korean missionaries: "We get treatment for physical wounds. But we're not used to getting check-ups to diagnose and treat wounds of our heart." He also strongly argued the importance of immediate intervention when a missionary is experiencing trauma and right after the incident occurs. Both Abraham and Daniel had to seek mental health professionals' help on their own because their sending mission agencies did not see the need for them to receive treatment for their trauma.

Desire for More Trained Mental Health Providers. Abraham, Esther, and Daniel all reported the need for mental health providers who understand a missionary's life and spirituality, as well as those who are well trained in mental health. Esther shared her personal story that she felt no one could understand her struggles when she came back to Korea after her left arm was amputated. She noted, "It's very hard for regular people to provide missionaries counseling. It's because there's no common ground. We need professionals who are specialized in counseling missionaries, and we need to raise them up." Abraham also commented, "I was able to connect with the psychiatrist, and the doctor diagnosed my traumatic stress level. I had been diagnosed and treated, which included medication, which I really needed at that time to manage my PTSD symptoms."

AN EFFECTIVE TRAINING MODEL FOR KOREAN MISSIONARIES

Based on the three missionaries' traumatic experiences and suggestions, I created a training model for mental health providers (e.g., psychiatrists, psychotherapists, and counselors) who plan to work with Korean missionaries. To offer effective member care for Korean missionaries, mental health providers need to be knowledgeable and aware of four aspects: psychology, theology, culture, and missionary life.

Figure 13.1. Four Aspects of Background Knowledge Necessary for Missionary Mental Health Providers

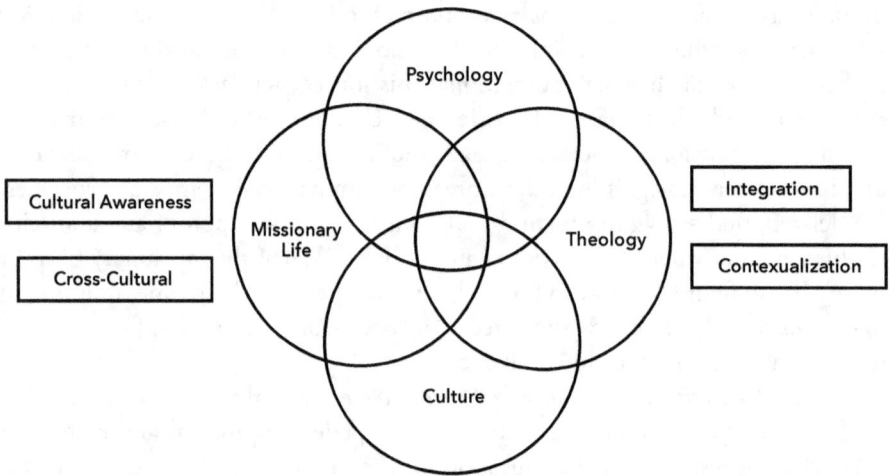

Integration of Psychology and Theology. When Korean missionaries face challenges and traumatic incidents, the initial thought that may come to their minds is that they have not sacrificed themselves for God and his mission enough or that they have done something wrong. Otherwise, God would have protected their families from being harmed while serving on the mission field. This belief may lead Korean missionaries to find the reasons for their suffering in their sin or wrongdoing. They tend to use the religious methods of prayer and

Scripture reading heavily because, compared to Western missionaries, they focus more on the spiritual aspect of their suffering than on the psychological aspects. Therefore, the importance of adequately preparing mental health providers for Korean missionaries to address spiritual and religious issues in their clinical work cannot be underestimated. They should not only be trained in psychology, but should also understand Korean missionaries' theological perspectives on suffering and hardship. Clinicians who plan to work exclusively with Korean missionaries should ensure that they receive ongoing training related to the integration of faith and mental health.

Cultural Awareness and Cross-Cultural Experience. It is critical that mental health providers for member care should be able to understand the unique life of a missionary—the stress and challenges they face on the mission field. Esther said that the best training for member caregivers is to experience cross-cultural stress and struggles. Particularly, being exposed to cross-cultural settings could be helpful for creating a better understanding of a missionary's life. Furthermore, there is also a great need for more bilingual mental health providers, as many missionary kids struggle to express their emotions and thoughts in Korean. Daniel strongly emphasized the importance of having a bilingual therapist for a Korean missionary family whose children do not speak Korean fluently and whose parents have difficulty speaking English. He commented, "The sessions were done in English, and because I was not fluent in English, every time I was brought up in the conversation, I felt guilty. I felt like she would be talking badly about me and that everything happened because of me." If mental health providers were bilingual and had cross-cultural experience (or were at least willing to learn about other cultures), it would greatly help Korean missionary families.

Contextualization. Most current member care systems and therapy materials developed thus far are for North Americans. Therefore, mental health providers for member care need to know how to contextualize the Western-oriented therapy approaches into the Korean cultural context, as well as the missionary culture. For example, Korean missionaries tend to express their emotional distress (e.g., depression and anxiety) through somatic symptoms, while Westerners emphasize affective complaints primarily. Another Korean cultural aspect that mental health providers need to take into consideration when addressing Korean missionaries is traditional gender roles. In many households, the husband serves as the head of the family and makes all major decisions. In addition, many Korean missionaries strongly believe that problems should be resolved within the family. Therefore, when missionary kids seek professional help outside the family without telling their parents, parents may be offended. Mental health providers, particularly Western member care givers, must take into consideration the individual's and/or family's experience of hierarchy within the Korean context. This consideration will aid in devising the most effective strategy for easing Korean missionaries' fear.

CONCLUSION

The growth of the missionary movement in Korea is well known. Currently, Korea is one of the major missionary sending countries in the world. However, this remarkable growth has not been seen as all positive.[4] Korean churches have heavily focused on the number of missionaries being sent to the mission field. As a result, many Korean missionaries have not been sufficiently cared for by their sending churches and mission agencies. They have had to survive on their own. There is an urgent need to develop a member care system for Korean missionaries that is culturally relevant and sensitive. Specifically, to help Korean missionaries effectively, the mental health providers need to be trained not only in psychology, but also in theology, missionary life, and cross-cultural awareness. Currently, there are few opportunities for member caregivers to receive this type of holistic training. When the sending/supporting churches and mission agencies are willing to invest their finances and time in the development of member care and more well-trained professionals commit their lives to member care, we may keep Korean missionaries from preventable attrition and enhance their well-being not only physically but also emotionally, relationally, and spiritually.

RESPONSE by PAMELA DAVIS

The chapter presented by Dr. Kim, "God's Wounded Servants: Exploring the Lived Experiences of Trauma," highlights the significance of traumatic experiences Korean missionaries encounter. Dr. Kim proposes that the rapid growth in numbers of Korean missionaries, coupled with the inherent dangers of missionary work, have led to experiences of missionary trauma being inadequately addressed. Further, she suggests the need to design and implement a robust program of member care for Korean missionaries, including professionally trained counselors who are bilingual. In this brief response, I will seek to amplify the need for bilingual, professionally trained counselors, and I will promote the need for enhanced pre-field assessment and pre-field training for Korean missionaries.

During my twenty-two years as a missionary in Asia, I experienced firsthand the need for professionally trained Korean counselors, as I often had the opportunity to counsel Korean families at both *The Well* and *Cornerstone Counseling* in Chiang Mai, Thailand. I soon realized that my inability to speak Korean left me at a disadvantage to understand the family context. My lack of understanding also created a disadvantage for the Korean families I served, as it was difficult to apply my Western counseling training to the Korean family experience. I often found

---

4   Steve S. C. Moon, "The Recent Korean Missionary Movement: A Record of Growth, and More Growth Needed," *International Bulletin of Missionary Research* 27 (2003), no. 1: 11-17; Steve S. C. Moon, "The Protestant Missionary Movement in Korea: Current Growth and Development," *International Bulletin of Missionary Research* 32 (2008), no. 2: 59-64.

myself thinking, "I'm missing something, but I don't know what!" Although we had one bilingual Korean counselor on our staff at *Cornerstone,* there were far more Korean missionaries seeking counseling than one person could manage.

Indeed, the need for bilingual, professionally trained counselors requires a sustained and cooperative effort among missionary sending agencies, on-field missionary counseling centers, and universities. Universities and missionary sending agencies could collaborate to create scholarship programs that support Korean students who wish to become missionary counselors. Sending agencies could identify current missionaries who desire counselor training and could subsequently support an extended study leave for them. On-field counseling centers such as *The Well* and *Cornerstone* in Thailand or *Olive Tree* in Turkey could designate a number of current internships for Korean interns, so that the constructs of psychology, theology, culture, and missionary life may be integrated during training. This proposed multidimensional solution, which requires a long-term perspective, has the potential to yield long-term benefits.

Moving beyond the member care suggestions proposed by Dr. Kim, I would go further to promote the importance of pre-field assessment and pre-field training for Korean missionaries. Robust pre-field assessment will allow sending agencies to understand how missionaries with traumatic experiences in childhood might respond to future traumatic events. This is not to suggest that missionary candidates with experiences of childhood trauma should be rejected for missionary service; instead, this knowledge will allow sending agencies to provide better support to their missionaries. Several prior studies have suggested that organizational support, and in particular pre-field training, enhances a missionary's ability to be resilient after experiencing negative on-field events.[5] Therefore, I would propose that pre-field training should include a focus on coping with stress and trauma, as well as an understanding of how adverse childhood events impact adult functioning.

May Dr. Kim's research become a call to action for those who care for, support, and send Korean missionaries. While concerted efforts have been made to increase the availability of member care services to Korean missionaries, it seems more needs to be done. Missionary counseling centers, sending agencies, and universities could seek to intentionally support professional counseling training for bilingual Koreans, thereby creating a clear path for trained mental health professionals to serve Korean missionaries on the field. Truly, it is bilingual member care workers, professionally trained in counseling, who will be most able to provide contextualized care, as Dr. Kim emphasized.

Additionally, Korean missionary sending agencies may wish to consider the importance of pre-field assessment and pre-field training as ways to promote

---

5   Claire Camp et al., "Missionary Perspectives on the Effectiveness of Current Missionary Practices," *Journal of Psychology and Theology* 42, no. 4, (2014): 359-368; Cynthia Erikson et al., "Social Support, Organisational Support, and Religious Support in Relation to Burnout in Expatriate Humanitarian Aid Workers," *Mental Health, Religion & Culture* 12, no. 7 (2009): 671-686.

resilience among their cross-cultural workers. As has been noted by missionary researchers, there is little that we can do to prevent exposure to traumatic events that so many missionaries seem to experience.[6] Traumatic experiences are common in the dangerous places that missionaries serve. There is *much* that we can do, however, to promote resilience among Korean missionaries.

QUESTIONS FOR REFLECTION

1. How do you grapple with the theological issue presented by Dr. Kim that we are all called to suffer, but that those who are suffering need member care?
2. What barriers do you see to having more professionally trained Korean member care workers?
3. What barriers do you see to implementing a more robust pre-field assessment and training process?

---

6   Robert Bagley, "Trauma and Traumatic Stress Among Missionaries," *Journal of Psychology and Theology* 31 (2003): 97–112; Frauke Schaefer et al., "Traumatic Events and Posttraumatic Stress in Cross-cultural Mission Assignments," *Journal of Traumatic Stress* 20, no. 4 (2007): 529-539. doi:101002/jts.20240.

14

SPIRITUAL RESOURCES IN DEALING WITH TRAUMA

by FRAUKE C. SCHAEFER AND CHARLES A. SCHAEFER

Missionaries leaving for cross-cultural ministry expect hard work, challenging cultural adjustments, spiritual battles, and often poverty. They may not always be aware that Christian work in various host countries also includes higher exposure to serious health risks, accidents, crime, violence, and even persecution. Studying the frequency of traumatic events among missionaries, we found that compared to sending countries, certain overseas locations pose a much higher risk of severe and recurrent traumatic events. An overwhelming majority of missionaries in West Africa, 71.1 percent of men and 64.2 percent of women, experienced more than three severe traumatic events in their lifetime.[1] In comparison, in the US, only 9.5

---

1 Frauke C. Schaefer, Dan G. Blazer, Karen F. Carr, Kathryn M. Connor, Bruce Burchett, Charles A. Schaefer, and Jonathan R. T. Davidson, "Traumatic Events and Posttraumatic Stress in Cross-Cultural Mission Assignments," *Journal of Traumatic Stress* 20 (2007): 534–535.

percent of men and 5.0 percent of women experienced that level of trauma.[2] In West Africa, 20.6 percent of missionaries suffered post-traumatic distress that affected their relationships and ministry, with women generally being more affected than men.[3] In two very high-risk sub-groups, as many as 28 percent were affected with post-traumatic distress.[4] Trauma is a reality in missionary service. Our organizations, as well as our workers, need to be prepared for it. The awareness of spiritual resources to deal effectively with trauma is key for missionaries and their supporters. God desires to be with us in suffering. He entered it himself, and by doing so made way for new life. Effective support deepens the connection with God and makes way for growth in suffering. Growth, in turn, promotes health and resilience.

The mental overload after severe trauma not only affects human minds psychologically (intrusive, numbing, and hyperarousal symptoms), but also spiritually. The emotional effect of trauma can make it hard to feel connected to God. Besides this, trauma challenges our deepest convictions about God, ourselves, others, our purpose, and calling. It rattles our spiritual foundations and pushes us into wrestling with life's deepest questions. These impacts can shake the spiritual foundations of Christians in ministry. Missionaries and their supporters need to be equipped with resources that help them journey together through the emotional and spiritual struggles caused by trauma.

CASE STUDY A

After an armed robbery occurred in their home one night, a missionary couple and their young children were deeply shaken. Understandably, they did not feel safe at home any longer, and they found it difficult to sleep. Sounds and flashlights in the dark set off strong stress responses, because they triggered memories of the robbery. Though desperately needed, the comforting presence of the Lord was hard for them to sense, even though they fled to him in prayer. Why did God feel distant right now? Had he not promised to be with them in trouble and to send his angels to watch over them? Why had he allowed this? They suddenly felt very alone and in need of trustworthy companions. They felt vulnerable and weak, as well as upset and in pain.[5]

Spiritual Resources—Community, Grace, Lament

A key spiritual resource traumatized workers need is a supportive Christian community, able to respond to their vulnerability and weakness with grace and prepared to accompany them in a way that helps them reconnect with God.

---

2   R. C. Kessler, A. Sonnega, E. Bromet, M. Hughes, and C. B. Nelson, "Post-Traumatic Stress Disorder in the National Comorbidity Survey," *Archives of General Psychiatry* 12 (1995): 1048-1060.

3   F. C. Schaefer, et al., "Traumatic Events and Posttraumatic Stress," 536.

4   Ibid.

5   For confidentiality and illustration purposes, case studies in this chapter are adapted and are a composite of multiple missionary stories.

1. *Community—when alone and afraid.* When trust is shattered after trauma such as this robbery, the very presence of trustworthy companions will provide comfort and a sense of being securely held and connected. This tangible presence often becomes the gateway for feeling God's presence again, too. The supportive community must first be present, provide practical support such as safe shelter, and attend to physical needs like food, drink, and medical care. It also needs to assist in crisis care and essential communication. For Paul, the first missionary, the mere presence of believers after his stoning had a hugely restorative effect: "But after the disciples had gathered around him, he got up and went back into the city" (Acts 14:20). Research shows that the severity of post-traumatic stress reactions is buffered by effective community support.[6] Building supportive communities on the field and establishing crisis care protocols are excellent preparations for harvesting this benefit. Above all, it pleases the Lord, whose greatest desire is that his followers love each other (Matt. 22:35–40). There are potential pitfalls if supporters would provide well-meant advice or speak biblical truth prematurely, before attentive listening. The traumatized first need to be heard in their distress, doubts, and questions. Only then will they be ready to receive advice. Our souls feel more warmly and securely held by people who listen, understand, and connect with our experiences. In entering human suffering our Lord, himself, gave us this great gift of being able to "empathize with our weaknesses" (Heb. 4:15). People start to heal when they realize that the Lord and human companions understand and connect with them in their pain and weakness.

Organizational applications: An important way in which a caring community can buffer post-traumatic stress is by relieving the person for a time from some ongoing responsibilities.[6] This relief assures that the person has time to process, rest, and heal. Healing may require counseling care. Since isolated placements and very small teams can make community support very challenging, and taking time away could be detrimental to ministry, organizations sending missionaries into trauma-prone areas do well to intentionally place them as teams, so that teammates can support and stand in for each other when someone needs time to recover.

2. *Grace—when vulnerable and weak.* Most people do not want to feel or appear vulnerable or weak, so they go to great lengths to repress and hide it when it occurs. Traumatic trigger reactions create fear, a sense of being out of control, and feeling weak. This is often hard to accept for those affected. However, experiences of weakness are human. When Jesus entered our humanity, he, himself, experienced vulnerability and weakness, and because of it reached out to the Father and his disciples for support: In Gethsemane he sweats, prays urgently, and seeks prayer support while facing suffering and death. When our hearts start to judge missionaries for "sweating" or expressing weakness after stress and trauma, we are not in line with

---

6 C. R. Brewin, B. Andrew, and J. D. Valentine, "Meta-analysis of Risk Factors for Posttraumatic Stress Disorder in Trauma-exposed Adults," *Journal of Consulting and Clinical Psychology* 68 (2002): 748-766.

this biblical understanding of humanity. Superhuman expectations of missionaries are unrealistic. In fact, vulnerability is part of God's design: "But we have this treasure in jars of clay to show that this all-surpassing power is from God and not from us" (2 Cor. 4:7). This design is most effective at making the glory of Christ known in this world. We serve the one who said to Paul, "My grace is sufficient for you, for my power is made perfect in weakness" (2 Cor. 12:9). We tend to assume we will bring the most honor to God by remaining strong and unperturbed in suffering. However, according to the Bible, spiritual strength grows as love and grace are received in weakness. Only by reaching out to God and others, showing vulnerability just like our Lord, will our hearts become filled and empowered. This takes the focus away from us and our human strength and puts it straight on the Lord and his glory.

We marvel at the wisdom displayed in Kintsukuroi (golden repair), the centuries-old Japanese art form of fixing broken pottery with a special lacquer dusted with gold and silver. It clearly recognizes the brokenness of the object and beautifully incorporates its repair instead of covering it up. God's intent with us is similar. We do not need to cover up brokenness, but instead let it be seen and touched by the Great Artist and his earthly followers. As broken pieces yield to gentle hands, so traumatized people experience safety in grace-filled relationships. Graceful supporters will accept raw emotions from missionaries, such as fear, anger, doubt, guilt, and sadness, with understanding, comfort, and normalization rather than with criticism or judgment. After feeling understood and cared about, sufferers will open their hearts with increasing trust. The golden art of loving with Christ's grace will deeply affect and encourage the traumatized person.

It is hard to be with sufferers in places of turmoil. We may be tempted to tell them "you should not feel like that" or "you should not think like that," and try to apply a "quick fix" to their distress. We need to remember that we are standing on "holy ground" when we love and encourage a vulnerable person. The Lord is present with both the sufferer and the supporter. God is certainly involved in his work of repair and growth, even if it is not immediately obvious.

Suffering and traumatized workers often feel shame and fear judgment for their frailties by their families, supporters, and organizations. They cannot perform as they would like to. The more their distress is met by a social culture of grace, the more likely they are to heal and grow. One way to build a grace-filled culture in a church or organization is to provide information about normal responses to trauma (emotionally and spiritually) and to explore with them biblically how the Lord works in the midst of suffering.[7]

---

7 F. C. Schaefer and C. A. Schaefer, eds., *Trauma and Resilience: A Handbook* (Fresno, CA: Condeo Press, 2012); Korean translation: *Suffering and Grace* (Seoul: Timothy Publishing House, 2016). Relevant sections: Karen Carr, "Normal Reactions After Trauma," 43ff and Appendix B "Common Reactions to Trauma," 201ff; Scott Shaum, "Reflections on a Theology of Suffering," 1ff.

3. *Lament—when upset and in pain.* The missionary family that was robbed not only lost the items that were taken from their home, but also their sense of safety and their belief that the Lord would safeguard them while they ministered. All losses hurt, and an experience that seems to indicate that the Lord is not fulfilling dearly held expectations is upsetting and confusing. Imagine missionary parents who bury their children due to consequences of being on the mission field! The enormous pain of losing a child will be compounded by weighty questions asked of God, such as, "Why did you allow this? Where were you?" The missionary parents may experience self-doubts about their decision to serve overseas. There will likely be hurt and anger. Intense upset and pain make it hard to connect with others and God. This is where the practice of lament helps.

In lament, pain and upset are expressed outwards, rather than held inside. When people hold strong emotions in, a part of them disconnects and withdraws. Expressing strong feelings, however, can help to reconnect. In prayers of lament, the sufferer, at times together with a group, brings distress and petitions to God. The Psalms are full of raw expressions of pain, upset, doubt, and anger.[8] As the sufferer gives words to feelings in the presence of God and others, connections are rebuilt. Answers to weighty questions are not needed at this point, since lament accomplishes what is most important: restored connections. As we see in the Psalms (e.g., Psalm 73), once connection is restored, changes in emotions and perceptions happen in due course. This is why encouraging lament, providing resources for lament, and lamenting together are such vital spiritual resources after trauma and loss. Listening to lament surely needs our willingness to hear emotions that are neither "positive" nor harmonious. Imagining these feelings as released into the heart of God, who has an immeasurable capacity to hold, keep, and return his love and promises, will help us to be present with the sufferer, and not take the weight of suffering onto our own hearts or shoulders. Then we can stand together in hope for God's loving and patient work.

CASE STUDY B

After the church shooting that killed national Christians and injured expatriate workers, the faithful missionary felt emotionally numb. The carnage she had witnessed was completely overwhelming. She felt "bad" about not feeling much, when she thought she "should" feel much more. She also felt a long way away from God. Had he abandoned her? Was he punishing her for something she had done wrong? What on earth was God doing? The shooter happened to be a person she had known, somebody to whom her team had ministered. What a betrayal! He had used the information gained about the church to harm them. She noticed anger rising in herself and vengeful imaginations flooding her mind. She knew she should forgive and had the earnest desire to do so. But, right now, honestly, she would not have minded taking revenge. She thought it was horrible that she even

---

8   F. C. Schaefer and C. A. Schaefer, eds., "Spiritual Resources in Dealing with Trauma," in *Trauma and Resilience: A Handbook* (Fresno, CA: Condeo Press, 2012), 157-162.

felt this way. She tried hard to forgive and felt at times that she had succeeded. But did her bouts of anger with memories of the shooting mean she had not forgiven and perhaps was disobedient to the Lord?

Spiritual Resources—Reconnecting with God, Remembering God's Truth, Forgiving

After trauma, emotions are often numbed, or shut down. Not only that, the way we think about the world, God, and ourselves is shaken up. Relationships can be affected by anger and distrust, depending on who seems responsible for what happened: the perpetrator(s), God, or ourselves.

1. *Reconnecting with God—when numb and depressed.* Shut down, numbed emotions effectively protect humans from becoming overwhelmed with shame, fear, and pain. Unfortunately, numbing also shuts down the experience of peace and joy. Many of us notice the presence of God through the peace and joy it creates in our hearts. However, when hearts are like dull musical instruments that cannot sound the tones of peace and joy any longer, we can easily confuse the absence of the tone with the absence of its origin, God's presence. How can we help someone with a dull emotional instrument, such as the missionary after the shooting, to connect with the abiding presence of the Lord?

Jesus tended to his traumatized disciples on the road to Emmaus (Luke 24: 13–35). They had just witnessed the violence and humiliation of their master and friend on the cross. Jesus listened a lot, asked questions, and gradually opened their understanding. Though they walked together for hours, they were unable to recognize him. Only when Jesus broke the bread were they able to see him for who he was. One reason for this is neurobiological. Numbed trauma victims can feel safe and connected when they tap into this reality with their senses (seeing, hearing, touching, smelling, tasting). That certainly happened with the breaking of the bread. Before their trauma, the disciples had enjoyed deep connection with the Lord when breaking bread. Upon arrival in Emmaus they saw, touched, and tasted the broken bread again, which allowed them to connect emotionally with Jesus' presence. In a similar way, we can help traumatized missionaries to reconnect with the Lord's presence. We can ask them: "What helped you in the past to feel the Lord's presence? Is there a song, an image, a verse, an experience of God's faithfulness and presence? How about communion?" When the person has identified what helped, we can then encourage him or her to sing or listen to the song they named, look at the image or imagine it, read the verse, connect with the experience, or partake in communion. The renewed realization of connection will bring hope, comfort, and strength. When people are unable to regain a feeling of connection with God, we can gently remind them that the abiding spiritual reality is the Lord's ongoing presence around them and that the Holy Spirit is present in them, even when they cannot feel him because of their numbed emotions.

2. *Remembering God's truth—when feeling punished or abandoned.* Difficulty feeling God's presence during a very painful time can lead to a sense of abandonment at the very moment when God is needed most. This is a very confusing experience for believers! Our human minds race to all sorts of explanations to make sense of it. Some conclude that God has withdrawn because he is displeased with them or their actions. The conclusion that the painful incident is a punishment for a sin is then not far off; and doubting God's love comes soon after. Research shows that a sense of abandonment or punishment by God and doubting his love ("negative religious coping") worsen the level of distress after adverse life events.[9]

How can we respond when Christians struggle with this sense of abandonment? Jesus cried out "My God, my God, why have you forsaken me?" (Matt. 27:46) when the sin of the world was placed upon him. He certainly understands abandonment. We can encourage Christians to bring their sense of abandonment to the Lord, which usually creates renewed connection. Also, there are many biblical promises assuring believers of the abiding presence of the Lord (e.g., Isa. 49:15-16). Those promises can be gently spoken as assurance.

How about the sense of being punished by the Lord? Though suffering can be a consequence of sin, the Gospel affirms that Jesus already paid the penalty for all our sins. When Jesus was asked by his disciples about the man born blind, he said: "Neither this man nor his parents sinned, but this happened so that the works of God might be displayed in him" (John 9:3). Looking at the blind man before him, Jesus did not focus on any past sins, but on the opportunity this suffering brought for the work of God in this man's life. Though God sometimes imposes painful consequences for sinful behavior as an effort to turn our hearts back to him, the Bible clearly shows that suffering and sin are not directly related (e.g., Job). Though interpreting trauma generally as punishment may seem to provide a sense of order or control in chaotic circumstances, assuming that all suffering results from sin is not biblical.

All missionaries will be better prepared for trauma if they study the Bible and personally grapple with a biblical theology of suffering.[10] Understanding it before facing trauma will greatly aid them in the confusion after trauma. Talking about theological matters to people who have been recently hurt, is usually not very helpful. And the frequent "why"- questions (e.g., "Why did you allow this to happen, God?") typically are not questions of the mind, but rather outcries of a soul in pain. Outcries, initially, need presence. Later, theological input is more fruitful.

3. *Forgiving—when hurt and betrayed by another.* When trust is broken, and mutual commitment betrayed, the personal, relational violation will add severity to the impact of the trauma. Anger, rage, vengefulness, or bitterness will add

---

9 K. I. Pargament, B. W. Smith, H. G. Koenig, and L. Perez, "Patterns of Positive and Negative Coping with Major Life Stressors," *Journal for the Scientific Study of Religion* 37 (1998): 710-724.

10 See Scott Shaum, "Reflections on a Theology of Suffering," in *Trauma and Resilience: A Handbook,* F. C. Schaefer and C. A. Schaefer, eds. (Fresno, CA: Condeo Press, 2012), 1ff, Appendix A. Worksheet, 197.

emotional pain on top of traumatic distress. Research shows that hostility and anger are associated with increased post-traumatic symptoms, while the ability to forgive is associated with less.[11] In his teachings, Jesus emphasized the importance of forgiveness and linked asking for God's forgiveness with our willingness to extend forgiveness to those who offend us: "And forgive us our debts, as we forgive our debtors" (Matt. 6:12, KJV). Certainly, the Lord's emphasis on forgiving is with our benefit in mind. Working toward forgiveness is vital for healing; however, with interpersonal trauma and betrayal, as in the church shooting, it is more challenging than we may expect. Understanding of the forgiveness process can help when we accompany people who seem to be stuck along the way. In our counseling work, we meet Christians who tell us about being violated and quickly add, "but I have forgiven." Their ongoing emotional struggles, however, tell a different story. Would it not be great if we could just decide in our minds to forgive and it would be done? With abuse or violence by a trusted person, the pain can be so deep that the victim has a desire to "just move beyond it." However, forgiving without fully facing the relational hurt and betrayal is like using a short-cut in a race. For a short moment, we feel as if we arrived at the desired goal, only to realize we need to return and take the longer path forward. The violated person may not be ready, yet, to face the intense anger and rage within and may wonder whether feeling such emotions would be acceptable for a Christian. Consider: What did Jesus feel when he saw his Father's House violated and misused by salespeople? He certainly felt anger! Feeling anger often indicates that something we are experiencing does not seem right. Without feeling anger, we may not find the vigor to resist, confront, and set limits. Similarly, with hurt: When we are unable to feel hurt, we may stay in a destructive situation too long. After letting hurt and anger into their hearts, victims usually can work through them and then let them go for God's sake, surrendering revenge into his just and trustworthy hands. However, after forgiving once, it is common that the same feelings recur with memories or triggers related to the trauma. This is not a sign of unforgiveness, but rather that, as humans, we need to retrace our steps of forgiveness again and again when we become newly aware of other aspects of the injury, or when our pain grows again. Intentionally forgiving helps the forgiver to heal, and over time, it will become easier to forgive.[12]

A frequent misunderstanding is a belief that biblical forgiveness necessarily includes reconciliation, meaning the full restoration of the original relationship. It does not! The wisdom of reconciliation should be considered after forgiving. Reconciliation requires the offender's true acknowledgment of responsibility for

---

11 C. V. O. Witvliet, K. A. Phipps, M. E. Feldman, and J. C. Beckham, "Posttraumatic Mental and Physical Health Correlates of Forgiveness and Religious Coping in Military Veterans," *Journal of Traumatic Stress* 17 (2004): 269-273.

12 For more details about the forgiveness process, see F. C. Schaefer and C. A. Schaefer, eds., "Spiritual Resources in Dealing with Trauma," in *Trauma and Resilience: A Handbook*, 162-168.

the offense (not just a superficial "sorry" or excuse), and sincere (not manipulatively stated) commitment to change. Once those conditions are met, trust building can gradually be attempted.[13]

CONCLUDING REMARKS

Effective emotional and spiritual support for missionaries after trauma is characterized by a supportive Christian community responding to vulnerability and weakness with grace and encouraging lament before God and trusted people. Effective support assists missionaries in emotionally connecting with God and gently reorients them to God's truth, supports developing a biblically based theology of suffering prior to further risk exposure, and accompanies people in the forgiveness process. In difficult circumstances in which the traumatized person's distress is severe or does not resolve, effective support includes the encouragement to pursue professional Christian counseling.

RESPONSE by MEESAENG CHOI AND HUNN CHOI

INTRODUCTION

As Drs. Frauke and Charles Schaefer point out, trauma is a reality in missionary service. Numerous articles, magazines, and books deal with the issue of missionary trauma. As we began writing this response paper, we entered "missionaries" + "trauma" into the Google search engine to see how many results we would find: 544,000 results! Using Asbury Seminary's library search tool, "trauma" appears as part of the title of an academic journal 194,384 times; of a magazine, 66,089 times; and of a book, 8,496 times.[14]

Numerous approaches to dealing with trauma exist, but the Schaefers have chosen a spiritual one: "Missionaries and their supporters need to be equipped with resources [especially, spiritual resources] that help them journey together through the emotional and spiritual struggles caused by trauma." They view mental and emotional overload not merely as psychological problems but primarily as spiritual ones: "Trauma challenges our deepest convictions about God, ourselves, others, our purpose, and calling. It rattles our spiritual foundations and pushes us into wrestling with life's deepest questions." The Schaefers believe, "Effective support deepens the connection with God and makes way for growth in suffering. Growth, in turn, promotes health and resilience," of which both are also key issues for missionaries. In their paper, they present all together six spiritual resources

---

13 See footnote 12. See also: Lewis Smedes, *Forgive and Forget* (New York: HarperCollins, 1996).

14 Frauke C. Schaefer and Charles A. Schaefer are the editors of, as well as contributors to, the book, *Trauma & Resilience: Effectively Supporting Those Who Serve God* (Fresno, CA: Condeo Press, 2012).

with two fictitious case studies: for Case Study A, 1) community, 2) grace, and 3) lament, and for Case Study B, 1) reconnecting with God, 2) remembering God's truth, and 3) forgiving. These six resources, in our (respondents') personal view, can be utilized in any given traumatic situation.

CASE STUDY A

In the first case, after a traumatic armed robbery, a missionary couple and their young children experienced post-traumatic stress disorder. They felt unsafe in their own home and had difficulty sleeping. At night, sounds and flashlights caused them intense stress. Though trying hard to lean on God in prayer for his comforting presence, they felt abandoned, vulnerable, weak, upset, and in pain.

First, the Schaefers address the importance of "effective community support." A supportive Christian community that can respond to vulnerability and weakness with grace and accompany traumatized missionaries in a way that helps them reconnect with God is crucial. When feeling alone and afraid and suffering in the wake of trauma, what missionaries need is a community of love and care: a community that hears them, receives them, understands their hurts and fears, and helps them reconnect with God. Such a community can help the hurting missionary to grow, heal, and develop resilience. Supporting missionaries as they pursue growth and healing post-trauma seems to us a type of debriefing, or, follow-up care provided after a crisis event—a component of member care that the Schaefers do not mention. When a missionary experiences trauma in the field, a member of the community—either professional or non-professional—with spiritual sensitivity and maturity, can take the initiative and offer a debriefing. When the debriefing is effective, the positive outcomes can be numerous. To name a few, debriefing can help the missionary process events and feelings; debriefing can provide relational support, ending isolation; it can enhance the missionary's connectedness, facilitate change, provide an opportunity for growth through sharing and being heard, bring rejoicing and glory to God through shared victories, and communicate to the missionary a powerful message of love, respect, and value. Debriefing will help missionaries reconnect with God in the wake of traumatic suffering.

Secondly, the Schaefers view human frailty—for example, vulnerability and weakness—as traits designed by God so that we must rely on him for his all-surpassing power and strength. Our spiritual strength grows as we receive love and grace in our weakness. One should not hide one's brokenness but yield to the loving hands of God and his people, receiving support and Christ's grace. Christian grace is a social grace, and "a social culture of grace" is a means of healing and growth. Rightly, as the Apostle Peter commands, we ought to be of one mind, sympathetic, loving as brothers/sisters, tender-hearted, and humble (1 Peter 3:8), especially toward those in suffering.

Thirdly, the Schaefers offer lament as a helpful—indeed, vital—biblical practice. To lament is to connect with God in an outward expression of inner pain, as Jesus exemplified in his emotional outcry from the cross. A community of supporters, in solidarity with those who are hurting, can provide a needed presence without taking the weight of suffering onto their own hearts or shoulders, by envisioning the missionary's painful feelings being released into the heart of God. They can stand together with the missionary, having hope in God's loving and patient work. Carving out space for lament in the community of faith provides the suffering with a powerful ministry of presence that is desperately needed in our hurting world.

CASE STUDY B

In the second case study, a fatal church shooting emotionally crippled a faithful missionary. She felt overwhelmed, guilty, angry, vengeful, unforgiving, confused, numbed, abandoned by God, and betrayed by the shooter, as she had known him. Once again, the authors offer three spiritual resources for healing: reconnecting with God, remembering God's word, and forgiving.

First, the Schaefers offer that reconnecting with God is crucial because numbness and depression caused by trauma provide protection from an overwhelming sense of shame, fear, and pain, but also shut down the experience of peace and joy. Jesus' way, as shown on the road to Emmaus, was to listen, ask questions, help to understand, and commune. As the breaking of the bread functions neurobiologically to help the traumatized disciples reconnect with Jesus, surely, the things that have helped traumatized missionaries in the past to feel God's presence, such as songs, images, and verses reflecting one's personal experience of God can also help a traumatized missionary regain a feeling of connection with God.

Secondly, the Schaefers note that a sense of abandonment or punishment by God and doubts about God's love increase the level of distress felt by traumatized individuals. Rightly, the sound biblical understanding of sin and suffering can resolve unnecessary pain and hasten healing and recovery. As the Schaefers recommend, not only can the traumatized persons bring their feelings of abandonment to Jesus because he himself experienced God's abandonment on the cross, but they can also seek scriptural help by reading the Bible for God's promises of abiding presence. Further, a healthy biblical understanding of suffering and its association with sin can deter missionaries from misunderstanding God's intended ways.

In our view, studying the Bible for a good theology of suffering, while exercising daily devotion to God's word and prayer (e.g., hearing, reading, studying, memorizing, and meditating on Scripture) is crucial but not sufficient for a healthy life and ministry. Those who have been traumatized need not only a good theology of suffering but also a good theology of life, based on a theology of atonement, a theology of the cross, a theology of trauma, a theology of victimization, a theology of Christ's return, and so forth. In addition to Scripture study, fasting, prayer, church attendance, worship, and, most importantly, application of God's word can provide the continued emotional and spiritual strength necessary for finding a new path. Lastly, in supporting the healing of traumatized missionaries, ensuring that a ministry of presence precedes the ministry of the Word—"theological input," in the Schaefers' words—is well-advised.

Thirdly, the Schaefers stress the importance of forgiveness because it decreases post-traumatic symptoms, such as hostility and anger, and is vital for healing. However, forgiveness is a process, not a single act with an immediate result. Deep emotional wounds may require a person to repeat the act of forgiveness, because new aspects of one's wounds can surface with the passing of time, renewing one's pain. Intentional forgiveness is a needed step toward healing, and it will become more comfortable over time. In extending forgiveness, the victim does not excuse the offense or minimize the harm but chooses to lay it at the foot of the cross. Once again, a good theology of the cross is critical. Forgiveness is a choice and an act of obedience; prompted by the Holy Spirit, it will result in a supernatural change of heart. The power and benefits of forgiveness could be further elaborated.

A FEW SUGGESTIONS

We would like to highlight a few augmenting suggestions. First, the Schaefers' discussion of missionary healing underemphasizes the role of the Holy Spirit. They refer to the Holy Spirit only once. As Christians, we know and experience the God of unconditional love and acceptance, through the transforming experience of *communitas* with Jesus, in the power of the Holy Spirit. Secondly, the importance of worship, both corporate and individual, is missing from the paper. The role of worship in the process of recovery and healing could be further explored. Thirdly, the resurrection motif is not mentioned. Jesus endured traumatic suffering and violent crucifixion, but as declared by the prophets, he rose from the dead. Admittedly, the most traumatic and crushing experience we know of is Jesus' suffering and crucifixion. Jesus is the traumatized one *par excellence*. The cross was a place of some of the most extreme kinds of trauma. Jesus was crushed and traumatized spiritually, physically, emotionally, and mentally. However, the power of trauma is destroyed on the cross. Jesus took upon himself sin, infirmity, sickness, and trauma because of his great love for us. The cross that symbolizes suffering, shame, trauma, and death does not have the last word, because Jesus rose from the dead. To all who suffer, the cross is the perfect symbol of the ultimate hope of transformation and restoration because of this resurrection.

15
HAPPINESS AMONG KOREAN MISSIONARIES AND ORGANIZATIONAL CARE IN THE MISSIONS COMMUNITY

by EUNJUNG UM

INTRODUCTION

When living under the shadow of idealized or exaggerated constructs of what it means to be a missionary, mission workers often become timid and lonely. Social psychologist E. Tory Higgins presents in his study of self-discrepancy and emotional vulnerabilities that those who experience discrepancies between actual and ideal self-states experience emotions associated with dejection (disappointment, dissatisfaction, and sadness). Similarly, those who experience discrepancies between actual and expected self-states feel emotions associated with agitation (fear, threat, and restlessness).[1] Higgins' study states that the emotional experience of self-discrepancy is a product of beliefs about oneself and others, formed in the context of social relationships.

Missionaries who follow the Great Commandment of Love and the Great Commission of Mission often experience such self-discrepancies within their communities. In Yoon Hee Kim's research on Korean missionary depression, 63 percent of the study participants had experienced depression in the past, and 21 percent were depressed at the time of the research.[2] From the social constructivist's perspective, scholars of narrative therapy view psychological distress as an internalized discourse formed out of social interactions.[3] Positive psychologists Peterson and Seligman present in their social science research that community virtues influence the happiness and well-being of the members.[4] The influence of the community is closely linked to the happiness, satisfaction, and well-being of the individuals. Especially in Korea's relationship-oriented culture, the belief system of the community influences missionaries' self-concepts quite significantly, either in a positive or negative direction.

Further, Park and Hwang have verified that the organizational culture has a significant effect on the subjective well-being of the members of the organization.[5] Member care is a movement that promotes a culture of caring within mission organizations. The movement reminds the mission community that not only the pursuit of missions but also the life of the missionary is invaluable. However, the member care movement has not yet penetrated deeply into missional organizations, and there exists within them a tendency to view missionaries' mental health concerns only as the psychological or spiritual problems of individuals. "Well-being" refers to an ontologically good state of life, to happiness and health

---

1. E. Tory Higgins, "Self-Discrepancy: A Theory Relating Self and Affect," *Psychological Review* 94, no. 3 (January 1987): 319.
2. Yoon Hee Kim, "Korean Missionary's Depression and Biblical Counselling" (Master's diss., Chongshin University, 2013), 9-12.
3. Jill Freedman and Gene Combs, *Narrative Therapy: The Social Construction of Preferred Realities* (New York: Norton, 1996), 101-103.
4. Christopher Peterson and Martin Seligman, *Character Strengths and Virtues: A Handbook and Classification* (Washington, DC: American Psychological Association, 2004).
5. Seul Gi Park and Jin Soo Hwang, "The Impact of Organizational Culture on Subjective Well-being in the Hotel Industry," *Journal of Hotel Resort* 14 (Feb. 2015): 329-345.

in the multidimensional realms of life. Taking into account the particularity of missionaries, Keckler presented a comprehensive picture of wellness, involving one's spiritual, social, emotional, physical, occupational, and intellectual (educational) life.[6] Andrews found that missionaries' well-being correlates with spiritual, family, and ministry satisfaction.[7] In their understanding of missionary well-being, the Dodds incorporated—even from the early days of member care—the dimensions of the individual, the mission organization, and the multicultural environment. Because a missionary's work depends on his or her calling, sharing common values with the mission community is of utmost importance for the mission worker. Considering the Korean cultural tendency to value the group more than the individual, the well-being of the mission organization will be crucial for the well-being of the Korean missionary.

Assuming that a missionary's happiness and quality of life are associated with both the values of the respective mission community and the missionary's interactions with that community, this paper asks the following questions. What is the status of the subjective well-being of Korean missionaries? How satisfied are they in their ministries? What is the state of their emotional health? What relation do those factors have to the organization's member care? What psycho-social factors lead missionaries to feel either happiness or dissatisfaction in their ministry work?

METHODS

Participants. A total of 215 missionaries who attended the sabbatical debriefing at Heartstream Resources Korea between 2013 and 2017 agreed to participate in the research. With the unreliable data excluded, 154 of the Korean version of SPARE (K-SPARE) and 183 of the Korean version of the Self-Evaluation (K-SE) responses were collected. A total of 195 participated in the study.

Instruments. The research data were collected, using the Self-Evaluation and the SPARE Assessment Tool (SPARE). The Self-Evaluation instrument, developed by Schubert; and SPARE, developed by Dodds,[8] were translated into Korean with some modifications to the questionnaires. The Korean adaptation of SPARE examined seven dimensions: relating to the holistic well-being of the individual, these five—Spiritual (S), Physical (P), Actualizing (A), Relational

---

6 Wade T. Keckler, Glen Moriarty, and Mark Blagen, "A Qualitative Study on Comprehensive Missionary Wellness," *Journal of Psychology and Christianity* 27, no. 3 (2008): 205-214.

7 Leslie A. Andrews, "Spiritual, Family, and Ministry Satisfaction among Missionaries," *Journal of Psychology and Theology* 27, no. 2 (Summer, 1999): 107.

8 Larry Dodds and Lois Dodds, *Foundation of Missionary Care* (Liverpool, PA: Heartstream Resources, Inc., 1993). To be published. For further details on SPARE, refer to Lois Dodds, Laura Mae Gardner, and Alice Chen, *Global Servants: Cross-cultural Humanitarian Heroes*, vol. 3 (Liverpool, PA: Heartstream Resources, Inc.), 140-153. On missionaries' depression, refer to Esther Schubert, *What Missionaries Need to Know about Burnout and Depression* (New Castle, IN: Olive Branch, 1993).

(R), and Emotional (E); and regarding organizational and cultural well-being—Organizational (O), and Cultural (C). The K-SPARE scale ranged from 1 (low) to 10 (high), with higher scores indicating a greater degree of the subjective well-being. The internal reliability (Cronbach's alpha) of K-SPARE's total scale score was 0.828. The K-SE consisted of subscales to assess the participants' levels of satisfaction in ministry and psycho-emotional states. Based on factor analysis, ministry satisfaction was identified using seven scaling questions, categorized into three factors, i.e., (1) ministry environment, (2) ministry resources, and (3) ministry relationships.[9] It also included two open-ended questions. A 4-point Likert style scale, ranging from 4 (satisfied overall) to 1 (dissatisfied overall) was used, with higher scores indicating greater degrees of satisfaction. The Cronbach's alpha for K-SE's total score was 0.783; for the ministry environment subscale, 0.759; for ministry resources, 0.701; and for ministry relationships, 0.695. The open-ended questions were (1) What brings you happiness in your ministry? and (2) What is unsatisfactory or what do you want to develop in your ministry? The subscales regarding the participants' psycho-emotional states were measured using nine scaling questions to assess depressive symptoms based on the DSM-IV criteria (e.g., depressed mood, recurrent thoughts of death, recurrent suicidal thoughts and or plans) and twelve either-or choices (e.g., contented-discontented, pleasant-irritable).

Procedures and data analysis. Convenience sampling was used to select the study participants. The data were collected through interviews and through questionnaires that were distributed during debriefing sessions given by the researcher. The data were then analyzed, using IBM SPSS Statistics 25. A factor analysis was conducted to check the validity of the variables, and Pearson's correlation coefficient for the relationship between them was calculated on K-SPARE and K-SE. The participants' characteristics, psycho-emotional states, and levels of happiness or dissatisfaction in ministry were assessed with the frequency analysis. To find out whether there exists a difference in subjective well-being and ministry satisfaction depending on the availability of organizational member care, the participants were categorized by two groups, self-referral type and organizational referral type, and their mean differences were analyzed with a T-test. The self-referral group was comprised of missionaries who participated in debriefing on their own, without member care in their organizations. The organizational referrals were missionaries with member care in their respective organizations, who participated in the debriefing process through the member care referral process.

---

9   The seven scaling questions for identifying ministry satisfaction in K-SE covered the following: (1) ministry environment (environment, safety on the job or in location), (2) ministry resources (motivation and feelings about work, resources to work, financial resources or rewards), and (3) ministry relationships (relationships with coworkers and leaders, support from organization and peers).

RESULTS

The genders of the participants were almost evenly distributed, with males constituting 45.6 percent and females 54.4 percent. The participants ranged in age from their 20s to their 70s, with 40s to 50s (45.1 percent) being the most common. Ministry experiences ranged from 2 to 29 years in length. Table 15.1 shows the number of K-SPARE and K-SE participants according to their referral types, further breaking down the data by mission organization type.

Table 15.1. Number of Participants according to Referral and Organization Types

Referral Type	SPARE N (percent)	Self-Evaluation N (percent)
1. Self-referral	23 (14.9)	31 (16.9)
2. Organizational referral	131 (85.1)	152 (83.1)
2-1. Denominational mission organizations	26 (16.9)	36 (19.7)
2-2. Korean mission organizations	29 (18.8)	35 (19.1)
2-3. Local church mission organizations	13 (8.4)	14 (7.7)
2-4. International mission organizations	63 (40.9)	67 (36.6)
Total	154 (100)	183 (100)

Correlation of subjective well-being. A correlation analysis of the variables of the K-SPARE scale for 154 subjects showed a positive correlation. Organizational well-being correlated most with actualizing ($r = .470$), relational ($r = .466$), emotional ($r = .455$), and physical ($r = .403$) well-being. Emotional well-being correlated most with spiritual ($r = .595$), relational ($r = .566$), actualizing ($r = .517$), organizational ($r = .455$), and physical ($r = .403$) well-being (Table 15.2). This result indicates that the well-being of a missionary is related not only to the individual dimension but also to the organizational dimension.

Table 15.2. Correlation Coefficient of K-SPARE Variables, Mean, SD (N=154)

Well-being	1	2	3	4	5	6	M	SD
1. Spiritual	1.00						6.44	1.775
2. Physical	.506**	1.00					6.12	1.792
3. Actualizing	.553**	.412**	1.00				6.44	1.824
4. Relational	.321**	.200*	.353**	1.00			6.57	1.930
5. Emotional	.595**	.403**	.517**	.566**	1.00		6.36	1.946
6. Organizational	.330**	.403**	.470**	.466**	.455**	1.00	6.45	2.090
7. Cultural	.349**	.320**	.408**	.286**	.297**	.311**	7.31	1.479

*P <.05 **p<.01

The study participants' subjective well-being scores averaged 6.5, with nearly half (41%) scoring lower than 6. (A score lower than six on the K-SPARE scale is interpreted to mean that the missionary's situation requires attention and preliminary intervention.) However, about 32% of the respondents scored at least eight points, reflecting a relatively healthy state. Among the different dimensions of well-being, cultural well-being ($M=7.31$, $SD=1.47$) ranked highest, and physical well-being ($M=6.12$, $SD=1.78$) ranked lowest. Between these two groups, the self-referral group had a lower sense of well-being, on average, than the organization-referral group (Table 15.3). A statistically significant difference in organizational well-being (*self-referral: M=4.61, SD=2.210, organizational referral: M=6.77, SD=1.900, t -4.911, p. .000 p<.05*) was found by conducting a T-test to evaluate the difference of subjective well-being between the two groups (Table 15.4).

However, none of the following traits made a significant difference in the organizational well-being scores: male/female, single/married, pastor-missionary/lay-missionary, or amount of time in the ministry. Comparing the mean difference between the group with the highest well-being status in the organizational referral group and the group with the lowest well-being status in the self-referral group revealed significant differences in organizational and physical well-being.[10]

---

[10] An independent samples T-test was conducted to evaluate the mean difference. Physical well-being, t -2.595, p .014. Organizational well-being, t -3.550, p .001. The mean difference is significant with p<.05.

Table 15.3. K-SPARE Subjective Well-Being Variables' Mean, SD according to Referral Types

Referral Types (N)		M SD	S Spiritual	P Physical	A Actualizing	R Relational	E Emotional	O Organization	C Cultural	SPAREOC Total
Self-Referral (23)		M	6.00	5.74	5.96	6.09	6.26	4.61	7.13	5.9689
		SD	1.859	1.888	2.011	2.172	2.137	2.210	1.517	1.45109
Organizational Referral	Denominational Mission (26)	M	6.12	5.81	6.08	6.35	6.19	6.00	7.12	6.2363
		SD	1.883	1.789	2.226	2.314	1.855	2.315	1.774	1.41944
	Korean mission (29)	M	6.38	5.62	6.28	6.90	6.14	6.62	6.76	6.3842
		SD	1.678	1.656	1.869	1.543	1.866	1.840	1.550	1.19651
	Local church mission (13)	M	7.23	7.31	6.69	6.62	7.46	7.15	7.62	7.1533
		SD	2.048	1.437	1.377	1.938	1.808	1.772	1.502	1.06180
	International mission (63)	M	6.60	6.37	6.79	6.68	6.35	7.08	7.65	6.7859
		SD	1.661	1.763	1.578	1.839	1.961	1.697	1.194	1.16758

Table 15.4. K-SPARE Subjective Well-Being T-test according to Referral Types

Well-being	Mean		SD		T	P
	S. Referral (n=23)	Org. Referral (n=131)	S. Referral	Org. Referral		
Spiritual	6.00	6.52	1.859	1.756	-1.297	0.197
Physical	5.74	6.18	1.888	1.773	-1.100	0.273
Actualizing	5.96	6.53	2.011	1.784	-1.396	0.165
Relational	6.09	6.66	2.172	1.880	-1.309	0.193
Emotional	6.26	6.38	2.137	1.919	-0.274	0.785
Organizational	4.61	6.77	2.210	1.900	-4.911*	0.000*
Cultural	7.13	7.34	1.517	1.476	-0.628	0.531

Ministry satisfaction. The study participants' satisfaction levels (K-SE) were analyzed for responses of "somewhat satisfied" (3) and "satisfied" (4). The following are the percentages of participants who reported being "somewhat satisfied" (3) or "satisfied" (4) with the indicated areas: "ministry environment" (75 percent), "ministry resources" (76 percent), and "coworker relationships" (65 percent). The indicated percentages of participants reported being "satisfied" (4) in the following areas: "ministry environment" (38 percent), "ministry resources" (42 percent), and "coworker relationships" (32 percent), the lowest satisfaction being in coworker relationships. The mean difference between groups was analyzed with a T-test, assuming that there would be a difference in the participants' levels of satisfaction depending on the availability of organizational member care. The results showed that the participants of the group who had access to member care had significantly higher ministry satisfaction, compared to those without member care. The levels of satisfaction with "ministry resources" and "ministry relationships" were significantly higher, whereas there was no significant difference in the satisfaction with "ministry environment" (Table 15.5).

Table 15.5. Ministry Satisfaction T-test according to Referral Types

Ministry Satisfaction	Mean		SD		T	P
	S. Referral (n=31)	Org. Referral (n=152)	S. Referral	Org. Referral		
M. Environment	3.034	3.076	.680	.842	-.254	.800
M. Resources	2.919	3.196	.707	.640	-2.055*	.041*
M. Relationship	2.483	2.962	.724	.871	-2.854*	.005*

Psycho-emotional well-being. An analysis of the K-SE missionaries' emotional states revealed that nearly half (49 percent) of the participants had depressive symptoms. Among them, 13 percent were severely depressed. The most common symptoms of depression were those of a depressed mood, a diminished sense of interest or pleasure, fatigue or loss of energy, and decreased concentration. Regarding their states of mind, 30 percent percent answered that they were "discontented," "irritable," and "grouchy;" and 37 percent, "driven," "melancholic." When asked to describe their state of mind, 8 percent of the respondents answered "unhappy," while 66 percent answered "happy." Sixty-seven percent responded that they were "optimistic," "future-oriented," and had a "positive self-image;" 22 percent percent said that they were "past-oriented" and that they had a "negative self-image."

Happiness and dissatisfaction on the mission field. The participants' experiences of happiness in ministry were categorized into five high-level themes and eight sub-themes, as listed in Table 15.6. Seventy percent of the responses regarding happiness in ministry had to do with the local people, the highest happiness being associated with nurturing the locals (46 percent) and building relationships with the locals (24 percent). Participants experienced happiness when seeing the local people convert and change and when seeing them grow as leaders through discipleship. Participants also reported that they experienced happiness when sharing intimate fellowship and emotional empathy with the locals and when receiving recognition, respect, hospitality, and care from the locals. Forty percent of the responses were associated with mission competence, such as engaging in opportunities to achieve their missionary visions (29 percent) or growing and developing on a personal level (11 percent). Twenty percent of the responses were associated with "spirituality;" the missionaries experienced spiritual happiness through devotional practices, such as worship, prayer, Scripture reading, and spiritual fellowship. Some participants responded that they felt happiness especially when worshipping with the local people. The rest felt spiritual comfort and happiness through supernatural spiritual experiences (9 percent), experiencing the power of the Spirit and of God's presence, or witnessing God's work. Thirteen percent associated happiness with "coworker relationships," which involved collaboration, support, and caring. Nine percent associated happiness with "ministry outcomes," such as attaining contributions, recognition, or achievements within their ministries.

The participants' experiences of dissatisfaction in the field of ministry were categorized into a total of five high-level themes and eleven sub-themes, as listed in Table 15.6. Fifty-one percent of the respondents answered that their dissatisfaction was the greatest with regarding to "mission competence and attitude." Nearly half (43 percent) of the respondents said that they were not competent enough to perform the ministry. Sources of dissatisfaction included language problems, identity confusion, loneliness, isolation, alienation, lack of motivation, lack of leadership, and personality traits such as timidity and passivity. The remaining (8 percent) responded that they needed to change their attitudes toward the ministry. Work-oriented ministry, result-oriented ministry, project-oriented ministry, excessive zeal, mannerism, and laziness were also found to be damaging to one's happiness in ministry.

Table 15.6. Themes and Sub-themes of Happiness and Dissatisfaction in Ministry

HAPPINESS (multiple responses: N=180)		DISSATISFACTION (multiple responses: N=174)	
Themes	Sub-themes (N, percent)	Themes	Sub-themes (N, percent)
1. Nurturing relationships	(1) nurturing the locals (82, 45.6 percent) (2) relationships with the locals (44, 24.4 percent)	1. Competence	(1) competence (75, 43.1 percent) (2) attitude (14, 8.0 percent)
2. Mission competence	(3) missionary participation (53, 29.4 percent) (4) self-development & growth (20, 11.1 percent)	2. Coworker relationships	(3) ministry coworkers (35, 20.1 percent) (4) the local people (20, 11.5 percent) (5) sending organization and church (21, 12.1 percent) (6) spouse (9, 5.2 percent)
3. Spirituality	(5) devotional practices (19, 10.6 percent) (6) the work of the Holy Spirit (16, 8.9 percent)	3. Mission Policy	(7) mission strategy (24, 13.8 percent) (8) mission resource (19, 10.9 percent) (9) mission environment (18, 10.3 percent)
4. Coworker Relationships	(7) coworker relationships (24, 13.3 percent)	4. Spirituality	(10) spirituality (15, 8.6 percent)
5. Ministry Outcomes	(8) Ministry Outcomes (16, 8.9 percent)	5. Ministry Outcomes	(11) Ministry Outcomes (10, 5.7 percent)
Total	274, 152.2 percent	Total	260, 149.3 percent

Forty-eight percent of the participants were not satisfied with their "coworker relationships," within which percentage, "ministry coworker relationships" was the greatest subcategory (20 percent). Many studies have already revealed that conflicts are the main reason people drop out of the ministry. Similarly, authoritarian leadership, one-way communication, a lack of mentoring, a lack of unity, a lacking understanding of member care among the leadership, and unfavorable peer relationships were the causes of dissatisfaction among the participants in this study. Eleven percent of the responses regarding dissatisfaction had to do with the local people, such as seeing no changes in them, lacking kinship or intimacy with them, and experiencing passive attitudes in the local churches and among church leaders. Twelve percent of the respondents expressed dissatisfaction with their sending organization and church relationships. Regarding the sending organization, the missionaries' issues included communicating with the headquarters, experiencing prejudice, lacking personal fellowship, having ambiguous ministry or work assignments, having an excessive amount of work and feeling fatigued, lacking member care, and receiving insufficient support. On the other hand, regarding the sending church, the missionaries' issues included not being trusted, experiencing a lack of communication or a weak church presence, and having no personal fellowship. If the dissatisfaction with the sending organization was related to administration, the dissatisfaction with the sending church was more about relationship. The rest (5 percent) had to do with the missionaries' spouses: spousal leadership, communication, and conflict. Thirty-five percent of respondents said they experienced dissatisfaction and grievance related to "mission policy," specifically, an insufficient mission strategy (14 percent), insufficient mission resources (11 percent), and a limited mission environment (10 percent). About "spirituality," 9 percent of respondents said that they experienced spiritual exhaustion, conflict, and doubt about their calling. They perceived spiritual laziness, ungodly living, and spiritual warfare as crises. Whereas the main factor of missionaries' happiness was intimacy, homogeneity, and unity with locals and peers, their dissatisfaction was caused by lack of competence, resources, and relationships.

CONCLUSION

A Christian community is a group that shares beliefs and values, and Christian happiness is based on a sense of community identity. Therefore, a community lacking in care cannot help its missionaries recognize their self-worth or sense their significance to the group. The effectiveness and the well-being of missionaries are not dependent only on the missionaries' individual qualities but are nurtured and promoted when a missionary's philosophy and values are shared with the mission community. Korean missionaries perceive happiness through relationships. Spiritual happiness comes through the feast of love that God has prepared for those who are called. Contradiction, however, lurks within this feast. At times, colleagues who should be working in tandem with a missionary turn out to be rivals and strangers. Conflicts among missionaries weaken community ties and cripple both the missionary and the whole community.

Many Korean missionaries are dissatisfied with their competence and mission resources. Mission agencies need to provide practical solutions to promote and develop missionary competence, as well as provide the needed missionary resources, so that their missionaries can be happy in the ministry. Ten to fifteen percent of the missionaries who participated in the current study would require special care and therapy to obtain full emotional recovery. Around 30 percent are in a relatively healthy state, but it would be difficult to say that they are all happy enough. Perhaps less than 5–10 percent of missionaries enjoy happiness, while living altruistically under constrained conditions.

Among the results of the study, it was interesting to note that the church mission organizations had the highest level of well-being among the groups with member care support. The group of participants classified as "church mission" participants consisted of both sending churches and sending organizations. The "church mission" worker has a dual organizational membership, serving with a missionary organization that a church has designated; the "church mission" worker is thus part of both that missionary organization and the affiliated church. This construct prevents the potential danger of a church sending missionaries on its own. The organizational structure of a church mission organization is considered to have a particularly positive impact on the quality of life of missionaries, because it delegates expertise to the mission agencies, while maintaining enhanced member care within the churches. In this respect, an alternative model of missionary care that promotes the well-being of Korean missionaries would be based on community relationships and enhanced by church care.

Another noteworthy finding is the mean difference between the cultural well-being scores of international mission agencies and the same scores of Korean mission agencies: international missions organizations had a higher average score than Korean mission organizations. Considering that the subjects were all Koreans with same cultural background, it is likely that the multicultural elements of the international mission organizations influenced the cultural intelligence (and, therefore, the cultural well-being) of the members.

The Great Commandment of Love and the Great Commission of Mission are not just appendices to the fundamental beliefs or ideals of the community. We receive God's love, as the Son did from his Father: "You are My beloved Son, in You I am well-pleased." When we are filled with God's love and, so, find happiness, we will be fully ready to take on our mission.

QUESTIONS FOR REFLECTION

1. Find examples of cross-cultural ministers who enjoy mentally healthy and happy lives. What are the psychological, spiritual, and social capital you find in them?

2. What are the creative methods and tools to develop missionary competence and resources?

3. What needs to be improved to increase the happy population in the mission community?

4. What are the theological lessons and insights in Jesus' teachings on happiness in the parable of the grapevine (John 15) and in the Sermon on the Mount (Matthew 5)?

RESPONSE by Lois A. Dodds

Eunjung Um writes for us an illuminating and significant chapter related to the happiness of Korean missionaries. Her research findings are relevant to missionaries and agencies in other cultures, as well. The study enlightens us about the huge need for and the importance of churches and mission organizations providing member care, showing how member care and organizational health increase both the perceived and actual well-being and happiness of Korean missionaries. The author's analogy of "living under the shadow" of idealized constructs is apropos.

Ms. Um raises excellent questions. She relates her study to the "member care movement," noting the tendencies of agencies to address only psychological or spiritual problems. I believe her observation touches a "raw nerve," alerting us to the benefits that can be achieved through a more holistic approach to member care.

The influence of community, as studied by other researchers, is reaffirmed. Ms. Um's work validates why it is imperative to prepare candidates with appropriate tools to enhance their community and individual relationships. It shows why it behooves us, from whatever church, mission, or culture, to attend lavishly to keeping our community life healthy. Some of the study findings are expected, such as that missionaries in denominational missions experience more happiness, likely due to the greater unity of shared values. The association between missionary happiness and denominational connection possibly also reflects the stronger sense of identity explored in *Am I Still Me?* [11]

The inventories Eunjung Um uses have been relevant for twenty-seven years at Heartstream, particularly the self-assessment for depression and burnout, by missionary psychiatrist Dr. Esther Schubert, which includes factors associated with happiness. Ms. Um astutely gleans the nuggets revealed by the SPARE-OC model.[12] This model assumes that "well-being" encompasses the primary dimensions of human development.

We truly need to take to heart (and head!) Ms. Um's finding that " … the higher the missionary's sense of belonging and unity with the organization, the higher the missionary's self-actualization and emotional stability." This is a strong indicator of why a person belonging to an agency/mission, rather than going it alone as an independent missionary, is so crucial. In our world in Heartstream, we see this validated in hundreds of cases. From the first days of our Intensive Care Programs almost thirty years ago, it became obvious that individuals who had supportive churches that actually understood them and prayed for them, along with families who similarly supported them, made much more rapid gains during their treatment for crises and burnout. In one program (1994) involving only single missionaries, when asked the reason why they were reluctant to leave at the end of the program, the participants said, "We don't have anywhere we want to go—our families don't understand us and will say, 'Are you going to get a real job now?' and our churches don't really know us or care about us."

Um's research validates the importance of churches not sending missionaries out without an agency. Regarding benefits of relating with multi-cultures, she says, " … international missions organizations had a significantly higher average score than Korean mission organizations … It is likely that the multicultural elements … influence the cultural intelligence (and therefore, the cultural well-being) of the members."

Hugely significant are the findings that lowest levels of satisfaction correlate with coworker relationship problems. Why do we need to wait even another minute to reinforce through training the positive, transferable personal attitudes and skills already identified? Another finding worthy of emphasis is how organizational structure can have "positive impact on the quality of life … because it delegates expertise to the mission agencies, while maintaining enhanced member care within the churches."

---

11 Lois A. Dodds, "Am I Still Me? Challenges to Identify for Cross-cultural Workers, Immigrants and Refugees," AACC World Congress of Christian Counselors, Nashville, TN (Forest, VA: AACC, 2013), and other conferences, www.heartstreamresources.org.

12 This model was created by Drs. Lawrence and Lois Dodds at Heartstream Resources, 1994.

Surprising is that the dimension of "cultural well-being" ranked highest in importance for the 32 percent scoring eight or above on the SPARE scale, while "physical well-being" ranked lowest. A future study might explore this further.

Highly significant is the finding that "seventy percent of responses regarding happiness in ministry had to do with local people, especially ... *nurturing* ..." The powerful dynamic of care between ministry workers and the local people, often overlooked, is well worth noting. Hopefully, leaders will take this dynamic to heart in assessing the outcomes of ministry. This vital interpersonal connection is the heart of ministry. In one case close to me in Latin America, leaders were astounded when 1,000 locals showed up for the *despedida* of a missionary they "let go." "Why are you sending her home?" they asked, "She is the one who is most like us!"

In the 70 percent noted above, "intimate fellowship" and "emotional empathy" were key aspects of mission workers' relationships with locals. This, too, illumines the value of teaching and training transferable relational attitudes and skills.

Also notable for agencies is that 51 percent said their dissatisfaction related to "mission competence." (This is not specifically defined but seems to relate to the individual's competence to do the job.) Our experience with hundreds of missionaries from many cultures bears this out. One veteran couple of a long-established mission said, after twenty years' service, "No one knows what we do well enough to tell us if we are succeeding." Thus, either the job description was hazy, or the leaders did not stay abreast of the couple's work.

Ms. Um's conclusions call us all to a much higher standard for living out God's love in mission contexts. Let us foster joy and love!

The study raises important questions about the psychological health of missionaries as it relates to their self-perceptions and their experiences of community.

QUESTIONS FOR REFLECTION

1. Since Korean culture, as described by Ms. Um, is more "relationship oriented, the belief system of the community influences missionary self-concepts quite significantly ..." To what extent is this true for other cultures?

2. Is the meaning of "actual" as used here understood by the Korean audience to mean "actualizing" or "making real" one's human potential?

3. If "fulfillment" rather than "happiness" were measured, would we see the same results?

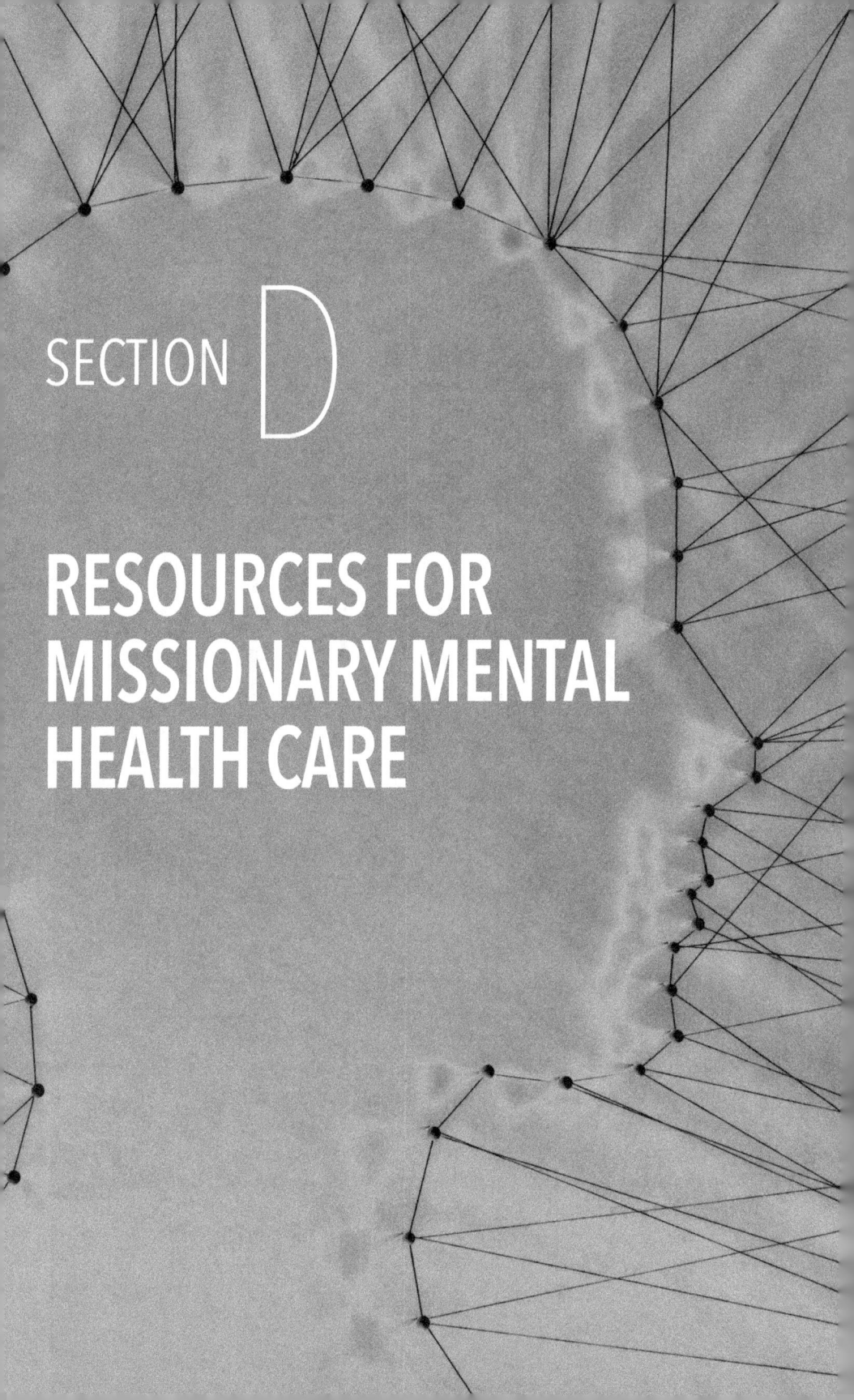

SECTION D

RESOURCES FOR MISSIONARY MENTAL HEALTH CARE

16

ORGANIZATION-CENTERED MEMBER HEALTH

by Brent Lindquist

A CASE STUDY

Mission A is struggling, although you might not easily see it. Financially, it is steady, and it has a good reputation in the church. It prides itself on its vision and purpose and has remained true to them over these long years. So what is the problem? Within the membership, numerous issues are simmering. People come and go with no explanation. No one admits to struggling with emotional issues. Decisions often come from the top down, and people have given up questioning them. Numerous people feel they just have a job, not the calling they used to have. A few of the young leaders have left to start their own organizations. Others have wondered if they should, too.

What organization am I describing? Several missions like this exist today in multiple places around the world.

A potential cautionary tale …

I think my middle name must be "fools rush in" (as in "fools rush in where angels fear to tread"). Throughout my professional career, I have been one of the first to catch a vision and run with it. Long ago, that vision was to talk about mental health applications in missions at a time when "psychology" was a negative word. Over time, positive attitudes about the mental health field have become increasingly mainstream, and many of us do not face the same sorts of issues we would have in the past. However, several peoples and cultures still look on emotional issues and their treatment as problematic. For the last few years, I have been preaching about the need for people to see the mission organization as a resource for mental health, as opposed to being seen as an adversary to it. And, once again, I have been a target.

And now? Now I am stepping into the arena of mental health in the Korean context. I am trying not only to address personal mental health, which on some leadership levels is taboo, but also to address issues in the health of the Korean organization itself. I have been told that I am taking a potential risk to my professional reputation in doing this. From my perspective, I have little to lose— I am over the hill, closer to heaven than I used to be. Frankly, I care little or at least less about my professional reputation—my reputation as a follower of Jesus is what drives me.

As an older community member, I am fine with my utterances being dismissed as the ramblings of an old man sitting by the city gate. But, I trust that some of these ideas or questions might just stimulate a needed dialogue among decision-makers.

Who am I to speak to Korean issues?

My mentor and coworker for twenty years, Donald N. Larson, PhD,[1] taught me that all languages (and cultures) are at once very similar, somewhat similar, and dissimilar to one another. I have had many interactions with Koreans and Korean-Americans over the years, as friends, employees, peers, and clients. In many ways, I am struck by the similarities we share, and I am struck again by our differences. But it is our similarities that drive me to make my comments. As you read and think, remember to grace me with a bit of flexibility regarding any naïveté, and confront my ideas where necessary. But also think through my words, and maybe after reflection, some of them will make more sense. Thank you!

HOW DID WE GET HERE? A SHORT HISTORICAL STORY

Member care came into being as a response to a need. Missionaries were hurting, having problems, and leaving the field. Most of those problems fell within the categories of stress, conflict, danger, relationship problems, burnout, and moral failure. Seeking help for these problems, and frankly also seeking to avoid

---

1   Donald N. Larson taught at the Toronto Institute of Linguistics and at Bethel College, and together we taught a pre-field orientation program at Link Care Center for almost twenty years, until his passing. Many of my quirky ideas grew out of our time together.

embarrassment, missions became a bit more open to considering psychological explanations and treatments for their struggling workers. Also, some people who had been hurt on the field started working in member care to prevent others from experiencing the difficulties they had experienced.

During this time, mission leadership did not pay a lot of attention to the emotional side of things. Basically, the assumption was that people would do their jobs and no one would have any significant emotional problems. For mission workers, stress came with the territory, and often, the older generation had gotten through their problems on their own. The leadership did not want to coddle or protect the new generation by giving them too much care, help, or support. However, this sink-or-swim mentality caused tension and distrust between missionaries and their leaders. When mission leaders did offer or provide treatment to their workers, the missionaries often perceived it as discipline or even punishment. Finally, because of the nature of the treatment provided, that of psychotherapy, for instance, treatment was confidential and did not include the direct addressing of interpersonal or work environment issues. That, unfortunately, has continued to a large extent, even up to today.

The dilemma, then, is that people are getting help, but the how and why are not necessarily apparent. This is not to say that personal emotional growth and psychological compassion are insignificant. But mission organizations still need to address how the insights gleaned from individual therapy can be utilized for the improvement of each organization as a whole.

The great misstep in missions was when organizations and their leaders took (and continue to take) a "hands-off" approach to helping people. In other words, let the counselors or the pastors take care of the missionaries; the organization's focus should be on the organization. To a certain extent, that approach may work well if the counselor understands the theology and the missiology in the global strategy of the mission. But nothing takes place in a vacuum, and sometimes what may make good sense as a treatment approach in the United States, for instance, may not play well in another cultural context, or in a particular mission context. In addition, ignoring what is happening on an individual level with its missionaries leaves a mission organization with insufficient data for shaping, overseeing, and guiding the ministry.

This is not to say that the mission organization should become enmeshed in the therapeutic world of the missionary. Professional distance for confidentiality and privacy needs to be maintained. But there are many appropriate ways to use missionaries' thoughts and experiences to better integrate health and healthy relationships into the organization's climate and culture.

A HEALING COMMUNITY

From my perspective, it seems like we have solved one problem—that of helping the hurting missionary—with some pretty awesome solutions. But I think because of our emphasis on the individual, we have created another problem, in that we have not looked closely enough at what it takes to have a healthy organization. In my current work as a consultant to Missio Nexus, I talk about member health and development, as opposed to member care. "Member care" carries a counseling connotation, while for me, "member health" or "member development" has a big-picture, organizational "feel": the organization is tasked with creating a healthy environment from which to provide services and resources to its members. Unfortunately, the organizations that allow self-development do not usually think how that development might help the organization or improve its effectiveness.

I think we are dealing with at least five critical problems when we look at the missionary organizational climate:[2]

1. Suspicion or ambivalence about authority. (If we each have equal access to God, why do we need leaders to get in the way?)
2. The past determining one's behavior and expectations. (I was hurt before. Is my default setting to expect the same of my current mission?)
3. Confusion about what to expect of mission organizations. (Do I expect my organization and leaders to meet all my needs?)
4. A desire or hope to do away with administrative control, without understanding the problems that such a lack creates. (Do I understand all that organizations do for me or even protect me from?)
5. The right to privacy superseding everything. (Do I understand the information it takes to run an organization?)

So, what would a good/effective/efficient organization or community look like? Or, what makes for a healthy workplace?

Where does one start? Most US descriptions of healthy workplaces are based on a business, church, or mission, which means that there is a headquarters staff (that is, people in close proximity to each other, who have regular, daily interpersonal relationships). A mission, which has dispersed people globally, is complex: its expectations are difficult to identify. Out of many dozens of characteristics I have reviewed, I have tried to condense healthy characteristics into the following:[3]

1. An environment of trust. A healthy organization manages to convey to all its people that it operates from a base of trust. While leadership may make decisions, regular staff largely believe that their concerns, needs, and issues are taken into account.
2. Communication. A healthy organization possesses multiple styles and levels of communication, so that everyone is kept up-to-date on

---

[2] These characteristics come out of my over thirty years of training and consulting with mission organizations. It is difficult for me to tag them to a specific document or citation.

[3] I started out my search for these with a simple Google search. Over some months, these six points evolved. I probably should have listed each link, but that might have been longer than the paper. I apologize for this omission. Anyone could probably find the same resources online by Google-searching terms like "healthy organizations." I found a dearth of resources written for Korean contexts directly.

issues, news, and other significant matters. The people have a sense that what is communicated is accurate and that what one contributes to the communication is conveyed where it is supposed to go.

3. Connected and empowered team members. In most contexts, people work as a member of a team, and they have a sense that their activities and efforts contribute to the outcomes and impact of the organization.

4. A focus on priorities and purpose, not just policy. A healthy organization at all levels understands what its primary purpose and priorities are. It operates along those lines to the best of its ability.

5. Wellness/balance. A healthy organization provides its people opportunities to grow and develop outside of the organizational arena.

6. Evaluation and change. An organization regularly evaluates how it is doing and makes changes as necessary.

While there are many characteristics in the literature, I think I have caught most of the components with these six points. What strikes me is that in healthy organizations, there is a dynamic interplay between the individual and the organization, and both benefit from their relationship. The health of the individual will only go so far without the organization's encouraging implementation of parallel healthy practices.

How does this translate to Korean organizations? My experience here is limited. Care should be taken not to draw too many conclusions from my comments alone.

From my perspective, I see many similarities and differences between US and Korean organizations.

The two kinds of organizations are similar, in that it is easy for them to become more policy driven than purpose driven. Also, they are both dealing with the complexities of generational change. New organizations developed by younger leaders are taking prominence. Established organizations are having to make big changes.

Korean and US organizations are different, in that it seems like mental health is still a taboo subject in the Korean context, or at least people tend to perceive mental health issues more negatively in the Korean context. What this means is that it is sometimes difficult to provide the kind of care in an overt fashion that helps not only the individual but the whole organization. Mental issues or illnesses are seen as failures of spiritual and psychological mechanisms and cause great "loss-of-face." They reflect poorly not only on the individual or family, but also on the entire organization.

Let's look at my condensed, six-point list to determine some questions one might ask in seeking to improve the health and effectiveness of both kinds of organizations.

COMPONENTS FOR PROMOTING ORGANIZATION-WIDE HEALTH

An environment of trust. There are two sides to the trust issue. There is organizational behavior in general. By this I mean: do individuals believe their organization behaves in a trustworthy fashion? There is also the personal issue of trust, which is expressed by the individual's feelings that they can trust the organization when dealing with them personally.

I see big differences between these two perspectives. Generally, most members of a Christian organization, such as a mission, believe that the organization behaves in a trustworthy fashion. It manages its books, does not engage in fraud, and stewards its resources well. In most organizations, trust problems seem to occur primarily between the individual and the leadership, especially in populations where there has been a history of interpersonal conflict, disagreement, or emotional difficulty or mental illness.

The common principle that seems to be operating within all these organizations is that people use their pasts to inform their expectations of the present and future. If they came from any environment of distrust in leadership, whether it was parental or organizational, it seems they are ready to see the same problems in their current relationships.

This, for me, is the basic problem influencing all organizational relationships. If we cannot bring this to the surface and address it, it will impact, usually for the worse, the future course of all organizations. Both US and Korean organizations regularly fail at this, for both similar and different reasons. While we US organizations believe we are more democratic, I think an authoritarian leadership style is common among both Korean and US organizations.

Communication. Perhaps I should say that trust and communication go hand in hand. One cannot have a healthy organization without either one or the other. What is good, healthy communication? For me, it is an environment where all parties can communicate their wishes, needs, and ideas in honest dialogue. Differences of opinions and perspectives are sought and are included in the search for answers. Disagreements are common, if not frequent, as they serve to sharpen the discussion. The result may not be unanimous, but people feel that they had a say, and they do not hold grudges against each other. Conflict is managed, if not resolved.

I am not confident that I can accurately gauge the particulars of Korean organizational communication. Korean organizations may have utilized a more hierarchical style that worked in the past but would be problematic with the generational changes occurring today.

Connection and Empowerment. Healthy organizations strive to make their people feel connected and involved. Logo shirts might be good advertising, but for the organization's members, they are also a statement of solidarity. They express commitment and loyalty by telling others about their organization and encouraging them to become involved.

Organizations can empower their members by providing opportunities for growth and development in skills both related and not related to the organization. Although such opportunities can be academic or business related, they can be related to health and spiritual development, as well.

I think all organizations need to do more than they are doing to foster connections and empowerment among their workers. Too frequently, they define "development opportunities" as the opportunity to get a degree, which may be completely disconnected from the ongoing effectiveness of the organization.

Priority and purpose. It seems that a natural developmental process in organizational life is to start with a clear purpose, and then have a policy-centered approach take over. To a certain extent, this is unavoidable because of fiduciary or legal requirements. But that does not mean that the purpose cannot continue playing a prominent role. My insurance agent has the company vision statement covering the entire wall of the large office, where over forty staff members look at it all the time. My Rotary Club recites the 4-Way Test at each meeting (right before we say the Pledge of Allegiance), which is another way of keeping our purpose central.

In my consulting with Missio Nexus Mission Agencies,[4] I help them make their Member Health strategy and philosophy organic to their daily functioning. I challenge them—in whatever they are doing, deciding, or allocating—to consider the people of their organization. We also go further, pushing Member Health into their missiology.

Keeping the Member Health vision and strategy organically involved in the daily life of the mission has multiple benefits. First, it focuses the mission on the most important part of any organization—its people. But an important second function is that in cases where decisions must be made that might not be people-centered (as in legal or fiduciary issues), the organic approach to Member Health prompts mission leadership to explain to its people what is going on.

The lively dynamic between purpose and policy exists in all organizations. Regular reviews by the members, from my perspective, are one useful way to ensure the striking of an appropriate balance between the two.

Wellness/balance. Healthy organizations work to ensure that their environments maintain and, in the best cases, enhance member health. For example, an organization might promote member health by building a fitness center. But in a global mission, distributing fitness plans would be a more efficient approach to promoting physical health. Other components of a mission's efforts to promote health might include ensuring Sabbath opportunities and assisting members with transition planning (whether for home assignment or retirement).

Evaluation and change. Healthy organizations need to ensure that their evaluations are not done in a vacuum. That is, do they have effective mechanisms

---

4 One of my numerous hats is to function as a "Mission Advisor" for Missio Nexus member agencies (https://missionexus.org/new-mission-advisors/). In this role, I help agencies around the world look at how they integrate Member Health into their organizational structure, as well as their resulting national church structures.

to make the changes that the evaluations identified? Can they communicate the results expeditiously, so that members can understand and anticipate the upcoming changes? This process may be difficult for many US organizations. Americans tend to be blunt and direct in their feedback, and for many leaders, receiving such feedback can result in defensiveness.

I wonder how the same process would work in Korean contexts. How would the face-saving mechanism operate in an open evaluation context? It seems that an open evaluation could be more difficult to achieve, when tensions are running high and many people, as is common in Asian contexts, value the avoidance of criticism. The process of change may need to be much more explicit in such organizations, so that people can see constructive outcomes from their feedback.

SUMMARY AND CONCLUSIONS

This chapter has attempted to illuminate the necessity of developing an organization-centered approach to member health. Member Care, as it has developed, has effected many positive changes, but it has focused too exclusively on individual and family approaches. Member Care has also emphasized clinically oriented treatment approaches, and the confidentiality of the therapeutic hour has meant that applications of treatments are not as available to organizational growth and change as they could be.

I have attempted to identify key indicators of organizational health, noting some similarities and differences between Korean and US organizational aspirations and climates. These indicators of organizational health are based on surveys and studies of US organizations, so their direct application to Korean organizations needs further research.

However, I believe a global constant stretches across all cultures, dictating how groups and organizations thrive and develop. While each organization is unique in its personality and achievements, all organizational climates, cultures, and changes begin with the leader. The leader is essential to begin, maintain, and follow through on the values and guidelines of the organization. His or her styles of relating and leading will be reflected in the organization, whether on a personal or policy level.

The crisis in US missions is how to encourage health in a rapidly changing context and through constant crises on the field, accounting as well for generational differences. We could also note the pressures placed on our theology and doctrine by constantly shifting cultural values.

However, I am optimistic about the changes that must be made, because God always seems to call up new leaders to run the race, and new and great things happen. In many US missions, younger leaders are already making needed organizational adjustments. Brand new organizations are also appearing.

Of the Korean context I am less certain, but only because of a lack of knowledge. If hierarchical systems exist, are they capable of adjusting to the younger generations' involvement? What would that look like? Perhaps it would be helpful to instate some transitional leaders, who could manage the changes better because they are not invested in the historical hierarchy. Do such leaders exist? Or were they driven out earlier because of the entrenched systems? Alternatively, could the current leadership develop a clearer understanding of the health components of an organization and begin establishing mission environments that are conducive to open communication? One example of such openness within an Asian context, as well as within churches and mission agencies, is Ivan Liew's book, *Churches and Missions Agencies Together*.[5]

Implementing better services for people and de-stigmatizing mental health issues may help an organization tremendously, but change needs to be implemented from the top down too, not just from the bottom up.

RESPONSE by Nam Yong Sung

I appreciate Dr. Lindquist's contribution. Many approach member care issues as personal matters, yet he boldly attempts to "illuminate the necessity of developing an organization-centered approach to member health." This is a valuable contribution for mission organizations. I agree with his "Components for Promoting Organization-wide Health," which include: 1) An environment of trust; 2) Communication; 3) Connected and empowered team members; 4) A focus on priority and purpose, not just policy; 5) Wellness/balance; and 6) Evaluation and change. I would only add that any mission organization should be a spiritual community, defined by shared vision and calling.

SIMILARITIES AND DIFFERENCES

Dr. Lindquist noted the similarities we share and differences we carry. Although each person and organization is unique, we do not have to emphasize our differences. Too much emphasis on the differences among missionaries and organizations may mislead our mission community. Preferences, choices, and methods may be different, but human activities tend to be very similar. For example, no culture treats marriage and funeral ceremonies lightly, but methods of honoring such ceremonies differ across cultures.

In differentiating a shame culture from a guilt culture, Koreans are more inclined toward a shame culture, in which people are heavily concerned about the views of others. In line with that, Koreans tend to perceive mental illness negatively. I agree with Dr. Lindquist's statement that "mental issues or illnesses are seen as failures of spiritual and psychological mechanisms and cause great 'loss-of-face'" and "reflect poorly not only on the individual or family, but also on the entire organization." However, Koreans are beginning to recognize mental illness as a sickness that requires medical attention and do not feel as much shame as they did in the past. In terms of Americans being

---

[5] Ivan Liew, ed., *Churches and Missions Agencies Together: A Relational Model for Partnership Practice* (Fresno, CA: Condeo Press, 2017).

"blunt and direct in their feedback," Dr. Lindquist seems to be curious about how Koreans would respond in an open evaluation context. I do not think that there is much difference between us these days. If a judgment is fair, I believe most will accept it without reservation. Currently, multidimensional evaluation is quite common and widely accepted in Korea.

In their social organization, Koreans are more hierarchical, while Westerners are more horizontal. Koreans tend to think holistically, while Westerners tend to think analytically. Koreans seem to withhold their views, while Westerners seem to express their views without hesitation. This seems to have been the general perception of the differences between these two cultures. To a certain extent, the differences we perceive are true and proper. But nowadays, many Koreans, especially those of younger generations, function more horizontally, think analytically, and express their views without hesitation. The hierarchical system in Korea is being changed to become more horizontal. In a nutshell, people around the world are living in an increasingly monocultural environment. One can easily find cafes throughout small, rural villages in Korea.

TWO IMAGES OF HUMAN BEINGS

Dr. Lindquist worries about "stepping into the arena of mental health in the Korean context." He states, "I am trying not only to address personal mental health, which on some leadership levels is taboo, but also to address issues in the health of the Korean organization itself. I have been told that I am taking a potential risk to my professional reputation in doing this." I understand his fear, but I assure him that he does not need to worry about it. Koreans have already recognized the need to address mental health medically and are trying to respond appropriately.

We need to understand that all human beings have two different images within them. First, we were created in the image of God (Gen. 1:26–27). At the same time, we were born in the image of man (Gen. 5:3). As bearers of the image of God, human beings possess health, beauty, order, and glory by nature. But as bearers of the image of man, human beings are prone to sickness, wickedness, disorder, and disgrace. The sin nature we inherited from Adam causes us to distrust others and to try to control them, causing disorder. Thorns and thistles in different forms are sprouting everywhere. We are not free from the various dark symptoms the image of man brings. We can both cure and cause disease because of the two images that we as humans bear.

SPIRITUAL COMMUNITY

Dr. Lindquist talks about "member health and development, as opposed to member care." I fully agree with his thoughts. To assume that missionaries are not prone to mental illness and sinful behavior is incorrect. All human beings are susceptible to all kinds of illnesses, including mental illnesses. In order to develop a healthy organization, we must build a spiritual community. A purpose driven community, rather than a work driven community, needs to be the goal of any Christian organization.

1. Worshipping communities build spiritual communities. The prophet Isaiah saw the glory of God (Isa. 6:1–4). This is what worship is all about. He then received a calling from the Lord (Isa. 6:8). When the Lord said, "Whom shall I send? Who will go for us?" he said, "Here am I. Send me." Likewise, when people see the glory of God in worship (Isa. 66:18), they will proclaim his glory among the nations (Isa. 66:19). Dr. Lindquist points out that "numerous people feel they just have a job, not the calling they used to have." If we lose our vision, our mission organization may do more harm than good to its members. We need to emphasize restoring our calling and awakening our souls through worship. This is one way to avoid becoming "more policy driven than purpose driven."

2. We should seek to be a restoring community for our missionaries. Devoted missionaries can become victims of mental illness, family conflict, addiction, and other evidences of our fallen state. We must restore those wounded ones gently, knowing that we can also fall into the same pit (Gal. 6:1). Developing healthy, graciously restorative organizations should be one of our top priorities. Reductionism is dangerous. Defining a person on the basis of a single shortcoming or failure distorts the reality of the person's nature. The missionary calling of those suffering from mental illness should not be dismissed but restored and sustained.

3. Being a problem-solving community helps, as well. Dr. Lindquist lists five critical problems that missionary organizations may encounter. I would like to comment on only two of them: first, "suspicion or ambivalence about authority;" and second, "confusion about what to expect of mission organizations." Anticipating the former, we need to create a non-threatening environment, where burdens may be shared without fear of possible punishment. James, Jesus' brother, urged us to confess our sins to each other and pray for each other so that we may be healed (James 5:16). On the basis of this word, even the Pope of the Catholic Church confesses his sins to priests regularly. We can have that kind of confessing community by sharing our problems. Secondly, regarding "confusion about what to expect of mission organizations," if our expectations exceed reality, we are likely to be disappointed. A way to achieve a satisfactory outcome may simply be to balance expectations with reality. It is important to have clear guidelines by which members can figure out what to expect from the organization and its leaders. Communication among missionaries is vitally important.

4. A community of mutual respect is also essential. Dr. Lindquist concludes that he is "optimistic about the changes that must be made, because God always seems to call up new leaders to run the race, and new and great things happen." However, I believe younger leaders are likely to encounter problems that older leaders have never faced before. This is not merely due to leadership styles or systems but, primarily, to our sinful nature. If one problem is solved, another problem emerges because of the organizational changes. Of course, we need to work hard to make our organizations suitable for missionaries and our visions. Still, we must admit that no one is good enough, except for God alone (Mark 10:18).

Many find fault with hierarchical systems. Malcolm Gladwell, in his book *Outlier*, persuasively argues the dangers of the hierarchical structure within Korean culture. Without a doubt, we are concerned about it. However, the hierarchical system is not always harmful, and it does have positive aspects. We abhor authoritarianism, yet we need to respect the authority of leaders. As long as we respect the authority of those in leadership positions, I believe the system goes well for all who are involved. Moses was a leader within a hierarchical system, yet he was well respected. We need to build a community of authority, not a community of authoritarianism; a community of respect, not a community of selfishness.

I have mentioned four types of communities that can foster spiritual community. There is a need to place more emphasis on a spiritual environment, rather than on systems or policies. We need to make our organizations reliant on God, the source of wisdom. As we read from the book of Ezekiel, the water that revives whatever it touches flows from the threshold of the temple (Ezek. 47:1–12). Let us come near to the throne of the Lord in worship and see the glory of God.

FLOURISHING COMMUNITY

Dr. Lindquist points out the characteristics of healthy organizations. I strongly agree that "in healthy organizations, there is a dynamic interplay between the individual and the organization, and both benefit from their relationship." Maintaining strong communication without barriers among members means less problems are likely to arise. Allowing members to pursue their visions within a cooperative environment can help produce a flourishing organization. If organizations encourage each missionary's ministry initiatives, they can reap positive change for those around them, including the missionaries themselves. Furthermore, if each missionary suggests ways to help achieve the organization's vision through the missionaries' own fieldwork, all members may develop healthfully as a result. Our organizations can flourish as communities where members thrive and prosper, when we maintain an open relationship between our organizational visions and the particular visions of the missionaries themselves.

QUESTIONS FOR REFLECTION

1. Can you point to mission organizations that have been transformed into supportive mission communities?
2. What can you advise about mission organizations comprised of missionaries from many nationalities and cultures? Can an agency born in an era of American triumphalism ever truly accommodate as full and valued members men, women, and families from Korea or elsewhere?
3. How do these ideal mission organizations deal with the mental illness of non-Western members and their families?

17

A STUDY ON THE EMOTIONAL STRESS AND MENTAL HEALTH OF RETIRED KOREAN MISSIONARIES

by JAE-HON LEE AND SUNG IL MOON

THE MENTAL HEALTH OF MISSIONARIES

The importance of caring for the mental health of missionaries working overseas is well established in North America, thanks to the pioneering efforts of works such as Mae Gardner's *Mental Health and Missions,* that laid the foundation for missionary care in the seventies. Further, the number of missionary care programs has greatly increased since then.[1] One of North America's most recognized centers for research on the health of missionaries is the Missionary Health Institute in Toronto, Canada. Established in 1936, this institute not only provides services for physical illness and overall health, but also provides counsel on mental well-being. The organization emphasizes the importance of research and providing services that stem from various research endeavors.[2]

In Korea, Protestant churches have actively sent missionaries abroad since the seventies. As a result, currently, over 20,000 Korean missionaries are working at various international locations.[3] However, in Korea, there exists almost no system to promote or to care for the mental health of these missionaries.[4] Churches are faced with the reality that they cannot adequately support team missions and other missionary efforts. Consequently, not only are many missionaries are finding it hard to continue with their missions, but many are also left wondering about their ability to complete the various responsibilities essential to their own personal lives.[5]

Many Korean missionaries lack support and have to deal privately with preventable mental conditions such as stress. Some face mental health problems that have already reached serious levels. Unfortunately, objective research on these matters is lacking. Only a few reports have been published, mostly based on the personal experiences of a particular missionary or mission specialist. For the last several years, various missions groups have attempted to monitor and to provide counseling for the missionaries working overseas. This development is welcome, indeed, but the scope of such services is still extremely limited and in no way close to satisfying the overall demand.

---

1   Hyeong Guen Choi, "Building Missionaries' Member Care System," *Mission and Theology* 28 (2011): 86-88.
2   Missionary Health Institute, accessed November 10, 2018, http://missionaryhealth.ca.
3   Hyeong Guen Choi, "Building Missionaries' Member Care System."
4   Bangkok Forum Committee, *The 11th, 12th Bangkok Mission Forum: Korean Missionaries' Retirement and Mental Health* (Gyeonggi, Korea: Heavenlyseeds, 2015), 34-53, 66-76, 121-204.
5   Steve Sang-Cheol Moon, "Missions from Korea 2013: Microtrends and Finance." *International Bulletin of Missionary Research* 37, no. 2 (2013): 96-97. http://www.internationalbulletin.org/issues/2013-02/2013-02-096-moon.pdf. See also: Steve Sang-Cheol Moon, Hee-Joo Yoo, and Eun Mi Kim, "Missions from Korea 2015: Missionaries Unable to Continue Ministry in Their Country of Service." *International Bulletin of Missionary Research* 39, no. 2 (2015): 84-86. http://www.internationalbulletin.org/issues/2015-02/2015-02-084-moon.pdf.

RETIREMENT AND THE MENTAL HEALTH OF KOREAN MISSIONARIES

The missionaries who have served for the last thirty years or so are now retiring and returning to Korea.[6] And the mental health of these retired missionaries has the potential to become a great problem for the Korean mission movement as a whole.

Retirement poses social and cultural changes that include a shift in the social and relational roles of the retirees because of their decreased abilities. Danger arises when losses in the retiree's life lead to social and psychological stress that could negatively affect mental health. In general, retirement, on one level, means the pursuit of leisure and the freedom from responsibilities pertaining to one's occupation or career. On another level, it can also cause stress, especially when retirement leads to financial pressure or loss of self-esteem. Such situations can threaten mental health. According to some reports, many retirees, because of financial difficulties or loneliness, return to work within two years of retirement. Sometimes, the length of retirement is almost equal to the length of one's working career. Therefore, it is worth noting that the time after retirement is just as important as the time leading up to it.[7]

However, in Korea, it is very difficult to find reports on emotional stress or research on the mental health of retired missionaries. Thus, no one can discuss the exact situation with objective accuracy. Meanwhile, missionaries and mission specialists working abroad are constantly reporting the seriousness of the problem. Such reports are contributing to the recognition of the problem, a better understanding of the situation, and the desire to find solutions.

THE NEED FOR RESEARCH BASED ON EVIDENCE

As noted, in Korea, there have been no previous efforts to examine the emotional stress or the mental health of retired missionaries by the professionals working in the mental health field. Towards remedying this situation, the research team has conducted in-depth interviews with retired missionaries who have returned home from abroad in order to accurately assess their emotional stress levels and to examine the state of their overall mental well-being.

In such an examination, it is imperative not only to minimize the researchers' mistakes but also to refrain from subjective judgments. While analyzing the contents of conversations collected through interviews, the research team attempted to set aside tentative concepts or categories for the time being and concentrated on the categorization of concepts that were repeatedly observed.[8] By repeating this process two to three times, the team tried to gain new insights on the problem.

---

6 "Worldwide Mission Ministry," General Assembly of The Presbyterian Church of Korea, accessed November 10, 2018, http://www.pckwm.org.

7 Korean Association for Geriatric Psychiatry, *Geriatric Psychiatry* (Seoul: Choongang Munwha Co., 2014).

8 Young Hwan Cho, *Qualitative Study: Methodology and Cases* (Seoul: Educational Science Co., 1999).

IN-DEPTH INTERVIEWS

For the purpose of this research, the team chose to interview missionaries who had retired after working for at least six years in various international locations. The research team, after outlining the purpose of the study, obtained a list of thirty-eight candidates who met all the requirements from the General Assembly of the Presbyterian Church in Korea's Global Mission Society, Korean Baptist Church, Onnuri Church, NamSeoul Church, Korea World Mission Association, Overseas Mission Fellowship in Korea, Global Mission Fellowship, Global Bible Translators in Korea, and The Paul Mission International.

All the missionaries who participated in the interviews signed written agreements and granted us permission to record our conversations. The interviews were conducted at whatever locations the missionaries preferred.

Before the interviews, the missionaries were asked to state their missions locations, as well as their genders, ages, and numbers of years doing missionary work. For information regarding their post-retirement mental health, the participants were surveyed on the four basic categories of mental health: depression, anxiety, trauma, and quality of life.

Aside from the two main researchers, a worker from the mission organization who is familiar with such works also participated as an assistant. The time allotted for the interviews averaged about an hour but was extended as needed. For each participant, one or two interviews were conducted. All interviews were recorded, transcribed, and examined. The participants were given a prepared questionnaire to answer. The subjects who have answered similar questions were permitted to compare their results. The researchers participated in the interviews as indirect observers. Without insisting on any specific locations, the interviews were conducted between June and October of 2018.

The detailed interview process, including the list of interview questions, is delineated below.

> **Introduction:** Greetings and introductions are made. General conversation follows, as well as an explanation of the research purpose and method.
>
> Main and supplementary questions: For each question, the subject should be able to express his/her experiences, thoughts, situations, and actions.
>
> **Main questions:**
> How long has it been since you retired from missionary work? (How are you spending your time at the present?)
>
> Please share with us how you spend your time in your retirement.
>
> Supplementary questions (in case there are no easy answers to the main questions, consider asking the following):

Please think about your life before and after your work as a missionary. What is the first image that comes to your mind?

Please share with us good experiences or difficult experiences you had after retiring. (Ask for specific examples or episodes.)

What kind of changes have you experienced after retirement (physical, emotional, financial, spiritual, with family members, relationship with others, etc.)?

When faced with difficulties in your retirement, what was the thing that helped you the most (physically, emotionally, financially, spiritually, with family members, relationship with others, etc.)?

In our conversations, what do you want to emphasize as the most important?

Conclusion: Tell the participant that the interview has come to an end and ask the participant if he/she has left anything out or wants to add something. Explain to the interviewee the possibility of further interviews and ask if he/she would agree to them. Thank the participant, and then end the interview.

THE EMOTIONAL STRESS AND MENTAL HEALTH OF RETIRED KOREAN MISSIONARIES

The research team defined emotional stress as psychological, social, spiritual, and physical difficulties caused as result of the inability to deal effectively with everyday situations. In accordance with the interview results, emotional stress was categorized as follows:

- Practical Problems (raising children, housing/house, financial matters, jobs)
- Family Problems (parent-children relationships, spousal relationships)
- Spiritual/Religious Concerns
- Physical Problems

Meanwhile, for the state of retired missionaries' mental health, the research team made use of the American Mental Health Association's internationally recognized *Diagnostic and Statistical Manual of Mental Disorders* (*DSM-5*) in order to better assess the existence or the seriousness of the subjects' mental disorders.[9] This was done to obtain objective and evidence-based data that could be compared to the results of similar research projects to be done in the future.

---

9 American Psychiatric Association, *Diagnostic and Statistical Manual of Mental Disorders 5* (Washington, DC: American Psychiatric Association, 2013).

RESULTS AND CONSIDERATIONS

The research team has successfully conducted detailed interviews with eleven retired male missionaries and analyzed the findings to look into their emotional stress levels and the state of their mental health. It was not realistic to interview all subjects who met the requirements. Also, considering selection bias and other limiting factors, it is difficult to say that the results can be applied to all retired Korean missionaries. But even with these limitations, the research team, based on the findings, would like to make the following conclusions.

First: The greatest sources of emotional stress, or distress,[10] for the retired missionaries we interviewed were financial anxiety and limited opportunities to participate in social activities. Finding affordable housing was especially difficult for the missionaries. This problem perpetuates the difficulties faced by the subjects in everyday situations and this, in return, perpetuates the negative effect on their emotional state.

Second: The subjects also faced distress in their relationships with their spouses and in their other social interactions, due to loneliness and the feeling of isolation. However, this problem did not seem to have serious negative effects on the subjects' day-to-day lives. Most subjects were finding solutions for this concern by utilizing their inner psychological strength and keeping contact with friends and colleagues. Still, if the subjects become unable to keep up with various changes and losses as they get older, this problem could pose greater threat to their mental health.

Third: The desire of the retired missionaries to share their experiences and wisdom with the churches was very strong. Sadly, the fact that there are only limited opportunities to do so was a source of distress for the retirees. Many retirees regretted that strict hierarchy and the inflexibility of Korean churches limit opportunities to share their experiences and knowledge. This finding is also in accordance with the fact that many retired missionaries felt limited in their opportunities to participate in social or church activities.

Fourth: In terms of experiencing depression, anxiety, and psychological trauma, most retired missionaries were doing better than we expected. Compared to the general public, they were also more likely to say that they are satisfied with the quality of their lives. This result is also supported by the structured examination of the subjects' mental health conducted during their interviews.

Fifth: It is possible that a small number of retired missionaries are facing serious mental health risks and, thus, urgent efforts need to be made to better analyze their situations and to intervene on their behalf. The majority of participants reported that they knew or had heard of other retired missionaries who were suffering from serious depression or other mental illnesses.

---

10 Kyeong Bong Koh, *Stress and Psychosomatic Medicine* (Seoul: Ilchogak, 2011): 17-24.

The difficulty in finding housing—noted in the first conclusion—has also been repeatedly reported in other research and by professional organizations.[11] The current research project approached this concern with consideration to the subjects' mental health and concluded that subjectively, this has become the greatest source of psychological stress to the retired missionaries.

In the field of mental health, housing and income directly affect one's subjective well-being.[12] Income can limit one's ability to adjust to medical needs or different styles of life. If one has sufficient income, one can probably afford more opportunities to participate in various activities and thus have a better chance at reducing one's stress. In order to have financial stability after retirement, one needs to make sufficient income during one's career and save enough of it before retiring.

However, according to the retired missionaries who participated in the interviews, most of their financial support came to an end the moment they retired, leaving them with considerable financial strain. Such difficulty and worries stemming from financial difficulty have led to negative moods and may eventually cause a deterioration of their mental health. Recently, bigger churches and mission organizations have started pensions and other financial support systems geared to support retired missionaries, but even these are very limited in scope and come short of securing the psychological stability of retired missionaries. The discussion about the correlation between mental and physical health may come later, but it is no overstatement to emphasize that stability in housing and other basic financial matters is paramount to maintaining one's mental health.

Another threat to mental health is loneliness or the lack of mutual interaction in a social setting.[13] According to recent studies, the danger of physical deterioration as result of lack of social interaction is greater in men. That is, women are more likely to invest in cultivating friends and thereby make better social relationships, while men are more likely to invest in their careers and as result, are less concerned with developing social relationships.[14] In many instances, social relationships and support networks are the protectors of mental health, none more so than the relational support of spouses and family members.

Missionaries returning to Korea after retirement are less likely to have maintained sufficient social support networks that they can rely on. Considering the special emphasis Korean missions place on the outward results of the missionary efforts, the possibility is high that most retired missionaries may

---

11 Yoon Il Hwang, "A Study for Post-Retirement Plans for P.C.K Missionaries," *Mission and Theology* 28 (2011): 189–220.

12 Korean Association of Neuropsychiatry, *Textbook of Neuropsychiatry*, vol 3. (Seoul: Iamis Co., 2017), 687–723.

13 Daniel A. Girdano, Dorothy E. Dusek, and George S. Everly, Jr., *Controlling Stress and Tension: A Holistic Approach* (Upper Saddle River, NJ: Prentice-Hall, Inc., 1979), 3–7.

14 Korean Association of Neuropsychiatry, *Textbook of Neuropsychiatry*.

not have invested enough time or effort in finding and maintaining sufficient family or social support. Many gatherings of retired missionaries are limited to a small number of people bound by personal friendship, and there are almost no support systems to help improve the spousal relationships of aging missionaries.

Regular and systematic meetings for retired missionaries would go a long way toward helping them maintain and expand their social relationships. Continued services, including couples counseling provided by mental health professionals, could also become a part of the solution. Unlike North American culture, the Korean culture traditionally places importance on keeping "face." Consideration of this cultural value should result in organizations approaching retirees' relational needs not only on the organizational level, but also on the personal level.[15]

It is true that social relationships are maintained, as well as expanded, by social activities. Many retired missionaries feel, however, that their activities within the church are greatly limited and, consequently, they become frustrated that they can no longer effectively participate in social activities. This frustration becomes another significant source of stress. Individual churches may vary, but the Korean church culture, which often focuses on the main pastor, may result in church structures or procedures that limit the retired missionaries' ability to be fully involved in church activities. Decreased self-esteem after retirement may also contribute to the missionaries' becoming less enthusiastic about participating in church activities.[16] Whatever the reasons, if the analysis points to the fact that the psychological chasm between the retired missionaries and the church has grown larger, then mental health professionals need to step in and assist in improving the communication between the two groups.

Fortunately, according to the research, the state of mental health and the quality of life for the majority of the retired missionaries seem comparatively satisfactory. Along with the detailed interviews, the participants were asked to fill out a survey or screening measurement[17] on depression, anxiety, and their satisfaction in life. In general, the subjects' state of mental health was reported to be positive and no clinically serious problem was found. In the interviews, the researchers could identify hitherto mentioned psychological difficulties, but on the other hand, they also noted the missionaries' efforts to be flexible in finding biblically faithful solutions.

Finally, another point that requires attention is that the majority of retired missionaries also directly or indirectly reported having fellow missionaries who were suffering from or at risk of succumbing to mental disorders. Of course, the researchers could not meet and listen to all those reported to be in this situation and make objective

---

15 Sang Chin Choi and Seung Yeob Yu, "Multifaceted Analyses of Chemyon (Social Face): An Indigenous Korean Perspective," *The Korean Journal of Social and Personality Psychology* 6, no. 2 (1992): 137-157.

16 Won-Gue Lee, "Openness and Closure of the Korean church," *Christian Thought* 288 (1982): 71-84.

17 Sung Kil Min, Kwang Il Kim, and Il Ho Park, *Korean Version of WHO Quality of Life Scale Abbreviated Version (WHOQOL-BREF)* (Seoul: Hana Medical Press, 2002).

conclusions, but the fact that similar cases are being repeatedly reported means that larger numbers of retired missionaries may be suffering from mental illnesses that are not yet realized by the church. The examination of the true situation should be pursued as soon as possible, allowing the cooperation of the church and professionals to help remedy the situation.

On several points, the scope of this research is somewhat limited. As already mentioned, the number of retired missionaries who agreed to participate in the research was not enough to make far-reaching analyses. After obtaining the list of candidates from churches and mission associations, the researchers got in touch with individual candidates and asked them politely to participate in the interview, but only a small number of them finally agreed, making it very difficult for the researchers to recruit enough subjects. Then again, it could be that other researchers may be faced with similar difficulty when delving into the mental health of another group of people.

In Korea, stigma surrounding the topic of mental health is comparatively greater than it is in Western countries and, therefore, Koreans participating in interviews on that topic tend to become a bit defensive in their answers.[18] This hesitancy of Koreans to discuss mental health concerns is also evident in the fact that the number of Koreans receiving mental health services is significantly lower in Korea than it is in the Western countries. Thus, one challenge of this research project was conducting interviews with mainly older subjects. Also, the researchers cannot overlook the fact that some participants may have given false answers to give an impression of health, for the sake of saving face.[19]

According to the survey they completed, both mental health and quality of life seemed comparatively satisfactory for the majority of the retired missionaries who participated in the study. But based on the analysis of the interviews, that satisfactory state could be said to fall on the borderline. Individuals who were the focus of others' attention and had social responsibilities tended to report the state of their mental health as good. It may be that retired missionaries in general have similar tendencies. In the subsequent analysis of the findings of this research, these points should be taken into consideration.

Another point is that this research only dealt with male missionaries. However, there are many female missionaries who have retired after years of dedicating their lives to international missions. There are also spouses of male missionaries who are coworkers in the mission field. This research is limited by not including the perspective of these women.

---

18 Ministry of Health and Welfare Korea Suicide Prevention Center, *2015 White Paper on Suicide Prevention* (Seoul: Korea Suicide Prevention Center, 2015).

19 Kyu Han Bae and Ki Jae Lee, *Survey Research Methodology* (Seoul: KNOU Press, 2003), 96-101.

A SUMMARY AND A SUGGESTION

This research, as far as the researchers know, is the first study conducted on the state of retired Korean missionaries in terms of their emotional stress and mental health. By monitoring and observing the subjects through in-depth interviews, the researchers tried to identify and categorize common concepts that can serve as the groundwork for further studies, as well as laying ground for systematic analysis and arriving at objective conclusions based on as many scientifically verifiable facts as possible.

Because of several limitations, the researchers caution about arriving at some interpretations. Still, the research succeeds in identifying sources of stress for the retired missionaries and especially puts emphasis on the need to better examine the reality and to intervene on behalf of those missionaries who are yet to be identified and who are on the verge of succumbing to mental disorders. The researchers suggest that professionals involved in the Korean churches waste no time in further examination and finding of solutions on this matter.

In the future, with help from churches and missionary organizations, more systematic efforts should be made to conduct further research that includes women and larger numbers of retired missionaries to obtain more and better data on this subject.

RESPONSE by Liz Bendor-Samuel

INTRODUCTION

Dr. Lee's and Rev. Dr. Moon's research case study refers to several overlapping domains that are of interest to this gathering. These include Mission Member Care, the experience of retirement and aging, reverse culture shock, and attitudes toward mental health issues. My observations are guided by the authors' views, my personal connections over the years with Korean mission workers, and several available articles.

MISSION MEMBER CARE (MMC)

Mission Member Care for retirees is but one element in a systemic approach to the support of long-term cross-cultural workers. Whole-person MMC includes provision of, and referral to, resources for the promotion of the physical, mental, and spiritual well-being of the mission worker in both the home and host countries.[20]

---

20 See, for example, Debbie M. Hawker, John Durkin, and David S. J. Hawker, "To Debrief or Not to Debrief Our Heroes: That Is the Question," *Clinical Psychology and Psychotherapy* 18, no. 6 (Nov./Dec. 2011): 453–463.

The authors of this case study note that MMC is relatively new in the Korean church scene and has developed since Korean cross-cultural mission experienced explosive growth in the 1980s. They identify particular *practical needs* among the first generation of late twentieth-century Korean mission workers, who are now aging and retiring.

Retirees who participated in this study described financial stress as a primary problem, especially with reference to the cost of housing. It is too late to seek solutions to this issue at the time of retirement. Organizational mission support stops at the time of retirement, and personal financial savings and pension plans are variable. This stress is in itself a logistical one, which needs to be taken seriously by Korean churches and mission organizations. Churches may be in a position to give loans or provide housing and continue to support missionaries until a source of income is identified, perhaps from pensions or part-time employment.

As with mission workers from many countries, it may be that at the time of departure overseas, they are encouraged by their churches to "give up everything for God." This will affect a new worker's ability to ask about long-term financial provision and pension plans, having a natural reluctance to be perceived as "unspiritual."

In the UK, for example, expats in general, and mission workers in particular, face challenging financial pressures on return from abroad. Davies reports that UK expats neglect pension planning—it is often low on the priority list prior to departure—and find their financial "lifeline" wanting on return.[21]

The policy of mission workers keeping a home property and renting it to tenants in their absence may be both a prudent stewardship of assets and a means of financial security on their return.

EXPERIENCE OF RETIREMENT AND AGING

It is helpful to separate the issues of *retirement* and *return* in reflecting on this study cohort.

Attitudes toward retirement and aging may be explored by considering Erikson's Developmental Stage Eight, where he contrasts the possibility of experiencing "Wisdom and Ego Integrity" with that of "Despair" in the years of late adulthood and retirement, ages sixty years and over.[22]

Erikson posits the psychological existential question of this stage in life as: "Is it okay to have been me?" As Christians, we will have a spiritual view to integrate here: "How does God view me and my work?" It is the time of life when we reflect on our accomplishments, and there will be a resulting sense of personal integration ("Ego Integrity") if we consider ourselves successful in God's eyes as well as our own.

---

21 Paul Davies, "New NHS Charges Hit Missionaries," *Professional Adviser*, Feb. 2017: 6–7, https://www.eauk.org/current-affairs/news/new-nhs-charges-hit-missionaries.cfm.

22 Simon Hearn et al., "Between Integrity and Despair: Toward Construct Validation of Erikson's Eighth Stage," *Journal of Adult Development* 19, no. 1 (Jan. 2012): 1–20. http://dx.doi.org/10.1007/s10804-011-9126-y.

On the other hand, if we evaluate our lives as unproductive, failing to accomplish God's calling and goals, then feelings of despair, depression, and hopelessness may dominate. Frustration with ourselves can lead to projection of anger toward God, the "system," our organization, our church, our spouse, our family, or our friends (see "Reverse Culture Shock" below).

The cohort in this study are senior male missionaries who have been retired for more than six years and are, thus, not new to retirement. They will have already negotiated this Developmental Stage more or less "successfully," with more or less support from their families, friends, churches, and organizations.

It would be interesting to see where the cohort members score themselves on the Erikson Stage Eight "Wisdom and Ego Integrity"/"Despair" axis, as a self-administered tool, both retrospectively and currently. The study authors note that members refer in their interviews to retired colleagues known to them, who may well be near the "Despair" end of this axis (see "Attitudes toward Mental Health" below).

Newly retired missionaries would be an interesting group to research, coming fresh to Erikson's self-questioning, typical of Stage Eight as described above.

How can retired long-term mission workers be involved with the new "Silver Missionary" workforce, as a source of mutual inspiration and benefit?[23]

REVERSE CULTURE SHOCK

Craig Storti identifies factors that affect the experience of return and the negotiation of Reverse Culture Shock.[24] The experience of age and previous life transitions, including returns from overseas, may make it easier to negotiate later transitions; alternatively, it may result in depression and a sense of cumulative loss. The emotional work involves dealing with the idealization of the home culture and the expectation that it will not have changed.

In Dr. Lee's and Dr. Moon's study of male missionary retirees, there are elements of "stuckness" reflected in the interviews with the cohort, where "adjustment" to the practical and emotional effects of low income, in particular, may not yet have been achieved. This is a significant issue at six years after retirement, later than the usual timescale of one to two years.

In another aspect of Reverse Culture Shock for mission workers, Jordan highlights the issue of lacking opportunities to share about mission experiences in the mission worker's home church.[25]

---

23 Jae Kyeong Lee, "South Korea's Great Missionary Movement–God's Sovereignty, Our Obedience," Korea Baptist Convention, Feb. 9, 2018, https://www.imb.org/2018/02/09/south-korea-mission-movement/.
24 Craig Storti, *The Art of Coming Home* (Boston: Intercultural Press, 1996, 2001, 2003).
25 Peter Jordan, *Re-entry: Making the Transition from Missions to Life at Home* (Seattle: YWAM Publishing, 1992).

Beaver views the issue from a social science perspective,[26] while Lee reflects on the reverse migration of diaspora Koreans from the USA and China particularly[27] (see also Suh[28]).

Equally, retiring mission workers may face "bittersweet" reactions from family and friends, when the loved ones' expectations have been in some way disappointed.

Convening groups of retired missionaries, so they can share their experiences and support each other, would help individuals and couples to address common issues of identity and role within the church and within society. Mission networks may be drawn on to convene these groups.

General debriefing post-retirement provides a "one-off" space for mission workers' personal exploration of these significant subjects, whereas pastoral counseling may be appropriate for longer-term support.

ATTITUDES TOWARD MENTAL HEALTH

The authors note the stigma attached to mental health issues in the Korean context. This was reported by Park et al., in a study of adult Koreans' attitudes to mental health services.[29]

Missionaries are respected as mature Christian leaders and, as such, are not expected to fall prey to depression, anxiety, or marriage disharmony; neither are they expected to seek support from mental health professionals.

The authors note the difficulties of accurately gauging the cohort members' mental well-being, although it seems that the interviews were revealing, allowing greater latitude in response than the self-administered questionnaire.

In the UK, too, mental health challenges have only been considered a "respectable" conversation topic within the last three to five years, as public figures, such as the British royal family, have begun speaking out about their own experiences and enthusing others about the benefits of therapy. The President of the UK Royal College of Psychiatrists wrote in a national newspaper in 2017 that younger members of the royal family were "breaking mental health taboos for a new generation."[30]

---

26 Michael J. Beaver, "The Effect of Modernity on Korean Sojourners and Korean Non-sojourners: Shift in Cultural Identity and Self-construal and Reentry Adaptation" (doctoral dissertation, Capella University, 2008).

27 Helene Kim Lee, "Bittersweet Homecomings: Ethnic Identity Construction in the Korean Diaspora" (doctoral dissertation, University of California, 2009).

28 Stephen Suh, "Nostalgic for the Unfamiliar: US-Raised Koreans and the Complexities of 'Return'" (doctoral dissertation, University of Minnesota, 2016).

29 Jee Park, Seong-Jin Cho, Jun-Young Lee, Jee Sohn, Su Seong, Hye Suk, and Maeng Cho, "Impact of Stigma on Use of Mental Health Services by Elderly Koreans," *Social Psychiatry and Psychiatric Epidemiology* 50, no. 5 (May 2015): 757–766.

30 Simon Wessely, "Princes William and Harry Break Mental Health Taboos for a New Generation," *The Guardian*, April 19, 2017, https://www.theguardian.com/commentisfree/2017/apr/19/princes-william-harry-taboos-mental-health.

National health policy has been working steadily toward this end.[31]

It would be interesting to note the perspectives of women missionaries and of younger missionaries in future studies, regarding their readiness to share about mental health challenges.

CONCLUSION

In the context of Mission Member Care, there is a newly evident need for considering the practical and financial challenges that face Korean missionary retirees. Pensions and property-owning should be included in mission organization policymaking (in conjunction with the missionaries and churches), to address these challenges from the start of the missionaries' association with the organization.

Preparation for the experiences of retirement and aging can be intentionally and fruitfully considered long before the calendar turns to the year of return and may include interaction with new "silver" missionaries.

Perspectives on reverse culture shock on return to Korea may also be intentionally and fruitfully explored prior to experience. Wherever possible, retiring missionaries can be encouraged and taught both to plan satisfactory closure in the host culture, as well as a fulfilling adjustment to identity and role in the home culture.

Korean societal attitudes toward mental health issues are opening up, and returning missionaries will reflect this to a growing degree, as they identify appropriate mental health support, whether in the short, medium, or long term.

In future studies, it will be significant to interview women missionaries, both singles and spouses, as well as to investigate the experiences of new retirees.

The authors are to be commended for breaking new research ground in the Korean mission scene, where there are opportunities for vital research, strategic thinking, and policy development.

QUESTIONS FOR REFLECTION

1. How could mission organizations and churches develop practical and financial strategies for missionary retirement?

2. How may currently retired missionaries be integrated into the ministry of their home churches?

3. How may support for returning missionaries be developed to fully explore the emotional and spiritual sequelae of reverse culture shock?

---

31 Chris Heginbotham, "UK Health Policy Can Alter the Stigma of Mental Illness, *The Lancet* 352(9133) (Oct. 1998): 1052-1053. See also, S. Parker, C. Robertson, N. Allen, J. Beezhold, A. Bhutto, R. Laverack, L. Parry, L. Piper, R. Smith, T. Wade, "Creating an Educational Intervention to Raise Mental Health Awareness and Tackle Stigma in Adolescents in the UK: 'Headucate,'" *European Psychiatry* 28, supplement 1 (2013): 1.

18

RETIREMENT PLANS FOR KOREAN MISSIONARIES:

A CASE STUDY OF NAMSEOUL CHURCH

by JINBONG KIM AND J. NELSON JENNINGS

INTRODUCTION

At the KGMLF 2017 gathering, Andrew Walls remarked that "God was perhaps quietly preparing the church in Korea for a special place in world mission."[1] According to his analysis, the remarkable surge of Korean missions had its roots in the miraculous growth of financially self-supporting Korean churches and the "Pentecost" of Korean Christianity's early twentieth-century revival movement. Furthermore, South Korea has experienced rapid economic growth and technological development, backed by Koreans' infamous fervor for education. All these factors were combined with an "awareness of the world outside and a global consciousness," which gave momentum for remarkable mission activity, according to Walls.[2]

Indeed, the number of Korean missionaries has grown rapidly, skyrocketing through such benchmarks as 100 in 1980, 1,000 in 1989, 10,000 in 2002, and 20,000 in 2012.[3] In recent years, however, the rate of increase has dwindled to 0.69 percent (145 persons more than the previous year), its lowest in 38 years.[4] As of 2018, there were 21,220 Korean missionaries serving in 159 countries.[5]

According to recently published data, the membership of the major Korean church denominations has also been steadily shrinking.[6] The reasons for the decline in membership in Korean churches include demographic changes in Korean society (with the lowest fertility rate among OECD nations), the sustained state of disrepute of the church in the society, and the aging church's failure to deliver practical messages to the younger population.[7]

Along with decreasing memberships, a significant number of Korean churches are facing financial challenges. It is now difficult to deny that the momentum for missions, once robust, is starting to decline. An accompanying challenge is that more than half of Korean missionaries will be retiring in ten years.[8] Just prior to

---

1 Andrew F. Walls, "Migration in Christian History," in Jinbong Kim et al., eds., *People Disrupted: Doing Mission Responsibly Among Refugees and Migrants* (Pasadena, CA: William Carey Library, 2018), 35-39.

2 Ibid.

3 Steve Sang-Cheol Moon, *The Korean Missionary Movement: Dynamics and Trends, 1988-2013* (Pasadena, CA: William Carey Library, 2016), 5-11.

4 Ibid.

5 Steve Moon, "Toward True Globalism in World Missions" *Lausanne Global Analysis*, Volume 8, Issue 1 (January 2019), https://www.lausanne.org/content/lga/2019-01/toward-true-globalism-in-world-missions?utm_source=Lausanne+Movement+List&utm_campaign=43bab89480-Lausanne_Global_Analysis+-May2018&utm_medium=email&utm_term=0_602c1cb67d-43bab89480-91713649 (accessed April 17, 2019).

6 Jinbong Kim, "Rethinking Retirement and Creative Aging among Korean Protestant Missionaries." D. Ics., diss., Grace Theological Seminary, 2016, 228-230.

7 Ibid.

8 Jinbong Kim, "Korean Missionary Retirement Survey," in Jonathan J. Bonk et al., eds., *Family Accountability in Missions: Korean and Western Case Studies* (New Haven: OMSC, 2013), 259-273.

that large-scale retirement, namely, in seven to eight years, Korean society will have turned from an "Aged Society" to a "Super-Aged Society," in which more than 20 percent of the population will be elderly. Then there will be a sudden surge in the retirement of Korean missionaries, for which Korean churches and mission organizations should specifically prepare.[9]

In the midst of such rapid changes occurring throughout Korean churches and society, at least one exemplary church in Seoul has faithfully maintained its mission policy for more than forty-five years. In particular, the church implements well prepared policies on missionary retirement that most Korean churches and mission agencies do not have. The name of the church is NamSeoul ("South Seoul") Church. Before describing NamSeoul Church's practices in detail, we invite you to consider the story of a Korean missionary whose church support looked much different.

THE CASE OF MISSIONARY DANIEL

Daniel,[10] who lived in Seoul, was invited as a mission candidate to a church in Busan and served the church for about a year. In early 1994, Daniel got married; he and his new wife had a wonderful commissioning ceremony in the church; and then they left Korea. The missionary couple wanted to serve through an international mission agency, so they went to England to prepare for the English qualification test required by the organization. The sending church supported 60 percent of the couple's living expenses and the full tuition for studying English.[11] Their first son was born during the eight months in which they were preparing for the English test. After the English test, they went to France to study French, the official language of the mission field where they were headed. While they were studying French in southern France, the sending church requested Daniel to come to Korea immediately. The reason was that he had failed to pass the English exam and could not join the international agency as originally planned.

It took two days for Daniel to arrive in Busan. No one from the church came out to pick him up. The sending church was difficult to locate, since it had recently moved to a new address. Daniel finally arrived at the meeting room in the church around 9 p.m. Several church elders and the senior pastor gathered for the "hearing" that went on for about one hour. Daniel had already been judged to be an incompetent missionary by the sending church, and he was scorned and discredited as an unsuccessful missionary who had failed even before entering

---

9   Kim, 2016, 228–230.

10 Daniel is a false name, and he was not a NamSeoul Church missionary.

11 Daniel was a member of the General Assembly of the Presbyterian Church in Korea. At that time, the mission organization required raising a monthly sponsorship of $2,400 for a family of four to depart for a mission field in Africa. The qualification to be a missionary's sending church was to provide more than 60 percent ($1,440) of the total required financial support.

the mission field. The church immediately ceased all financial sponsorship of Daniel's family and severed all relationships. Daniel's family experienced extreme financial difficulties and excruciating mental distress. Time passed, and a Korean American church in the United States began to support Daniel's family while they served in the mission field. Even though the church was a trustworthy and dependable sending church for Daniel's family, the church's mission policy changed, and after eight years, all financial support was discontinued.

THE RELATIONSHIP BETWEEN THE MISSIONARY AND THE SENDING CHURCH IN KOREA

According to a survey of 346 missionaries conducted in 2013, more than 20 percent of Korean missionaries do not have sending churches or major sponsoring churches.[12] Even the missionaries with sending churches have been exposed to cancellation of the support for various reasons. The reasons for such cancellation include the sending church's disappointment in the performance of the missionary and change in the mission policy of the church, as we have seen in the case of Daniel. In addition, the cancellation is more often than not caused by the financial difficulties of the sending church.

With Korean churches' memberships and budgets both down, it has become much harder to find a sending church that can support mission candidates. If Korean churches do not experience revival over the next ten years, Korean missions will eventually face a major crisis.

One especially key point in that crisis is that most Korean churches have taken almost no measures to care for retired missionaries. More than half of all Korean missionaries will be retiring within the next ten years. In 2026, by which time those returning missionaries will have returned to their home country, Korea will have become a super-aged society. Even now, the Korean government's welfare policy for the elderly is a major social issue. Many elderly people cannot afford to retire, finding welfare provisions inadequate.[13] Looking ten years ahead, the welfare policy for the elderly will be an even greater matter of concern for Korean society.

Unfortunately, most Korean churches and mission organizations have not made specific preparations for retiring missionaries.[14] The exceptional policy and practices of NamSeoul Church can thus serve as a valuable model for other Korean churches, as well as churches around the world, to consider.

---

12 Kim, 2013, 259-273.

13 Eun-Jee Park and Yun-Hwan Chae, "Old and Broke, More Koreans Forgo Retirement," *Korea Joongang Daily*, November 12, 2018.

14 Global Mission Society in Korea has sent more than 2,500 missionaries, and has had more than 900 main supporting churches. However, there are few supporting churches that have their missionary retiring preparations. WEC Korea has had 462 active members in 2018, but there is no specific financial preparations for their retiring missionaries.

CHARACTERISTICS OF THE MISSION POLICIES OF NAMSEOUL CHURCH

NamSeoul Church was established in Seocho-gu, Seoul on July 4, 1975, under the guidance of Reverend Jung Gil Hong. The ensuing senior pastors have been Reverend Chul Lee (1996–2012) and Reverend Jongboo Hwa (2012-current). This study will not attempt to examine NamSeoul Church in its entirety, but rather will focus on the church's policies and practices for retiring missionaries, as part of the church's overall approach to missionary member care.

1. Mission Policies and Practices Centered on Laity. Based on a white paper published by the church and a survey conducted particularly for this study, one special feature of NamSeoul Church's mission policy and practice is the obvious laity-centered approach.[15]

The church's Overseas Missions Committee (OMC) was established on August 29, 1976, prior to the organization of the church session. Lay church members have always been at the center of that committee, which lead the overall mission of the church. The mission budget is made up of special offerings of church members and is controlled under a special account budget. Other aspects of NamSeoul Church's lay-led mission policy include the following: (1) consistency in administering ministry policy despite changes in church leadership and other difficult disruptions; (2) the lay members of the church have continued to participate in voluntary devotion and loving care for mission support and management; (3) as a result, not only has the number of adult church attendees steadily increased over the past eighteen years, but the annual mission offerings have increased as well.

In July and August of 2017, NamSeoul Church self-analyzed the short- and long-term trends of its missions efforts. The data show that, overall during the eighteen years from 1998 to 2016, the church members increased 1.39 times (there are about 4,000 people attending Sunday worship service currently), the number of missionaries increased 1.82 times, and the mission offerings increased 2.56 times (toward an approximately $1 million [USD] mission budget), respectively. The report concluded, "The sustained and steep growth of the mission offerings led to the growth of the church's mission work. And the stability of the mission budget will be the driving force for the future mission work."

Specifically, for this study, a questionnaire survey was conducted of NamSeoul Church members who attended worship services at 10:30 A.M. and at 7:30 P.M. on Wednesday, July 4, 2018. A total of 120 respondents participated in the survey. To the question, "NamSeoul Church members are well aware of, and they actively cooperate with, the missionary policies of the church," 16.8 percent answered "strongly agree" and 50.7 percent answered "agree." In other words, 65 percent of

---

15 For more information on the surveys of the NamSeoul Church, refer to the Appendix in this volume.

the responding members were not only well-acquainted with the church mission policy but were also actively cooperative. Conversely, only 2.5 percent of the respondents answered negatively with "disagree." As NamSeoul Church has been pursuing its lay-centered mission policy for the past forty-three years, church members clearly have had a deep interest in the church's mission policies and have been supportive of them.

2. Policies and Practices for Retiring Missionaries. How many Korean churches have stipulated retirement provisions for missionaries and have provided church-wide care and sustained financial support for retired missionaries? The KWMA Secretary-General's response to "the present situation and future of the Korean church mission" at the KGMLF forum in 2017 was telling: "The preparation for the retiring missionaries in Korean church? There is none."[16]

NamSeoul Church's policies and practices for retiring missionaries are a welcome exception to the just-mentioned dire assessment. Indeed, NamSeoul Church may represent a model that churches outside Korea as well would find helpful for becoming a church that effectively implements retirement policies and practices based on God's mercy and love for missionaries.

Here, then, are the policies and practices for retiring missionaries at NamSeoul Church.

First, the stated purpose of making provisions for a retiring missionary is "to honor retirement as a missionary, and to provide for a stable and basic life after retirement." The church defines a retired missionary as a person who has served twenty years or more in the mission field, is over seventy years old, and who has been recommended by the OMC and approved by the session. As of January 2019, NamSeoul Church has eight retired missionaries. The chairperson of OMC gives a glimpse into the motivation for the church's mission policies for retiring missionaries through his confession, "It is our church's concern to look after the missionaries with the spirit of compassion and love of God."[17]

Min Young Jeong, a missionary who retired after thirty years of service since being commissioned by NamSeoul Church in 1985, confesses as follows: "The NamSeoul Church is a very good church that faithfully supports the missionary with trust and love. Not a few churches send missionaries and then cancel their support for various reasons. It is also hard to find churches that have concrete measures for retiring missionaries and practice them. In this regard, NamSeoul Church has a very special mission." Clearly NamSeoul Church has much to teach others through its striking demonstration of the love of God to retiring missionaries.[18]

---

16 Special panel on "Korean Mission and the Future," 4th KGMLF in Sokcho, South Korea, November 10–14, 2017.
17 Interview, July 10, 2018.
18 Interview, June 15, 2018.

Second, the church continues to support the retired missionary financially with the same monthly amount it provided while the missionary was serving in the field. The same amount is paid even if one spouse within a married missionary couple passes away. NamSeoul Church's policy also stipulates that the initial allowance for resettlement after retirement can be up to 5,000,000 (KRW, over 4,500 USD) for a missionary couple, and up to 4,000,000 (KRW, over 3,600 USD) for a single missionary.

The results of the survey further show NamSeoul Church's generosity in its financial support for retired missionaries. To the question, "The sending church must continue to support the missionary after retirement," 35 percent of the respondents answered "strongly agree," and 49.2 percent answered "agree." Only 3.3 percent of respondents answered "disagree," and no one replied "strongly disagree." The monthly support of 700,000 (KRW, over 600 USD) by NamSeoul Church for each missionary might not be unusually high compared to other sending churches. However, apparently, it is quite unusual that a church continues to sponsor its missionaries with the same financial amount, even after retirement.

According to the analysis of Um Eun Jung, sustained and strong missionary sponsorship and support greatly influence missionary ministry and mental health.[19] In this respect, NamSeoul Church sets an excellent example for other churches to follow in regard to its policies and practices of missionary care.

Third, a retired missionary continues to be called a "missionary," not a "retired missionary." The (retired) missionaries are assigned to small groups within the church, so as to ensure they continue to receive prayer support, care, and attention. Clearly, NamSeoul Church exemplifies a very important member care spirit that sustains the "sense of belonging and pride of a missionary" by continuing to support and care for the missionaries even after retirement. NamSeoul Church holds Missions Committee meetings twice a month, and missionaries are invited to give a mission report, pray together, and encourage each other.

3. Detailed Provisions and Policies for Missionary Member Care. For the past thirty to forty years, Korean churches have focused on finding, training, and sending missionary candidates. Whereas the churches and mission agencies used to think that sending missionaries overseas was what mission work was all about, they have begun to realize how important it is as well to take holistic care of missionary families. Sherwood Lingenfelter, who attended the first KGMLF gathering in 2011, pointed out the following: "My observations of Korean missionaries at Fuller suggests that their churches are very strong to articulate a global vision, mobilize their people to go, and prepare them for the specific mission task, such as church planting. Yet, few of them have seriously considered how to care for the wounded and the organizational casualties of their mission force."[20] Several years have passed

---

19 See Eunjung Um's paper on page 181 in this volume.

20 Sherwood Lingenfelter, "Response to SaRang Community Church," in Jonathan Bonk et al., eds., *Accountability in Mission: Korean and Western Case Studies* (Eugene, OR: Wipf and Stock, 2011), 148.

since Lingenfelter made his remarks, but still, interest in missionary member care is lacking among Korean churches.

In fact, many Korean missionaries are burdened with the responsibility of finding sponsorship to cover the cost of ministry expenses, sabbatical expenses, and expenses involved in educating their children. In these areas, NamSeoul Church has concrete financial support plans for the missionaries.

For the expenses of settlement when missionaries arrive in a mission field, the church will provide 3,000,000 (KRW, over 2,700 USD) for a couple, 2,000,000 (KRW, over 1,800 USD) for a single, and 5,000,000 (KRW, over 4,500 USD) for a family of three or more, respectively. Also, the church has set a budget of $1,800 (USD) for a couple, $1,360 (USD) for a single, and $2,700 (USD) for a family of three or more for their second-term preparations. The church also provides 50 percent of the airfare for departure for the first term and for the second term following sabbatical. The same 50 percent of the airfare is provided if the missionary must return home for a family member's urgent hospitalization or for a family's funeral service. Further, 50 percent of the return airfare for a retiring missionary is provided. In addition, the church meticulously arranges and executes medical insurance support for missionaries. Particularly noteworthy is that a medical examination is provided once every two years for up to 300,000 (KRW, or over $270 per person). On top of that, the church supports up to 70 percent of uninsured medical expenses.

Of the respondents to the previously described 2013 survey of missionaries, 16 percent had had no medical examination available to them, and 22 percent had had health check-ups only every four years. Of the sizeable number of missionaries returning home because of illness, many would find it difficult to acquire assistance from their sending churches for medical expenses.[21]

Lastly, NamSeoul Church provides financial assistance to missionaries for various family and education-related expenses. The church encourages contributions to a scholarship fund to offset the educational expenses of missionary children. They have specific mission budget allotments for various congratulatory or condolence gifts, such as 500,000 (KRW, over 450 USD) for a missionary's wedding, 300,000 (KRW, over 270 USD) for a missionary child's wedding, 300,000 (KRW, over 270 USD) for a parent's or child's funeral expenses, and 3,000,000 (KRW, over 2,700 USD) for a missionary or a spouse's funeral expenses. For language education, the church can send 200,000 (KRW, over 180 USD) per month for up to two years after sending. If education and training is needed during the sabbatical year, the church supports those expenses for up to one million won. If the NamSeoul Church Mission Residence is not available during a missionary's sabbatical, the church will support 20,000 (KRW, over 18 USD) per day (600,000 KRW, over 545 USD per month) for accommodations. NamSeoul church's detailed mission policies were made through long-term

---

21 Kim, 2013, 259-273.

experience and constant revision of regulations. In particular, they have tried to make better mission policies for their retried missionaries for years.

There is no denying that church growth in Korea has been stagnant for the past twenty years and is now declining. Without the revival of the church, there can be no vigorous missionary activity. The number of missionaries in Korea is actually on the decline. However, the NamSeoul Church, founded forty-three years ago, is carrying out consistent lay-centered mission policy notwithstanding the changes in leadership or unexpected challenges that have arisen in the church. In particular, the aim of the church represented in the policies and practices regarding their retired missionaries sets an excellent example for many Korean churches that may focus on immediate results, as well as for other churches around the world.

Although NamSeoul Church has many outstanding features in its missionary support policies and practices, the following are some suggestions for the church's development toward even further maturity.

First, while the missions budget keeps increasing, the church needs to ponder the reason that there are not many long-term missionary devotees among young adult members in their twenties and thirties. Perhaps the church needs to adjust its monthly sponsorship amount for missionaries. Today, it is difficult to expect young people to commit themselves as long-term missionaries while burdening them with the daunting task of raising money for their manifold expenses. If the sending church supports at least 60–70 percent of the living expenses of the missionary, it is likely that the accountability relationship between the missionary and the sending church will be strengthened. The example could be cited here of Dr. Jonathan Bonk's church in Canada that has been giving $4,000 (CAD) every month for more than twenty years to support five refugee families from Congo. What might Korean churches say to this when they take pride in the large number of missionaries sent, while spending so small an amount on their mission budget?

Second, NamSeoul Church has only one part-time staff member in the OMC, which oversees and supports 140 commissioned and affiliated missionary families. Recently a full-time pastor from NamSeoul Church began serving in the OMC as well. However, he is also a full-time associate pastor of the church, so he has many other church ministries to look after.

Another challenging example comes from a British church member:[22] "Our church near London has commissioned fifteen units of missionaries. Yet I am fully dedicated to their member care as a full-time professional counselor. Of course, the church hired me as a full-time member care worker." Perhaps NamSeoul Church would do well to recruit additional full-time staff with expertise and experience.

---

22 Conversation at European Member Care Consultation in Malaga, Spain, March 17, 2018.

Finally, currently there are more than two million immigrants living in Korea, accounting for 4 percent of the total population. By 2025, over three million migrants, i.e., 8 percent of the total population, will be intermingled in Korean society.[23] NamSeoul Church could initiate new mission directives for such immigrants. In WEC Korea, for which NamSeoul Church Senior Pastor Jongboo Hwa serves as Board Chairperson, there are more than ten missionaries who returned from their fields to minister to immigrants in Korea. However, it is very difficult for them to find a sponsoring church. NamSeoul Church could create a department dedicated to immigrant missions and invite the necessary professionals to lead the way for multicultural social missions.

CONCLUSION

In 2030, missionary John returned to his homeland after thirty years of mission work. His wife was deeply depressed by the tremendous stress experienced during their ministry in a Muslim country. His daughter, a college student, had to take a leave of absence from school to earn tuition. His sending church stopped all financial support upon his return and retirement. Unfortunately, he had no retirement fund. He did not have the national pension fund that most Koreans had. Worse, he had no place to stay in the long term. He applied for government-funded, permanent rental housing but had to wait at least two to three years to receive a placement. He could not work because of chronic illness. Even without the illness, he was over seventy years old, and a job was hard to find for a person who had returned home after thirty years of living abroad. One day, turning an empty gaze toward the sky in Seoul that was clouded with fine dust, he lamented his miserable situation and felt a suicidal impulse.

The fictional missionary story above will not come to be realized among the missionaries sent by NamSeoul Church. The church serves retired missionaries with the mercy and love of the Lord. The OMC, organized from the church's earliest days, has been operating well for forty-three years, with the dedication and love of lay people. Most of the members of the church are well aware of, and actively cooperating with, the missionary policies of the church. Perhaps most impressively of all, out of respect for retired missionaries, the church members are supporting the monthly living expenses of eight retired missionary units. As a church family, NamSeoul Church tries to enfold their retired missionaries into the church community.

It is the missional duty of sending churches and mission organizations to provide their retired missionaries with basic living expenses and practical support

---

23 Park, Si Nae, "Development of the Survey on Immigrant's Living Conditions and Labor Force" *Migration Statistics Research* 22, no. 1 (2017): 2.

for accommodations. NamSeoul Church serves as an encouraging example of a congregation that serves their retired missionaries, walking with them on their way to receive their crowns prepared by the Lord in Heaven.

QUESTIONS FOR REFLECTION

1. What are the differences between the policies and practices of NamSeoul Church and those of your church regarding retirement and member care?
2. Are there specific provisions for the retirement of missionaries in the missions policies at your church? If not, why?
3. As it is important to send the missionaries to the field, it is also very important to provide proper care for them (and their families). In what specific way is your church providing care for the missionaries that you have sent?
4. The Korean churches have stopped growing and are even showing decline. Likewise, the commissioning rate of the missionaries is also stalling and might soon turn negative. What do you think is the reason for this?
5. In Korea, there are more than two million migrants. What are the things your church is doing to share the Gospel with them? Have you made an acquaintance with any of the migrants, and are you sharing the love of the Lord with them?

RESPONSE *by Lawrence Fung and John Wang*

INTRODUCTION

Member care has been an important topic in recent discussions among all parties in the mission circle. For a potential missionary candidate, how member care is done reflects the sending agency's attitude toward its missionaries. For a missionary who is entering the last few years of service, after all these years of "forgetting what is behind and straining toward what is ahead,"[24] retirement planning has suddenly become a necessity. Given the recent economic growth in Korea, retirement has become a costly dream for many missionaries, who spent the golden years of their career in poor countries with little income and limited savings. The case study of NamSeoul Church is a beautiful story of how these challenges have been overcome by a local church. The analysis yields valuable lessons for our missiological community. We will offer our response in three areas and raise several questions for further exploration.

---
24 Phil. 3:13.

A LAITY-CENTERED APPROACH

According to the description in the paper, NamSeoul Church organized its mission committee only one year after the church's founding. This unusual piece of history points to the church's early emphasis on overseas missionary work. In addition, its laity-centered approach to missions not only became a part of the church's identity; it became the church's strength: taking thoughtful measures to care well for its missionaries. The authors note two areas of advantage: 1) mission policy consistency and 2) active volunteer involvement. These reflect the outstanding features of churches that do well in mission, as suggested by George Miley: commitment for the long-haul and taking ownership.[25] Policy consistency prevents the frequent or random cancellation of missionary support, thus allowing missionaries to focus on their work in the field. The active involvement of church volunteers allows the church to mobilize the congregation to provide help and care to the missionaries, including those who come back for retirement.

While it is beautiful that this laity-centered approach has made a deep imprint in NamSeoul Church's history and has proven to be a strength of its overall missionary work, it is not a norm in most other churches. Having a laity-centered approach to missions as part of the church's history is an advantage—one that is difficult to reproduce in other church contexts. In the end, NamSeoul's legacy serves to remind other pastors and church leaders to invite their members to participate, including in the area of decision making for future missionary endeavors.

Diaspora Chinese churches in general take a top-down approach to decision making, whether they are led by lay leaders or pastors. But younger members may not accept this top-down approach and are ready to challenge the old way, once they assume leadership positions in the church. This would usually be the case if younger leaders were to take over their church's mission committee; they would likely be open to adopting new policies that could affect the church's relationships with its missionaries. Leadership training and discipleship are therefore essential for ensuring policy consistency and for maintaining a mission emphasis in the church.

A HIGH VIEW OF THE MISSIONARIES

Apparently NamSeoul's laity-centered approach helps strengthen the traditional high view of the missionaries. Church members tend to appreciate and respect the sacrifices the missionaries make. They realize that while they were pursuing economic growth and living in comfort, their missionaries willingly went to poorer countries to live under modest and sometimes even dangerous conditions. In contrast, our experience in working with new missionaries from diaspora Chinese churches, especially those who come from large cities like

---

25 George Miley, "The Awesome Potential for Mission Found in Local Churches," in Ralph Winter and Steven C. Hawthorn, eds., *Perspectives on the World Christian Movement: A Reader* (Pasadena, CA: William Carey Library, 2009), 748.

Seoul, gives us another picture. Many potential missionaries inquire about fringe benefits and retirement plans in their application interviews with the mission agency. Some megachurches have no problem providing retirement plans for the missionary candidates they support. But candidates from regular, midsized Chinese churches have difficulty raising enough financial support to provide for their retirement. It is important that issues regarding one's benefits and retirement are raised at the beginning of the missionary sending process. However, these concerns should not be the main focus of discussion in one's application interview.

THE GENEROSITY OF THE LOCAL CHURCH

NamSeoul Church's commitment to continuing their missionaries' financial support post-retirement is truly commendable. Indeed, when the missionaries return to Korea for retirement, most of them will realize that Korea has become a nation with a high standard of living. A higher level of financial support may be needed for missionaries to retire in Korea than they needed in most of the countries where they served. Unfortunately, a lack of growth in church membership is usually associated with lower levels of financial support for missionaries. However, coupled with the simultaneous reduction of missionary candidates, the demand for financial support may be reduced, as well. The simultaneous reduction of both a church's financial resources and its number of missionary candidates might actually prevent a church from needing to decrease the support it can offer each missionary. Still, the downward trend in church growth is a dangerous sign; Korean churches need to prepare for possible decreases in both membership and financial resources and begin seeking ways to reverse them.

A QUESTION ON AGENCIES

What would be the role of the mission agencies? The NamSeoul case study does not say much about sending agencies. If missionaries are sent directly by their churches, then those churches assume all responsibility for the missionaries' retirement, and volunteers become an essential part of the missionary support infrastructure. However, if a mission agency is involved, then a collaborative structure must be established, and expectations must be clearly understood and agreed upon by the agency, the sending churches, and the missionary.

A QUESTION ON GOVERNMENT

How can Korean missionary retirees tap into the government-sponsored social safety nets of health insurance, social security income, and public housing? How can the retirees cope with Korea's economic development, its increased cost of living, and a general reduction in missionary support? Over the past few decades, Korea has successfully transformed from a war-torn and agriculture-based society into an industrial and economic giant. Although its citizens enjoy highs levels of income, the byproduct of such economic growth is a higher cost of living. With the return of retiring missionaries, a single church, especially one that does not have the size and infrastructure of NamSeoul Church, would need to tap into the social safety nets offered by the government—health insurance, social security income, and public housing. If the church or agency could assist retiring missionaries in navigating through the complicated systems of social benefits, it would be of tremendous help to those who are nervously preparing for their return to Korea.

QUESTIONS ON PERSONAL ISSUES

What about spiritual and psychological well-being? The focus of the paper is on financial support. However, when missionaries come home, many of them are experiencing reverse culture shock. Some may have difficulty adjusting to the technology, language, or culture in Korea. These are situations where local churches like NamSeoul Church could offer their help. In addition to providing peer support through their church members, local churches can also offer professional and pastoral intervention. They can strive to be places that offer comprehensive emotional, psychological, and spiritual support to their retired missionaries.

What about parental care in a super-aged society? Another situation that is unique to some of the Asian countries, especially where the Confucian influence is strong, is the concern for parental care.[26] This concern is even more serious for countries facing super-aged societies, like Korea. Retired missionaries find themselves sandwiched between their parents' traditional mindset of expecting their children to care for them in their old age and the westernized, younger generation's mindset of not feeling responsible to support their retired parents. How to help these missionaries, who are thus caught in the middle, may be an area for further exploration.

How can churches utilize the wisdom and experience of their retired missionaries, especially in domestic, cross-cultural ministry (e.g., teaching missions or language training) or in diaspora ministry? Missionaries with many years of interactions and experience with other cultures are treasures for the Korean church. Since an economically strong Korea attracts more and more foreigners to come as immigrants, refugees, foreign students, and guest workers, ethnic communities have formed all over the country. Retired missionaries are ideal candidates for using their cross-cultural expertise to help the local church reach out to these communities. Perhaps, after seeing their returned missionaries actively engaging in ministry, local churches will become even more enthusiastic about continuing their support well into retirement.

---

26 Sunny Hong, "Caring for the Parents of Missionaries: A Case Study of Global Bible Translators," in Dwight P. Baker and Robert J. Priest, eds., *The Missionary Family: Witness, Concerns, Care* (Pasadena, CA: William Carey Library, 2014), 60-78.

CONCLUSION

Member care is an important topic for our generation. We can learn some valuable lessons from this case study on how NamSeoul Church cares for its missionaries. As we face the challenge of Korea's changing Christian landscape, coupled with its changing societal landscape, we will begin to realize that there are many more member care issues to be explored. Let us hope that many more churches will exhibit the same spirit of care as NamSeoul Church and that they will adopt a variety of effective practices for welcoming missionaries who return to Korea for retirement after years of faithful service in the mission field.

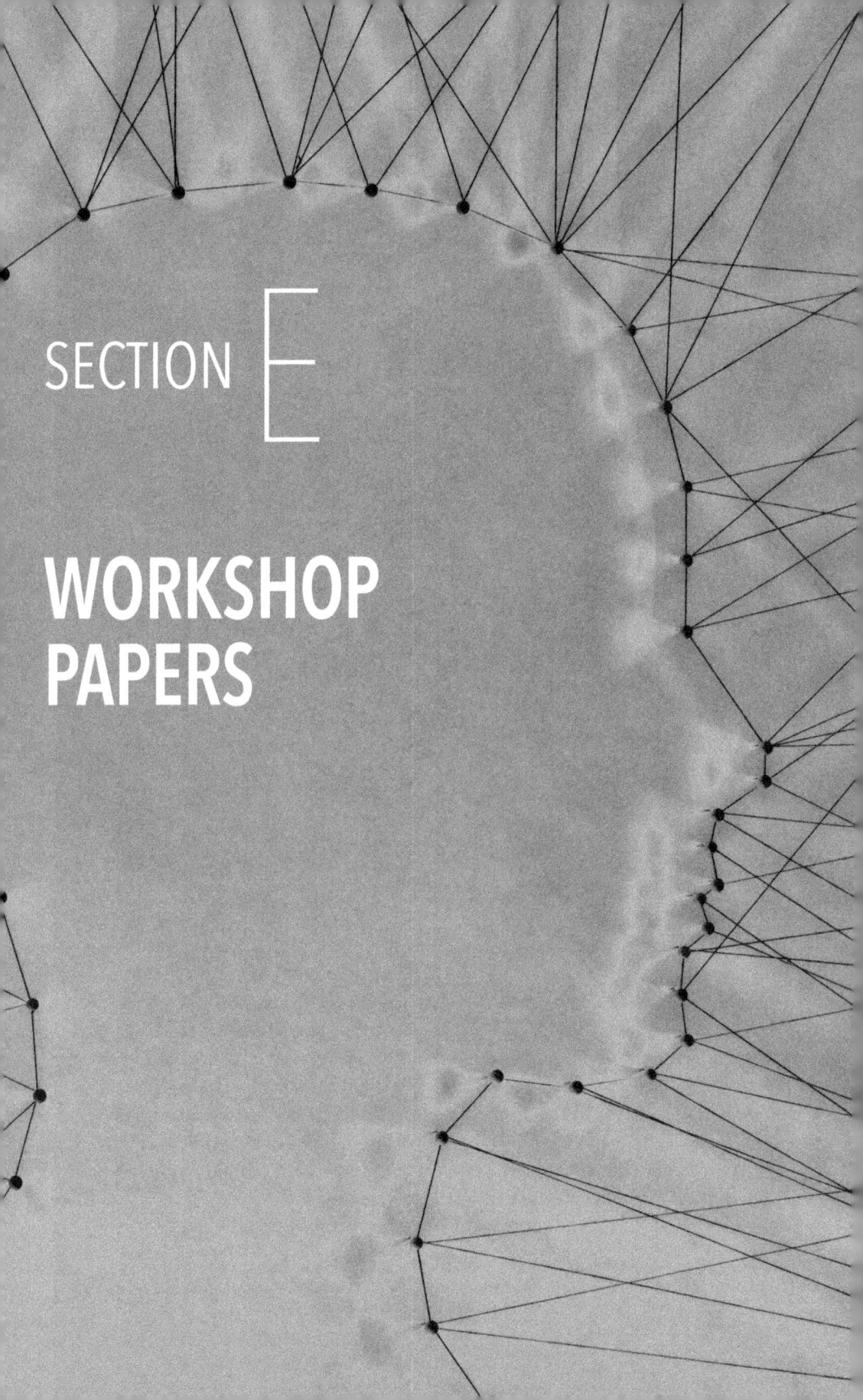

SECTION E

WORKSHOP PAPERS

19

DEPRESSION IN THE OLD TESTAMENT

by MICHEL G. DISTEFANO

Depression is just one of the afflictions discussed in this forum, but it occurs in conjunction with many, if not all of the others. As with any affliction, we are expected to pray: "Any prayer or supplication by any person ... who knows the affliction of their own heart, and who spreads their hands towards this house—might you hear it ... and forgive them ... and grant it ... for you know their heart, indeed, you alone know the hearts of all the sons [and daughters] of men" (1 Kings 8:38–39).[1] The Bible often speaks about depression and its treatment. This paper will explore biblical teaching on depression and compare it to a modern diagnosis and treatment, all in an effort to show that the Bible can help to restore and heal Christians who are afflicted with depression.

---

1 Unless otherwise stated, translations from the Hebrew Bible are my own, based on the standard scholarly lexicons. I use the English versification.

MY BACKGROUND AND EXPERIENCES

I have a medical background as a registered nurse, so I studied psychiatric disorders and did rotations on psychiatric wards. Even though I chose another area of nursing to work in, I maintained an interest in those disorders, especially depression. After working as a nurse, I got a PhD in Hebrew Bible, and, due to my own struggles with depression, I have been drawn towards signs, symptoms, and cases of depression in the Bible. I am also writing a book on a related topic. Dr. Jon Bonk knows all of this, so he invited me to write this paper and to include some of my personal experiences. I praise God for the forum topic and for the awareness and healing it will bring.

OVERVIEW OF A MODERN DIAGNOSIS

The Mayo Clinic defines depression as "a mood disorder that causes a persistent feeling of sadness and loss of interest. Also called major depressive disorder or clinical depression, it affects how you feel, think and behave and can lead to a variety of emotional and physical problems. You may have trouble doing normal day-to-day activities, and sometimes you may feel as if life isn't worth living."[2] In contrast to the American Psychiatric Association that states, "Symptoms must last at least two weeks for a diagnosis of depression,"[3] the Mayo Clinic does not specify a minimum length of time in order to establish a diagnosis. It simply says symptoms must be "persistent." Therefore, the Mayo Clinic could diagnose a case of depression even if symptoms presented themselves for less than two weeks. I find this minimal time requirement to be more in line with biblical teaching and more compassionate than the two week requirement. Although in many cases it is hard to tell how long episodes of depression last in the biblical accounts, the Bible does describe depression that is persistent, that lasts at least two weeks, and that lasts much longer. It also describes recurrent depression. Personal experience has also taught me that recurrent depression, once triggered, can become deep and debilitating very quickly, even within two hours, let alone two weeks, and it must be so for many others as well.

OVERVIEW OF A BIBLICAL DIAGNOSIS

The Bible uses several phrases for depression. An excellent example is in Nehemiah 2:2: "Why do you look so ill-disposed and you aren't sick? This can be none other than melancholy" (literally "sadness of heart,"[4] cf. 1 Sam. 1:8). Here bodily sickness

---

2 "Depression, major depressive disorder," Mayo Clinic, accessed April 2, 2018, https://www.mayoclinic.org/diseases-conditions/depression/symptoms-causes/syc-20356007. Unless otherwise stated, Mayo Clinic quotations are either from this address or its subfolders.

3 "Depression," American Psychiatric Association, accessed April 2, 2018, https://www.psychiatry.org/patients-families/depression/what-is-depression.

4 "Heart" is the Hebrew word used for "mind," where thoughts and feelings (emotions) come from. So, "sadness of heart" is a mental illness.

and mental illness are mentioned in the same sentence. Other phrases for depression are "shortness of spirit," i.e., despondency (Exod. 6:9), "bitterness of soul" (1 Sam. 1:10), and "losing heart" (1 Sam. 1:15). There may even be an allusion to the diagnosis of mental illness in ancient Israel: "The most devious of all is the heart, and its disease—who can diagnose it?"[5] (Jer. 17:9).

Other phrases for a depressed mood are variously translated as a heart that is faint, broken, crushed, wounded, pierced, distressed, agonizing, and writhing; as a soul that is crushed, melted, distressed, restless/turbulent, and languishing; and as a spirit that is faint, broken, crushed, and languishing. Most of these phrases occur in the individual lament Psalms. There were many attendant circumstances in the Old Testament that caused or led to sadness and sorrow, or to a depressed mood, manifested by a fallen face, discouragement, tears, groaning, emotional anguish, despair, and lament, with loss of friends and support leading to isolation and loneliness, eventually leading to numbness and loss of interest in daily life, including loss of appetite, and finally, to thoughts or attempts to end life. Examples will be given below.

MODERN SIGNS AND SYMPTOMS AND THEIR BIBLICAL COUNTERPARTS

The Mayo Clinic states that "although depression may occur only once during your life, people typically have multiple episodes." During these episodes, symptoms occur most of the day, nearly every day, and may include:

1. Feelings of sadness, tearfulness
2. Anxiety, agitation or restlessness
3. Sleep disturbances, including insomnia
4. Tiredness and lack of energy
5. Reduced appetite and weight loss
6. Loss of interest in most or all normal activities
7. Frequent or recurrent thoughts of death, suicidal thoughts

Other signs and symptoms include "hopelessness, anger, trouble thinking or concentrating, feelings of worthlessness or guilt, and fixating on past failures or self-blame." I ordered the signs and symptoms to show how depression becomes progressively worse, affecting normal life activities and eventually threatening life itself.

The number of biblical verses that correspond to these modern signs and symptoms are legion. Some verses present generalizations about depression, while others describe particular individuals who were depressed, which correspond to

---

5 Translation by M. Dahood in his notes on Ps. 69:21 (Hebrew): Mitchell Dahood, *Psalms II: 51-100*, AB 17 (New York: Doubleday, 1968), 161.

modern case studies in depression. There is also a biblical genre that is saturated with depression, that is, lament. The general statements are observations about depression in others, while the case studies and laments include statements by those who have suffered through it themselves.

GENERAL STATEMENTS ABOUT DEPRESSION

1. "You fed them tears as food, and made them drink tears" (Ps. 80:5, a community lament).
2. "Anxiety in the heart of a man makes him depressed" (Prov. 12:25).
3-6. Alluding to Job's condition in general, Elihu describes a depressed person "suffering on his bed, with continual strife in his bones, his appetite loathes bread and his throat loathes his favorite food, his flesh vanishes from sight and his bones, once unseen, are stripped of flesh [and visible], and his soul draws near to the pit/grave" (Job 33:19-22). "Strife in the bones" is an image of extreme agitation; continual strife causes sleep disturbances. Finally, extreme loss of interest in normal activities occurs when one is bedridden.

CASE STUDIES

For this short paper I have chosen Hannah, Amnon, Hezekiah, Jeremiah, and Job for case studies in depression, skipping Jacob, Joseph, Moses, Saul,[6] Ahab, Elijah, and others. I have also skipped the book of Lamentations.

Hannah was depressed because the Lord had closed her womb and she was childless. Her depression was persistent as she watched her rival bear sons and daughters (1 Sam. 1:4–6), and it was especially intensified every year at God's house (the tabernacle) in Shiloh, when her rival provoked her mercilessly, verbally abusing her (1:7). Hannah exhibited the following signs of depression: sadness and tears; loss of appetite (1:7, even though a sacrificial meal with the best of foods was on offer), including not drinking wine or beer (1:15); anxiety (1:16); and, a sad face (1:18). Her husband diagnosed her with melancholy ("sadness of heart," 1:8), and she diagnosed herself with depression ("losing heart," 1:15). After taking some food, still bitter of soul and crying profusely, she prayed at the tabernacle because of her affliction (1:10–11), pouring out her soul (1:15). God answered her with Samuel, as well as with three more sons and two daughters (2:21).

Amnon, a son of David, was depressed because he was in love with Tamar and thought he could not be with her (2 Sam. 13:2, 4; contrary to what Tamar thought, 13:13). He exhibited the following signs of depression: he was anxious

---
[6] Saul may have had bipolar disorder.

(13:2); he made himself ill; and, he looked downcast and dejected (13:4). This lasted day by day (13:2, 4). Then he and a friend developed a ruse to say he was sick in bed, was not eating, and needed Tamar to make bread for him so he could eat. It is likely that in the actual illness (depression) he did lose his appetite, and his genuine signs and symptoms added credibility to the ruse of being sick in bed. Of course, there is nothing in Amnon's behavior that commends itself. He could have been noble and dealt with the situation differently. Nevertheless, he was genuinely depressed.

Hezekiah became terminally ill and was told to inform his house that he would not recover (he would die and not live, Isa. 38:1). Signs of Hezekiah's depression included profuse weeping (38:3; cf. God heard his tears, 38:5) and turning his face to a wall, a sign of loss of interest in life (38:2; cf. Ahab's depression, which included loss of appetite and turning his face toward a wall, 1 Kings 21:4–5, 7). After Hezekiah prays and God relents, Hezekiah reflects on his illness and recovery and says he was bitter of soul (38:15) and was very bitter (38:17). He says he was anxious all day and night (38:13–14—a difficult passage, but it probably means that Hezekiah made sounds like a lion and various birds as God was bringing him to his end). And, God broke all of his bones (38:13), meaning that he was tired and exhausted. Hezekiah prayed, and God granted him fifteen more years.

JOB

Job is afflicted with the loss of his flocks, servants, and children (Job 1). Then he is afflicted with a grave skin disease (Job 2). We do not know how much time intervened between these events or what occurred during this period. For instance, Job may have begun the grieving process for his children during this time. However, given that grief and depression may present with the same signs and symptoms, it is important to note that in Job's speeches he does not grieve for his children or servants. As opposed to reminiscing about them and experiencing profound sadness at their loss, a normal part of the grieving process,[7] he focuses on himself and loathes his own life (7:16; 9:21; 10:1). Job only mentions his children in a positive light once (29:5), part of his remembrance of the days before affliction.[8] If grief over the loss of his children intensified Job's depression, he did not mention it. Another important thing to note is that Job is not simply describing symptoms of his skin disease. Based on the evidence, it would be very difficult to establish a differential diagnosis of a certain skin disease with depression as one of its complications. Since Job says he is depressed, I interpret the inward symptoms as ones of depression. Overall, this approach seems to coincide with Job's focus on his mental anguish—anguish about his righteousness, about lack of comfort, about verbal abuse, and about God.

---

7   "Complicated Grief," Mayo Clinic, accessed September 15, 2018, https://www.mayoclinic.org/diseases-conditions/complicated-grief/symptoms-causes/syc-20360374.

8   Otherwise, Job only alludes to their deaths in the context of teaching on guilt and punishment (21:19), an issue raised previously by his friends (8:4).

We do know that all of these events occurred over a period of months, beginning with the losses described in chapter one (7:3; 29:2). Job gives many speeches in dialogue with his friends during these months. At times the speeches are stylistically elevated—one gets the impression that they were prepared beforehand, possibly written down (16:4), and that Job and his friends met at various intervals to argue and counter-argue (cf. 23:2, "even today …"). At other times, Job's speeches are raw, terse, and a bit unpolished.

In his first speech (Job 3), one week after he was inflicted with disease, Job's depression has already reached the stage where he has thoughts of death—he curses the day he was born, wishes it was blotted out from record, wishes he had died in his mother's womb and was stillborn (3:11), or that he had been a miscarriage (3:16). If he were dead or had never been born, he would have rest (13) from his present suffering. He is bitter of soul—"Why is life [given] to those who are bitter in soul, who are waiting for death, but it does not come, and who search/dig for it more than hidden treasures?" (Job 3:20–21). He is also agitated, restless, and weary without strength (3:17, 26), and he sighs at the sight of food, meaning he has lost his appetite (3:24). One note of interest is that Job and Isaiah have some of the most difficult passages to translate in the OT. In Job, grammatical relations are not always supplied, similes and metaphors are not always clear, and sometimes they are mixed. One example is Job's loud groans/roarings poured out like water, probably a reference to profound crying with tears (Job 3:24). These translation difficulties may have to do with Job's depression. Even if he had time to think about his speeches or write them down, he would have had trouble thinking, concentrating, and expressing himself, all well-known symptoms of depression.

Job's depression persisted throughout those months. In broad terms, he is filled with bitterness (9:18), he swears on oath that he would not abandon his lament, he asserts that he would speak about the bitterness of his soul (10:1) and that God has written bitter things against him (13:26). His spirit is broken (17:1), he is short of spirit, i.e., despondent (21:4), and his soul is poured out (30:16). Signs and symptoms of depression that he exhibited during those months were: Job's face was reddened with tears, with dark shadows around his eyes (16:16, 20); his eyes eventually became expressionless from deep sorrow (17:7); his lyre played laments and his flute the sounds of weeping and wailing (30:31); he was anxious and restless: "My inner organs/being are/is in turmoil and not at rest, days of affliction confront me" (Job 30:27); he had sleep disturbances, including insomnia: "Nights of trouble have been appointed for me, I am filled with tossing/restlessness until the light of dawn" (7:3–4); he was tired and lacked energy: "What is my strength that I should remain hopeful? Do I have the strength of stones, or is my flesh made of bronze?" (6:11–12); he lost his appetite (6:6–7), wasted away (7:16), his limbs were a shadow of their former selves (17:7), and his skin and flesh clung to his bones (19:20).[9] Job lost interest in normal life activities partly due to a forced social isolation. His brothers distanced themselves, friends became estranged, his kin and acquaintances forgot him, and his circle of confidants abhorred him (19:13–14, 19).

---

9 Admittedly, some of these symptoms could be due to a combination of the skin disease and depression.

He was in anguish because of the verbal abuse he experienced, even from young boys (19:18). Job mentions verbal abuse in many places (16:20; 17:2, 6; 19:18; and, 30:1, 9). He was especially bitter about the fact that he was a counselor and comforter who everyone listened to, who sat at the head like a king (29:21–25), but now the dregs of society were abusing him (30:1–15). He expresses hopelessness—his days come to an end without hope (7:6; cf. 17:15; 19:10).

Finally, Job had frequent and recurrent thoughts of death, and suicidal thoughts. Besides cursing the day he was born, wishing he had not been born, and wishing his birth day had been blotted out, all in his first speech, Job later says he would choose suffocation and death over his deep agony (7:15), and laments again, "Why did you bring me out from the womb? Would that I had stopped breathing and no eye had seen me; or, that I had never been, or that I was carried from the womb to the grave" (10:18–19). He also mentions that he is near death (10:20–22), in one place saying his days are few (10:20; cf. 14:1), in another that he has a few years left (16:22). Sometimes Job complains that he has not yet lived out his days, lamenting his impending death because he wants to live. So, during months of depression, Job vacillates between lament and wanting to die, and complaint and wanting to live.

PERSONAL REFLECTION ON JOB'S DEPRESSION

Even though Job was written thousands of years ago, I am met with the same thoughts that I have had, sometimes word for word, including: God has hedged or walled me in (3:23; 19:8); I have become a target for his arrows (16:12–13); I have become a joke (12:4); the righteous are a joke (12:4); God has hidden his face; he has become my enemy (13:24); and, he has turned cruel (30:21). More than any other book, Job describes the inner struggles of someone afflicted with depression. His thoughts illustrate the emotional instability and intellectual debility of a severely depressed person alternating between little hope and much despair. Since I empathize so much with Job, I described his depression in the present tense. This is not much different than someone empathizing with a lament Psalm and praying it themselves. It is encouraging to me that whoever edited the book of Job did not expunge the rawness of emotion, the questioning of God, the controlled anger, the sarcasm, indeed, the whole pathos and nuance that only someone who is or has been depressed can fully appreciate.

God instigated and then allowed Job's afflictions, and so the events that led to Job's deep depression. Therefore, he was actually accomplishing one of his works in Job's depression. This personal discovery helped me to finally acknowledge that God is responsible for the events that led to mine. I know that he orchestrated my depression, including blessing the day of my birth, forming my personality, perhaps afflicting me with depression in my DNA, and finally, being in control of the events in my life. So, I affirm that God is real and near, even during depression.

It also strikes me that God's perspective is so different than mine. Satan argued that Job only worshipped God because of the things he gave to him—riches, social position, family, and health. Of course, Job suffered the loss of these things with severe attendant depression, but he still worshipped God. So, from God's perspective, Job's suffering had something to do with his own glory. I hope to see that glory one day, and then my present momentary suffering will be forgotten.

DEPRESSION IN THE PSALMS OF LAMENT

We find all the signs and symptoms of depression in the most common form of prayer in the Psalms, the so-called Psalm of Lament. Laments are prayers that complain or protest about ongoing affliction. They ask or imply "How long?" and sometimes "Why?"—protesting against what God is doing. The individual laments describe sickness[10] and enemies in general terms that could be applied to specific cases, by those who knew the afflictions of their own hearts. Even in cases where the affliction is a punishment for sin, the lament or complaint is that the affliction continues after confession of sin and asking for forgiveness. These laments exhibit all the signs and symptoms of depression. I will go through the lament Psalm 102, followed by a summary listing that reveals just how prevalent depression is in these laments.

Psalm 102 is entitled, "A prayer for someone afflicted, who is weak/fainting, and who before Yahweh pours out his lament/complaint." He exhibits the following signs and symptoms of depression: his heart "is struck/blighted like grass, and dried/withered" (102:4); he mixes his drinks with his weeping tears (9); he is distressed/agitated (2), and stays awake to keep watch all night (7); God weakened his strength (23), and he withers away like grass (11); his bones are scorched like a hearth (3), meaning he is extremely tired and exhausted; he has lost his appetite and lost weight: "My heart is struck ... I forget to eat my bread. Because of my groaning noises, my bones cling to my skin" (Ps. 102:4–5); and, he is verbally abused: "My enemies taunt/revile me all day long, they mock me" (8).

"When one laments, the spirit grows faint," i.e., the lamenter becomes depressed (Ps. 77:3). As a group, the approximately forty-seven individual laments[11] exhibit all of the signs and symptoms of depression.

1. There is sadness and tearfulness: "You put my tears in your leather bottle; are they not [also] recorded in your scroll?" (Ps. 56:8). "I am weary with my sighing/groaning; I soak during the entire night my bed, with my tears my divan I drench. My eye swells up from sorrow" (Ps. 6:6–7). "I have grown tired with my calling out,[12] my throat is hoarse, and my eyes are bleary,[13] waiting for my God" (Ps. 69:3).

---

10 These symptoms are so general that they do not suggest a differential diagnosis of any disease with depression as a complication. Taken as a whole, the laments seem to present depression more than any other illness.

11 Pss. 3, 5-7, 9-10, 12-13, 17, 22, 25, 26, 28, 31, 35-36, 38-43, 51, 54-57, 59, 61, 63-64, 69-71, 77, 86, 88, 94, 102, 109, 120, 130, 137, 140-143 = 47 laments. There are also at least six community laments, 44, 60, 74, 79, 80, 83, and possibly as many as fourteen, depending on the commentator (e.g., Gottwald, adding 58, 85, 89, 90, 108, 123, 126, 144).

12 English translations and lexicons can cause confusion when they translate "calling out" as "crying [out]." In some cases, "calling out" can be accompanied by crying tears, e.g., Ps 39:12; 69:3. Also, a lament Psalm that does not specifically mention weeping probably assumes it, i.e., weeping accompanied calling/crying out. But, translations and lexicons should differentiate between these two terms/phrases.

13 Translated "bleary" by M. Dahood, *Psalms II: 51-100*, 156.

2. The affliction itself causes anxiety and restlessness: "I am restless in my lament, and disquieted ... My heart flutters[14] within me" (55:2, 4). Bones, meaning the inner being and soul, are dismayed/panicking (6:2). Both of these verses probably describe a panic attack. A panic attack is certainly in view in Ps. 38:10, "My heart throbs violently/palpitates, my strength leaves me."

3. Sleep disturbances occur during times of lament: "Evening, morning, and midday I lament and moan" (55:17). "My tears have been my food all day and night" (42:3). "I stretched out my hand during the night, without it growing numb ... when I lament, my spirit is faint" (77:2–3; see also 22:2 and 6:6 for all-nighters).

4. One who laments becomes tired and exhausted: "All of my bones have become dislocated; my heart has become like wax, melted within me. My strength has dried out like a potsherd" (Ps. 22:14–15). Dislocated bones are a metaphor of extreme tiredness and lack of energy. "My years are consumed with sighing/groaning, my strength totters/gives way" (31:10).

5. Eventually, a lamenter loses appetite, ingests tears as food (42:3), strength begins to fail, and the body deteriorates/wastes away (31:9–10). Fasting often accompanies lament, and the body becomes lean/emaciated, without any fat on it (109:24).

6. Someone who laments often experiences forced social isolation: "I am estranged from my brothers, a stranger to my mother's sons" (69:8). "You have distanced far from me loving friend and companion, my acquaintances [now] are the darkness" (88:18, cf. v. 8). It is difficult to maintain an interest in life's activities with only darkness as friends. Some call Psalm 88 the saddest Psalm of all.

7. The lamenters complain frequently about impending death or going down to the pit/grave.

VERBAL ABUSE

One of the main complaints in the Psalms of Lament is verbal abuse. In fact, sometimes it is the only complaint besides a vague allusion to enemies who are the abusers. Psalm 69:20 says, "Reviling/taunting[15] has broken my heart and I have become sick." This sickness is depression. Similarly, Psalm 109:22 says that lies, accusations, hateful words, taunts, and curses (mentioned in the lament) pierce/wound the heart. The Bible does not underestimate the destructive and debilitating power of negative words, especially when they are sustained (e.g., Ps. 35:15, "without ceasing"), become unbearable, and the target asks, "How long?"

General terms for verbal abuse in the individual laments include mocking, deriding, insulting, taunting/reviling, slandering, defaming, deceiving, telling lies, tearing to pieces (meaning slandering), gnashing teeth, cursing, and, possibly, reciting magic spells against the complainant. The community laments add scorning, spurning, and giving false testimony. The abuse can be so persistent

---

14 Translated "flutters" by M. Dahood, *Psalms II: 51–100*, 28.
15 M. Dahood translates, "[Verbal] Abuse ..." Dahood, *Psalms II, 51–100*, 154.

that the target becomes despised (22:6), a proverb (69:11), and an abomination (88:8). Various similes and metaphors accentuate the destructive intent and power of verbal abusers, including, "their throat is an open grave" (Ps. 5:9), their mouths are opened wide like a roaring lion tearing and devouring its prey with its fangs (22:13; 57:4, 6; cf. 124:6), their words are like the poisonous venom of a snake (58:4; 140:3), and their words are burning hot coals (120:4). The most striking metaphors are those that depict words as weapons—words are drawn swords (Ps. 55:21), tongues are sharp swords (57:4), swords are in their lips (59:7), teeth are spears (57:4) and arrows (57:4; 58:7), and bitter words are drawn arrows that are released and let fly (64:3–4).

Notice that all the similes and metaphors of verbal abuse imply words can inflict mortal wounds. In some cases this could be quite literal, as false accusations and testimony could lead to a death sentence. Murder plots also occurred outside the workings of the legal system. In any case, the intent is always to harm, even to murder. From the perspective of the complainant, verbal abuse can lead to a wounded heart, and to the signs and symptoms of depression.

VERBAL ABUSE IN MY LIFE

At this point I am reminded of my own depression and how words can be deadly weapons. I was verbally abused every day for at least a few hours, for seven years straight, and practically every time I visited my family after that. I know from experience that verbal abuse is like a whip ripping the flesh off your back, which stays bloody and raw. In that state, it does not take much to invoke excruciating pain again. I even wrote this in a letter to my parents without knowing at the time that the Bible describes verbal abuse as "a whip of the tongue" (Job 5:21). I cannot explain it, but I feel like I have been murdered and the whole integrity of my psyche has fallen apart. In addition, when trying to come to terms with it later, opening up and talking to others about it, all I wanted was a bit of empathy and compassion, but instead I was verbally abused again. Many would-be counselors among my family and church friends let me down. I know now that many others who were hurting and dying inside have been counseled with worthless and hurtful words. Unwise, ungracious, and unfeeling counselors who are not sensitive to verbal abuse during treatment of depression may exacerbate an ongoing episode of depression or trigger a new one. Even fellow Christians can be guilty of this. I know because I, shamefully, verbally abused a depressed brother on one occasion. I will discuss accountability below, but as a reminder, let us all be mindful of the power of words, how they can harm and can even murder (e.g., Jesus talks about name calling in the context of murder, Matt. 5:21). There is already enough of this from non-believers and enemies.

JEREMIAH

Jeremiah suffered from personal depression and grief for the nation. Regarding his depression, he was particularly sensitive to verbal abuse. He complains that he was subjected to verbal abuse for announcing God's words, including taunting/reviling (15:15) and cursing (15:10). He said that his "pain was endless, his wound incurable, which refused to be healed," and he sat alone (15:17–18). God also commanded him not to marry or to have sons and daughters (16:2), or to go to the house of feasting to eat and drink, i.e., go to parties (16:8); so, he also experienced a forced social isolation. The verbal abuse and isolation gradually grew worse. Because he spoke the word of Yahweh, announcing violence and devastation, everybody reviled/taunted, scorned, and derided him all day long, and he was a laughingstock all day long (Jer. 20:7–8). He also heard people, including his friends, defaming and denouncing him (20:10). Eventually he cursed the day he was born and the man who delivered the good news of his birth to his father (20:14–17). He wishes that the man had killed him while he was still in the womb and that his mother's womb was still his grave. He laments, "Why did I go out from the womb to look on trouble and sorrow?" (20:18; cf. 15:10).

To conclude this section, I set the bar high to find examples of depression in the OT, i.e., individual cases or genres that mentioned most if not all of the seven signs and symptoms from the Mayo Clinic's list. However, if one lowers the bar, depression is present in many other parts of the Bible where affliction, oppression and persecution are mentioned. In short, depression in the Bible affected men and women, leaders—including judges, prophets, and kings—and commoners, rich and poor, the righteous and the wicked (at least with reference to particular events), the wise and the foolish, and those physically sick or otherwise healthy in body. It also affected whole groups of people, e.g., Israel as slaves in Egypt, Israel as a vassal nation on their own land, and Israel as refugees and displaced persons in exile. The community laments in the Psalms deal with depression on a national scale, but I do not have enough time or space to describe them.

CAUSES

The Mayo Clinic states, "It's not known exactly what causes depression. As with many mental disorders, a variety of factors may be involved." Current research suggests that biological risk factors are involved, including genes, altered neurotransmitter functions, and anatomical changes in the brain, as well as other risk factors that can lead to or make someone more vulnerable to depression, including family history of mental illness, psychological makeup, and environmental factors. Environmental factors are usually traumatic events, such as major losses—of a loved one, a home, one's livelihood, reputation, health, or safety, or events such as verbal abuse and physical or sexual assault. A risk factor describes a correlation, not a necessary cause. The reason for this is simple: modern medicine looks at the general population and observes that not everyone who experiences the same traumatic event or shares another risk factor develops depression. But, risk factors that trigger the development of actual depression in particular cases are often referred to as causes. It is in this sense that the Bible mentions causes of depression, i.e., it describes actual cases.

The Bible declares that God is ultimately responsible for events. Focusing on the types of events that lead to depression, it says in many places that God orchestrated those events. For example, he sold Joseph into Egypt, he incited and allowed Satan to afflict Job, he closed Hannah's womb, he told Hezekiah he would not recover, and he told Jeremiah what to preach, and commanded him to be somewhat alone. In each case, the biblical characters were aware that God did it. Those who lamented asked God how long he would keep doing it. In some cases, the biblical characters were also given insight into why God did it. For example, Joseph came to realize that he was sold as a slave to preserve life in a great deliverance from famine (Gen. 45:5–7; 50:20). I want to stress, though, that even if there is a redemptive purpose for suffering and depression, e.g., a form of discipline or testing, more often than not we do not know why God ultimately causes or allows events that trigger depression. This is important for counseling those who are depressed. Job thought that at the very least he was being tested, and he was correct, but he did not know about the heavenly councils where God instigated the entire drama. And, even though we, the readers, know about the councils, in the end we do not know exactly why God did what he did to Job.

TREATMENT

The Mayo Clinic says, "More than just a bout of the blues, depression isn't a weakness and you can't simply 'snap out' of it." Job says something similar about snapping out of his depression: if he decided to leave off his sad countenance and be cheerful, he knows that it would be a ruse, that God would continue what he was doing, and the pain would still lie underneath the fake smile (Job 9:27ff.).

The Mayo Clinic continues and says, "Depression may require long-term treatment." Very briefly, modern medical treatment for depression amounts to prescribing a healthy lifestyle in general—diet, exercise, and sleep, and progressively intensive and invasive treatments for depression in particular. Psychotherapy, the general term for talk therapy, is often sufficient for mild cases of depression, drug therapy is added in moderate cases, and finally, ECT (Electroconvulsive Therapy) or TMS (Transcranial Magnetic Stimulation) is added in severe cases. It is said that most depressed persons respond to medical treatment.

The focus of biblical treatment is talk therapy—prayer and counseling. The latter corresponds to modern psychotherapy. The Mayo Clinic even "encourages participation in spiritual practice, if appropriate. For many people, faith is an important element in recovery from depression—whether it's involvement in an organized religious community or personal spiritual beliefs and practices."[16] As an aside, it is encouraging that this statement justifies what we are studying in this paper.

---

16 "Depression: Supporting a family member or friend," Mayo Clinic, accessed April 17, 2018, www.mayoclinic.org/diseases-conditions/depression/in-depth/depression/art-20045943.

PRAYER

The primary biblical treatment for depression, which was mentioned at the beginning of this paper, bears repeating: "Any prayer or supplication by any person ... who knows the affliction of their own heart, and who spreads their hands towards this house—might you hear it ... and forgive them ... and grant it ... for you know their heart, indeed, you alone know the hearts of all the sons [and daughters] of men" (1 Kings 8:38–39). I chose this verse about prayer, or talking to God, because of its emphasis on the heart—the sufferer knows the affliction of his or her own heart, and God knows their heart. A depressed person with a sad heart, or who is faint of heart or broken hearted, whose heart is distressed, crushed, wounded, pierced, agonizing, or writhing, who has any of the signs and symptoms of depression, and especially someone who was the victim of abuse, is often reluctant to share his or her heart, especially the intimate details of often shameful events. They often feel excessive guilt, and develop a low self-esteem and feelings of worthlessness, which leads to withdrawal, isolation, feelings of loneliness, and to feelings and outbursts of anger. This has certainly been my experience. I think many depressed persons are reluctant to seek medical treatment exactly because it involves telling someone some of their deepest and darkest secrets, and often the deepest and darkest secrets of others. They are afraid they will be judged, which will lead to even more deep depression. The gift of God is that he already knows our hearts, and he still invites us to pray with him. So, he accepts us, he will forgive us, and he will grant our requests.

We also must have realistic expectations of how God grants requests to heal depression. He did grant Hezekiah's request quite quickly. In Hannah's case, she was depressed for years while her rival had sons and daughters. We do not know if she prayed for children earlier, or if she added something new to her prayer in 1 Samuel, when she vowed that she would dedicate her child to the Lord. Joseph was sold as a slave, cried tears of affliction, endured false accusations, named his children as expressions of his depression, and missed his father whom his soul was bound up with. Joseph suffered through these afflictions for twenty-two years before he was given understanding about why God did it.

There is also a subtle warning for those who do not pray in their depression, e.g., in the cases of Amnon and Ahab. Without humbling ourselves in prayer, our depression can turn into anger and hatred turned outward and directed at others.

ACROSTIC LAMENTS

The Book of Lamentations is a lament about the fall of Jerusalem, more specifically, it is a series of laments about it. Its first four chapters are composed as acrostic laments, that is, each line of every lament begins with a successive consonant of the Hebrew alphabet. Lamentation 3 is composed of three consecutive laments, each its own acrostic. There are also two acrostic laments among the individual

Psalms of Lament, Psalms 9–10 (partial) and Psalm 25. An acrostic is an artificial rubric or organizing principle used in the case of laments to try to bring some order, analysis, and comprehensive understanding to a severe depression. In the deepest depressions in the Bible, the person becomes silent or non-verbal, with groans, sighs, and whispers, alternately sounding like the growling of a lion or the chirping of a bird. The destruction of Jerusalem was so severe, and the attendant depression so severe, that the author of Lamentations had to search for a means to begin talking about the disaster and its consequences, a type of cathartic exercise. One suggestion I have is that depressed persons write their own acrostics about their depression. I have done this myself, and I offer the following as an example for others to talk to themselves about the affliction of their own hearts.

I am/have/etc.: a) anxious, in anguish, angry, apathetic, alone; b) broken hearted; c) callous, catatonic, comatose; d) depressed; e) excruciating pain; f) flat affect; g) groan; h) helpless; i) insignificant, insomnia; j) joke; k) killed; l) lonely, low self-esteem; m) murdered; n) numb; o) order—crisis of emotion and mind; p) poor in spirit, panic attack; q) questions; r) restless; s) sad; t) tears; u) unburdening my soul; v) vulnerable; w) wounded; x) x-; y) y-; z) zombie. This exercise is very helpful for me when I am deeply depressed, including filling out the details. It helps me to reflect on a biblical and medical account of my condition. I also began an acrostic for treatment: a) afflicted, if anyone is afflicted, pray ... ; b) blessed are the poor in spirit, for theirs is the kingdom of heaven; c) call to the Lord and he will answer you.

THE LAMENT PSALMS

Although we do not know how the liturgy worked exactly, the individual Psalms of Lament were at least sung, chanted, or read, and the priests and the complainant(s) read and/or repeated different parts. These official laments are saturated with the signs and symptoms of depression, and depressed individuals could identify with their complainants and receive the same official answer from God as they did, through the priest. So, another suggestion that I have is using the Psalms of Lament as healing liturgies in the church today, with depressed individuals or small groups of them reciting their respective parts of a Psalm—the part of the sad, the poor in spirit, the tired and weary, the lonely, or the isolated, and counselors reciting the other parts, so that the Church would support them with hopeful words, and with deeds of kindness. This exercise would also help a depressed person move from private prayer to a non-threatening liturgical prayer, even perhaps toward a willingness to start counseling and pouring out their heart to another believer.

COUNSELING

The Bible also offers the counsel of the wise. The wisdom tradition amounted to observations about the nature of things, including human nature—things like right and wrong, success and failure, friendship and enemies, and, most importantly for us, happiness and sadness. Some of these observations correspond to modern psychotherapy when they address distorted thinking and problem solving. The counsel regarding depression is more general in Proverbs, and more particular in the book of Job.

Proverbs addresses the seriousness of depression and its healing: "A man's spirit can endure sickness, but who can bear a broken/downcast spirit?" (Prov. 18:14). Likewise, "Anxiety in a man's heart depresses/weighs him down" (Prov. 12:25). The same proverb continues, "But a good word gladdens it [the heart]." I am glad that there is a direct link in Proverbs 12:25 between depression and general healing. "Words of kindness are like honeycomb, sweet to the throat (possibly soul), and healing to the bones" (Prov. 16:24). It cannot be stressed enough how the wisdom tradition recommended soothing and well-chosen words for general healing and disavowed ill-chosen words that induced strife or quarrels, or that caused other harm. I do not have the space to show how the Bible views belittling, sarcasm, gossip, lies, taunts, reproaches, reviling, false testimony, and other harmful words as weapons that destroy people, actually murder them. Sometimes people use such words inadvertently or jokingly. But since most depressed persons are very sensitive to negative words, counselors need to take extra care in choosing their words and avoid using them as any sort of weapon. Anything negative will just keep feeding the depression. "There is one who speaks thoughtlessly, like the stabs of a sword, but the words of the wise bring healing" (Prov. 12:18).

The book of Job provides the best example of how *not* to counsel a depressed person. As a wise man himself, Job describes the type of counsel he had expected from his friends—he expected them to be gracious and compassionate (Job 19:21). Also, "A discouraged/despairing man [expects] *ḥesed* from his friend" (Job 6:14). *Ḥesed* is difficult to translate, but includes the idea of faithfulness and loyalty, and love and kindness. If their roles had been reversed, he would have strengthened/encouraged them (16:4–5). Instead, they attacked him with words as weapons—they grieved and crushed him with words (19:2), which were full of wind with no end (16:3)—no end to their wisdom theologies and words of judgment. In the end, Job called them "worthless healers" (Job 13:4) and "comforters who do harm" (16:2). Job's friends did well when they were silent for a week, observing Job's immense sufferings and just being with him. But they failed miserably as soon as they opened their mouths, turning from comforters to accusers. It is even comical. Job's suffering is so great that he loses his appetite, becomes emaciated, lacks sleep, is nearing death, sometimes prefers death and suffocation to living, or to have not lived in the first place, and struggles intellectually and emotionally with the cause of it all. Yet, his friends even make callous remarks about his dead children, that they also sinned and deserved their punishment (8:4; 21:19).

ACCOUNTABILITY OF CHURCH LEADERS AND SUPPORT SYSTEMS–TREATMENT

I recommend the following based on my own study of the Bible and my own experience of depression and its treatment. Much of it will serve just as a reminder to many of you.

1. Recognize that depression is prevalent in the Bible and the church, with a wide spectrum of triggers or causes, and signs and symptoms. It exists either as a single diagnosis or as part of a dual diagnosis with another disease or syndrome. Recognize that fellow church leaders may also have depression.

2. Be like God, who is near to the broken hearted, and who heals those who are crushed in spirit (Ps. 34:18) and broken hearted (Ps. 147:3).

3. Recognize that a severely depressed person may be non-verbal and non-expressive with flat affect. They may be so troubled that they cannot speak (Ps. 77:4). They also may not be able to pray with words, either alone or in the company of others. They may just groan, sigh, or make indistinct noises that resemble whispered growling or chirping. This calls for patience and great listening skills. Job himself counseled his counselors to be silent, and said that would be their wisdom (Job 13:5).

4. Be patient in prayer. Accept that a depressed person might pray in groans too deep for words, and/or in emotionally charged words.

5. Biblical Counseling.

    Be patient in counseling. Proverbs 14:10 says, "The heart knows the bitterness of its own soul." Depressed people are often victims of shameful, often unspeakable abuse, so it is difficult for them to talk about it. And, as my wife has observed, abuse "reverberates in the soul," so they often still feel bitter about it.

    I believe that a counselor should be a righteous man or woman whose own prayers can accomplish much (James 5), that they should recommend prayer to a depressed person, and that they should emphasize the forgiveness of sin that is promised to an afflicted person in 1 Kings 8:38-39. Every depressed believer knows they have sinned. I would say that most are more aware of their sins than other believers, which often develops into an unhealthy sense of guilt that leads to deeper depression and feelings of worthlessness. Do not focus on the guilt and punishment of sin, but on the forgiveness of sin.

6. Medical Intervention.

    Interestingly, the Mayo Clinic recommends that if someone is reluctant to seek medical attention, they should speak with a minister, or spiritual or faith leader in their community. No doubt it does so to recommend a form of psychotherapy, and also with the hope that such leaders have had training in psychiatric disorders and would recommend the medical profession if needed.

Since biblical teaching on depression corresponds in many ways to modern teaching, especially in the areas of diagnosis and psychotherapy, I would recommend biblical prayer and counseling as therapies, either on their own or in conjunction with modern psychotherapy. Many believers who suffer from mild depression have found prayer and counseling to be sufficient treatment and intervention for it. However, many others who suffer from moderate to severe depression have required further treatment, either alternative psychotherapies, medications, or ECT or TMS. Biblical counselors can successfully treat undiagnosed cases of mild depression. Beyond that, most biblical counselors do not have the qualifications to diagnose and treat moderate to severe cases of depression.

7. Be persistent. Depression is often recurrent, and healing is often an alleviation of symptoms, not a full cure. On the other hand, Joseph seems to have been cured of his depression, but it took at least twenty-two years. Also, depressed persons who experienced childhood or adolescent trauma often suffer from incomplete growth and development. They may take the better part of a lifetime to come to terms with these traumatic events.

ACCOUNTABILITY OF CHURCH LEADERS WHO ARE DEPRESSED

As I mentioned, church leaders may become depressed. Depression may be unrelated to ministry, i.e., it would have occurred irrespective of a chosen vocation, a result of heredity, a natural disposition (Jeremiah's sensitivity comes to mind), personal issues, and/or exposure to trauma or affliction. However, depression may be related specifically to the ministry, i.e., it may occur with environmental factors associated with ministry and leadership, particularly some of those discussed in this forum, including exhaustion, burnout, loneliness, verbal abuse, persecution, failure, guilt (whether real or imagined), and self-recrimination. All of these have their counterparts in the OT. For example, Elijah was exhausted and burnt out, had an extreme low after an extreme high, thought he was the only one left, thought he had failed and said he was no better than his fathers, and asked that his life be taken. Jeremiah suffered from verbal abuse and loneliness, wished he had not been born, and wished he had not been called. Although it could lead to crises of personal faith, biblical theology, and hands-on ministry, church leaders who recognize that they are depressed should seek at least the biblical treatment, and adjust their faith and ministry to the presence of this affliction in the church.

In closing, when Dr. Jon Bonk invited me to write this paper he said that "my experiences would enhance the credibility of writing on the biblical material and models." Part of my personal experience has included knowing Jon himself. He (along with Jean) prayed for me and has been all the good things that a listener, counselor, friend, brother, and father should have been to me. I do not think he realizes just how much he has contributed towards my healing. So, I thank him for that, and for the opportunity to raise awareness of such an important issue in the church.

20

MISSIONARY KIDS: WHO ROCKS THE CRADLE?

by LOIS A. DODDS

THE MK'S CRADLE

A child's parents and the relationship the parents have with each other create the cradle in which their child is sheltered and developed.

The most powerful influence in the development of a person is the family which rears him or her. The family may be either the cradle of eminence of the cradle of emptiness… . Parental backgrounds and styles, the degree of nurture or neglect, the coherence and function of the family system, communication habits, and attitudes arise within the family. The family is the microcosm of culture. It is the center in which the self develops and the earliest and most lasting learning takes place. Later relationships usually repeat patterns learned within the family.[1]

---

1 Lois A. Dodds and Laura Mae Gardner, *Global Servants: Cross-cultural Humanitarian Heroes*, vol. 1, *Formation and Development of These Heroes* (Liverpool, PA: Heartstream Resources, 2010), vviii.

I am deeply indebted to the Goertzels[2] for this concept of "cradle." In studying the families of 400 distinguished persons, they discovered parental qualities and styles leading to either "eminence or emptiness." This work influenced me enormously as a parent bringing up three missionary children (MKs) in the rain forest of Peru.

To discuss the MK's well-being and adjustment without examining the family of origin, the cradle of development, is inadequate. Problems that occur in an MK's life are rooted first in the family and the parents' adjustment, before they are "acted out" in the cross-cultural or multicultural context. We must ask, "How healthy are the parents? What are they modeling in their interactions and attitudes that the MK is emulating? Are the parents adjusting by growing beyond themselves and the home culture in a way that models for their children how to thrive? Have they become "metacultural" persons?[3]

The cradle of the missionary kid (MK) is woven by strands of the parents' own development: their character, ability to love and to bond with the child, relationships to God and others, communication skills, and other key "ingredients" in their own formation and adjustment. The cradle is woven thread by thread, strand by strand, word by word, action by action, by reaction and response. To the extent that a mother and father love and nurture their relationship, the cradle of their child's development becomes more or less safe and stable.

The parents and the cradle they create are embedded in the home culture of the parents.[4] The Korean culture is known to be "monocultural," due to the nation's geography. Koreans generally have little exposure to other cultures. As long as the MK parents are still at home in Korea, the church and the extended family cradle the parents, assuring them of love, attachment, belonging and support. We might say there are many strands that, woven together, create and support the cradle, assuring the child a fairly secure place in the world.

Once a couple decides to go abroad, their own cradles are endangered, as they are separated from home and, thus, lose many supportive strands. Some of the woven strands loosen, and the strength of the parents' cradles is diminished. Therefore, it is imperative for the church and the extended family to understand this phenomenon before they send the couple out: the couple will be faced with having to not only weave a new cradle to shelter their child, but also to strengthen their own cradles of support. The parents' relationship will now become the primary cradle for the children, the next generation. If we do not help the parents of the nuclear family to create a safe and secure cradle, the whole family will be endangered. The children (MKs) will find it difficult to grow any healthier than are mom and dad and their love relationship.

---

2   Victor and Mildred G. Goertzel, *Cradles of Eminence: A Provocative and Eye-Opening Study of the Childhoods of over 400 Famous Twentieth-Century Men and Women* (Boston: Little and Brown Co., 1962).

3   Dodds and Gardner, *Global Servants*, 109.

4   Ibid., xxiii.

A STRONG CRADLE IS WOVEN OF LOVE

The famous cradle in which Moses was set afloat provides a useful model for us.[5] Because of his mother's devotion to her baby and to God, Moses grew up in a bicultural setting, amazingly nursed and nurtured by his birth mother and taught in the very household of Pharaoh by his daughter! This mother-child bonding allowed him to retain his Jewishness, while adapting to and learning the ways of Pharaoh and the Egyptians. This prepared him for the unique role God planned for him—being fully Jewish, yet equipped for effectiveness in the larger cultural context.

Parental love: The love relationship of the parents becomes the model for the children, as well as the "ground" in which they are to grow. We must therefore do everything possible to help the couple develop a very strong relationship of love. Central in this is their own formation, especially their ability to love and to express love in ways that strengthen each other and their children. This means that before going to the field, they must *already* demonstrate character and personal strengths, such as positive communication, effective expressions of love, and relational effectiveness in settings beyond the home culture alone.

Home culture: Any person must be grounded in the home culture before being able to grow beyond it. Positive human formation demands rootedness, groundedness, in one culture and one family before the person has the strengths and capacity to grow beyond the self. Just as a child who learns to read and write in his or her mother tongue can more readily transfer those skills to a second language, it is the same with parenting skills. Though people may blame "being missionaries" for dysfunctions in the nuclear family, the problems most likely originated in the family pre-field and then went on to affect missionary adjustment.

One does not "give up" one's attachment to the home culture; rather, one grows in a way that extends beyond it to accept, understand, and acculturate to the host culture(s). Just as we must know ourselves as individual persons in order to grow beyond ourselves and be able to give ourselves away to others,[6] so too we must be grounded and healthy in the home culture in order to extend beyond it. What parents model for their MKs is crucial, for the children take their cues from the parents.

WHO STRENGTHENS THE CRADLE?

The agency, church, and extended family need to create training and policies that promote healthy parenting, strengthened to grow healthy children. In the cradle are centered language, character development, personality types, and mental health. The resiliency of the MK is determined largely by how the parents model responding to adversity and how they embrace other-culture attributes.

---

5   Exodus 2:1-10.

6   Dodds and Gardner, *Global Servants*, xxiv and 67

They must learn to live effectively as Koreans but within the host culture(s). Foremost is what parents model in relationships—respect, openness, good communication, *the ability to love and to express love* and to bond with the other.

To reach the highest levels of human development, the children must have good models and be validated in their own efforts to be loving and accepting. This does not mean accepting everything in the host cultures. It means learning to love persons in spite of cultural aspects we do not endorse. The openness of the parents to the larger world provides a model for children, who can gain resilience in the struggles the cultural differences create. Parental relationships, the cradles of growth, lead either to limited life effectiveness or healthy development and effectiveness. The MK, and the parents themselves, can learn to overcome adversity in the process of struggling to acculturate and become persons "beyond themselves," *so they become more than who they were in the home culture.*

Teaching knowledge and skills pre-field predicates the family being healthier on the field. Such teaching might include the use of resources such as "Ten crucial outcomes of the family of origin,"[7] "Two paradigms for parenting and relating to people,"[8] and "Ten gifts to give your children."[9] Such pre-field training for parents could change MK life outcomes dramatically. Imagine mission agencies giving as much preparation time to family strength as to language study! Which would be most enduring?

TRANSPORT AND TRANSFORM THE CRADLE?

Will the suggestions presented above change the cradle and the one who grows within it? Yes, for sure. But that change is an essential process for one's becoming effective across cultures. If the cradle is *transported with no subsequent transformation,* there will be a serious compromise in effectiveness. All this means that neither the MK nor the parent couple will ever fully fit into their home culture again. *They will return to Korea as modified Koreans, with a broader identity than when they left.* This undeniable reality can be painful upon reentry. Both churches and agencies should prepare the families for this change, this "enlargement" of themselves into the "emerging selves" they become while growing in new soil.

As parents model their struggle to become effective in the new "ground" of the host culture, the MK's identity is formed by learning from them how better to communicate and extend love and acceptance to others. This means mom and dad must themselves be growing, as they become more and more effective. If they get stuck somewhere in the process of learning to love each other and love their hosts, their children will probably get stuck, too. The MK observes

---

7 Ibid., 5-6.
8 Ibid., 7-8.
9 Lois A. Dodds, "Ten Gifts to Give Your Children," *Eternity*, vol. 30, no. 12 (Dec. 1979): 26-29. Reprinted numerous times in various journals and languages. Korean language translation by Child Evangelism Fellowship, 1984.

the adaptations parents make and unknowingly internalizes what the parents model. We found early on in our member care work that when a marriage has a "crack" in the foundation, it quickly becomes a "chasm" under the weight of field stress.[10] This distances parents, so they cease to appreciate and affirm each other. When this happens, a family is in trouble and needs immediate intervention to rebuild their relationship. MKs, if caught in the chasm, will suffer.

In contrast, a family whose relationships are visibly secure and loving *can bring persons to Jesus—the best outworking of the Gospel.* When my husband, a highly trained physician, and I went to Peru, we expected our vital *work* to bring people to Jesus. But it was how our family life reflected God's love that brought people to him.

WHO ROCKS THE CRADLE?

Many forces rock the cradle beyond a gentle, parental pace. Unforeseen powers can create havoc, most notably these four:

Team and organization. The organization one joins has more power to influence and shape one's life than does the host culture, as the former provides structure, accountability, and definition for one's ministry. Teams, too, exert powerful influence. Koreans, typically, serve in cross-cultural and multicultural teams whose relationships affect them profoundly. Sadly, the reported 70 percent of relationships wracked by conflict bring dire outcomes.[11] Missionaries who end up in "treatment" are almost universally driven to do so by negative team relationships. A healthy team, in contrast, primes members to grow, providing an atmosphere of affirmation, cooperation, and belonging.

Host cultures. Every family must contend with host governments, who, in myriad ways, rock the cradle. When it comes to circumstances determined by national governments, missionary parents cannot guarantee stability for their children, as so many factors can contribute to family and ministry pressure. Such pressures sometimes make very rough waves, almost swamping the cradle. However, this situation creates unique opportunities for growth, for facing and working through challenges along with the children. The vulnerability or resilience of the MK is greatly shaped by the parents' ability to withstand and compensate for the forces rocking the cradle.

The MK who learns to transcend these forces will demonstrate lifelong effectiveness and resilience. Emerging from pressured, host government situations with positive attitudes leads to growth. Resentment or attributions of malevolence toward the hosts can endanger the future well-being of the child. A ten-year-old I recently debriefed after evacuation believed the host government was wrong. He attributed to them very

---

10 Lois A. Dodds and Lawrence E. Dodds, "Love and Survival: Personality, Stress Symptoms, and Stressors in Cross-cultural Life" (presentation, American Association of Christian Counselors Conference, Dallas, TX, Oct. 19, 2000), http://www.heartstreamresources.org.

11 Dr. John Powell of the Mental Health and Missions conferences reports this, in person. It is echoed by others.

dark motives. He was "*not a guest*" he insisted; "*he lived there,*" and "*they were unfair!*" "The government should have given back our money spent for visas!"

Unbidden events. Wars, evacuations, displacements, natural disasters, calamities—all of these bring disruption, threatening the stability of the cradle. Sudden separation from one's host-country home, friends, school, pets, and even beloved trinkets have a high impact on both parents and MKs. At such times, the injurious outcomes can be mitigated by parental efforts to restore equilibrium.

Relation to the cosmos. The placement of a kingdom family in the cross-cultural or multicultural world involves shifting each family member's understanding of the cosmos—the realm of God and his purposes in the world.[12] We might say that everything from the cradle to the cosmos changes. Such an enormous shift carries high potential for the distortion of one's perceptions—or an unparalleled opportunity to mature one's perceptions. It will challenge one's ethnocentrism and ideally open one to larger realities, such as that God has created all persons everywhere in his image, equally valuable to him. One must give up any assumptions of who in the world is "best," in part because false assumptions can lead to conflict and diminish one's effectiveness. Learning to work through assumptions to overcome conflict and to grow in love enables one to develop and mature, thus becoming more effective. It takes effort to sort out the differences and consider the large variety of approaches, but doing so opens us to loving those who are different and recognizing the universal human needs common to all the family of God.

REGAINING EQUILIBRIUM

A cradle is built for movement. It is not meant to be static. Thus, the cradle must rock for change to happen. But it has to regain equilibrium from excessive rocking to be a safe place of comfort and growth. For the MK, the parental relationship will remain the stabilizer. For parents who create the MK's cradle, the home culture will remain their stabilizer. The home culture becomes a stronger stabilizer if the constituency accepts the changed identities of the families they sent out—*valuing the ones they sent out as now "more than," rather than minimizing them as "less than."*

Creating reentry opportunities that value and affirm the changes is important. The church and agency, as well as the extended families, must *receive the MK back "as one of us" who has grown beyond our cultural boundaries.* They can proudly say, "We have given one of us to become a world-class, kingdom-inspired person, equipped for the harvest."

---

12 Lois A. Dodds and Lawrence E. Dodds, "Stressed from Core to Cosmos: Needs and Issues Arising from Cross-cultural Ministry" (presentation, American Association of Christian Counselors Conference, Philadelphia, PA, March 22-23, 1995); also presented at AACC Conference, Pittsburgh, PA, Sept. 22-23, 1995. Later published in *Christian Counseling Newsletter*, Fall 1995 (Liverpool, PA: AACC). Also presented for the Association of Church Mission Committees (ACMC) at various regional meetings. This has been the most read of the Dodds' works.

Through being well grounded in the home culture, both parents and MKs have strength to venture into the larger world, to move beyond monoculture. Though this changes both parents and MKs, the role of the solid home culture remains vital as a springboard for MKs to enter the larger world. From out of the "monoculture," the sent person emerges to become effective in the broader world—a multicultural person. He or she becomes able to bridge two worlds, two or more cultures, for the sake of the Gospel.[13] In this, we acknowledge that the MK has a unique "third" culture, a fusion of the parents' and the host's cultures.

NEVER FULLY THE SAME

The very first day of our SIL training, our beloved professor, Dr. Calvin Rensch, said, "Starting today, you will never fully belong. You will never fully belong to the people to whom you go, and you will never fully belong again to those you leave." I remember the shock I felt, hearing that there would be no going back. I recall our painful journey of learning this truth. We have witnessed this awkward truth even among veteran missionaries. But having made the journey, we discovered that the greater "belonging" is to the family of God. Now, we can fall out of the sky into any country and find brothers and sisters in our greater, far-extended family. It has been worth giving up the one, for we have gained the many.

RESILIENCY DYNAMICS FOR MKS[14]

Growing up abroad in a healthy cradle prepares the MK for life success. Some dynamics are that MKs are:

Accustomed to multicultural settings, so they can feel at home and have a sense of belonging with a wide group. We see this phenomenon when MKs go to college. No matter where they come from or have lived, they flock together as a family and form strong bonds out of a common identity as Third Culture Kids (TCKs).[15] Our daughter's wedding party included more than a dozen MKs from various countries, lovingly collected by her and her MK husband. It was endearing to see their strong bonds!

Able to adjust to other multicultural settings. Some MKs recently told me that on furloughs, living in the inner cities of their home countries felt just right because there were many cultures represented in their schools and neighborhoods.[16]

---

13 Dodds and Gardner, *Global Servants*, 45-46.
14 Dodds and Gardner, "Resiliency–Essential for Effectiveness," in *Global Servants*, vol. 2 (Liverpool, PA: Heartstream Resources, 2011), http://www.heartstsreamresources.org, 56-59.
15 David Polluck and Ruth Van Reken, *Third Culture Kids: The Experience of Growing up among Worlds* (Yarmouth, ME: Nicolas Brealey Publishers with Intercultural Press, 2001), 119; also Cindy Loong, ed., *Growing Up Global: What a TCK's Life is Like* (Hong Kong: Shepherd International Church, Ltd., 2008).
16 Dodds and Gardner, *Global Servants*, 109.

More independent, especially with travel, thus adjusting more quickly to being away from home. Hanging out in a college dorm, one readily sees the difference between students who travel and students who do not.[17]

More at ease with adults because they have lived in community rather than in age-segregated sub-cultures. They are more accustomed to relating to adults. This is an enhancement when entering the "back home" culture.

More international ease. I know two-year-old MKs whose play is all about visas, passports, and money exchange.

Know more languages compared to peers in the home country. This prepares them for more life opportunities.

Expanded global awareness. My son-in-law, an MK from Chile, told his parents after his first date with my MK daughter: "She is the first girl I've met who understands the world! That's the girl I'm going to marry!"

VULNERABILITY DYNAMICS[18]

Being out of touch with one's home culture, with "cultural literacy gaps," such as not knowing about popular songs, television programs, movies. Not knowing culture cues "back home" is embarrassing. This can lead to feelings of "not fitting in" and puzzlement at the values and behavior of home-country peers. One of our sons was baffled by behaviors of his US friends at college. When he decided to view them from the perspective of anthropology, as the foreigners, he found his adjustment easier. The more monocultural the home country, the more likely it is that small errors lead to a sense of being misunderstood or even alienated.

Less sense of belonging to a place, as typifies TCKs.[19] They may not know what to say when people ask, "Where are you from?" They may not have a permanent home.

Identity issues may be unresolved.[20] Due to being in many cultures, solid identity formation may be delayed or solidified too soon. (John Marcia hypothesizes four identity stages, all of which relate to MKs.[21])

More frequent separation from parents can have dire consequences. One MK left behind in America at age twelve "for her education" was placed in a family with no understanding that she was in reality Japanese. In the era of ship travel, the extended absences of her parents had negative, lifelong consequences. (We want to be careful

---

17 Personal experience of my children and grandchildren at three Christian universities.
18 Jonathan Bonk, et al., eds., *Family Accountability in Missions* (New Haven, CT: Overseas Ministries Studies Center Publ., 2013), 5-13. Esther Baeq poignantly illustrates many of these in her life narrative.
19 David Polluck and Ruth Van Reken, *Third Culture Kids*.
20 Lois A. Dodds, "Am I Still Me? Challenges to Identity for Cross-cultural Workers, Immigrants, and Refugees" (presentation, AACC World Congress, Nashville, TN, Sept. 11-14, 2013). Also available in booklet form from http://www.heartstreamresources.org.
21 Lois A. Dodds, "Resiliency and Vulnerability: Longevity and Effectiveness in Cross-cultural Ministry," *AACC Newsletter* 20, no. 4 (Liverpool, PA: Heartstream, 2012), 22-25, http://www.heartstreamresources.org.

not to judge well-meaning parents "back then" who followed the lead of even secular families, at a time when higher emphasis was placed on formal education than on the value of family-togetherness and its significance in child formation.) We have learned in our generation both the hurtful outcomes of separation and the benefits of family-togetherness. This issue is especially agonizing for Korean families because the school system is unlike most others. The overseas family may have to trade the developmental benefits of keeping the family together for the detrimental effects of sending the child away in order to seek the hoped-for benefits of educating the MK in the Korean system.

Feeling alone and misunderstood, especially when it seems to the MK that he or she has been abandoned, that "God's work" is more important to the parents than is the child.[22]

Less proficiency in one's mother tongue due to one's speaking many languages. Recent research shows the importance of understanding the mechanics of bilingualism for young children.[23] This may mean that the MK feels less understood. A Korean family who attended a Heartstream program told me their child had not even one playmate who spoke Korean. Such experiences may lead MKs to have less ability to express their deep emotions, which could contribute to later depression or alienation.

Out of step educationally. This has been well documented for Korean MKs.[24]

SUMMARY

It is impossible to have healthy MKs unless one first has healthy parents. We must take this so seriously that as missions and churches, we prepare candidates pre-field for the rigors of family life and love relationships with the same dedication we give to language and culture training. In the long run, a loving, healthy family, in which parents model *how* to love, is more credible and effective than any other factor in the missionary endeavor. Any crack in the marriage relationship becomes a chasm within the host culture, due to the extreme stresses of cross-cultural missionary life. Many winds blow the cradle of parental love, sometimes with gale force, and the family can fall. Teaching missionary families how to have strong relationships with effective communication enables MKs to develop securely, to be transformed into "more than Korean"—into "Korean-Plus"—and to more effectively reflect Jesus.

Appendix

A helpful self-assessment questionnaire regarding adjustment is available.[25]

---

22 Jonathan Bonk et al., eds., *Family Accountability in Missions*, 7.

23 Tracey Tokuhama-Espinosa, *Raising Multilingual Children: Foreign Language Acquisition and Children* (Westport, CT: Bergin and Garvey, 2001).

24 Bonk, et al., eds. *Family Accountability in Missions*, 75-101. See especially chapter 3: "The Education of Missionary Children: Challenges and Opportunities."

25 Dodds and Gardner, *Global Servants*, 21.

21

HOW TO BUILD A MULTICULTURAL MISSION— OPPORTUNITIES AND CHALLENGES:

A CASE STUDY OF WEC KOREA

by Kyung Nam Park and Kyoung A Jo

WEC (Worldwide Evangelization for Christ) International was founded in 1913 by Charles Thomas Studd, one of the "Cambridge Seven." WEC International has always been a pioneer mission, sharing Jesus across cultural barriers where he is least known. Our vision is to see Christ known, loved, and worshipped by the unreached peoples of the world. Our mission is empowered by the Holy Spirit, with a sense of urgency and a commitment to work with others: we proclaim the Gospel by word and deed, so that people come to a living faith in Jesus Christ as Savior and Lord and become his disciples; we gather believers around Christ, establishing churches in the Word of God, so that they make disciples in their communities and beyond; and we mobilize for missions—recruiting, training, sending, and caring for workers in fellowship with the wider church.[1]

WEC International Korea (the sending branch in Korea—referred to in the rest of this paper as "WEC Korea") was established in 1997 to recruit Korean missionaries into WEC. At that time, ten Korean members were working in WEC, recruited through other sending offices. By the end of December 2018, WEC Korea had sent 487 workers to over forty countries. Even though WEC Korea has a short history, it has become one of WEC's major national sending branches. We would like to reflect on what factors have contributed to bringing so many people into WEC, what challenges we face, and what we have learned.

THE CURRENT SITUATION AS VIEWED BY STATISTICS

WEC has over 2,300 members (long-term workers), including retirees, from fifty-six different countries. Among the 2,300 members, around 1,900 are actively involved in ministries[2]—and 462 of them are Korean. Koreans thus make up over 24 percent of the active WEC International membership, members from the UK, the USA, and Brazil making up the next highest percentages. This is a unique phenomenon among international mission agencies that use a standardized selection process. WEC's ratio of traditional sending countries (TSC as below) to non-traditional sending countries (NTSC as below) is 59.2 percent: 41.8 percent.[3] This is a result of WEC's strong emphasis on building multicultural fellowship.

Among WEC's active Korean members, 378 are married, and eighty-four are single. We also have 394 MKs (missionary kids). Most of our workers are working among unreached people groups. During the past eight years, we have sent out an average of 16.8 new members per year.

---

1   WEC International, "Core of WEC" (WEC International, 2016), 2.
2   These 1,900 are called "active members."
3   Traditional sending countries, in this case study, are those countries within WEC that actively sent missionaries before 1980.

Figure 21.1. WEC Korea's Membership Trend

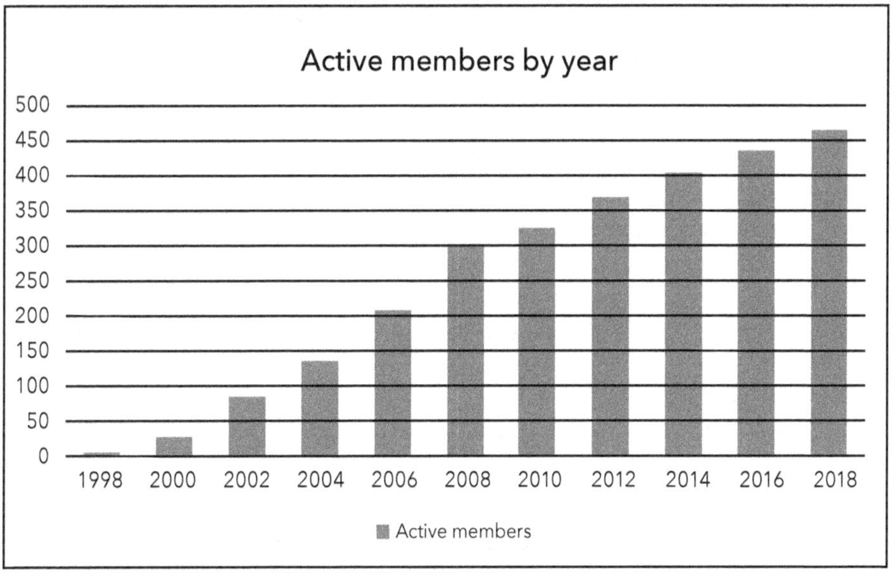

Active members by year

(Bar chart showing active members from 1998 to 2018, with values rising from near 0 in 1998 to approximately 460 in 2018.)

FACTORS CONTRIBUTING TO KOREAN INVOLVEMENT IN WEC

Advance preparation—God's provision. We are a community of God's people drawn from various backgrounds and cultures, reflecting the diversity of the global church.[4] So, we desire to work in multicultural teams, embracing the benefits and challenges this brings to our organization and team building.[5]

Dieter and Renate Kuhl (WEC's International Secretaries, 1984–96) placed a strong emphasis on multiculturalism. They shared their conviction that a greater influx of "Third World missionaries"[6] would strengthen WEC.[7] In fact, WEC decided to open a Korean sending base in 1986, but the base did not open until 1997, due to matters of timing and staffing. WEC Korea was founded on the basis of the organizational calling for internationalization and established a firm, long-lasting foundation of Korean involvement in WEC. In 1989, 58 WEC members (4.1 percent) were from NTSC; by 1998, the number had grown to 153 (8.6 percent); in 2008, it was 555 (25.3 percent); and now, 794 (41.8 percent) of WEC's members are from NTSC. This is a result of God's provision for Korean members and for WEC International.

---

4 WEC International, "Core of WEC," 4.
5 WEC International, "Practice of WEC" (WEC International, 2016), 4.
6 This is old terminology for "the majority world" or "global south."
7 Evan Davies, *Whatever Happened to CT Studd's Mission?* (Gerrard's Cross, UK: WEC Publications, 2012), 87.

Mobilization through an emphasis on the ethos of WEC. WEC emphasizes certain core principles as a spiritual community and as a missions organization. The following principles, known as the "Four Pillars of WEC," are core to the way we seek to live in order to honor Christ and fulfill our God-given mission. The four core principles are faith, holiness, sacrifice, and fellowship. We recognize that living out these principles is possible only through the indwelling of Christ and the transforming work of the Spirit.[8] Further, we consider one's commitment to living out these principles as part of the calling to WEC.

Byungkook and Boin Yoo, who founded WEC Korea and served from 1997 to 2008 as its directors, also placed a strong emphasis on the four core principles and were themselves wonderful examples of what it looks like to live them out. Their work had a huge impact on many young people. Eventually, these young people joined WEC, and WEC Korea grew rapidly—from having three workers in 1998 to having 311 (297 active) in 2008—an amazing work of the Holy Spirit. We still place a strong emphasis on the four core principles and on living radically as messengers for God. These values have continued to promote continuous organizational growth for WEC Korea.

In his thesis, Jongsun Lee reported the top three reasons for joining WEC: its ethos and lifestyle, its ministry know-how, and its team work and equality in decision making.[9] Further, a 2019 survey[10] reveals the top three reasons our members joined WEC: the ethos of WEC and the example of WEC missionaries, the purpose of WEC, and WEC's teamwork / multicultural team. Interestingly, the survey participants noted that WEC's shared ethos and its valuing of the team were the most helpful elements for adjusting to the field. These ranked as even more important than cross-cultural training and candidate orientation, which we will discuss below.

Training and education for multiculturalism: candidate training. WEC has a conviction that well prepared people will be able to serve as good and effective workers. WEC runs missionary training colleges (MTC) in five countries (previously six). Candidates can study the Bible, theology, missiology, and practical ministry skills in a multicultural setting. Almost all instructors are WEC missionaries. So, candidates can develop their knowledge and practical skills on the basis of WEC's ethos. It is very helpful for Koreans who wish to serve with WEC to learn how to communicate, to identify "who I am," to understand cultural differences, and to live and to do ministry together

---

8   WEC International, "Core of WEC," 3.

9   Jongsun Lee, "A Study on the Korean Missionaries' Adjustment to the Multicultural Team of WEC International" (ThM thesis, Hapdong Theological Seminary, 2014), 45.

10 A short survey was done in March 2019, with seventy-four members (M:F=55:45) responding. Of the respondents, 77 percent had been serving in WEC for more than five years, and 50 percent of the total number of respondents had been with WEC for more than ten years. Percentage of respondents serving in leadership roles: 23 percent. Percentage of married respondents: 78 percent (22 percent were single). Percent working on a multicultural team: 85 percent. Percent working on a team in which the majority of team members were from non-traditional sending countries: 47 percent. Percent working on a team in which members from traditional sending countries are dominant: 46 percent.

with those who are from other cultures. So, WEC Korea sends most of its candidates to WEC colleges abroad. The training consists of either a one-year or two-year program in English. Usually, candidates spend one to two years in Korea studying English while maintaining employment at their own jobs and, afterward, go abroad to receive their training. According to Lee's report, 87.5 percent of WEC's trained members agreed that MTC training is helpful for adjustment.[11] In our experience, workers trained in MTC can adjust better to their local cultures and to working alongside the WEC team.

Each sending office runs a candidate orientation (CO). The length of the orientation is eight weeks or more. Currently, WEC Korea runs a twelve-week program. Each sending office may decide on the length of the CO. The various COs' curricula consist of certain common components. "The Ethos of WEC" is the most important component. It helps candidates to think deeply about both spiritual formation and character formation. In addition, candidates receive orientation regarding "how to build a multicultural team," for example, considering issues like cultural diversity, effective communication, peacemaking, and rooting one's identity in Christ. This process helps candidates to develop a better understanding of multiculturalism. Most Korean candidates have received this cross-cultural training before joining their COs, so the COs provide time for the students to reflect on what they learned in MTC.

The CO of WEC Korea has a strong emphasis on character and spiritual formation; it takes some time for candidates to understand how to apply the knowledge and experiences of cultural diversity they gain during MTC and CO into real life and ministry. In application, it is not easy to overcome ethnocentrism without having a deep relationship with Christ and practicing self-denial in daily life. For this reason, the CO lectures and training focus on addressing self-identity and personal characteristics, identification with Christ, emotional health, spiritual formation, and so on. These constitute about one-third of the WEC Korea's CO contents. We also give lectures that present our past experiences as case studies. These case studies help candidates to gain a realistic, rather than theoretic or imaginary, picture of service on a multicultural team. Through CO, candidates thus become ready to begin their work within a multicultural team.

Training and education for multiculturalism: training experienced workers in their mission fields. Training experienced workers in their mission fields is also very important, especially for members from TSC. If the experienced workers in a field (especially those from TSC) never adjust their thinking or practices, it will be impossible for new workers to adjust within their teams. When my wife and I[12] studied in New Zealand, one of our professors (who had lifelong mission experience) said to us, "If WEC is unable to change, new workers from Korea will be unable to stay and adjust to WEC." We did not know what our professor's statement meant at that time, but WEC did start changing,

---

11 Jongsun Lee, "A Study on the Korean Missionaries' Adjustment to the Multicultural Team of WEC International," 49.

12 Kyungnam Park.

in both training and structure. Around 2006, WEC started educating its candidates on "the cultural differences between TSCs and NTSCs," providing leadership training, regional and international conferences, and even field conferences. Through the efforts of a couple who have a passion for building harmonious multicultural teams, WEC also started providing peacemaking training in 2008. Now, all training modules in WEC include these elements, and even in-the-field workers receive the training. This enables all the members of WEC to develop a similar mindset and more fully to understand WEC's organizational identity. It also enhances the mutual understanding between members from TSC cultures and those from NTSC cultures, improving communication between them, as well.

Strengthening member care. International leaders of WEC have realized that care for NTSCs' members was very different from care for TSCs' members. So, the international office appointed a member care consultant and has been making efforts to develop member care that is appropriate to each culture.

For WEC Korea, member care was the burning issue in 2008. WEC Korea grew rapidly, but a proper member-care system had not yet been established, and there was a lack of care providers. Without an appropriate level of member care, many challenges and even conflicts arose in various fields. These challenges were like growing pains. Starting that year (2008), WEC Korea began to strengthen its candidate screening process, now also running multilayered psychologic tests. Since 2008, we have been treating the candidate's selection process and training time as the starting point of member care. Between 2009 and 2011, we worked to organize the administration of member care and to set up member care goals.

During our 2011 annual conference, we took time to brainstorm together. More than 100 members participated. Our time together revealed several areas of member care that we would soon need to develop. We decided to create a member care system based on our findings. The goal was to help our members develop the fruit of the Holy Spirit and grow in inner strength, personality, ministry, and good relationships. As a result, we hoped to see all workers become healthy, resilient, and influential as missionaries. It was a turning point for WEC Korea, at which we stopped focusing only on mobilization and began to focus on mobilization and care together.

We encouraged talented workers to receive training in counseling, spiritual direction, debriefing, MK care, and any other area related to member care. We also developed connections with a number of member care centers. It helped us to learn more and to take care of our members in various ways. In the beginning, it was not easy to introduce our workers to outside care centers and counseling. For Korean members, it was not acceptable to receive counseling or even to talk about heart issues. Traditionally, discussing such topics was regarded as shameful, and people assumed that Christians should not receive counseling. However, we had a conviction that counseling is a kind of common grace, and well cared-for workers could serve the kingdom more effectively. So, our leaders took the initiative to share their own experiences. Thankfully, as a result, some members did go through counseling and became willing to receive care. They then gave positive feedback about these experiences. So, eventually, member care has become acceptable among Korean members. Now, counseling, coaching, spiritual formation and directing, and psychologic evaluation for new workers and workers on sabbatical are regular practices in WEC Korea.

In January 2018, we took time to brainstorm again regarding future areas for our next leader to focus on. We listed the five most frequently mentioned items, of which member care was fifth. It was amazing. We did not expect to see that much improvement in such a short time, but our Korean members felt that they were receiving member care quite well. Of course, there are areas of care that we need to develop more. However, God has been using our sincere efforts to touch people's hearts.

In the 2019 survey, care and help from one's team or fellowship with one's teammates (mutual care) ranked as the third most significant factor in adjusting well to a team or a field. This team support ranked even higher than did English language training. The results could be biased, since 85 percent of respondents had spent more than five years in WEC and could therefore be underestimating the importance of the English training. Still, WEC's recent emphasis on member care has apparently brought about some major change.

CHALLENGES TO BUILDING A MULTICULTURAL ORGANIZATION

The attrition rates. In spite of huge efforts to take care of our members, our overall attrition rate is 17.5 percent for the last twenty-one years. The reasons for attrition are listed in Table 21.2. Unpreventable reasons, such as getting married or taking issue with one's denomination, make up 3.6 percent of the attrition, so the actual rate should be seen as 13.9 percent.

Table 21.2. Reasons for Resignation between 2000 and 2018

Reason for resignation	Number (% of total recruited members, 591)	2000–2008	2009–2013	2014–2018
Different vision & ministry goal from team/field	17(2.9)	2	8	7
Conflict with individual or team	22(3.7)	8	11	3
Personal issue (health, long standing personal issue, etc.)	21(3.6)	6	6	9
Denominational issue—not allowing dual membership	10(1.6)	2	0	8
Changed calling for mission	16(2.7)	0	8	8
Marriage	11(1.9)	4	4	3
Family issue (marriage relationship, MK, parents, etc.)	7(1.2)	2	4	1
Total resignations	104(17.5)	24	41	39

The most frequently listed reason is conflict (22 of 104: 21.2 percent). If you also include the number who noted a "different ministry goal" (17 of 104: 16.3 percent), teamwork related reasons are listed most frequently (39 of 104: 37.5 percent). Personal issues ranked next highest (21 of 104: 20.2 percent), followed by a changed missionary calling (16 of 104: 15.4 percent) and family issues (7 of 104: 6.7 percent).

The history of WEC Korea could be divided into three eras: the period of explosive mobilization (1997—2008), the period of transitioning toward structured care (2009—2013), and the period of using structured care (2014—2018). The current member care system was established between 2010 and 2012.

WEC places a high value on teamwork. This means we need to share a team vision and have common goals. It is rare that a worker engages in ministry individually, so most workers have the benefit of facing challenges alongside a team of companions. Recently, conflict is declining within WEC Korea. This is a result of multiple efforts, including strengthening our candidate screening process and introducing pre-field training modules on teamwork, peacemaking, and cross-cultural communication. In addition, whenever relational or personal issues surface during a candidate's application process, we recommend that the person receive counseling before going into the field. This provides applicants with the opportunity to reflect and to strengthen their areas of weakness. Through additional training in WEC Korea, a candidate can also develop a deeper understanding of multicultural teams. Unfortunately, regarding WEC Korea's attrition rates, the number of those reporting a change in mission calling has increased. It is possible that these cases may stem from relational issues. However, the overall rate of attrition due to relationship-related issues is decreasing.

Almost all workers who reported resigning due to personal issues were accepted into WEC Korea before 2009, which means they did not go through the multilayered screening process or receive pre-field member care. In the future, it will be helpful to evaluate the impact of our strengthened candidate screening process. During the last five years, the number of resignations due to personal issues has decreased. One reason for this could be WEC Korea's emphases on maturity, character, integrity, and missionary accountability, especially with regard to personal healing through counseling and member care. Some have responded well, but others have refused to receive guidance or assistance and have left the organization.

In the 2019 survey, one question asks, "Have you ever wanted to resign from WEC? If yes, why?" Surprisingly, 44 percent of respondents answered "yes" but said they have tried to overcome that desire during recent years. People shared various reasons for their desire to resign, along with various solutions to their concerns. Some of their solutions included having a humble attitude, being patient, denying self, and remembering the calling to WEC.

Beyond understanding of cultural diversity. During last twenty years, Korean members have adjusted quite well within the international culture of WEC, and WEC in turn has accepted Koreans well. Today, many Koreans serve as leaders in WEC. They are comfortable with the cultural diversity and serve while understanding that communication can be conducted quite differently from one culture to the another. However, some areas remain in which Koreans still need to grow.

The areas of communication and decision making still pose some challenges for Koreans. The challenge of language lies not just in grammatical correctness or one's way of communicating, but also in the culture surrounding the language. Koreans are familiar with hierarchical decision making, but this stands in contrast to decision making through conversation and discussion. Today's Korean team members are decreasingly traditional, but traditional Korean culture still impacts their teamwork. The presence of different communication styles still presents some challenges for mission teams. For example, many Korean members and leaders tend to think and plan independently, because we are trained that we need to have clear, complete thoughts and ideas before presenting them to others. Thus, Koreans may avoid consulting their teammates mid-planning. They may tend to present ideas to their team quite late in a planning process. Incidentally, the team might regard such seemingly delayed participation as reflecting one's lack of belonging to the team or even as a lack of integrity. This cultural difference in communication and decision making can be a problem on WEC teams, since WEC team members work very closely with each other. So, we have tried to educate our members in this area. Some of them feel it is not an easy challenge to address. In particular, when a Korean member becomes a team leader, the other team members could interpret their Korean leader as too authoritative or as uncommunicative.

WEC was started in the UK and, later, expanded. So, WEC has its roots in a low-context culture. (Korean culture is a high-context culture.) Through training, Koreans have learned how to communicate with those who are from low-context cultures. In a low-context culture, written information is important, which means that English language ability is a very important element for one's adjustment and personal growth in WEC. Of course, language is a part of communication. Lee also pointed this out.[13] Actually, communication involves multiple elements: cultural assumptions, ways of thinking, values and belief systems, and so on. Since communication is such a complex act, we need to consider how to improve in this area continually.

Currently, any WEC member will acknowledge the importance of having a multicultural team. We respect each cultural background and try to learn each other's cultural values. However, we need to go further: finding a biblical culture that reflects the kingdom of God. Respondents in the 2019 survey said the same thing. To build up a multicultural team is not easy, but attempting to do so is valuable. We can learn and grow into the fulness of Christ through building up a multicultural team, and a multicultural team can illustrate to people what the kingdom of God looks like.

Conflict resolution. A conflict is always a challenge to building up multicultural teams, but it is also an opportunity to grow and to glorify God, as well. A conflict will bring up issues that have been lurking under the surface. When we overcome the

---

13 Jongsun Lee, "A Study on the Korean Missionaries' Adjustment to the Multicultural Team of WEC International," 55-57.

challenge, our team will become stronger and more effective. Usually we think that differences bring conflict. However, personal factors are more responsible for conflict than are differences between people. Lee pointed out that immature personalities induced the most conflict, rather than cultural or lifestyle differences.[14] So, it is essential for us to consider ways that we can help our members to grow, both spiritually and emotionally.

In addition, we need to handle conflict well. WEC uses peacemaking principles and practices, which help us deal with interpersonal issues and bring people together through forgiveness, but reaching reconciliation is still very challenging. The traditional way of resolving conflict in Korea is to cover it up and leave it behind. At some future point, we may meet again and express our apology in a cultural way, rather than clearly asking for forgiveness and acceptance. So, some Korean members could find it difficult to exercise peacemaking principles. Recently, resolving a conflict that occurred between Koreans was also a challenge, due to the difference in the involved parties' levels of adaptation to international culture. This is another area in which we need to grow.

CONCLUSION

In spite of many challenges, building a multicultural team is a valuable endeavor. Doing so reflects the kingdom of God and provides us with opportunities to grow spiritually, emotionally, and socially. When we have unity across different cultures, we become the message of the gospel (John 17:22–23). In order to build each other up, we need to have Jesus' attitude, as described in Philippians 2:5. In his book, Evan Davies quotes Traugott Boeker, saying, "In the end what is crucial is the heart attitude of members and leaders from all nations to each other. What rules and regulations cannot do can be achieved by a spirit of love and respect for each other and our differences."[15]

Finally, Koreans need to help bridge the gap between members from TSC and newly joined members from NTSC. We have learned many important lessons during the past twenty-two years. At times, we have learned through trial and error, so we have a great deal of experience that can help our brothers and sisters from the majority world. We believe that God is preparing Koreans for the next season of harvest, so let us open our hearts to the guidance of the Spirit. Someone once said that internationalization is not having people join us at the dinner table but letting people come into the kitchen and all of us cooking food together. In the same way, we want to see people from the majority world coming into WEC's kitchen to make food together with us for the glory of God.

---

14 Ibid., 94.
15 Evan Davies, *Whatever Happened to CT Studd's Mission?* 142.

SECTION F

SUMMARIES

22

OUR PAIN IS NOT IN VAIN

by JUNG-SOOK LEE

I would like to give a special thanks to Dr. Jonathan Bonk for the extraordinary privilege to serve KGLMF in this capacity. Writing a concluding summary was a daunting and frightening task for someone who is not a specialist in this area. However, I accepted the challenge, so that I could learn more about this year's topic, which I believed critically important not only for missionaries working in cross-cultural contexts, but also for many Christian workers in various ministries at home. As I read each article, many times I found myself in the places of those people who were introduced as case studies or described in an episode, and I felt their pain poignantly. I prayed for the missionaries and their families who have gone through numerous, diverse difficulties and traumas. I reflected on how these same people become the "wounded servants" who will, in the end, "comfort those who are in any affliction, with the comfort with which [they themselves] are comforted by God" (2 Cor. 1: 4).[1] Our pain is not in vain in the Lord!

The papers regarding Korean missionaries' mental health almost unanimously pointed out two things: First, the mental health of Korean missionaries has a strong correlation with Korean society and its high-context culture.

---

1   ESV translation, with author's insertion of "[they themselves]" instead of the original "we."

Second, missionary member-care systems are desperately needed and must be more professionalized, in order to meet the urgent and dire needs of missionaries and their family members.

Let me elaborate on the first point. Korean society underwent a series of invasions and turmoil until the middle of the twentieth-century but experienced drastic changes in every aspect of life within the latter half of the last century. Koreans have achieved unprecedented economic growth within only decades, surprising the whole world. Nonetheless, it is also true that this growth may have come at the expense of other things. Having the highest suicide rate and the lowest birth rate among the OECD countries is just an example of the costs we are paying for our remarkable economic growth. There is a consensus that Korean Christianity has been one of the beneficiaries of the Miracle on the Han River in Korea, and the Korean church has henceforth achieved unheard-of levels of growth and wealth. The Korean government's systematic suppression of Shamanistic/Animistic religious activities, a strong aspiration of Westernization (more specifically Americanization), and evangelical Christian leaders' endorsement of government leadership in the 1970s and 1980s helped Protestant Christianity to be recognized as an acceptable alternative to traditional religions like Buddhism and Confucianism. Protestant pastors and leaders emerged as national figures, thanks to rapidly growing numbers of Christian Churches and believers. It is also undeniable that since 1980, a major mission movement has taken off, thanks to such growth, and the mobilization of capable young people for mission became possible in the post-1980 socioeconomic milieu.

Beginning with the new millennium, however, church growth began to stagnate or even reverse, and we found out that both non-Christians and a good number of Christians, especially among younger generations, did not trust the Protestant churches. Recent surveys regarding social trust toward religions in Korea[2] gave a strong warning signal to Korean Protestant Churches, as Protestant Christianity ranked third in social trustworthiness, following Catholic Christianity and Buddhism. The main reasons for the society's distrust of Protestant Christians have to do with an irrecoverable gap between their words and deeds, and with their materialistic and selfish lifestyles. In short, Protestant Christians are not considered true disciples of Jesus Christ but followers of the prosperity-gospel, whose values are fixed on earthly things, such as success, power, honor, wealth, and other material blessings. This phenomenon is often ridiculed in Korean media and literature and contributed greatly to the creation of a gruesome image of Protestant Christianity, namely, *Gae-dok-kyo*.

---

2 A Korea-based NGO, Trust Initiative Church and Society in Korea, has conducted annual surveys since 2008 to measure societal trust in the Korean church, and its result has been publicized. It was the first kind of attempt by the Korean church and Korean Christians to gauge the level of social trust that both non-Christians and Christians have for the church. Initially, it was criticized by evangelical Christians as a self-destructive behavior; however, it is more widely accepted now as the barometer for assessing the socially perceived trustworthiness of the Korean church, in comparison with Catholic Christianity and Buddhism.

The public's distrust of Protestant Christians is not totally fair, because the survey respondents' understanding of churches and Christians were often based on either wrong information or a lack of information. Further, Koreans' trust level toward religions or religious organizations is low in general.[3] However, we cannot ignore or neglect such negative views against Christians and churches in Korea. The existence of churchless Christians, namely, "Canaan" believers (a play on words, denoting Christians who have no church affiliation), is further evidence of problems in the Protestant church. The prevailing social distrust is one concern, but obvious problems—such as nepotism in leadership, embezzlement of church funds, sexual harassment, or many other types of *Gapjil*[4] within churches and mission fields—are another concern, which worries us greatly.

SOME CHARACTERISTICS OF KOREAN CHURCH CULTURE

In relation to the social distrust toward Protestant Christianity rampant in Korean society, let me describe some characteristics of Korean Christian (church) culture that have been shaped by the national ethos, from which no Korean missionaries are free. The following list are cultural values of which we Korean Christians need to beware and divest ourselves. For missionaries, it may be even more important to shed these characteristics, before leaving for a different culture. Otherwise, these tendencies could be a constant stumbling block to the missionaries themselves and to the native people in the mission fields.

1. Success over service, or, service for success. One of the most problematic and unchristian values that Korean Christians share is a success-oriented mentality. It has to do with a results-based evaluation of one's efforts and an emphasis on hard work, hurriedness, title seeking, and even cheating to get ahead. Let us look at the emphasis on hard work as a sample case. Since Korea as a nation was extremely poor when Christianity was introduced, hard work was highly needed and, hence, encouraged by early Korean Christian leaders, so that people could overcome absolute poverty. Christians in Korea have learned the value of working hard from childhood on. Personally, I remember singing a Korean hymn, "Samchunri bando keumsookangsan," often during Sunday school worship. It was written in 1907 by a national leader, Namgung Eok (1863–1939). Although this hymn now has Matthew 9:37 as the theme verse (possibly added),

---

3 Seung-hyun Choi, "Confidence in Religious Organizations 3.3 percent, 8 out of 12 Institutions," *Newsnjoy.or.kr*, Nov. 8, 2018, accessed Mar. 20, 2019, http://www.newsnjoy.or.kr/news/articleView.html?idxno=220874.
    Reportedly, the level of social trust in religious organizations ranked eighth out of twelve organizations, including government offices and the military (3.3 percent total confidence level in religious organizations).

4 *Gapjil* is the arrogant, authoritarian, and even violent attitude or actions of a person who has a higher position or more power than someone else. It is most often observed in company owners who behave like feudal Lords–quite a social scandal since the infamous "Nut Rage" incident of 2014.

the lyrics do not carry a sense of evangelism but of urgency to work for the nation (possibly for independence). It also says that doing so is God's call for us Koreans! Some believe that this hymn served like a national anthem in the church during the colonial period. No wonder singing it was prohibited in 1937, when it became the first hymn to be banned by the Japanese colonial government! This hymn, some also believe, greatly influenced the birth of the Sae Ma Eul (New Village) Movement song, "Jal Sala BoSe" ("Let Us Live Well") in the 1970s, which inspired Koreans to work hard and live well. Christians validated the value of hard work with Bible passages (Prov. 6:9–11; 24:33; 1 Thess. 5:14; 2 Thess. 3:10), which contributed to the fast transformation of Korean churches into self-supporting churches. Christian businessmen and women began supporting not only their own families but also the churches and their members. After the nation gained independence from Japan and suffered through the Korean War, the Sae Ma Eul Movement prepared a breakthrough for Koreans, by which they could become economically independent and further accelerate their national prosperity. The direct connection between hard work and success (or power and wealth) was emphasized and reinforced in the church and in theological schools without any criticism. I remember hearing pastors and lay leaders offer prayers for success during almost every public worship service I attended in my youth. One example was, "Lord, make our children to be the head, not the tail." The same idea of success is found without exception in all components of the Korean mission movement. So, what non-Christians have been criticizing about Christians and their churches is that Christians are as secular as non-believers are, if not more. It is often said that "Christians want everything, including heaven!" Korean Christians and their churches are understood as a religious power group, and instances of the Gapjil syndrome seen at home and even in the mission field may be explained by this connection between religion and power.

2. *Confucius over Jesus.* Korean Christianity has been known as a "Confucian Christianity" because of its patriarchal and hierarchical nature in church polity and ministry practices. Confucian culture is deeply embedded in Korean Christian families, and hence, the problems between missionary husbands and wives or between missionary parents and children share similarities, to a great extent, with those of Christian workers' families at home.

Some of this year's conference papers highlight that Korea is categorized as a "high-context culture" and *Noonchi* was developed over the centuries in Korea. *Noonchi* is crucially important in personal and work relationships and overrides the written manual at times. Because of the patriarchal and hierarchical nature of Confucian culture, *Noonchi* is most required of inferiors, women, younger people, and maybe the less educated, as well. In Korean churches, too, a hierarchical concept of church offices has developed. Among pastors—and among lay people in a church—rank, age, sex, marital status, education, and family background are denominators that decide who should lead and who should follow a step behind.

In old Confucian culture during the Joseon dynasty, "loyalty" to the king, "filial piety" toward one's parents, "trustworthiness" toward one's friends, and "respect" for one's elders were considered foundational virtues for human relationships. These virtues are certainly great by themselves and can help our lives to flourish; however, within our relationships, they unfortunately require blindness toward justice and the public good. Korean *Jeong* (a shortened form of *Injeong*, human affection) can be one example of such abuse. Confucianism as a religion no longer really exists in Korea, but dead Confucius has maintained an influential presence in Korean people's lives.

3. *Men over women.* Gender has become a huge concern in Korea lately. Due to a radical understanding of gender and the legalization of a third gender in the West, Korean society has jumped into the controversy over gender ideology, without first undergoing a proper discussion of gender. Taking time to discuss the concept of gender and its beginning may help many to reconsider what it means to be men and women in God's sight and, further, what it means to be raised as a man or as a woman at home and in society. The "nature vs. nurture debate" has a long history in the West and in Christianity throughout the ages. However, in Korea, this whole discussion has been confined to limited academic circles (mainly women scholars), and now the gender issue has become a hot topic because it directly relates to the possible inclusion of same-sex love in the antidiscrimination law. Gender studies, however, are necessary in Korea, as we observe that strong Confucian attitudes still prevail among men and women (more among those of middle age and above), while the millennials do not believe in such ideals anymore. This widens generation gaps further than ever. Early introductions to particular images and activities are commonly prescribed for children, depending on whether they are boys and girls, though individuals and families may differ in their specific practices. Such images being prescribed for each gender has resulted in inequality and has created various marital problems. Gender equality is something Christianity championed during its early years in Korea, but in recent years, churches have shown a cultural lag in terms of men's and women's roles in ministry. Obviously, in evangelical churches, there has been scarcely any female leadership among either the clergy or the laity for a long time, making women feel less appreciated and either less interested or simply blind when it comes to decision making within the church. On the other hand, women in the broader society have made remarkable advances.

Marital problems and sexual harassment among missionaries and pastors demonstrate that Christian ministers have not had a proper opportunity to learn and think about gender, sex, marriage, and family from an appropriate perspective. They do not know how to maintain a healthy companionship/ partnership with the opposite sex for God's ministry, whether they are in church or at home. Korean women in their twenties and thirties, since the Gangnam Station Murder case in 2016, are raising their voices against inequality and misogyny.

Many of them advocate for and enforce their interests with regard to women's rights, and church is not a place of exception. Many women of this age group have become indifferent to marriage and childbearing; meanwhile, pastors raise their voices in support of childbearing, based on Genesis 1:28, while at the same time fomenting a national crisis over their mis-handling of women. I do not intend to underestimate or to mercilessly criticize churches' good intentions toward women, but there is certainly another nationalistic campaign alive and well within the church that does not even come near to touching a good biblical message on men and women and their love. Also behind this campaign, I suspect, lies a hidden xenophobia or unwelcoming attitude toward refugees, migrant workers, and North Korean defectors.

Singleness is another thorny issue in Korean churches and possibly in the mission field, as well, although among Western Christian women, the missionary life has been considered an equal opportunity for ministry as early as the late nineteenth century.[5] Singleness has been one of the suffering concepts in Protestant churches since the Reformation. When Protestant reformers celebrated marriage in the sixteenth century, they were disapproving the misuse and abuse of the biblical teachings on singleness, which had been misinterpreted and misapplied, as is the case in the mandatory clerical celibacy of the Roman Catholic Church. Jesus Christ blessed marriage and family but also pronounced a new concept of family by saying that whoever does the will of God is his brother and sister and mother (Matt. 12:50; Mark 3:35; Luke 8:21). The Bible tells us of the urgency of mission and ministry for all who believe in him, and a special gift of singleness is given to some for such purposes, as 1 Corinthian 7 explains. The idea of a right or good age for marriage, especially for women, has to do with childbearing and is often stated expressly in Confucian Korea and in Confucian Korean churches. However, the primary estate of marriage is not just for reproduction or for remedying concupiscence (sexual desires), in contrast to the teachings of Augustine and the medieval theologians. The good of marriage should be understood as first of all companionship (Gen. 2:18); therefore, marriage requires spiritual, mental, and social maturity, as well as independence, in both the man and the woman. However, in Korean society, as family centered as ever, singles are not respected. Singles are being pushed into marriage by their parents, when their parents' own marriage does not demonstrate a promise of happiness. Churches are no different in this regard, and singles in the church feel marginalized.

4. *The nation over the kingdom.* This attitude is closely linked to the historical situation of Korea in the days when Korea's involvement in Christian mission was first beginning. In the late nineteenth century, Korea was too isolated to detect the dynamics of the world, where the expansion and colonial expeditions of Western countries and the struggle for hegemony between Eastern countries like

---

5   Ruth Tucker, *From Jerusalem to Irian Jaya: A Bibliographical History of Christian Missions* (Grand Rapids: Zondervan Academic, 1983 and 2004).

Russia, China, and Japan were already far advanced and ready to plunder Korea. When Japan annexed Korea, Korean Christians—with the support of some missionaries—became patriotic leaders, working for their nation's independence. This year, Koreans are celebrating the centennial year of the March First Movement of 1919, which is famous for having a high level of involvement from Christian leaders, including in the drafting of the Declaration of Independence. A proportionally large number of Christians also risked their lives to participate in Christian mission during the same few decades.

During and after the colonial period and the Korean War, Korean Christian churches have served as centers for praying and acting on behalf of the nation's destiny. Many Christians in their public and personal prayers earnestly beseech God for their nation's peace and prosperity. Pride in the nation's history of success is also strong in churches, and this pride presents as nationalistic arrogance to others, like migrant workers at home and native peoples in the mission fields abroad. Such a mentality prompts us to show arrogance, a *gapjil* attitude, frustration, and anger. Many of you have heard about the Wonsan Revival Movement in 1903, which triggered the famous Pyongyang Revival Movement in 1907. It is believed that the Wonsan revival began with the repentance of a Canadian physician missionary, Robert A. Hardie (1865–1949). In the summer of 1903, as a young and capable missionary, Hardie was full of anger and discouragement because he felt that his mission work in Wonsan was not producing results. Then, while he was studying the Bible and praying with some missionaries who were visiting Wonsan for vacation, he realized that he was viewing his work with a *Yangdaein* (洋大人, literally Big Westerner) attitude, which involved despising the "rice Christians" in Korea. Once he repented of his arrogance, a revival began and moved on to other parts of Korea.[6] Throughout the history of mission, there are not many Christian workers who have been truly free from national pride while serving in cross-cultural contexts, but maintaining nationalistic or prideful attitudes has never helped evangelism or furthered Christian mission.

Samuel H. Moffett (1864–1939) shared an episode of his accidental and unwitting participation in the 1919 independence movement. He began to research how some American missionaries were trying to stand with Koreans in 1919; he went on to publicize the atrocities committed by the Japanese police against peaceful Korean marchers, who were simply shouting for independence.[7] Despite the fact that missionaries were subject to and easily swayed by their government's interest and regulations, it was found that a good number of Western missionaries became close confidants of the independence leaders. And their choice provided Koreans with a good reason to trust Christianity over other religions. Unless we identify ourselves with heavenly citizenship and work

---

6   Robert A. Hardie, "God's Touch in the Great Revival," *Korea Mission Field*, vol. 10 (January 1914).

7   Samuel H. Moffett, "The Independence Movement and the Missionaries," *Royal Asiatic Society-Korea Branch*, vol. 54 (1979): 13–32.

for righteousness no matter what our national backgrounds, others will never see us as Christians who work for God's kingdom, but only as people who simply serve the interests of our own nations.

I remember preachers and mission mobilizers in the 1980s unanimously emphasizing that Korea is the chosen nation to lead the world in mission, citing 1 Peter 2:9. Korea's history of intermittent sufferings, resilient endurance, and historic success through hard work had all been God's providence, so he could raise up Korea to receive the baton of mission from America. Now, we can say thankfully that the Korean mission movement has been amazingly efficient and influential, on every continent and within a short period of time. But we also acknowledge that Korean missionaries have created various problems and have hurt themselves, when they have not undergone debriefing processes necessary to free them from their own cultural baggage.

RESPONSIBILITIES OF ORGANIZATIONS / SENDING CHURCHES

In this forum, we have clearly addressed the need for member-care systems that work to secure the mental health of missionaries and the further stability of their mission work. Member care starts with the missionary selection process and ends at retirement. During missionaries' field work, member-care systems (perhaps in coordination with external care providers) should be arranged to address the needs of the missionaries and their families. The availability of such services will help missionaries to seek help when they face difficulties. Even a short-term mission team composed of professional counselors would be highly encouraging. In June 2015, Torch Trinity Graduate University (TTGU) sent an "Angel Project" team, composed of faculty and students who were also licensed counselors, to Nepal about two months after a massive earthquake, so they could help people process the related traumas. Whereas there are only a few theological schools that provide Christian counseling programs in Asia or Africa, almost all Korean theological schools have a Christian counseling department. Therefore, it would be ideal if sending churches and organizations could work together with counseling departments or counseling centers in Korea to provide member-care teams that provide for missionaries' mental health needs.

Missionaries' mental health is also related to financial security, as presented. NamSeoul Church's exemplary case was very helpful in describing how to care for the missionaries we send, especially when they retire. Missionary students in my school often confide that taking the sabbatical year is not easy because of financial limitations. According to them, their financial support is reduced by up to 70 percent during their sabbatical leave, while their living expenses in Korea are higher than they are on the mission field. Unexpected expulsions from the mission field or other traumatic situations are not easy matters for missionaries to deal with gracefully. My own study of an American woman missionary in the early twentieth-century assured me that sending churches and mission organizations should take care of their missionaries. Mary Culler White (1875–1973) was sent to China in 1901 by the Methodist Episcopal Church, South in Atlanta through the Woman's Foreign Missionary Society of the Methodist Episcopal Church, South (WFMSMECS). She visited Wonsan in August of 1903 for vacation and there renewed her friendship with the missionaries who had been sent to Korea. It was then that the revival took place, while missionaries including Robert Hardie gathered together for prayers and Bible study. White served China until she was expelled by the Chinese government in 1943, at which time she returned home and continuously led a missional life until her death, serving the church in Georgia, by which she had been sent to China.

Reading the minutes and reports of the WFMS and Board of Missions of the Methodist Episcopal Church, South convinced me that we should take care of our missionaries more comprehensively. The Twenty-Sixth Annual Report of the Woman's Board of Foreign Missions reads,

> While rejoicing over what God, through this organization, has accomplished, we cannot close our eyes to the fact that our *representatives* [emphasis added] are overburdened, are breaking down, because the work presses upon them so heavily. They are distressed, too, for fear reinforcements longer delayed may injure the glorious success they have met. The situation is critical indeed. At home membership is not increasing as it should; candidates for foreign service are few, and those offering themselves are not yet fully equipped, and collections inadequate. These things cause apprehension. Only four graduates this year from the Training School applying for foreign work, while China itself needs four new missionaries at least … The first years—the trial years of our organization—have passed, and the self-denial and suffering of the missionaries should also be things of the past.[8]

SUGGESTIONS AND CONCLUSION

Like pastors' lives at home, missionaries' lives abroad should be protected by a certain standard, so that they can be effective in their ministries and in evangelism. The standardization and normalization of missionary life would help to protect missionaries from suffering under too much stress. It could also help to prevent the development of mental disorders when missionaries face challenging situations like expulsion or trauma. Providing proper care for missionaries' mental health is important not only for the missionaries themselves, but also for the mission

---

8 Methodist Episcopal Church, South, *Twenty-Sixth Annual Report of the Woman's Foreign Missionary Society for 1903-04*, Methodist Episcopal Church, South, Woman's Foreign Missionary Society (Louisiana Conference: 1954).

itself, since experienced missionaries are irreplaceable assets in the mission fields and within their organizations. So, in order to take care of Korean missionaries, I would like to suggest five areas, to which we should pay more attention. First, we must develop a self-critical understanding of who we are as Korean Christians beyond a personal inventory level, because none of us is free from our socio-historical context. Second, a normalization of our expectations of life seems to be necessary. A success-oriented culture has driven us to become people oriented toward success, hard work, achieving goals, and we have considered health, family, community, and even spiritual practices as simply a means to those ends. Third, our missionaries should be guaranteed vacation time, sabbaticals, and pensions for retirement. Recent statistics on the rising senior mission movement are encouraging in this regard. Fourth, a (united) member-care system needs to be required for every missionary sending body. Lastly, spiritual formation programs, such as a spiritual direction program or mentoring / coaching program, should be also required for missionaries. Spiritual well-being, mental health, and mission work are tightly interrelated, as many researchers have already argued.[9]

As I conclude, I remember Psalm 107:6–7 (ESV), "Then they cried to the LORD in their *trouble,* and he delivered them from their *distress.* He led them by a straight way till they reached a city to dwell in." Christians face diverse troubles, and troubles always get bigger when they encounter us, because we add our worries and fears to them. But God takes care of the stress and tiredness our troubles cause us, when we implore the Lord for mercy. As this pattern of facing trouble and then receiving the Lord's deliverance repeats in our lives, let us encourage one another by remembering God's promises in Matthew 11:28 (ESV), "Come to me, all who labor and are heavy laden, and I will give you rest" and 1 Corinthians 15:58 (ESV), "Therefore, my beloved brothers, be steadfast, immovable, always abounding in the work of the Lord, knowing that in the Lord your labor is not in vain."

---

[9] A recent research project is useful for understanding this issue. Hee-Ju Yoo, "영적 안녕감 증진을 위한 선교사 집단 심리 디브리핑 프로그램 개발: 기독교적 이야기치료 관점에서" ("Development of a Group Debriefing Program for Enhancing the Spiritual Well-Being of Missionaries: A Christian Narrative Therapy Perspective" (횃불트리니티신학대학원대학교) (PhD dissertation, Torch Trinity Graduate University, 2018).

23

"BUT WE HAVE THIS TREASURE IN JARS OF CLAY ...": MENTAL HEALTH AND GOD'S SERVANTS

by Jonathan J. Bonk

PERSPECTIVE

"But We Have This Treasure in Jars of Clay...": Mental Health and God's Servants

Some perspective on who and where we are in the history of Christian missions is helpful in a forum like this. At its birth, the tiny Christian church was immediately confronted with an existential crisis. Following the stoning of Stephen (Acts 7), "a great persecution broke out against the church in Jerusalem, and all except the apostles were scattered throughout Judea and Samaria" (Acts 8). You know the story of how one of the principle operatives in this fierce attempt to make sure that Jesus' followers were exterminated was a man named Saul. He would become the best known and most influential missionary of all time. His teaching and his methods have been applied and even emulated ever since.

It is difficult to imagine that Paul did not suffer trauma and post-traumatic stress disorder from the physical abuse, disappointments, and fatigue that dogged him throughout his career. Although he did at times have access to Dr. Luke, he did not have the luxury of naming and treating his conditions as we would today. His summary of the hardships and brutal mistreatment that he had experienced by the time he penned his second letter to the Corinthians—and things would get even worse for him in Ephesus—is difficult to read or imagine (2 Cor. 11:16—12:10).

> But whatever anyone dares to boast of–I am speaking as a fool–I also dare to boast of that. Are they Hebrews? So am I. Are they Israelites? So am I. Are they descendants of Abraham? So am I. Are they ministers of Christ? I am talking like a madman–I am a better one: with far greater labors, far more imprisonments, with countless floggings, and often near death. Five times I have received from the Jews the forty lashes minus one. Three times I was beaten with rods. Once I received a stoning. Three times I was shipwrecked; for a night and a day I was adrift at sea; on frequent journeys, in danger from rivers, danger from bandits, danger from my own people, danger from Gentiles, danger in the city, danger in the wilderness, danger at sea, danger from false brothers and sisters; in toil and hardship, through many a sleepless night, hungry and thirsty, often without food, cold and naked. And, besides other things, I am under daily pressure because of my anxiety for all the churches. Who is weak, and I am not weak? Who is made to stumble, and I am not indignant?
>
> If I must boast, **I will boast of the things that show my weakness.** The God and Father of the Lord Jesus (blessed be he forever!) knows that I do not lie. In Damascus, the governor under King Aretas guarded the city of Damascus in order to seize me, but I was let down in a basket through a window in the wall, and escaped from his hands.
>
> ... Therefore, to keep me from being too elated, a thorn was given me

in the flesh, a messenger of Satan to torment me, to keep me from being too elated. Three times I appealed to the Lord about this, that it would leave me, but he said to me, "My grace is sufficient for you, for power is made perfect in weakness." So, I will boast all the more gladly of my weaknesses, so that the power of Christ may dwell in me. Therefore I am content with weaknesses, insults, hardships, persecutions, and calamities for the sake of Christ; for whenever I am weak, then I am strong.[1]

One of the constants in the way Paul coped with difficulty was his theology of weakness. "I can do all things through him who strengthens me," he explained to the Philippian church (Phil. 4:13).

Today, more than 2,000 years later, the church is truly universal. Throughout most of Christian history, emissaries of the Gospel had neither the vocabulary nor the conceptual framework to describe or deal with mental illness that almost certainly manifested itself among them. There were no schools of psychology or psychiatry; there were no therapists; there were no treatment centers; post-traumatic stress disorder almost certainly existed.

Every culture and every era have their ways of understanding, describing, identifying, preventing, and coping with mental illness. You and I think of ourselves as relatively privileged, members of societies deeply conditioned by entitlements and expectations that would have been alien to most of our ancestors, and which are unknown to a majority of Christians in the world today.

So, as I briefly summarize the extraordinarily insightful case studies presented and discussed in this forum, we need to remind ourselves that had this gathering been convened 100 or 1,000 or 2,000 years ago, a very different set of analytical tools and concepts—mostly theological and pastoral—would have been marshalled to help us deal with our human frailties. And I believe that at rock bottom, these remain as our uniquely Christian and sure foundation.

In order to organize my thoughts, I have created a four-tier taxonomy of broad, logically progressive categories within which to arrange the case studies. The categories and criteria of inclusion are not mutually exclusive, and one can easily find plenty of overlap and a little repetition. In this concluding summation, I attempt to follow that progression.

THE FOUR CATEGORIES OF CASE STUDIES

1. Missionary disillusionment, discouragement, and depression. Three case studies seem to fit naturally within a larger frame of missionary disillusion, discouragement, and depression. **Dr. Ruth Maxwell**—with many years of personal experience as a missionary and as a caregiver for missionaries, serving in one of the oldest, largest, and most reputable mission societies, SIM International—knows what she is talking about.

---

1   2 Cor. 11:21–12:10 (NRSV).

Hers is not a rosy picture of intrepid missionaries conquering all, but a somber reminder that we have our treasure in jars of clay—a treasure that is from God, not from us. "Despair, discouragement, disillusionment, despondency, and disappointment" are the "norm" for missionaries (and probably for all servants of God) somewhere along the way. This was certainly true of Jesus, even though he was just a young man and no veteran of decades of cross-cultural service!

There is no detour around the great gulf separating *pre-service expectations* from *in-service realities*. This is probably true of all human beings who anticipate and then experience such things as marriage, children, vocation, and so on. Cognitive dissonance is a given. The gap between youthful naïve expectations and actual life is too wide to bridge and must be traversed on foot by the plodding pilgrim. Adding to the stress are the role expectations associated with the missionary vocation. Korean and Western societies have moved far beyond the expectations outlined by Paul when he said that he and his fellow missionaries were like prisoners "on display at the end of the procession, like men condemned to die in the arena" (1 Cor. 4:9). Living into the status of "missionary" and its associated roles is difficult, perhaps even impossible, for most of us. Whether the couple described by Dr. Maxwell ever surmounted their disillusion is left open, with Amber searching the Bible for clues on the way forward.

Dr. Kyunghwa Hong's excellent response affirms that darkness and loss of hope is all too common for missionaries who "adjust to a different culture while at the same time balancing family and ministry responsibilities." I think she is correct in her insistence that churches and mission societies move away from triumphalist reporting of "results" and instead focus on the missionary's interior and relational journey. She also proposes sensible aspects of systemic church and agency support of missionaries that would provide spiritual and emotional support through debriefing, counseling, and psychological testing. It seems to me that there are many occasions when proper pre-field training and perhaps a different kind of short-term, cross-cultural experience would remove the rose-tinted glasses from fledgling missionaries and their supporters, so that expectations do not collide so disastrously with on the ground realities.

Dr. Do Bong Kim provides an evocative account of Pastor Sorak's futile and ultimately devastating attempts to live up to his superman persona. Statuses and their accompanying clusters of roles and role expectations are both ascribed and earned. We can never escape our humanity or the brutal reality that we are only what those around us tell us we are. Becoming a missionary is one path to upward social mobility and all of the imagined benefits associated with higher social status. The missionary path has been one way of achieving high statuses within certain societies at certain times in their history.[2]

---

2 See C. P. Williams, "Not Quite Gentlemen: An Examination of "Middling Class" Protestant Missionaries from Britain, c. 1850-1900," *The Journal of Ecclesiastical History* 31, no. 3 (July 1980): 301-305. Published online, March 25, 2011, https://www.cambridge.org/core/journals/journal-of-ecclesiastical-history/article/not-quite-gentlemen-an-examination-of-middling-class-protestant-missionaries-from-britain-c-18501900/A0C2EE294A577DA3A397FB2F93E66D05.

But with these statuses come roles and the corresponding expectations described so vividly by Dr. Kim in this case study. These expectations become a kind of procrustean bed.[3] There is no escaping these roles. A missionary's behavioral and character traits are supposed to be consistent with his or her status. Role sincerity is crucial to missionary credibility. Those of us who make a living by being religious are often tempted to act and speak as if all the points we make are personal convictions. When this happens, *role insincerity* functions as a contradicting para-message.[4] In a success-oriented, driven culture such as you have in Korea and we have in many parts of the West, to be a pastor or a missionary is to bear an impossibly heavy burden of spiritual and cultural expectations. Dr. Kim wisely reminds us through his case study that role fulfillment associated with a certain status in one context (country "P") was no guarantee of effective or harmonious ministry among fellow Koreans in another (Canada). The "mental health care journey map for missionaries" was one enduring positive outcome of the physical, mental, and relational brokenness of Mr. and Mrs. Sorak. The response of **Dr. Kemper** reminds us that super-person "heroics" is built into the one-dimensional hagiographical accounts of missionaries that inspire youth and young adults to consider a missionary vocation, and such highly idealized, filtered accounts virtually guarantee eventual multiple-level failures and profound disillusion with themselves, their colleagues, and their calling.

The third paper in this cluster of case studies on missionary disillusion, discouragement, and depression is by **Dr. Jonathan S. Kang,** who writes insightfully about missionary anger from a Korean perspective. Anger, as Dr. Kang observes, is not a uniquely Korean problem. It is universal and runs across the entire gamut of homo sapiens. Nevertheless, those of us on the outside who have been privileged to count Koreans among our closest friends and colleagues readily agree with Dr. Kang that "Koreans are feisty, fiery, emotional, passionate ... easily angered" and in relentless pursuit of becoming "better and greater." He says that Korean *han* or volcanic "fire illness" (*ul-hwa-byung*) derives from Korean feelings of inferiority and envy at the relative success of

---

3 In the Greek myth, **Procrustes**, a son of Poseidon, had a stronghold on Mount Korydallos at Erineus, on the sacred way between Athens and Eleusis. There he had a **bed**, in which he invited every passer-by to spend the night. He would then set to work on them with his smith's hammer, stretching or mutilating them so they would fit in the bed.

4 Loewen relates the story of the healing of Pastor Aureliano's wife, who was ill with malaria. The missionaries "pretended" to believe James 5:14-15–"Is any one of you sick? He should call the elders of the church to pray over him and anoint him with oil in the name of the Lord. And the prayer offered in faith will make the sick person well ..."–but their prayer for her was not effectual. Later, the Indian pastors prayed for her healing, this time with the desired result. When the missionaries asked why they had not been invited to participate in the prayer, Pastor Aureliano explained that it had been evident that they did not really believe and that, according to the text itself, their prayers would be ineffective. (Jacob A. Loewen, "Missions and the Problems of Cultural Background," in *The Church in Mission: A Sixtieth Anniversary Tribute to J. B. Toews,* ed. A. J. Klassen (Fresno, CA: Mennonite Brethren Church, 1967), 289-292.

others, combined with the deeply ingrained social pressure to save face at any price (*che-myun*) in social and public relationships. Korean work-focus and task orientation with its emphasis on measurable *doing* rather than on less tangible *being* sets the stage for mental seismic pressures that give rise to rage volcanoes. I am not Korean enough to verify what Dr. Kang has written, but I have lived long enough to know with certainty that whatever Korean shortcomings might be, the world—especially the world of Christian missions—is greatly enriched through them.

2. Missionary relational dynamics and tensions. A cluster of four case studies relates more specifically to relational dynamics and tensions. One common current shared by these "illnesses" is their debilitating impact on interpersonal relationships. And since our Christian faith is a fundamentally *relational* faith—stressing reconciliation with God and reconciliation with one another—these case studies are worthy of our close attention.

Among the most intractable dividers among human beings is race and the visible markers of racial distinction. We should never underestimate our capacity even as Christians to succumb to the most egregious kinds of racism. We do well to recall that the "Christian" Papal Bull *"Inter Caetera,"* issued by Pope Alexander VI on May 4, 1493, played a central role in the Spanish conquest of the western continents ("New World"). The document provided a virtual carte blanche justification to Spain's claim of exclusive right to the lands "discovered" by Columbus the year before. And it laid the "Christian" theological foundations for the greatest genocide and land theft in the history of our world, the conquest of the Americas.[5]

---

5 David E. Stannard, *American Holocaust: Columbus and the Conquest of the New World* (New York: Oxford University Press, 1992). Stannard estimates that during the 400-year period from the first Spanish assaults against Arawak peoples of Hispaniola in the 1490s to the US Army's massacre of Sioux Indians at Wounded Knee in the 1890s, as many as 100 million indigenous inhabitants of what we now know as North and South America were obliterated in the most horrific genocide in the history of the world. It was perpetrated by white "Christians." In more recent times, we recall the Jewish holocaust, perpetrated by one of the most "Christian" nations of all time, Germany. Of course, one might argue that Hitler was no Christian, but we would have to agree that on the basis of German religious demography of the day, the vast majority of soldiers, military personnel, and civilian civil servants who conceived, managed, and implemented this vast system of murder would necessarily have self-defined as "Christian." Nor are such race-rooted mass murders restricted to white people. The genocide in Rwanda that occurred for 100 days between April 7 and mid-July in 1994 resulted in the Hutu slaughter of an estimated 500,000–1,000,000 Tutsis. Rwanda was and is a Christian nation, with 57 percent of the population self-defining as Catholic, 26 percent as Protestant, 11 percent as Seventh Day Adventist; the remaining population is either Muslim or indigenous. This means that both victims and perpetrators had to have been Christians. I say these things because it should not surprise us if, within a multi-racial mission community, there are tensions. These tensions are often dismissed as "cultural," and there is a cultural dimension. But beneath this is a concept of self-identity that is solidly racist, endogamous, and culturally and linguistically distinct, making difficult the kind of harmonious community to which Paul constantly urged early believers.

Dr. Soohyun Kim acknowledges the legitimacy of explanations proffered by intercultural studies, sociology, and psychology. Yet each is capable of only partially explaining or ameliorating the profound sense of "otherness" experienced by racial minorities in international mission organizations. The author concludes that while there are some significant strategic and theological benefits to Korean missionaries who persist within an international mission agency framework—and she even provides a helpful, six-point guideline for doing so—there is a steep personal identity price to be paid. **Patricia Toland's** insightful response constitutes a constructive "amen" to this. Will it be worth it to all parties involved and to the credibility of the Christian witness? Perhaps. But it is wondrously difficult for any culturally dominant understanding of "we" to genuinely accommodate "them."

Dr. Hyun-Sook Lee's case study reminds us that even within the context of a marriage in which husband and wife are shaped by similar cultural and social backgrounds and share a common theological understanding and missionary vision, there is plenty of room for relational conflict. Her penetrating insights reveal the ways that cultural conditioning and highly idealized gender and occupation role expectations—in both cases sharply at odds with biblical ideals and principles—undermine, erode, and destroy both marriage and ministry. **Rev. Ben Torrey's** response reminds us that a biblically informed "conversion" of both Confucian conditioning and church-mission role idealization and expectations is the only way off of the marriage- and ministry-distorting Procrustean bed of culturally driven expectations for both.

Dr. Nancy Crawford's case study on the neurodevelopmental disorders and mental health of missionary children is a logical complement to Hyun-Sook Lee's case study. Dr. Crawford's is a poignant reminder of the dilemmas faced by parents the world over: a child's needs inadequately addressed because of limited access to resources. This is by no means a uniquely missionary family problem. It is probably no exaggeration to say that missionary children have access to services and privileges well beyond those available to the children of ninety-nine percent of the non-missionaries among whom they live and work. But a Western or Korean missionary's culturally derived sense of entitlement and the awareness of alternatives in the treatment of Robert's ADHD or Rebecca's SLD back in their homeland acerbates the understandable sense of frustration and guilt. This dilemma has been a constant ever since the Protestant missionary movement began sending entire families abroad.[6]

---

6 Sarah Davis Comstock, a young mother and American Baptist missionary to Arakan (Burma), wrestled with the tension between missionary service and family responsibilities in a letter of anguished outpourings, dated 1842, almost 180 years ago:

"Our children are but another name for self. You are right in supposing that I have many anxious thoughts about their future lot; how many and how anxious, no human being can ever know ... As a general rule, I believe a mother's duty to her children is second only to her duty to her Creator. How far missionary mothers may be exempt from this rule, it is difficult to decide. I see no other way than for each individual mother prayerfully to

Dr. Crawford is among those whose service to missionary families is of inestimable value. Identifying and naming disorders marks the beginning of hope in understanding and coping with their deleterious effects and, perhaps, treating them. It will probably be some time before missionary families can expect to hear the words with which she concludes her case study. As **Jenny Pak** points out in her response, Korean missionary families face unique cultural obstacles to understanding and acknowledging, let alone treating, ADHD or LD. Not only do we all have much to learn, but the functional application of that knowledge to the well-being of our children will be relatively enhanced or stymied by the cultures to which we belong and for which we are obligated to acculturate our children.

I have included **Dr. Richard Winter's** thoughtful consideration of sexual addiction as the fourth paper in the cluster of papers relating to relational dynamics and tensions. Although there is debate among psychologists and psychiatrists about whether or not sexual addiction is a mental illness per se, there is no doubt that in Western societies at least, sex is an obsession that permeates advertising, education, literature, the arts, politics, and the public imagination. The sexual impulse in all creatures is one indication that the author of these enigmatic words in Ecclesiastes is correct: God has "set eternity in the hearts of men, yet they cannot fathom the work that God has done from beginning to end" (Eccles. 3:11).[7] Replication of ourselves through offspring is the only way that we can ensure some kind of existence into the future, whether one is a flea, a mouse, a cricket, a squirrel, or a rabbit: it is the sexual impulse that is the

---

consider the subject, and let her own conscience decide as to her duty. As to my own feelings on this subject, after long, serious, and prayerful consideration, I have come to the conclusion that it is best to send our eldest two back to America in the course of another year, should a good opportunity offer.... This surely forms the climax of a missionary's sacrifices....

"If it were not for the consciousness of doing right, of being in the path of duty, I could not, no, I could not sustain it.... Pray for me; pray for those dear children who are so soon to be orphans, an age, too, when they most need the watchful care of parental affection. This thought is at times almost too much for my aching, bursting heart to endure. Had not my ... compassionate Saviour added these two words: "and children" to the list of sacrifices for his sake, I might think it more than was required...."

"Shall we withhold our Isaac? No; may we rather strive to commit ourselves and our precious offspring in faith to his care, who has said, 'Leave thy fatherless children to me.' They are in one sense orphans. But if rendered so by what we feel to be obedience to our heavenly Father's will, will He not be to them a father and protector? Will He not more than supply the place of the most affectionate earthly parents?"

She sent her children back to the United States by ship in 1942. Dead from cholera less than one year later, she would never see them again.

Groves and Sarah Comstock began service in British-held Arakan (Burma) in 1835. Shortly after sending their two eldest children back to the United States, both died of cholera: she, in 1843, and he, in 1845. See Mrs. A. M. Edmond, *Memoir of Mrs. Sarah D. Comstock, Missionary to Arracan* (Philadelphia, PA: American Baptist Publication Society, 1854), 184-186. The sketch is taken from G. Winfred Hervey, *The Story of Baptist Missions in Foreign Lands, From the Time of Carey to the Present Date* (St. Louis, MO: Chancy R. Barns, 1884), 348.

7 Berean Study Bible.

best—though by no means certain—guarantee of some kind of continuity on earth. The same is true of self-conscious human beings, who are capable of flights of imagination, including sexual, but whose stake in the future is utterly reliant on their compulsion to reproduce themselves. According to popular myth, men think about sex every seven seconds. It would be difficult to prove or disprove such an assertion; suffice it to say that the sexual drive is not a compartmentalized but an integral part of human identity. It is not surprising if sexual awareness is a relative constant (depending on age, virility, culture, and social context).

As theologians early in Christian history understood, our great adversary cannot *create* anything; he can only pervert what God creates. He can only take what is good and distort or misdirect it, so that it no longer serves only good purposes. The sexual impulse is at the core of all biological life, including human life, because it is the basis of our survival beyond a single generation. As one author put it, "all of life is foreplay." Without sex, life comes to an abrupt end in a single generation.

We do not need to be reminded that widespread sexual abuse has existed in the Catholic Church since at least as far back as the eleventh century and has rocked the church in recent years. But evangelical missionaries, clergy, and other dedicated Christians are at least as susceptible to this addiction as anyone else, as the sad stories of child abuse in mission boarding schools or in church youth groups remind us.[8] Richard Winter's case study and his sober reminder that "we

---

8 See V. Hunter Farrell, "Broken Trust: Sexual Abuse in the Mission Community. A Case Study in Mission Accountability" (paper presented to the seminar on Mission-Missionary-Church Accountability Issues and Case Studies: Implications for Integrity, Strategy, and Dynamic Community; OMSC, New Haven, CT, Feb. 2011). In 1998, the GAMC's World Mission office received a report of sexual abuse by a retired Presbyterian missionary who had served in the Congo. An Independent Committee of Inquiry (ICI) was established "to investigate allegations of abuse of children in the Democratic Republic of the Congo (formerly Zaire) for the period 1945-1978. The Independent Committee of Inquiry functioned independently and made its report (including any recommendations for additional action) to the Executive Committee of the General Assembly Council." The specific mandate of the ICI was not disciplinary or for the purpose of establishing civil legal liability, but to "be essentially pastoral in nature, to help survivors, the well-being of the larger Christian community, the General Assembly level offices, and the integrity of the Presbyterian Church (USA)."

The ICI, in its final report in 2002, found that an ordained Presbyterian minister, who served as a missionary for thirty-three years, had, in fact, committed at least twenty-five acts of sexual abuse against missionary children at the Central School located in Lubondai, Congo. The Commission's thirty recommendations were received by the GAC, and it acted favorably upon all but one of the recommendations (#29, which was not feasible in a Presbyterian system of governance) and one sub-recommendation (#14-B, which raised legal issues beyond the mandate of the General Assembly Council). The GAC distributed the report publicly and took additional measures beyond those recommended by the ICI in an effort to increase awareness of the problem of child sexual abuse and to prevent future acts of abuse. During the ICI's investigation, allegations were received of incidences of abuse from former Presbyterian missionary children in other countries and time periods, especially Egypt and Cameroon. On June 27, 2003, the GAC Executive Committee chartered the Independent Abuse Review Panel (IARP) to investigate these and other allegations of abuse "in other mission fields, including Cameroon and Egypt."

all live on the edge of [sexual] addiction" is as timely as it is salutary, as is **Sun Man Kim's** fitting response.

3. Contextual contributory factors in missionary mental "illness." For the third group of papers, I have "illness" in quotation marks, because "illness" does not seem to necessarily apply to these case studies. Psychological duress and limits seem a more apt characterizations of the mental state of missionary experiences that push the limits of human duress and mental and psychological endurance. These four case studies seemed particularly reminiscent of the Apostle Paul's own experiences. Like Paul, the missionaries discovered that their calling was not the royal road to high status, security, creature comforts, and longevity. As I read these case studies, I had the feeling that I was treading on sacred ground ... that these were missionaries whose shoelaces I am not worthy to tie. Their lives constitute a kind of exegesis of the ministry of Paul.

Rev. Jeong Han Kim shares the wrenching stories of devoted missionaries serving in situations where authorities have done everything possible to make service in the name of Christ impossible or at least inconvenient. After years of investing their lives as families to linguistic, cultural, and social immersion in service to men and women whom they have come to love, they find themselves wrenched away from the people they love and returning to well-meaning but uncomprehending faith communities back home. Vocationally bereft, socially uprooted, and psychologically bewildered at an age when fresh beginnings are extremely difficult, they and their families must soldier on. It is heartening to learn of GMS's commitment to "customized care" for these wounded servants, but it is clear that there is only so much that any organization or church can do to ameliorate the deep hurt and shock suffered by these deported missionaries, as **Dr. Karen Carr** points out in her response.

The second case study in this cluster is **Rev. Stanley Green's** harrowing account of the kidnapping of Al and Gladys Geiser and their eventual release after fifty-six days of captivity. The case study shows the limits of principled agency policies and crisis management teams in these kinds of situations. Al Geiser's decision to return to

---

The Independent Abuse Review Panel (IARP) was mandated "to pursue the truth, encourage healing, and promote justice on behalf of those making allegations and those accused," and "to further the integrity of the mission and witness of the Presbyterian Church (USA)." The GAMC perceived the allegations of sexual abuse as inconsistent with Christ's valuing of children and as a threat to the integrity of the church's witness. For seven years, the IARP promoted its mandate and sought out witnesses, receiving and investigating 131 reports, involving eighty-one possible victims and forty-seven alleged offenders at mission schools in Cameroon, Congo, Egypt, Ethiopia, India, Mexico, Pakistan, Kenya, Zambia, and Thailand. It interviewed more than 200 victims, witnesses, and alleged offenders. In October 2010, the Panel issued a 546-page report detailing its findings: Independent Abuse Review Panel, "Final Report" (Louisville, KY, Presbyterian Church [USA], 2010).

Afghanistan to be in solidarity with his Afghan partner who did not enjoy the luxury of escape from high risk situations resulted in the death of both of them. Was this a waste? Not according to the logic of seeds, which must die before they can yield fruit (John 12:24). This case study not only touches on the enormous psychological strain and mortal risks of service in the name and spirit of Jesus in countries like Afghanistan, but on the limits of even the most enlightened denominational or mission agency policies in such situations. The story (and the Korean hostage incident alluded to by **Dr. Jinsuk Byun and Dr. Hyekyung Hong** in their thoughtful response) is reminiscent of the Apostle Paul's life and modus operandi (Acts 21:12; 2 Cor. 4, 6, 11), neither of which can be replicated at the level of mission agencies or churches, but which *have been* and *are being* emulated by some of God's exemplary servants throughout Christian history. Paul's life did not have a happy ending, surrounded by admiring and respectful care providers in a Christian retirement village on the shores of the Mediterranean. He spent this last days in a Roman dungeon, a frail old man whose battered body gained relief at last through execution. A waste? Not at all. As Kosuke Koyama reminds us, "Through Paul who was imprisoned, beaten, stoned, shipwrecked, threatened by all kinds of people, hungry, thirsty, cold and exposed, God touched the foundation of history, and he let Paul touch it too."[9]

Dr. Young Ok Kim's case study on "God's Wounded Servants" is a strong complement to these two case studies, written from broad, first-hand experience, as Dr. Kim's own ministry work focuses particularly on helping traumatized missionaries. She recounts the story of one missionary who was kidnapped and held, terrified, for fourteen hours by his captors. Because he was released unharmed, his mission agency found it difficult to empathize with his trauma. Her second story is about a single, female missionary in East Africa whose left arm was amputated after it was crushed in a car accident. Rather than empathizing with her trauma, those charged with caring for her seemed to downplay her shock and loss, since it was "only her left arm," leaving her feeling utterly abandoned. The subjects of her third story were the missionary parents of a young daughter whose school was in the region of a massive earthquake that killed more than half a million people. The daughter developed psychological problems that manifested themselves in severe eating disorders. Appeals to the mission society to allow the family to return home for proper treatment fell on deaf ears, leaving the father feeling helpless and depressed because he could not properly care for his child. Cases such as these are giving rise to more sensitive and functional member care policies that include more culturally aware mental health care providers, as **Dr. Pamela Davis** acknowledges. But Davis goes farther and proposes models of pre-field assessment and pre-field training for Korean missionaries.

The final paper in this section makes an excellent contribution to this grouping of case studies. **Drs. Frauke and Charles Schaefer** are a gifted missionary couple

---

9 Kosuke Koyama, *No Handle on the Cross: An Asian Meditation on the Crucified Mind* (London: SCM, 1976), 77.

with both training and experience in medicine, psychiatry, and psychology. As medical missionaries themselves, their discussion of spiritual resources for dealing with trauma is doubly credible, as it moves beyond well-intended but empty platitudes. Their counsel, based on deep knowledge and broad, first-hand experience, is wise, and should be studied carefully by every mission agency and missionary sending church, with a view to implementing their suggestions. Theirs is a practical, biblically rooted theology of care for the traumatized. Members of any mission or church community that internalizes and practices the six dimensions of the spiritual resources that they identify will be blessed indeed. These are the resources to which the most paradigmatic missionary of our faith, the Apostle Paul, had recourse, and so can we.

4. Resources for missionary mental health care. The Schaefer's paper is a natural segue to the fourth and final category in my taxonomy, four case studies that focus on resources and organizational structures that address missionary mental health in preventative, remedial, and proactively supportive ways. The report by **Dr. Jae-Hon Lee and Dr. Sung Il Moon** on their interviews with a few retired male missionaries to discern the "Emotional Stress and Mental Health of Retired Korean Missionaries," together with **Dr. Liz Bendor-Samuel's** response, points to the inadequacy of our evidence-based understanding of these crucial questions and to the potential of the interview model. The number of missionaries interviewed was not enough to be truly representative; only eleven retired men were interviewed, and those interviews were very limited in both scope and time. No women were interviewed; no adult children of the missionaries were interviewed. The method utilized is tantalizing and holds considerable promise, were it to include greater and more representative numbers of retired missionaries and their families, closest friends, and supporters. Support of such a venture would be money and time well invested.

Ms. Eunjung Um's case study on "Happiness Among Korean Missionaries and Organizational Care in the Missions Community" with the response by **Dr. Lois Dodds** is an excellent and illuminating research report. She is to be congratulated, and her research model should be emulated. In many ways, her research confirms what we already know at the most instinctive levels of our being. Human beings are relational creatures. Not only is it not good for us to be alone, but in the words of an Ethiopian proverb, "there is no me without you." The wholesomeness of the family and community that shapes our fundamental identities has a direct bearing on who we become and how we relate to others as adults. It comes as no surprise, then, that the more caring the church and mission organization, the greater the missionary's sense of belonging and well-being. The fact that Korean missionaries serving under the aegis of international mission organizations felt better cared for than their counterparts in Korean agencies seems counterintuitive. Knowing that one is an integral part of a caring community is essential for the healthy functioning of all human beings.

Also telling was the finding that the greater the degree of identification with and intimacy with the local community, the greater the missionary's sense of happiness. The story related by Lois Dodds of the astonishment experienced by mission leaders when "1,000 locals showed up for the *despedida* of a missionary they 'let go,'" is instructive and illustrates the difference between being "known" by an organization as an employee and *really* known as an integral member of a living community: "Why are you sending her home?" the community asked the agency functionaries; "she is the one who is most like us!"

Dr. Brent Lindquist's "Organization-Centered Member Care" case study and the response by **Dr. Nam Yong Sung** is a strong affirmation of the insights derived from Eunjung Um's research. Quite apart from his opening lamentation, springing from his engagement with less-than-appreciative persons and agencies—and I have every confidence that he has found at this forum deeply appreciative colleagues and coworkers—his observation that mission organizations "have not looked closely enough at what it takes to have a healthy organization" resonates with the other case studies in this cluster. His observations about organizational culture should be of special interest to mission organizations in Korea that are administered on a term-by-term basis by pastors and professors who have little, if any, field experience and who make important decisions that directly affect missionaries. Since missionaries are typically not well represented on these boards and, even if represented, have no real power, it is hard to imagine how missionaries themselves could have confidence in these distant, sometimes troublingly meddlesome power structures. To be a missionary serving in an organization led by armchair administrators over whose appointment one has no control is a recipe for mutual mistrust and more or less guarantees acerbation of missionary interpersonal and mental crises. The clear lesson from this case study and its response is that organizations must make member confidence and trust in administrative leadership a priority. If this means altering and even abandoning established structures and procedures, that is a small price to pay for the trust and well-being of rank-and-file missionaries.

Finally, all of us are beneficiaries of the inside look at NamSeoul Church's efforts to fashion a fair, workable retirement plan for its missionaries. **Dr. Jinbong Kim and Dr. Nelson Jennings** are to be commended for sharing this story, since its example is salutary and worthy of emulation by other mission-supporting congregations who are just beginning to think carefully about their responsibilities to aged servants of God. Having put their hand to the missionary plow, to look back just when their missionaries are most vulnerable is a shameful abrogation of responsibility. NamSeoul Church is an exception, and God is blessing the church for its commitment to doing the right thing. But following the example of NamSeoul Church's well-established retirement policies is complicated by the age demographics of both nation and church. One out of every five Koreans will soon be officially defined as "elderly" in a nation that has one of the lowest birth rates in Asia. The prospects for missionary retirees are grim. This case study suggests to me that the days of the relatively novel concept of missionary financial support from home churches and agencies may be coming to an end. Missionaries may need to be more like Paul—possessing aptitudes and trained in skills that enable them to make a living for themselves and for their colleagues (Acts 20:33–35). And in the interim, the number of missionaries sent will need to be sharply curtailed—not a multitude of missionaries but, like Gideon's little band, only those who can meet rigorous qualifying standards.

In their response, **Dr. Lawrence Fung and Dr. John Wang** raise important questions about parental care and the church's role in the missionaries' spiritual and psychological well-being in an age when Western, individualistic values have corroded the traditional sense of obligation felt by the young for the old.

CONCLUSION

I must mention with gratitude the healing concert offered by violinist Ms. Yoo Jin Jung. What a beautifully appropriate way to conclude this forum! To my knowledge the first music therapy mentioned in the Bible was rendered by David to King Saul, when Saul was in a state of deep depression (1 Sam. 16). The vocabulary of mental illness at that time was limited, and Saul's attendants diagnosed Saul's problem as the torments of "an evil spirit from God" (1 Sam. 16:14–23). The writer tells us that "Whenever the spirit from God came on Saul, David would take up his lyre [harp] and play. Then relief would come to Saul; he would feel better, and the evil spirit would leave him" (v. 23). People the world over still seek and find solace through the words and strains of music. Christians—and I among them—find their innermost selves deeply stirred, encouraged, and strengthened when they sing the great hymns of the faith, many of which were authored by men and women who were going through acutely painful suffering and loss at the time.

It is fitting that this summary should end as it began—with a testimony from missionary brother Paul (2 Cor. 4:1–18):

> Therefore, since it is by God's mercy that we are engaged in this ministry, we do not lose heart. We have renounced the shameful things that one hides; we refuse to practice cunning or to falsify God's word; but by the open statement of the truth we commend ourselves to the conscience of everyone in the sight of God. And even if our gospel is veiled, it is veiled to those who are perishing. In their case the god of this world has blinded the minds of the unbelievers, to keep them from seeing the light of the gospel of the glory of Christ, who is the image of God. For we do not proclaim ourselves; we proclaim Jesus Christ as Lord and

ourselves as your slaves for Jesus' sake. For it is the God who said, "Let light shine out of darkness," who has shone in our hearts to give the light of the knowledge of the glory of God in the face of Jesus Christ.

But we have this treasure in clay jars, so that it may be made clear that this extraordinary power belongs to God and does not come from us. We are afflicted in every way, but not crushed; perplexed, but not driven to despair; persecuted, but not forsaken; struck down, but not destroyed; always carrying in the body the death of Jesus, so that the life of Jesus may also be made visible in our bodies. For while we live, we are always being given up to death for Jesus' sake, so that the life of Jesus may be made visible in our mortal flesh. So death is at work in us, but life in you.

But just as we have the same spirit of faith that is in accordance with scripture—"I believed, and so I spoke"—we also believe, and so we speak, because we know that the one who raised the Lord Jesus will raise us also with Jesus, and will bring us with you into his presence. Yes, everything is for your sake, so that grace, as it extends to more and more people, may increase thanksgiving, to the glory of God.

So we do not lose heart. Even though our outer nature is wasting away, our inner nature is being renewed day by day. For this slight momentary affliction is preparing us for an eternal weight of glory beyond all measure, because we look not at what can be seen but at what cannot be seen; for what can be seen is temporary, but what cannot be seen is eternal.[10]

---

10 NRSV.

PARTICIPANTS

Mrs. Baek, Eun Young
Counsellor
Asian Mission
Seoul, Korea

Mr. Baker, Martyn
International Member Care Consultants
WEC International Palmerston North,
Manawatu, New Zealand

Mrs. Baker, Wendy
International Member Care Consultants
WEC International Palmerston North,
Manawatu, New Zealand

Mrs. Batsuren, Enkhbayar
Missionary
Assemblies of God in Mongolia
Taebaek, Gangwondo, Korea

Dr. Bendor-Samuel, Elizabeth (Liz)
Assistant Chaplain, Oxford Centre for Mission Studies, Counsellor and Spiritual Director, Oxford, Oxfordshire, UK

Dr. Bendor-Samuel, Paul
Executive Director
Oxford Centre for Mission Studies
Oxford, Oxfordshire, UK

Mrs. Bonk, Jean
Adviser
Global Mission Leadership Forum Inc.
Winnipeg, Manitoba, Canada

Prof. Bonk, J. Jonathan
President, Global Mission Leadership Forum Inc. Director, DACB Research Professor, Boston University School of Theology, Winnipeg, Manitoba, Canada

Dr. Byun, Jinsuk (Felipe)
Director
Global Missionary Training Center
Seoul, Korea

Dr. Carr, Karen F.
Clinical Psychologist
Barnabas International
Midlothian, Virginia, USA

Rev. Dr. Cha, Stephen
Lead Pastor, English Ministry
Onnuri Church
Seoul, Korea

Rev. Dr. Choi, Du Yol (Joseph)
Senior Pastor
Renewing Church
Yongin, Gyeonggi, Korea

Mrs. Choi, Eunkyung
Missionary in China
Hope
Seoul, Korea

Rev. Choi, Hunn
President
All Nations Mission Center
Lexington, Kentucky, USA

Dr. Choi, Hyung-Keun
Vice President
Seoul Theological University
Goyang, Gyeonggi, Korea

Rev. Chung, Jae-Chul
Pastor
Asian Mission
Seoul, Korea

Dr. Crawford, Nancy A.
Associate Professor of Psychology
Rosemead School of Psychology, Biola University, La Mirada, California, USA

Dr. Davis, Pamela
Associate Professor
Gordon Conwell Theological Seminary
Lake Wylie, South Carolina, USA

Dr. Distefano, Michel G.
Independent Scholar
Homewood, Manitoba,
Canada

Rev. Do, Yook Hwan
Director, Tyrannus International Mission
Onnuri Church
Yongin, Gyeonggi, Korea

Dr. Dodds, Lois A.
Founder and Director
Heartstream Resources USA, and International, Liverpool, Pennsylvania, USA

Rev. Green, Stanley
Executive Director
Mennonite Mission Network
Goshen, Indiana, USA

Mrs. Green, Ursula
Minister
Mennonite Mission Network
Goshen, Indiana, USA

Dr. Hong, Hyekyung (Grace)
Professor
Global Missionary Training Center
Seoul, Korea

Mrs. Hong, Junghee
President
EZER Community Fellowship
Seoul, Korea

Dr. Hong, Kyungwha
Professor
Torch Trinity Graduate University
Seoul, Korea

Rev. Hwang, Jong Yeon
Director, Acts29 Vision Village
Onnuri Church
Yongin, Gyeonggi, Korea

Rev. Ishkhuu, Rentsen-Ochir
Pastor and Missionary
United Mongolian Church in Seoul
Seoul, Korea

Rev. Dr. Jennings, J. Nelson
Mission Pastor, Consultant, and International Liaison, Onnuri Church
New Haven, Connecticut, USA

Mr. Jo, Daeshik
Elder
Onnuri Church
Seoul, Korea

Revd. Joung, Eimsook
Reverend, Pastor of St. David's Anglican Church, Fort Simpson, Northwest Territoires, Canada

Mr. Jun, Youngsoo
Elder, Chairman
Society for World Internet Mission
Onnuri Church, Seoul, Korea

Ms. Jung, Hyesun
Conductor and Counselor
The Lord's Church
Seongnam, Gyeonggi, Korea

Dr. Jung, Soonuk
Independent Researcher
Translator, KGMLF
Seongnam, Gyeonggi, Korea

Participants

REV. KANG CHEOLMIN
Missionary in China
Hope
Seoul, Korea

MRS. KANG, KYUNGHWA
Director, WEC Korea
WEC International
Seoul, Korea

MRS. KEMPER, ERIKA BARBARA
Freelance: Trainer, Psychotherapist and Adjunct Professor, United Methodist Church, Atlanta, Georgia, USA

MR. KEMPER, THOMAS
General Secretary
United Methodist Church Global Ministries, Atlanta, Georgia, USA

DR. KIM, DO BONG
Consultant, Holistic Healing Institute
SAM Hospital
Gunpo, Gyeonggi, Korea

REV. KIM, DONG HWA
Director, Global Bible Translators and Global Missionary Fellowship
Anyang, Gyeonggi, Korea

REV. KIM, HONG JOO
Director, Mission Headquarters
Onnuri Church
Seoul, Korea

MS. KIM, HYE JIN (LISELLE)
Staff, All Nations International Center
Assistant of KGMLF
Cheonan, Chungnam, Korea

MRS. KIM, HYEWON
Member & TCK Care Coordinator
SIM Korea
Seongnam, Gyeonggi, Korea

REV. KIM, HYUNCHEUL
Director, South Seoul Branch
Scripture Union Korea
Seoul, Korea

REV. KIM, JAEHYUNG
Director, WEC Korea
WEC International
Seoul, Korea

REV, KIM, JEONG HAN
Director, Crisis Management
Global Mission Society Missionary
Hwaseong, Gyeonggi, Korea

REV. DR. KIM, JINBONG
Managing Director, GMLF
Coordinator, KGMLF
Shelton, Connecticut, USA

REV. KIM, KYUNGSOOL (JOSHUA)
Director, SIM Korea
SIM International
Seongnam, Gyeonggi, Korea

DR. KIM, SOOHYUN
Psychiatrist, Volunteer Clinical Staff
Tumaini Counselling Centre (AIM)
Nairobi, Kenya

MS. KIM, SOOKHI
Lay Leader
Seungdong Presbyterian Church
Seoul, Korea

REV. KIM, SUN MAN
Senior Pastor
The Shalom Church of McKinney (KAPC), McKinney, Texas, USA

DR. KIM, YOUNG OK
President, Flourishing Lives Counseling Center, Korean American Wellness Association, Lisle, Illinois, USA

Rev. Kim, Won Tae
Senior Pastor
Suzi Joyful Church
Yongin, Gyeonggi, Korea

Rev. Kong, Paul
Asia-Pacific Regional Representative
UMC Global Ministries
Seoul, Korea

Rev. Kovoor, George Iype
Rector, St. Paul's Episcopal Church
Chaplain to the Queen Elizabeth II.
Darien, Connecticut, USA

Rev. Dr. Lawrence, Fung
Director
Gospel Operation International
Daly City, California, USA

Dr. Lee, Hyun-Sook
Director
Turning Point Counselling Center
Seoul, Korea

Rev. Lee, Jae Hoon
Senior Pastor
Onnuri Church
Seoul, Korea

Dr. Lee, Jae-Hon
Psychiatrist, Chairman, Department of
Psychiatry, Korea Rehabilitation Center
Seoul, Korea

Dr. Lee, Jung-Sook
President
Torch Trinity Graduate University
Seoul, Korea

Mr. Lee, See Young
Executive Committee Member
Senior Mission Korea
Seongnam, Gyeonggi, Korea

Mrs. Lee, Yongrae
General Counsel
Ezer Community Fellowship
Gimpo, Gyeonggi, Korea

Mrs. Lkhumbu, Dulamjav
Missionary
United Mongolian Church in Seoul
Seoul, Korea

Dr. Lindquist, Brent
President
Link Care Center
Fresno, California, USA

Ms. Lyman, Margaret
Interserve Missionary
Doctoral Student, Fuller Theological
Seminary, Tucson, Arizona, USA

Dr. Maxwell, Ruth L.
Consultant for Regional Leadership
and Development , SIM, Abbotsford,
British Columbia, Canada

Dr. Moon, Steve Sang-Cheol
Executive Director
Korea Research Institute for Mission
Seoul, Korea

Dr. Moon, Sung Il
Director
Sooyoung Counseling Center
Busan, Korea

Mrs. Mun, Shinhee
Missionary, GMS & GBT
Director, Shalom Counseling Center
Kuala Lumpur, Malaysia

Rev. Dr. Oh, Hwee Kiong
Deputy International Director
Gospel Operation International
Commonwealth Close, Singapore

Participants

Rev. Oh, Yungsup
Founder and Representative
Landmarker Ministry
Seoul, Korea

Dr. Pak, Jenny H.
Professor, School of Psychology, Fuller Theological Seminary, Diamond Bar, California, USA

Rev. Park, Daeyoung
Editor, "QT and Sermon"
Scripture Union Korea
Seoul, Korea

Rev. Dr. Park, Jinho
Director, Global Missionary Training Institution (GMTI)
Hwaseong, Gyeonggi, Korea

Ms. Park, Jung-ae
Manager of Missionary Care
Sooyoungro Church World Mission
Busan, Korea

Mrs. Park, Kiyoung
General Counsel
EZER Community Fellowship
Goyang, Gyeonggi, Korea

Dr. Park (Jo) Kyounga
Former Director, WEC Korea
WEC International Office from 2020
Seoul, Korea

Dr. Park, Kyung Nam
Former Director, WEC Korea
WEC International Office from 2020
Seoul, Korea

Mr. Park, Minha
Missionary with SIL & GMS
Field Mentoring Missionary
Kuala Lumpur, Malaysia

Rt. Rev. Parsons, David Wayne
Diocesan Bishop, Anglican Diocese of The Arctic, Yellowknife, Northwest Territories, Canada

Dr. Schaefer, Charlie
Licensed Psychologist
Barnabas International Staff
Chapel Hill, North Carolina, USA

Dr. Schaefer, Frauke
Psychiatrist, Private Practice
Barnabas International Staff and Duke University Consulting Faculty
Chapel Hill, North Carolina, USA

Mr. Shin, Hunseung
Elder and Head, Mission Committee
Onnuri Church
Seoul, Korea

Ms. Shin, Sun Han
Assistant Administrator
New Wave Ministries
Yongin, Gyeonggi, Korea

Dr. Sung, Nam Yong
Senior Pastor
SamKwang Church
Seoul, Korea

Dr. Takamizawa, Eiko
Professor
Torch Trinity Graduate University
Seoul, Korea

Dr. Toland, Patricia Lucille
Director, WEC Latino
Director, Latino Member Care
Forest Grove, Oregon, USA

Bishop. Torrey, Ben
Executive Director
The Fourth River Project, Inc.
Taebaek, Gangwon, Korea

Mrs. Torrey, Liz
Principal
The River of Life School
Taebaek, Gangwon, Korea

Mrs. Um, Eunjung
Co-director
Heartstream Resources Korea
Goyang, Gyeonggi, Korea

Ms. Wang, Linghuei
Clinical Counselor
The Well International
A. Hangdong, Chiang Mai, Thailand

Dr. Winter, Richard
Professor Emeritus
Covenant Theological Seminary
St. Louis, Missouri, USA

Rev. Dr. Wright, Christopher J. H.
International Ministries Director
Langham Partnership
London, UK

Dr. Yoo, Mary Hee-Joo
Senior Research Fellow
Korea Research Institute for Mission
Seoul, Korea

Rev. Zunduidorj, Bayaraa
Missionary in Korea
Assemblies of God Mongolia
Taebaek, Gangwon, Korea

CONTRIBUTORS

ELIZABETH BENDOR-SAMUEL, WITH her husband Paul and four sons, previously served with an international mission agency in the Muslim-majority world. Liz is British and originally trained as a GP (family physician). She has spent the last sixteen years in pastoral and integrative counselling practice, in Malaysia and the UK. Liz is a Registered Member of the British Association for Counselling and Psychotherapy. In addition to providing counselling in multi-faith and multiethnic contexts, she has established counselling services for two NGOs and a megachurch. Liz's current roles include private counsellor, spiritual director, Assistant Chaplain at the Oxford Centre for Mission Studies (OCMS), and assessor and mentor for cross-cultural mission personnel.

JONATHAN J. BONK is Research Professor of Mission at Boston University, where he directs the *Dictionary of African Christian Biography*. He is Executive Director Emeritus of the Overseas Ministries Study Center (1997–2013) and served as Editor of the *International Bulletin of Missionary Research* (1997–2013). He has authored five books (including *Missions and Money: Affluence as a Western Missionary Problem*); edited eight collaborative volumes; and published over one hundred scholarly articles, book chapters, reviews, and editorials. He is President of the Global Mission Leadership Forum and has been actively involved with the KGMLF since its inception. He and his wife are active members of the Fort Garry Mennonite Fellowship in Winnipeg, Manitoba, Canada.

JINSUK BYUN is a Presbyterian minister who served as a missionary in Ecuador from 1994 to 2002, focusing on leadership training and church-planting work. Since completing his doctoral studies at Trinity Evangelical Divinity School (PhD, ICS) in Deerfield, Illinois, he has been serving as the Director and as a professor at GMTC, a non-denominational, cross-cultural missionary training center, located in Seoul, Korea. Jinsuk is also a member of the WEA Mission Commission IMTN steering committee. He and his wife, Hyekyung Hong, have two adult sons.

KAREN F. CARR is a clinical psychologist who serves with Barnabas International as a trainer and consultant for missionaries and mission organizations. She was the Clinical Director of the Mobile Member Care Team, helping missionaries in crisis and providing crisis training for missionaries in West Africa for fifteen years. She and her team have trained hundreds of missionaries to respond to peer crisis situations. Dr. Carr has authored several articles and chapters on resilience and on responding to crises, also co-authoring the book *Trauma and Resilience,* which has been published in English and Korean and is currently being translated into Spanish. She resides in Virginia.

DOROTHY CARROLL is the copyeditor of this KGMLF publication. Previously, she worked for four years as the Editorial Assistant for *Missiology: An International Review* (2007–2011) and, as a freelancer, has edited five full-length publications, twenty doctoral dissertations, and multiple graduate level papers, proposals, and post-residency papers. She and her husband, Pastor Timothy Carroll, serve cross-culturally in their local church, which is seeking to become more hospitable to its highly diverse surroundings. Tim and Dorothy live just outside Washington, DC with their infant and three-year-old daughters.

JEONG-HO CHAE, MD, PhD, is Professor of Psychiatry, The Catholic University of Korea, Seoul St. Mary's Hospital, Korea. He is a founding President of the Korean Society of Traumatic Stress Studies (KSTSS); of the Korean Academy of Medicine for Emotion, Cognition, and Behavior; and of the Korean Academy of Meditation in Medicine. He has also served as President of Korean Society of Christian Psychiatrists (KSCP). Dr. Chae specializes in the research and practice of psychological trauma, anxiety disorders, stress-related disorders, depression, neurophysiology, brain stimulation, positive psychiatry, and affective neuroscience. He has authored over 400 scientific, peer-reviewed papers and chapters and published more than twenty books.

HUNN CHOI immigrated to America in 1974, during his middle school years. He majored in Aerospace Engineering at the University of Michigan and studied at Stanford University, later working for aerospace companies before enrolling in the MDiv program at Asbury Theological Seminary. After spending several years in ministry in New Jersey and Chicago, in 2002 he became a professor at Asbury Theological Seminary. He is the Senior Pastor of All Nations United Methodist Church, a multicultural, multiethnic, and multi-congregational church. He served as Associate Director of New Church Development of the Kentucky Annual Conference of the United Methodist Church (2005–2013). He is now finishing his PhD in Intercultural Studies at Asbury.

MEESAENG LEE CHOI, after graduating from Ewha Woman's University (BA) and Seoul Theological University (MDiv), served as Assistant Chaplain at Myongji University and Seoul Theological University. She came to the United States to study at Asbury Theological Seminary (Th.M.) and later, at Drew University (PhD in Historical Theology) while teaching at International Evangelical Seminary, NY. Since 2002, she has been raising next-generation leaders as Professor of Church History and Historical Theology at Asbury Seminary, an outstanding interdenominational and evangelical seminary. Since 2011, she and her husband, Rev. Hunn Choi, have served at All Nations Mission Center for Missionary-Pastor Member Care and Mission Research.

Contributors

JAE-CHUL CHUNG serves as Chaplain at E-LAND, a leading Christian business group in Korea. He is also Chairman of the Board for Asian Mission, a member-care mission agency founded by E-LAND. From 2002 to 2008, he lived in a Muslim nation in Southeast Asia, teaching the Bible and engaging in a business as mission. He is keenly interested in missionary member care, missionary reassignment and retraining, missionary care after retirement, and the community of missionary retirees. He serves Canaan Bridge Church, a church he planted for those who have left the church but still have faith.

NANCY A. CRAWFORD currently serves as an Associate Professor and as the Director of Clinical Training at Rosemead School of Psychology, Biola University in La Mirada, California. Prior to joining Rosemead in 2010, she served as a teacher and counselor-in-residence at Rift Valley Academy in Kijabe, Kenya for seven years and as a clinical psychologist at Tumaini Counselling Centre in Nairobi, Kenya for ten years. She joined Africa Inland Mission International in 1985 and remains an affiliate member, helping to facilitate the involvement of psychologists in member care.

PAMELA DAVIS served as a missionary in Asia for twenty-two years. She served as the Regional Member Care Coordinator for her mission agency, TEAM, and in this role coordinated oversight for the care of missionaries serving in eight countries in Asia. She also provided family counseling at both The Well Member Care Center and Cornerstone Counseling Foundation in Chiang Mai, Thailand, where she frequently counseled Korean missionaries. Currently, she is an Associate Professor and the Director of Graduate Programs in Counseling at Gordon Conwell Theological Seminary. She lives in Charlotte, NC and provides care for missionary families through her work at Carmel Counseling Center.

MICHEL G. DISTEFANO was a Neonatal Intensive Care nurse. He changed careers and taught Ancient Near Eastern Religions, including Israelite Religion, and beginning and advanced biblical Hebrew at McGill. He wrote *Inner-Midrashic Introductions and Their Influence on Introductions to Medieval Rabbinic Bible Commentaries*. His contribution to KGMLF 2019 coincides with his most recent interest in the parts of the Bible that deal with affliction, prayer, lament, wisdom, and healing. The Lord provided his wife with a good teaching job in southern Manitoba, and they moved to the countryside. He has worked ever since on their homestead, renovating a century-old house, repairing outbuildings, maintaining vehicles and a tractor, gardening, and chopping firewood. They have three adult children, two married and one at university.

LOIS A. DODDS is the co-founder and Director of Heartstream Resources for Global Workers. She served with her husband, Lawrence E. Dodds, MD, with WBT and SIL for twenty-three years before they founded HSR in 1992. She taught in thirty countries with Operation Impact of Azusa Pacific University, as well as in many other countries. She is the author of fifteen books, including the three-volume *Global Servants,* with Dr. Laura Mae Gardner, and hundreds of other materials related to the care of international workers. She has conducted over 40,000 hours of counseling with humanitarian workers around the globe. Her passion is to help restore the wounded, enabling them to thrive. Lois and her husband Lawrence have three children, eight grandchildren, and five great-grandchildren.

LAWRENCE FUNG serves as International Director of Gospel Operation International (GOI). He was born and raised in Hong Kong and began full-time ministry at Hong Kong Youth for Christ, serving as their Acting Executive Director and Asian Training Director. He received theological training and began serving at Cumberland Presbyterian Chinese Church (CPCC) in 1981. Rev. Fung then earned his Master of Divinity and Doctor of Ministry degrees from Golden Gate Baptist Theological Seminary, San Francisco. After serving as Senior Pastor of CPCC for over twenty years, he joined GOI in 2008 and went on to earn his Doctor of Intercultural Studies degree from Western Seminary in Portland, Oregon.

STANLEY GREEN is the Executive Director of Mennonite Mission Network, the mission agency of the Mennonite Church USA. He has served in mission agency leadership for the past twenty-five years and is also the Chair of the Mission Commission of the Mennonite World Conference. He has led congregations in South Africa, California, and Jamaica, where he and his spouse, Ursula Lucille, served as mission workers in the 1980s. Stanley has a postgraduate degree in Intercultural Studies from Fuller Theological Seminary in Pasadena, California. He has served on several boards and has traveled and ministered in more than eighty countries around the world.

KYU SAM HAN is the Senior Pastor of Choong Hyung Presbyterian Church in Seoul, Korea. Before his present service in Seoul, he spent eighteen years pastoring Korean American Churches in the US. Throughout his tenure as head pastor of three different churches, Rev. Dr. Han has constantly showed a burning desire for world mission in various ways, such as training local leaders, sending missionaries, and organizing mission strategy meetings. His major areas of concern remain with persecuted ethnic minority groups.

Contributors

HYEKYUNG HONG, after receiving missionary training at GMTC, served as a missionary in Ecuador, working as a nurse and administrator at a foundation for children with disabilities. Since her return to Korea, she has been serving as a professor and a counselor at GMTC. She earned her degrees in Nursing and Counseling at Yonsei University (BSN, MSN, ThM, ThD).

KYUNGWHA HONG is an associate professor of Christian Counseling at Torch Trinity Graduate University located in Seoul, Korea. Her higher education has focused mostly on understanding children, adolescents, and their environments. She earned her EdM and EdD in Human Development and Psychology from Harvard Graduate School of Education (Cambridge, MA, USA). She is currently a member of a research team for the Education Community Research Institute for Character and Citizenship. Her clinical experience includes counseling at-risk children, adolescents, and their families, and she has participated in short-term mission trips to Africa and South East Asia with professors and students of Torch Trinity Graduate University.

BARBARA HÜFNER-KEMPER IS a former missionary who worked for eight years with the Methodist Church in Brazil. Barbara specializes in stress reduction, burnout, anxiety, and other trauma-related conditions and has over twenty years of clinical experience. She serves as a cross-cultural trainer and conflict transformation consultant, working for church, government, and non-governmental organizations. In addition, Barbara offers life coaching services in English, Portuguese, and German at TACC at St. Luke's and teaches, as an adjunct professor, Bibliodrama and Conflict Transformation at Candler School of Theology, Emory University, Atlanta. She also works as a trainer and consultant at GIZ Deutsche Gesellschaft für Internationale Zusammenarbeit (Capacity Building International).

J. NELSON JENNINGS, his wife Kathy, and their children moved to Japan as church-planting missionaries in 1986. Jennings taught at Tokyo Christian University (1996–1999) and at Covenant Theological Seminary (1999–2011), then served at the Overseas Ministries Study Center (2011–2015) and with GMI (Global Mapping International, 2016–2017). Since September 2015, Jennings has served as Mission Pastor, Consultant, and International Liaison for Onnuri Church (Seoul). His publications include *Theology in Japan: Takakura Tokutaro (1885–1934)* (2005), *God the Real Superpower: Rethinking Our Role in Missions* (2007), and *Philosophical Theology and East-West Dialogue* (2000, co-authored with Hisakazu Inagaki). He has also been the editor of *Missiology* (2007–2011), *IBMR* (2013–2015), and *Global Missiology* (since 2018).

SOONUK JUNG participated in KGMLF 2019 as the translator. Fluent in Korean, English, and Japanese, Soonuk is currently a design research advisor to Acorn Publishing Company. In the past, Soonuk was a design strategist at Continuum, a global design consultancy, and an adjunct professor at KEPCO International Nuclear Graduate School. He has translated several books on presentation design, including

Garr Reynolds' *Presentation Zen* and Nancy Duarte's *Resonate,* into Korean. Married with three children, he currently lives in South Korea.

JONATHAN SHUNG KANG is the Executive Director of the Christian Counseling and Education Partners, Los Angeles, California and serves as a member care specialist at Friends of Missionaries. He holds two doctorates, in Educational Studies and Clinical Psychology. Jonathan is a "1.5 generation" Korean American minister and a licensed clinical psychologist, who is currently involved in supervising clinician interns and teaching graduate students. He provides psychological services to both Korean- and English-speaking clients and missionaries/ministers and to their families in a private practice setting.

THOMAS KEMPER is the General Secretary of Global Ministries of The United Methodist Church, responsible for missionaries, health ministries, evangelism, and church growth in the global context. The United Methodist Committee on Relief, part of Global Ministries, is the development and disaster response arm of the church. Kemper is a layman and the first person from outside the United States to lead a UMC program agency. Since his election in 2010, Kemper has promoted increasing internationalization of mission operations, opening regional offices and diversifying mission opportunities for young adults, creating mission and missionaries "from everywhere to everywhere." Previously, Kemper served as a missionary in Brazil through the German United Methodist Board of Missions, worked for the Evangelical Church in Germany, and was Mission Director for The German United Methodist Church.

DO BONG KIM is an ordained minister and is affiliated with the Korea Methodist Church. He was appointed to the Philippines as a missionary, working there from 1991 to 2003. After gaining hands-on experience in the mission field, he served briefly on the faculty at Union Theological Seminary. He is proud to serve as an educator of Clinical Pastoral Education in the Philippines, Canada, and Korea. He enjoys providing holistic care for individual patients as well as their families at the Sam Medical Center and is a renowned throughout Korea as a lecturer on hospice education. His passion for member care extends to both Korean and global mission networks.

JINBONG KIM, the Coordinator of KGMLF, proposed its creation in 2008 and is now the Managing Director of the umbrella organization, Global Mission Leadership Forum. After receiving training at Chongshin Theological Seminary and Chongshin World Mission Graduate School in Korea, he and his wife, Soon Young Jung, joined the Global Mission Society. They then pursued mission studies in England; he also interned at a church in France. In 1998, they joined WEC International and spent two terms working among Fulani Muslims in Guinea. After moving to New Haven in 2006, Kim served for six years as the Director of International Church Relations at Overseas Ministries Study Center. He and his wife are blessed with two sons.

Contributors

Jeong Han Kim began his missionary work in China in 2001. In 2007, he was appointed to lead the Missionary Risk Management Taskforce, while serving as Director of Missions at Global Mission Society (GMS) Headquarters. He moved to Taiwan in 2012 and, later, worked in mainland China. He has been in charge of Risk Management at GMS HQ since September 2017. Dr. Kim graduated from Chongshin Theological Seminary and Chongshin Graduate School of World Mission. He is married and has a son and a daughter.

Soohyun Kim, MD, is a volunteer clinical staff member at Tumaini Counselling Centre in Nairobi, Kenya, which is an on-the-field-counselling center for Christian workers and their families. As a Korean board-certified general psychiatrist, Soohyun loves working with Christian workers and their families who are facing various and unexpected challenges. She believes that on-the-field-counselling is imperative, since it is profoundly helpful in restoring people's resilience in the midst of extreme suffering. In addition to her clinical work, as a member of Africa Inland Mission International, Dr. Kim is passionate about sharing her perspectives on how to build well-balanced, multicultural communities.

Sun Man Kim is the founding pastor of Shalom Presbyterian Church of McKinney, Allen, Texas. He also preaches for "Today's Meditation," a radio program of Dallas Korean Network Radio Broadcasting. From 2012 to 2015, he served with the Overseas Ministries Study Center, New Haven, Connecticut, as a member of its board of trustees. In 2014, he served as the President of the Korean Church Council of Connecticut. He also worked for the First Korean Presbyterian Church of Greater Hartford, Manchester, Connecticut (2006–2016) and for the Reformed Presbyterian Theological Seminary of the East Flushing, New York, as a professor and member of its board of trustees (2010–2015). He is the author of *Expository Preaching on the Book of Revelation* (published in Korean through CLC Publication, Seoul, 2014).

Dr. Young Ok Kim served as a missionary with OM in India and Siberia and at OM Korea headquarters for ten years. She holds four master's degrees: intercultural studies from Chongshin University, theology, and marriage and family therapy from Fuller Theological Seminary, and clinical psychology from Wheaton College; as well as a doctoral degree in clinical psychology from Wheaton College. Dr. Kim is currently working as a clinical psychologist and serves as the president of the Korean American Wellness Association (KAWA, www.kawachicago.org) in Chicago, a non-profit organization. She is actively involved in providing member care for Korean missionaries via both in-person and online counseling. She wrote her doctoral dissertation on "Exploring the Lived Experience of Suffering Related to Traumatic Events among Korean Missionaries: An interpretative phenomenological analysis."

Hyun-Sook Lee has been a member of the Global Bible Translators (a Wycliffe organization in Korea) since 1984, along with her husband, who served as the founding Director. She has been serving as a counselor for missionaries for more than twenty-five years. Hyun-Sook earned her PhD in Christian Counseling from Baekseok University in Seoul. She is now serving as the Director of Turning Point Counseling Center in Seoul and as an adjunct professor of counseling at Midwestern Baptist Seminary in Missouri, USA.

Jae-Hon Lee is the Chair of the Department of Psychiatry at Korea National Rehabilitation Center, an adjunct professor at the Inje University in Korea, a lecturer of the Department of Psychiatry at the University of Toronto, and a psychoanalyst candidate at Toronto Institute of Psychoanalysis. He serves at God's Will Jeongeui Church in Seoul and has taught Chinese missionaries in Shanghai on the topic of mental health. His clinical and research interests include depression, anxiety, cultural psychiatry, effective psycho-social interventions for the minority population, psychoanalysis, and characterizing the association between body and mind. He has authored and translated texts and treatment manuals on anxiety and depression.

Jae Hoon Lee has served as the Senior Pastor of Onnuri Church, Seoul, since 2011. In the United States, he pastored the Chodae Community Church, Norwood, New Jersey, for four years. As an evangelist, he leads what is regarded as one of the most creative megachurches in South Korea. He has been influential in both Christian and non-Christian circles throughout South Korea through innovative uses of social media, art, and publishing. He also serves as the Chair of the Korea Lausanne Committee and the Chair of the board of trustees for Korea's Handong Global University.

Jung-Sook Lee is a professor at Torch Trinity Graduate University in Seoul, Korea, where she also formerly served as President. She currently serves as President of the Korea Association of Accredited Theological Schools (KAATS) and the Korea Association of Evangelical Theological Schools. She is a presidium member of the International Congress for Calvin Research, Vice President and Board Secretary of the Asia Theological Association (ATA), and a council member for the Oxford Center for Mission Studies (OCMS). She enjoys teaching and writing about the Protestant Reformation and its legacy, Christian art history, and Protestant mission history. She is an ordained minister and is married to Rev. Dr. Joseph Du Yol Choi. They have two adult children.

Contributors

BRENT LINDQUIST is a psychologist and serves as President of Link Care Center, a global ministry providing psychological and pastoral care and training to missionaries and pastors. He is a consultant in learning and member health for multiple organizations, including Missio Nexus and Crosswired, and helps organizations globally develop and enhance their services to missionaries and pastors. Brent has been married for forty-three years to Colleen, and they enjoy spending time with their two adult children, their children's spouses, and their four grandchildren.

RUTH L. MAXWELL provides leader care and coaching in SIM. She grew up in a missionary family in Nigeria and witnessed, through her parents, the value of caring for Christian workers. Her childhood included village life and boarding school. As a young adult, she faced the loss of her parents in a car accident. Five years in the Student Life Department at Prairie College (Canada) gave her invaluable experience in teamwork, discipleship, and leadership. During her thirty-three years with SIM, she worked in member care, leader care, mentoring, and discipleship through Bible studies, coaching, training, hospitality, and supporting others who were caring for Christian workers. Ministry has taken her to Canada, Liberia, Kenya, South Africa, Asia-Pacific, and now many places beyond those countries, via the Internet.

SUNG IL MOON is a pastor of the Presbyterian Church of Korea (PCK) and a registered psychotherapist (RP) in Ontario, Canada. He has served as Director of the Sooyoungro Counseling Center, which is affiliated with Sooyoungro Presbyterian Church at Busan, Korea. He previously served as a counselor for the Korean immigrant community and the international students in Canada, serving Toronto KOSTA (Korean Students All Nations) and working as a coordinator of the Centre for Asian-Canadian Theology and Ministry at Knox College in the University of Toronto. Rev. Dr. Moon continues to serve at theological schools in Canada and Korea, sharing his experiences and his knowledge of pastoral counseling and psychotherapy.

HWEE KIONG (SOLOMON) OH was a Land Surveyor by training. After working in the government sector for eight years, he decided to serve God in full-time ministry. Together with his wife, he worked alongside the locals to plant a church in Phnom Penh, Cambodia. Recently, Solomon completed his doctoral degree in Pastoral Ministries at Singapore Bible College. Rev. Dr. Oh now oversees missionaries deployed to South East Asia and East Asia.

JENNY H. PAK is an Associate Professor of Psychology at Fuller Theological Seminary and chairs the Cultural and Community Psychology Track. She also served as an elected board member of the Christian Association of Psychological Studies (CAPS) and the lead coordinator of the Cross-Cultural/International Track. She has traveled to Thailand, Turkey, China, and South Korea to teach, train, and provide counseling to missionaries and pastors. Her expertise in narrative analysis is utilized to research the impact of rapid culture change and trauma on identity and spiritual formation. She is the author of *Korean American Women: Stories of Acculturation and Changing Selves.* For over thirty years, she has been serving with her husband, who pastors a Korean congregation in Southern California. They have two daughters.

KYUNG NAM PARK and KYOUNG A JO served in West Asia as medical workers for an NGO. From 2011 to February 2019, they served as Korean Branch Directors of WEC International. They currently serve as deputy international directors of WEC International and are interested in developing member care and Christian spirituality for workers in a cross-cultural context. They have two children.

TIMOTHY KIHO PARK has been teaching Asian missions at Fuller's School of Intercultural Studies since 1996. He also served as Director of the Korean Studies program until 2015, when he became Director of Global Connections. Before coming to Fuller, Park served as a missionary in the Philippines for fifteen years. Park founded the Institute for Asian Mission (IAM) and Asian Society of Missiology (ASM), through which he works with other Asian missiologists to help Asian churches and missions through research, publication, consultation, and education. He also served as the head chairman of Asia Missions Association and now serves as President of East-West Center for Missions Research and Development.

CHARLIE A. SCHAEFER, PhD, is a psychologist and a staff member of Barnabas International, which exists to encourage and strengthen those in cross-cultural Christian service and their families. Charlie has lived in West Africa and served Christian workers there and in Europe, Central Asia, East Asia, and the Middle East. His special interests include transitions in life and ministry, relationships, marital and family health, trauma and resilience, burnout, men's issues, and talking about God's work in our lives. Charlie and his wife, Frauke, co-edited *Trauma and Resilience: A Handbook—Effectively Supporting Those Who Serve God* (2012). In addition to his ministry with Barnabas International, Charlie has a counseling practice in North Carolina, where he primarily works with people in Christian service.

Contributors

FRAUKE C. SCHAEFER, MD, a family physician from Germany, is also a psychiatrist and psychotherapist, who receiving her training at Klinik Hohemark, Germany and at Duke University in NC, USA. She worked in Nepal from 1990 to 1997 as a medical missionary with International Nepal Fellowship. She presently works part-time in private practice, mostly with missionaries and pastors, and is on staff with Barnabas International. She and her husband, Charlie, focus on clinical care, consultation, training, and support research in member care, both in the US and internationally. They edited and co-authored *Trauma & Resilience: A Handbook* (2012), a resource to support Christian workers who serve in cross-cultural environments. The book grew out of two published research studies (*The Journal of Traumatic Stress,* 2007; *International Journal of Psychiatry in Medicine,* 2008).

NAM YONG SUNG is the Senior Pastor of Samkwang Presbyterian Church, Seoul. He previously served as a missionary in Nigeria and is currently a Professor of Missions at Chongshin University's Graduate School of Pastoral Theology. Editor-in-chief of *Korea Missions Quarterly,* he has written several books and many articles. His books include *Research Methodology* (ChumTab Publishing, 2012), *365 Days of Missions in Prayer* (ChumTab Publishing, 2011), and *Mission Case Studies* (Life Book, 2006), all in Korean. He and his wife, Rachel, have two grown children.

PATRICIA LUCILLE TOLAND has served as a missionary since 1990 with WEC International. For the last twenty-one years, she has ministered primarily in Spanish-speaking Latin America, training Latino missionaries in a variety of mission schools, speaking in missions conferences, developing cross-cultural simulation camps, and mobilizing the Latino church. She is the founder of WEC Latino Latin America and is the Director of WEC Latino Global, which trains and sends Latino missionaries. She also formed and developed WEC's Latino Member Care Department and serves as the Director of the Member Care team. She teaches on intervention strategies for trauma and crisis, spiritual warfare on the mission field, leadership in honor and shame cultures, and other cross-cultural topics. She has written several published articles.

BEN TORREY, a member of Jesus Abbey in Taebaek, Gangwon-do, Korea is Executive Director of The Fourth River Project, Inc., preparing for the opening of North Korea. Ben grew up in Korea, where his father, Rev. Archer Torrey, worked first to reestablish the Anglican seminary following the Korean War and then, with his wife Jane, to found the interdenominational intentional community, Jesus Abbey. Ben and his wife Liz were called back to Korea in 2005 to build Jesus Abbey's Three Seas Center in Taebaek, as a place to prepare people to enter North Korea and share the love of Jesus as agents of reconciliation and healing. Ben also serves as the Syro-Chaldean Missionary Bishop for Korea. Since 2005, he has been writing a monthly column for the *Life of Faith* (Shinang-gye) magazine (Central Full Gospel Church [Yoido], Seoul).

EUNJUNG UM is Co-Director of Heartstream Resources Korea, serving cross-cultural workers of mission agencies and denominational missions. Before working in member care, Eunjung worked as a Practice Director of Human Dynamics, overseeing staff management and human resource consulting for her clients. Previously, she taught Christian Counseling courses at Nairobi Bible School in Kenya. She also taught at Seoul Theological University and served on the Korean staff with One Mission Society. Eunjung is a PhD candidate at Yonsei University Graduate School and holds a master's degree in counseling from Asbury Theological Seminary. She loves art and music and enjoys finding solitude in nature.

RICHARD WINTER is Professor Emeritus of Applied Theology and Counseling at Covenant Theological Seminary in St. Louis, MO, USA. He is also a psychotherapist/counselor, who received his training in medicine and psychiatry in England before serving on the staff and as a Director of the English branch of L'Abri Fellowship for fourteen years. He was a member of the Royal College of Psychiatrists in England and authored *When Life Goes Dark: Finding Hope in the Midst of Depression* (IVP 2012); *Perfecting Ourselves to Death: The Pursuit of Excellence and the Perils of Perfectionism* (IVP, 2005); *Still Bored in a Culture of Entertainment: Rediscovering Passion and Wonder* (IVP, 2002); and other books and professional journal articles. He is married with four children and nine grandchildren.

CHRISTOPHER J. H. WRIGHT is the International Ministries Director of the Langham Partnership, which provides literature, scholarships, and preaching training for Majority World pastors and seminaries. He worked as a professor of Old Testament at the Union Biblical Seminary in India for five years. His books include *Old Testament Ethics for the People of God; The Mission of God; The God I Don't Understand;* and *The Mission of God's People.* Chris was the chief architect of The Cape Town Commitment—the Statement of the Third Lausanne Congress in October 2010. He is an Honorary Vice President of Tear Fund, UK, and of IFES. Chris and his wife, Liz, have four adult children and ten grandchildren and live in London, as members of All Souls Church, Langham Place.

INDEX

NOTE: An "n" in the page number indicates that the entry appears in a footnote on that page.

A

Abraham 24, 126
Accountability in Missions (2011) ix, xxi
Acts Ministries International 125
Adam and Eve 24, 99, 115, 122-23
addiction, sexual 115-22
Afghanistan, missionary work in 144-53
Ahab (OT) 3, 9, 241, 250
Alexander VI (pope) 291
All Nations Christian College xviii, 26
Al-Qaeda 148
American Mental Health Association 212
American Psychiatric Association 239
Am I Still Me? (Lois Dodds) 193
Amnon (OT) 241-42, 250
Andrews, Leslie A. 183
Angel Project (Torch Trinity Graduate University) 283
anger, in Korean culture 59-71
Anyang city 134
Asbury Theological Seminary xvii, 177
Ascension, Mount of 8
Asian Mission xviii, xx, xxii
Assyrians 60-61
Atkinson, D. R. 79-80
Attention-Deficit/Hyperactivity Disorder (ADHD) 103-6;
  in Korea, 110-14
Augustine 116, 119, 281
Autism Spectrum Disorder (ASD) 109

B

Baal 3, 6
Baeq, Shinjong (Daniel) xx
Balisky, Lila ix-x
Balisky, Paul ix-x
Barresi, J. 81
Batalha, L. 78
bbali-bbali 67-68
bbali-maani 67-68
Beaver, Michael J. 220
Beersheba 4
Bendor-Samuel, Liz 217-21, 297, 307
Benjaminites 124
Bethel College 197n1

Bhagavad Gita 60
bitterness and resentment, of Jeremiah 14-17
Blagen, Mark 183
Boaz (OT) 125-26
Boeker, Traugott 274
Bonk, Jean 255
Bonk, Jonathan J. ix, xviii-xxii, 230, 239, 255, 276, 286-300, 307
Book of Heroic Failures, The (Pile) 22, 25
Buddhism 277
Byun, Jinsuk (Felipe) 154-57, 296, 307

C

candidate orientation (WEC) 269
Carmel, Mt. 3-5
Carr, Karen F. 141-43, 295, 307
Carroll, Dorothy xx, xxii, 308
Catholic Christianity (Korea) 277.
  See also Roman Catholic Church
Catholic University of Korea xi.
  See also Roman Catholic Church
CCI. *See* Crisis Consulting International
Chae, Jeong-Ho x-xi, 308
che-myun 65-66, 68-69, 291
Cho, Maeng 220
Cho, Nan-Sook 45
Cho, Seong-Jin 220
Cho, Yong Joong xx
Choenmin (Korean social class) 63
Choi, Hunn 177-80, 308
Choi, Meesaeng 177-80, 308
Chosun dynasty (Korea) 63
Christian Peacemaker Teams (Iraq) 148
Chung, Jae-Chul xviii, xix, xxii, 309
Churches and Missions Agencies Together (Liew) 204
CMT. *See* Crisis Management Team
CO. *See* candidate orientation (WEC)
Columbus, Christopher 291
Communication Disorders 109
community: spiritual 205-7;
  value of for missionaries 98-101
Confucianism 68, 113, 235, 292;
  values of xv, 91, 94, 96, 100, 277-281

Coram Deo faith   126
Cornerstone Counseling (Chiang Mai)   166–67
Counseling American Minorities   79–80
Crawford, Nancy A.   102–9, 292–93, 309
creation, and God's plan for husband and wife   99–100
Crisis Consulting International   147–48, 151
crisis management policy   155–56
Crisis Management Team   137, 142, 147–51
Cronbach's alpha   184
Cross-Cultural Connections (Elmer)   78n5

D

David (OT)   25, 126, 299
Davies, Evan   274
Davis, Pamela   166–68, 296, 309
debriefing, of missionary returnees   45–46
Declaration of Independence (Korea)   282
Demas (NT)   xiv
deportation   129–36, 141–43
depression: Elijah's experience of   3–10; depression, in the Old Testament   238–55
Developmental Stages (Erikson)   218–19
Diagnostic and Statistical Manual of Mental Disorders (DSM-5)   64n5, 212
disillusionment, of Jeremiah   12–14
Distefano, Michel G.   238–55, 309
Dodds, Larry   183
Dodds, Lois A.   xix, 183, 192–94, 256–64, 297–98, 310
Duranno Press   xx
Dyck, Gladys. *See* Geiser, Gladys

E

Edwards, Jonathan   56
Electroconvulsive Therapy (ECT)   249, 254
Eli (OT)   24, 123
Elijah   xviii, 142, 254; depressed and fearful   3–10
Elmer, D.   78n5
Emotionally Focused Therapy (Johnson)   80
emotional stress, and retired Korean missionaries   208–17
Eok, Namgung   278
Erikson, Erik   218–19
Ethiopia, Korean missionaries in   ix–x
Ethiopia, SIM missions in   ix–x
Evolutional Approaches (Sng, Williams, and Neuberg)   77–78

F

failure, in Peter's experience   24–32
Family Accountability in Missions (2013)   xxi
"Farewell to the Missionary Hero" (Peterson)   57
Father School   101
Federal Bureau of Investigation (FBI)   149–51
Fifty Missionaries Heroes Every Boy and Girl Should Know (Johnston, Julia H.)   56
Foster, Richard   123
Four Pillars of WEC   268
Fox, Tom   148
Fuller Theological Seminary   xii
Fung, Lawrence   232–36, 299, 310

G

Gae-dok-kyo   277
Gangnam Station Murder case   280
gapjil   69, 278–79, 282
Gardner, Laura Mae   96, 209, 259nn7–8
Geiser, Al (father)   145–56, 295–96
Geiser, Andrea (daughter)   145, 148
Geiser, Franklin (son)   145, 148
Geiser, Gladys (mother)   145–50, 152, 154–56, 295
Geiser, Kaitlyn (granddaughter)   145
Geiser, Mary (daughter-in-law)   145, 148
Geiser, Roland (brother)   149–50
General Assembly of Presbyterian Churches of Korea   211
General Assembly of the Presbyterian Church in Korea   224n11
Gergen, K. J.   80–81
Gideon (OT)   24, 299
Gladwell, Malcolm   207
Global Bible Translators in Korea   211
Global Mission Fellowship   211
Global Mission Leadership Forum   xviii, xxi, xxii
Global Mission Society (GMS)   128–42, 211, 297, 315
Global Missionary Training Center (GMTC)   154
Gnosticism   116
God, as Master Therapist for Elijah   6–10
Goertzel, Mildred G.   257
Goertzel, Victor   257
Good Samaritan   82
Grant, Robert   158–59
Great Commandment (love)   49, 57, 182, 192
Great Commission (mission)   49, 57, 182, 192
Green, Stanley W.   144–53, 295–96, 310
Guidelines of Recommendations for Deported Missionaries (GMS CMT)   142

Index

H

Hagar   24
han   63-64, 70, 72, 290
Han, Kyu Sam   310
Hannah (OT)   241, 249-50
Han River, miracle on   59, 277
happiness, of Korean missionaries   181-92
Hardie, Robert A.   282, 284
Hartz, Sarita   35
Hauenstein, Phillip   57
Hawker, Debbie   35
Heartstream Resources Korea   183, 193, 264
Hekmatyar, Gulbuddin   146
hero myth, and missionary service   48, 56-58
Hezekiah (OT)   241, 249-50
Higgins, E. Tory   182
Hisb-e-Islami   146
Holmes, Arthur F.   122
Holy Spirit   xiv, 20, 32, 67, 266;
  and member care   174, 180, 270
Hong, Hyekyung (Grace)   154-57, 296, 311
Hong, Jung Gil   226
Hong, Kyungwha   42-46, 289, 311
Hüfner-Kemper, Barbara   72-74, 311
Hwa, Jongboo   226
hwa-byung / ul-hwa-byung   64-65, 72
Hwang, Jin Soo   182

I

IBM SPSS Statistics 25   184
inferiority complex, among Koreans   65, 290-91
Intellectual Disorders   109
Inter Caetera (papal bull, 1493)   291
intercultural studies, value of   78-79
international missions, challenges of   75-84
Isaiah   206

J

"Jal Sala BoSe"   279
James (Jesus' brother)   3, 206
Japan, and occupation of Korea   63, 282
Jennings, J. Nelson   xviii, 222-32, 298-99, 311
Jeollado (region of Korea)   63
jeong   61-62, 68-69, 280
Jeong, Keung-Chul (Matthew)   xx
Jeong, Min Young   227
Jeremiah   xviii, 11-21, 248-49, 254-55
Jerome   116
Jerusalem   251
Jesus   xix, 6, 10, 16, 57, 123, 171, 175-76, 247;
  and anger   73-74;
  and his disciples   xiv, 57, 98, 174;
  and Peter   27-32
Jezebel, Queen   3-6
Jezreel   4, 5
Jo, Kyoung A   265-74, 316
Job (OT)   242-45, 249, 252-53
John (apostle)   29-30
John (epistle writer)   25, 32
Johnson, Sue   80
Johnston, Julia H.   56n6
John the Baptist   xix, 10
Jonah, as angry missionary   60-61
Jones, B.   78
Jongboo, Hwa   231
Joongin (Korean social class)   63
Jordan, Peter   219
Joseon dynasty   280
Joseph (OT)   126, 249-50, 254
Judas (NT)   27
Judges   124
Jung, Carl   125
Jung, Soonuk   xx, xxii, 311
Jung, Soon Young   xx
Jung, Um Eun   228
Jung, Yoo Jin   299
Jung, Young Hyun   xx

K

Kabul Crisis Management Team   148-51
Kang, Jonathan S.   59-71, 290-91, 311
Kang, Seung Sam   xx
Keckler, Wade T.   183
Kemper, Thomas   56-58, 290, 312
KGMLF 2011   ix, xviii, xxi, 228-29
KGMLF 2013   xxi
KGMLF 2015   xxi
KGMLF 2017   xviii, xix, xxi, 223, 227
KGMLF 2019   xx
Kidron Mennonite Church (OH)   146n3, 147-48
Kim, Do Bong   47-55, 289-90, 312
Kim, Hong Joo   xix
Kim, Jeong Han   128-40, 295, 313
Kim, Jinbong   xviii-xxii, 222-32, 298-99, 312
Kim, Mi Hyang   54-55
Kim, Soohyun   75-84, 292, 313
Kim, Sook Hee   xx
Kim, Sun Man   122-26, 295, 313

Kim, Yoon Hee   182
Kim, Young Ok   158-66, 296, 313
Kintsukuroi (Japanese art form)   172
Klamser, Bob   147-50
Korea, occupied by Japan   63, 282
Korea Crisis Management Service (KCMS)   155
Korean Academy of Child and Adolescent Psychiatry   111
Korean American Presbyterian Church (KAPC)   124
Korean Baptist Church   211
Korean Christian Psychiatrists Association   xi
Korean Institute for Special Education   112
Korean Ministry of Foreign Affairs   132, 135
Korean Ministry of Health and Welfare   111-12
Korean War (1950-53)   xiii, 63, 279, 282
Korea World Mission Association (KWMA)   211, 227
K-SE   184, 185, 188.
   See also SPARE Assessment Tool
K-SPARE   183-88.
   See also SPARE Assessment Tool
Kuhl, Dieter   267
Kuhl, Renate   267

L

Lamentations   251-51
Langham Scholars   xiv
Lapp, John F.   147-49
Larson, Donald N.   197
Learning Disorders (LD), in Korea   112-13
Lee, Chul   226
Lee, Eunha   45
Lee, Eun-Joo   94
Lee, Helene Kim   220
Lee, Hun-Sook   292
Lee, Hyun Mo (Tim)   xx
Lee, Hyun-Sook   90-98, 314
Lee, Jae Hoon   xix, xxi, 208-17, 297, 314
Lee, Jongsun   268-69, 273
Lee, Jung-Sook   276-85, 314
Lee, Jun-Young   220
Lee, Kwang Soon   xx
Lee, Kyunghee   xx
Lee, Sang Joon   xx
Lee, Shin Chul   xx
Lee, Wonjae   xx
Lee, Yoo-Kyung   94
Lee, Young Hoon   xxi

Liew, Ivan   204
Life of David Brainerd, The (Edwards)   56
limited access area missionaries   128-40
Lindquist, Brent   196-204, 298, 315
Lingenfelter, Sherwood   228-29
Linguistic Relativism   83-84
Link Care Center   197n1
Lot (OT)   123

M

March First Movement (1919, Korea)   282
Marcia, John   263
marital conflict, in Korean missionary couples   90-98
Martin, Raymond   81
Maté, Gabor   117
Maxwell, Ruth L.   34-42, 288-89, 315
Mayo Clinic   239-40, 248-49, 253
MCC. *See* Mennonite Central Committee
McGregor, Malcolm   xiii-xiv
Megachurch Accountability in Missions (2016)   xxi
member care, xii   50-51, 87-88, 133-34, 156, 159-66, 181-236
Member Care Network   50
Mennonite Central Committee   145
Mennonite Mission Network   145-56
mental health, of missionary children   102-9
mental health, of retired Korean missionaries   208-17
Mental Health and Missions (Gardner)   209
mental health care timeline   52-55
meritocracy, and Korean missionary service   48-52
Message, The (Peterson)   58
Methodist Episcopal Church, South   284
Minority Identity Development Model   79-80, 86
Missio Dei (MMN)   153
missionary children, mental health of   102-9
Missionary Crisis Management (KCMS)   155
missionary disillusionment   34-42
missionary family struggles   34-42
Missionary Health Institute (Toronto)   209
missionary kids, formation of   256-64
missionary training college (WEC)   268-69
Missio Nexus   202
Mission Member Care   217-18, 221
MMN. *See* Mennonite Mission Network
Moon, Sang-Cheol (Steve)   xx, 45
Moon, Sung Il   208-17, 297, 315
Moreau, Scott   xiv-xvi

Moriarty, Glen 183
Morning from the End of the Earth 51
Morris, Colin 58
Morten, G. 79-80
Moses 4, 8, 25, 207, 258
Motor Disorders 109
MTC. *See* missionary training colleges (WEC)
Mujahid, Zabiullah 152
myung-bun 69

N

Nahum 60
Najavits, Lisa M. 125
NamSeoul Church 211, 283, 298-99;
    mission policies of 222-32
Native Americans, ministry among 56
Neese, Brian 66n9
Nehemiah 239-40
Neuberg, S. L. 77-78
neurodevelopmental disorders, and missionary children 102-9
non-traditional sending countries (WEC) 266-67, 270, 274
Non-violent Communication (Rosenberg) 73-74
noonchi culture (Korea) 66-69, 73, 279
NTSC. *See* non-traditional sending countries (WEC)

O

Obadiah 5, 9
O'Brien, Brendan 149
Oh, Hwee Kiong (Solomon) 315
Olive Tree (counseling, Turkey) 167
OMC. *See* Overseas Mission Committee (NamSeoul Church)
OMSC. *See* Overseas Ministries Study Center
Onnuri Community Church xix, xxi, xxii, 211
Open Doors 130
Operation Mobilization 163
organization-centered member health 196-204
Outlier (Gladwell) 207
Overseas Ministries Study Center ix, xx
Overseas Mission Committee (NamSeoul Church) 226-27, 230-31
Overseas Mission Fellowship in Korea 211

P

Pak, Jenny H. 110-14, 293, 316
Park, Jee 220
Park, Kyung Nam 265-74, 316

Park, Seul Gi 182
Park, Shan-Eui 45
Park, Timothy Kiho xii, 316
Paul Mission International 211
Paul/Saul (NT) xiv, xix, xxii, 16, 25, 287-88, 295, 299-300;
    and community 98, 171;
    as vulnerable 58, 172
Pearson's correlation coefficient 184
People Disrupted (2018) xxi
Peter (NT) xviii, 178;
    and healing from failure and guilt 21-32
Peterson, Amy 57
Peterson, Christopher 182
Peterson, Eugene 58
Pharaoh 258
Pile, Stephen 22, 25
Polanczyk, Guilherme 110
pornography 117-21
Posttraumatic Stress Disorder 162-64
Prodigal Son 82
prosperity-gospel 277
Protestant Christianity (Korea) 277-78
Proverbs 252
Psalms 14, 18, 72;
    of Lament 173, 240, 245-52
psycho-cultural characteristics of Koreans 61-66.
    See also che-myun;
    han;
    hwa-byung;
    jeong;
    noonchi
Pyongyang Revival (1907) xiii, 282

R

Rahab (OT) 125-26
Rempel, Angela 148
Rempel, Erwin 148
Rensch, Calvin 262
retired Korean missionaries, mental health of 208-17
retirement plans, for Korean missionaries 222-32
Reverse Culture Shock 219-20
Reynolds, K. J. 78
Rice, Condoleezza 149
Roembke, Lianne 81-83
Roman Catholic Church: and sexual abuse 294;
    and singleness 281
Rose, Carol 148

Rosenberg, Marshall B.   73–74
Roth, John   146–47
Royal College of Psychiatrists (UK)   220

S

Sae Ma Eul Movement   279
Samuel (OT)   24, 241
Sangmin (Korean social class)   63
Satan   6, 249;
   hating the family   100;
   sifting Peter   29
Saul (OT)   299
Schaefer, Charles A.   169–77, 296–97, 316
Schaefer, Frauke C.   169–77, 296–97, 317
Schubert, Esther   183, 193
self-pity, of Jeremiah   17–20
Seligman, Martin   182
Seong, Su   220
Seoul Club   xx
Seoul National University Hospital   111
sexual addiction   115–22
Shakur, Al   145–46
Shamanism/Animism   277
Shin, Kyung-Seop   45
Shue, Terry   147, 149
Shukur, Al   149
Siegel, Daniel   81
SIL. See Summer Institute of Linguistics
SIM International   ix–x, 163, 288
Sinai, Mt. (Mt. Horeb)   7–8
Sng, O.   77–78
Social Identity Perspective (Reynolds, Subasic,
   Batalha, and Jones)   78
Sodom and Gomorrah   123
Sohn, Jee   220
Song of Songs   115, 123
SPARE Assessment Tool   183, 194.
   See also K-SPARE
SPARE-OC   187, 193.
   See also SPARE Assessment Tool
Special Education Act for Individuals with
   Disabilities and Others (SEAIDO)   112
Special Education Promotion Act (SEPA)   112
Specific Learning Disorder (SLD)   106–8
Stephen (NT)   xiv, 287
Stoltzfus, Rachel   147
Storti, Craig   219
Stott, John   82
stress, and missionary service in limited access areas
   128–40

Stringer, Jay   117–21
Struthers, William   117
Studd, Charles Thomas   266
Subasic, E.   78
Sue, D. W.   79–80
Suh, Stephen   220
suicide, in Korea   61
Suk, Hye   220
Summer Institute of Linguistics   262
Sung, Nam Yong   xx, 204–7, 298, 317

T

Taliban   152
Tamar (OT)   241–42
Taylor, William   26n3
Tennent, Timothy C.   xvi–xvii
Tertullian   153, 155
Third Culture Kids (TCK)   262–63
Thomas (NT)   4
Timothy (NT)   xiv
TMS. See Transcranial Magnetic Stimulation
Toland, Patricia Lucille   85–88, 292, 317
Too Valuable to Lose (Taylor)   26
Torch Trinity Graduate University   283
Toronto Institute of Linguistics   197n1
Torrey, Ben   98–101, 292, 317
traditional sending countries (WEC)
   266, 269–70, 274
Transcranial Magnetic Stimulation   249, 254
trauma: in missionary service   158–66;
   spiritual resources in dealing with   169–77
TSC. See traditional sending countries (WEC)
Tumaini Counselling Centre (Kenya)   102
Turning Point (member care organization)   97

U

ul-hwa-byung   290
Um, Eunjung   181–92, 297–98, 318
United Methodist Board of Global Ministries   56
US Special Forces   150

W

Wall, Andrew   xiii, 223
Wang, John   232–36, 299
WEC   163, 266, 268
WEC Korea   231, 265–74
Well, The (Chiang Mai)   166–67
West, Christopher   116
Wheaton College Graduate School   xvi

White, Mary Culler   284
Wiebe, Carl   152-53
Wiley, George   233
William Carey Publishing   xx
Williams, K. E. G.   77-78
Winter, Richard   115-22, 293-95, 318
Wired for Intimacy (Struthers)   117
Woman Revival Movement (1903, Korea)   282
Women's Foreign Missionary Society
   (Methodist Episcopal Church, South)   284
Wood, William B.   149
Worldwide Evangelization for Christ. *See* WEC
Wright, Christopher J. H.   xviii, 1-32, 318
Wynn, DG   xx

Y

Yale University Library   xx
Yangban (Korean social class)   63
Yangdaein ("Big Westerner") attitude   282
Yi dynasty (Korea)   63, 66
Yoido Full Gospel Church   xxi
Yoo, Boin   268
Yoo, Byungkook   268
Yoo, Hee-Joo   45

www.ingramcontent.com/pod-product-compliance
Lightning Source LLC
Chambersburg PA
CBHW071217080526
44587CB00013BA/1405